THE FAMILY, SEX AND MARRIAGE

Lawrence Stone was educated at Charterhouse School and Christ Church, Oxford. He was a lecturer at University College, Oxford, from 1947 to 1950, and a Fellow of Wadham College, Oxford, from 1950 to 1963. Since 1963 he has been Dodge Professor of History at Princeton University, and Director of the Shelby Cullom Davis Center for Historical Studies, also at Princeton, since 1969. Professor Stone has contributed numerous articles to learned journals and periodicals. His published works include *The Causes of the English Revolution, 1529–1642*, *Crisis of the Aristocracy, 1558–1641*, and (editor) *Schooling and Society*. He is also author of *Sculpture in Britain: The Middle Ages*, published in The Pelican History of Art series.

LAWRENCE STONE

THE FAMILY,
SEX AND MARRIAGE

In England 1500–1800

ABRIDGED EDITION

HARPER TORCHBOOKS
Harper & Row, Publishers, New York
Grand Rapids, Philadelphia, St. Louis, San Francisco
London, Singapore, Sydney, Tokyo, Toronto

THE FAMILY, SEX AND MARRIAGE IN ENGLAND 1500-1800. Copyright © 1977, 1979 by Lawrence Stone. All rights reserved. Printed in the United States of America. No part of this book may be used or reproduced in any manner whatsoever without written permission except in the case of brief quotations embodied in critical articles and reviews. For information address Harper & Row, Publishers, Inc., 10 East 53d Street, New York, N.Y. 10022.

First HARPER PAPERBACK edition published 1979.

ISBN: 0-06-131979-1

92 93 94 95 MPC 19 18 17 16 15 14

To my family, without whom . . .

Contents

List of Graphs

List of Illustrations

The problems, being existential, are universal; their solutions, being human, are diverse ... The road to the grand abstractions of science winds through a thicket of singular facts.

(C. Geertz, *The Interpretation of Cultures*, New York, 1973, p. 363)

Acknowledgements

Some of the basic ideas in this book were presented to the Columbia University Seminar on the Nature of Man, the Social Science Seminar at the Institute for Advanced Study at Princeton, a *Past and Present* Conference in London, and the History Department Colloquium at Princeton, to the members of all of which I am grateful for some very trenchant criticisms and helpful suggestions. Without them I would never have eliminated some of the more extravagant claims and implausible hypotheses, and would never have got clear in my own mind the essentials of my very complicated argument. I am particularly grateful for constructive suggestions from Robert Darnton, W. J. Goode, Margaret Mead, Robert K. Merton, Theodore K. Rabb and Edward P. Thompson. I also owe a great debt, of a somewhat ambiguous kind, to Clifford Geertz. He has provided me with invaluable intellectual stimulus and new insights, and has also driven me to think out where my craft as an historian differs from his as an anthropologist. The main themes of the book and some of the evidence were presented to students and faculty at Cambridge University as the Trevelyan Lectures in November 1975. From the reactions of the audience, especially those of J. H. Plumb and E. A. Wrigley, I also learned much. None of these persons and groups, however, should be assumed to be in agreement with the argument, for which I must, alas, take full responsibility.

I am also grateful to Michael MacDonald, who generously allowed me to make use of some of his unpublished findings from the casebooks of the Reverend Richard Napier; to the archivist at Brasenose College, Oxford, who permitted me to examine transcripts of the Legh MSS; to Miriam Slater, who has allowed me to quote from her unpublished dissertation; and to Natalie Davis, whose mimeographed bibliography on 'Society and the Sexes in Early Modern Europe' drew my attention to many sources I should otherwise have missed. Ansley Coale very kindly answered a number of technical questions about demography. For financial support for this project,

ACKNOWLEDGEMENTS

I am indebted to the National Science Foundation (Grants GC28832X and GS39877X) and to the Princeton University Research Board. A preliminary version of Chapter 4 of this book was published by the University of Pennsylvania Press, to which I am grateful for permission to reproduce a revised and expanded text. P. Laslett kindly provided me with the figures for pre-nuptial conceptions and illegitimacy for Graphs 10 and 11 from his *Family Life and Illicit Love in Earlier Generations*. R. B. Latham kindly allowed me to read the proofs of the last volume of his definitive edition of Pepys' *Diary*, which include the previously expurgated passages. I am also grateful to Mrs V. B. Elliott for supplying me with some information from her work on Kent marriage records of the early seventeenth century. For individual references and suggestions I am indebted to P. Clark, M. H. Crawford, N. Z. Davis, D. H. Fischer, E. Gilliam, P. Goubert, A. T. Grafton, L. H. Rosenband, M. Shanley, Morton Smith, S. R. Smith, M. Smuts, S. E. Spock, L. A. Tilly, S. Watkins, C. S. Weiner, and others whose names I have doubtless overlooked.

I am very grateful to my devoted secretary, Mrs Betty Ann Berry, who typed and retyped version after version of an increasingly illegible and bulky manuscript with remarkable speed, accuracy and palaeographical skill. Finally, I owe a very large debt to my wife. It is, naturally, from interaction with her that I have learned whatever I know at first hand about the ups and downs of family life. She has read the manuscript several times and provided me with a not always welcome stream of suggestions and criticisms, most of which I have accepted, and some rejected. She helped me with the horribly tedious chore of checking footnotes, and in doing so managed to eliminate a number of serious misinterpretations caused by over-hasty reading of documents.

Throughout the book, spelling, capitalization and punctuation have been modernized, on the grounds that the gain in readability far outweighs the loss in accuracy of transcription. In the period of Old Style dating, the year is taken to begin on 1 January.

LAWRENCE STONE

Princeton, N.J.

Preface to the
Abridged Edition

A book which weighs 3 pounds 6 ounces, is 800 pages long and costs £16 or $30 is clearly in need of abridgement if it is to reach a wide audience. This edition is therefore approximately half the size of the original. The principles upon which the cuts have been made are as follows. All extraneous matter, intriguing diversions from the main line of the argument, has been severely pruned. Most sections treating the lower classes have been particularly ruthlessly trimmed, since, as reviewers were quick to point out, the evidence here was very weak. This edition is therefore even more closely concerned than the original with the top levels of society, the upper mercantile and professional classes, the squirarchy and the aristocracy. Space has been saved by cutting out all but the most striking and illuminating of the mass of examples that were used to buttress each point. All the scholarly apparatus, the references and the bibliography have been omitted, as well as about half of the graphs and a third of the plates. The opportunity has been taken to correct errors of fact and grammar and typographical slips, and also to insert one or two telling new quotations.

It should be obvious that although this abridgement offers a faithful rendering of the original, it is inevitably much simplified, and the evidence provided is suggestive rather than conclusive. Anyone wishing to test the validity of any argument or the source for any fact should refer to the original edition.

In making this abridgement, I have been much helped by suggestions from my wife.

LAWRENCE STONE

Princeton, N.J.
May 1978

PART ONE

Introduction

CHAPTER ONE

Problems, Methods and Definitions

'The public life of a people is a very small thing compared to its private life.'
> (G. d'Avenel, *Les Français de mon Temps*, Paris, 1904, p. 1)

'To judge fairly of those who lived long before us ... we should put quite apart both the usages and the notions of our own age ... and strive to adopt for the moment such as prevailed in theirs.'
> (Lady Louisa Stuart, *c.* 1827, in *Letters and Journals of Lady Mary Coke*, ed. J. A. Horne, Edinburgh 1889, I, p. xxxv)

'We have very little of correctly detailed domestic history, the most valuable of all as it would enable us to make comparisons ...'
> (*The Autobiography of Francis Place*, *c.* 1823–6. ed. M. Thale, Cambridge, 1972, p. 91)

1. THE PATTERN OF CHANGE

The subject of this book can be stated fairly simply. It is an attempt to chart and document, to analyse and explain, some massive shifts in world views and value systems that occurred in England over a period of some three hundred years, from 1500 to 1800. These vast and elusive cultural changes expressed themselves in changes in the ways members of the family related to each other, in terms of legal arrangements, structure, custom, power, affect and sex. The main stress is on how individuals thought about, treated and used each other, and how they regarded themselves in relation to God and to various levels of social organization, from the nuclear family to the

21

state. The microcosm of the family is used to open a window on to this wider landscape of cultural change.

The critical change is that from distance, deference and patriarchy to what I have chosen to call affective individualism. I believe this to have been perhaps the most important change in *mentalité* to have occurred in the Early Modern period, indeed possibly in the last thousand years of Western history.

The four key features of the modern family – intensified affective bonding of the nuclear core at the expense of neighbours and kin; a strong sense of individual autonomy and the right to personal freedom in the pursuit of happiness; a weakening of the association of sexual pleasure with sin and guilt; and a growing desire for physical privacy – were all well established by 1750 in the key middle and upper sectors of English society.

Further stages in the diffusion of this new family type did not take place until the late nineteenth century, after a period of nearly a century during which many of the developments that have been described had gone into reverse. When forward movement picked up again at the end of the nineteenth century, it involved a spread of the domesticated family ideal up into the higher court aristocracy and down into the masses of artisans and respectable wage-earners who composed the bulk of the population.

This is not the first time that problems of this sort have been studied, for they are similar to some of those with which both Max Weber and Jacob Burckhardt wrestled more than three-quarters of a century ago. They too were obsessed with the complex inter-relationships thanks to which changes in culture emerged from changes in religion, social structure, political organization, economics, literacy and so on. Neither Weber nor Burckhardt solved these problems either to their own or to posterity's full satisfaction, and I cannot hope to succeed where scholars of such pre-eminent distinction have partly failed. But it is worth making a new effort, using a much narrower focus, in a different national context and in the light of another seventy-five years or so of historical scholarship, if only because these issues are so central to the evolution of Western civilization.

Early Modern English society was composed of a number of very distinct status groups and classes: the court aristocracy, the county gentry, the parish gentry, the mercantile and professional elite, the small property owners in town and country, the respectable and struggling wage-earners, and the totally destitute who lived on charity and their wits. These constituted more or less self-contained cultural units, with their own communication networks, their own systems of value and their own patterns of acceptable behaviour. Internal cultural divisions between social groups ran much deeper than they do today, when the differences are as much between generations as between classes. As time went on and as writing and printing spread to become the main vehicle for the diffusion of ideas, the degree to which different social strata used or were affected by this new means of expression brought with it still more marked divisions. The result was less the supersession of one family pattern and set of familial values by another than the provision of a widening number of quite different patterns.

Attitudes and customs which were normal for one class or social stratum were often quite different from those which were normal in another. Such changes as took place sometimes affected one class but not others; for example, the rising rates of pre-marital pregnancy and illegitimacy affected the peasantry, the artisans, and the poor in the late eighteenth century, but not the upper middle class, the gentry and the aristocracy. Other changes, for example the drift towards a more child-oriented attitude, affected different groups at widely different times, taking a century or more to flow from one to another. Other powerful influences were confined to a single class. Thus possession of property to be handed down vitally affected family structures and marriage arrangements among the propertied classes, but left the propertyless masses untouched. Conversely, the pressures of urbanization and industrialization profoundly affected the poor, but hardly impinged on the lives of the nobility in any significant way. Even religion, which was so powerful a force in the early seventeenth century and again in the nineteenth century, affected the more literate middling social strata far more deeply than the pleasure-seeking court aristocracy or the illiterate poor. Magical beliefs remained deeply embedded in the minds of the lower ranks who constituted the majority of the population, so that the religious enthusiasm of the age created a dissociation of sensibility rather than a restructuring of the values and beliefs of the society as a whole. Once again, there was a fragmentation of cultural norms. Stratified diffusion of new ideas and practices is the key to any realistic understanding of how family change took place. Generalizations about family change have therefore always to be qualified by a careful definition of the class or status group, the literate or the illiterate sector, the zealously godly or the casually conformist, which is under discussion. Patterns of behaviour found in the leading sectors of value-change, the professional and gentry classes, do not necessarily apply to the court aristocracy, the urban lower-middle class, the rural smallholder, or the landless labourer.

Simple models of family evolution may work perfectly well for primitive and culturally homogeneous societies unaffected by the technology of printing, the social consequences of demographic growth or the rise of capitalism, the economic consequences of gigantic wealth alongside abject poverty and unemployment, and the intellectual consequences of Puritanism, Newtonian Science and the Enlightenment. But they will not work for so sophisticated, so diversified and so changing a society as seventeenth- and eighteenth-century England, where there is a plurality of cultural worlds, and a consequent plurality of family styles and values. Thus of the three ideal types of family which have been identified, each overlapped the other by anything up to a century, and none of them ever fully died out.

2. EVIDENCE AND INTERPRETATION

Every possible type of evidence has been examined to pick up hints about changes in values and behaviour at the personal level. The greatest reliance has been placed on personal documents, diaries, autobiographies, memoirs, domestic correspondence, and the correspondence columns of newspapers. Other sources which have been used are the more popular and most frequently reprinted handbooks of advice about domestic behaviour, before 1660 written mainly by moral theologians and after 1660 mainly by laymen, with doctors becoming increasingly prominent after about 1750; reports of foreign visitors; imaginative literature, concentrating on the most popular novels, plays and poems of the day; art, especially conversation-pieces and caricatures; architectural house plans showing circulation patterns and space use; modes of address within families, between husband and wife and parents and children; folk customs such as bundling and wife-sale; legal documents such as wills, inventories, marriage contracts, and litigation over divorce or sexual deviation; and finally, demographic statistics about birth, marriage, death, pre-nuptial conception and bastardy.

To identify and describe changes in values, this rag-bag of evidence has been picked over and the finds assembled to try to create a coherent composite picture. The principal weakness of the data base does not lie in sampling, since most of the readily accessible surviving personal documents and of the most popular didactic, literary and artistic works have been examined. The preservation rate of the first is poor, and undoubtedly there has survived only a fragment of what once existed. But there is no reason to suppose that there is any inherent bias between what was kept and what was thrown away, except that much correspondence of an explicitly sexual or embarrassingly intimate character has undoubtedly been destroyed. It can therefore be assumed that what we have today is fairly representative of what has been lost, and that what is in print is representative of what still remains in manuscript. The one sampling weakness is that an examination of manuscript wills and marriage contracts for the eighteenth century has not been undertaken, although such material before 1660 has been carefully sifted.

Interpretation is more of a problem, since the most revealing materials, namely diaries, memoirs, autobiographies and letters, can rarely be checked from an independent source. We have, for example, no records kept by Mrs Pepys or Mrs Boswell to act as controls on the accuracy of the reporting of their husbands, who were the two greatest diarists in the English language. This material needs to be treated with the same critical scrutiny which the historian gives to documents in political history: an exchange of love letters needs to be handled with exactly the same sceptical caution as an exchange of diplomatic notes – no more, no less. But these personal records are peculiarly difficult to interpret. As E. H. Carr has warned, 'no document can tell us more than what the author of the document thought – what he thought happened, what he thought ought to happen or would happen, or perhaps only what he wanted others to think he thought, or even only what he himself thought he thought.' A good deal of this kind of material, unfortunately, probably falls into the last two categories. A second difficulty is that these are highly personal documents and, therefore, often very idiosyncratic, reflecting the quirks and quiddities of the individual psyche of the author, as well as the shared norms of social and moral behaviour of persons of his social class, education and time. They must, therefore, be examined in bulk, to make sure that one is not taking the exception for the rule, given the known wide variations of family patterns even within a single class at a certain time in a limited area.

Autobiographies are particularly suspect forms of evidence. This is partly because some tended to copy stereotyped models from the past such as St Augustine, Plutarch, Seneca or Marcus Aurelius, while others developed new stereotypes, like the Quaker model; partly because they were often very selective in what they recorded, being written with a view to placing the authors in a good light for posterity and leaving the world with some useful moral lessons; partly because even when they appeared most frank and intimate, like Rousseau's *Confessions* or Casanova's *Memoirs*, they were often involved in deliberate fantasy or role-playing.

The nature of the surviving evidence inexorably biases the book towards a study of a small minority group, namely the literate and articulate classes, and has relatively little to say about the great majority of Englishmen, the rural and urban smallholders, artisans, labourers and poor. But the consequences are mitigated by the fact that everything suggests that the former were the pacemakers of cultural change. Distortion of the record can be avoided if it is always remembered that the principle of stratified cultural diffusion and the persistence of distinctive, class-determined sub-cultures are the two keys to a proper understanding of the complicated history of family evolution in any society as socially differentiated as Early Modern England.

This problem is compounded during the sixteenth and early seventeenth centuries by the extreme loquacity of the Puritans and their compelling anxiety to commit their thoughts and beliefs to paper. An even more serious difficulty is caused by the dramatic increase in the amount and type of printed material and a substantial increase in literacy and in the capacity to handle the language, especially by women. Fortunately, there is also sufficient independent evidence from advice books and contemporary comment to make it fairly certain that the change is in the message, not merely in familiarity with the medium.

Any generalization inevitably runs into the objection that any behavioural model of change over time imposes an artificial schematization on a chaotic and ambiguous reality. This is, of course, true in the sense that a survey of family types at any one moment in time will reveal the same complexities as a geological survey. Strata are piled upon strata in layers that earth movements have pushed and pulled out of place, so that older formations lie on the surface in places, while very recent formations are beginning to develop here and there. Similarly, older family types survive unaltered in some social groups at the same time as other groups are evolving quite new patterns. There will, therefore, be a plurality of coexisting types, without there being any single pattern predominant among all social classes, or even necessarily within a single class. Model building, therefore, involves an attempt to identify Weberian ideal types out of the welter of historical evidence, and to highlight features which seem to have been dominant in certain social groups, but were far from universal at any given time.

The historian of the family is faced with the usual problem, but in its most intractable form, of how best to interweave fact and theory, anecdote and analysis. As Lévi-Strauss has well said, 'biographical and anecdotal history ... is low-powered history, which is not intelligible in itself, and only becomes so when it is transferred *en bloc* to a form of history of a higher power than itself ... The historian's relative choice ... is always confined to the choice between history which teaches more and explains less and history which explains more and teaches less.' This book oscillates between analysis, which tries to explain, and anecdote, which tries to teach, in the perhaps vain hope that it may thus be possible to have the best of both worlds.

In dealing with the anecdotal material, the alternatives are to offer brief extracts from a large range of sources, or to use selected case studies to illustrate a point in depth. In this book the second method has been adopted, since in so sensitive an area as family relations only fairly detailed accounts can bring out the nuances of the situation. This choice has been deliberately made in full awareness that the method is open to the charge that the case studies selected are unrepresentative of the whole sample. All that can be said in defence is that a deliberate effort has been made to find representative examples and to eliminate exceptional sports.

3. DEFINITION OF TERMS

In order to understand what follows, it is first necessary to define with some care what is meant by 'family', 'household', 'lineage', 'kin', 'marriage' and 'divorce'. On close inspection these apparently simple words turn out to have complicated and ambiguous meanings.

The word 'family' can be used to mean many things, from the conjugal pair to the 'family of man', and it is therefore imperative to begin with a clear definition of what the word will mean in this book. Here it is taken as synonymous neither with 'household' nor with 'kin' – persons related by blood or marriage. It is taken to mean those members of the same kin who live together under one roof.

A household consists of all persons living under one roof. Most households included non-kin inmates, sojourners, boarders or lodgers, occupying rooms vacated by children or kin, as well as indentured apprentices and resident servants, employed either for domestic work about the house or as an additional resident labour force for the fields or the shop. This composite group was confusingly known as a 'family' in the sixteenth and seventeenth centuries. It was because of their legal and moral subordination to the head of the household that no one, not even the Levellers, suggested that the electoral franchise should be extended to children or servants or women. They were not free persons.

In a society almost entirely without a police force, the household was a most valuable institution for social control at the village level. It helped to keep in check potentially the most unruly element in any society, the floating mass of young unmarried males; and it provided the basic unit for taxation. No wonder both Church and state looked on marriage with approval, and the sixteenth-century moral theologians spoke eulogistically about it as 'appointed by God Himself to be the fountain and seminary of all other sorts and kinds of life in the Commonwealth and the Church'.

In the Early Modern period, living-in servants were not the rarity that they are today, but a normal component of all but the poorest households. From the time of the first censuses in the early sixteenth century to the mid-nineteenth century, about one third or more of all households contained living-in servants.

The lineage are relatives by blood or marriage, dead, living, and yet to be born, who collectively form a 'house'. The kin are those members of the lineage who are currently alive and who by virtue of the relationship are recognized to have special claims to loyalty, obedience or support. It was the relation of the individual to his lineage which provided a man of the upper classes in a traditional society with his identity, without which he was a mere atom floating in a void of social space.

As this traditional society eroded, however, under the pressures of church, state, and a market economy, different values came to the fore. These included the interest of the state in obtaining efficient and honest servants who were best fitted for their tasks; the interest of the individual in obtaining freedom to maximize his economic gains and freedom to pursue his personal goals; and the claims and interests of intermediate organizations, such as churches and professional groups. These new values undermined allegiance by the kin, and the result was a crisis of confidence among the aristocracy.

As one proceeds further away from the Highland zone and closer to London, and further down the social scale through gentry, bourgeoisie, peasants and artisans, the concept of kinship carried less and less of the baggage of ideological commitment to 'honour' and 'faithfulness', etc., to which most great magnates and their followers paid more than mere lip-service. In these less exalted circles, lineage meant little, and kinship was more an association for the exchange of mutual economic benefits than a prime focus of emotional commitment. Further down still, among the propertyless, the community of friends and neighbours was probably more important in both respects, especially in the urban environment.

In the Early Modern period, marriage was an engagement which could be undertaken in a bewildering variety of ways, and the mere definition of it is fraught with difficulties. Up to the eleventh century, casual polygamy appears to have been general, with easy divorce and much concubinage. In the early middle ages all that marriage implied in the eyes of the laity seems to have been a private contract between two families concerning property exchange, which also provided some financial protection to the bride in case of the death of her husband or desertion or divorce by him. For those without property, it was a private contract between two individuals, enforced by the community sense of what was right. A church ceremony was an expensive and unnecessary luxury, especially since divorce by mutual consent followed by remarriage was still widely practised.

It was not until the thirteenth century that the Church at last managed to take over control of marriage law, to assert at least the principle of monogamous indissoluble marriage, to define and prohibit incest, to punish fornication and adultery, and to get bastards legally excluded from property inheritance.

Although by the sixteenth century marriage was fairly well defined, before 1754 there were still numerous ways of entering into it. For persons of property it involved a series of distinct steps. The first was a written legal contract between the parents concerning the financial arrangements. The second was the spousals (also called a contract), the formal exchange, usually before witnesses, of oral promises. The third step was the public proclamation of banns in church, three times, the purpose of which was to allow claims of pre-contract to be heard (by the seventeenth century nearly all the well-to-do evaded this step by obtaining a licence). The fourth step was the wedding in church, in which mutual consent was publicly verified, and the union received the formal blessing of the Church. The fifth and final step was the sexual consummation.

But it cannot be emphasized too strongly that according to ecclesiastical law the spousals was as legally binding a contract as the church wedding, although to many laity it was no more than a conditional contract. Any sort of exchange of promises before witnesses which was followed by cohabitation was regarded in law as a valid marriage. In remote areas, especially the Scottish border country, Wales and the extreme south-west, the betrothal ceremony itself, the 'handfast', continued to be treated by many of the poor as sufficient for a binding union without the blessing of the Church. There is some evidence that even in the Lowland zone quite large numbers of the poor were not getting married in church in the late seventeenth century. Indeed the church wedding had not been elevated to the position of a sacrament until 1439, and it was only in 1563, after the Reformation, that the Catholic Church first required the presence of a priest for a valid and binding marriage.

The Anglican Church naturally did not recognize this Catholic innovation, and since it took no measures of its own, the situation was left in considerable confusion. As the Anglican Church tightened its grip on society in the sixteenth and seventeenth centuries, both the laity and the clergy came increasingly to regard the wedding in church as the key ceremony, but the civil lawyers who ran the courts continued to recognize the spousals before witnesses.

Spousals could take two forms, one of which was the contract *per verba de futuro*, an oral promise to marry in the future. If not followed by consummation (which was assumed to imply consent in the present), this was an engagement which could be legally broken by mutual consent at a later date. If followed by consummation, however, it was legally binding for life. The contract *per verba de praesenti*, however, by which the pair exchanged before witnesses such phrases as 'I do take thee to my wife' and 'I do take thee to my husband', was regarded in ecclesiastical law as an irrevocable commitment which could never be broken, and which nullified a later church wedding to someone else.

To make matters worse, the canons of 1604 stipulated that a church wedding must take place between the hours of 8 a.m. and noon in the church at the place of residence of one of the pair, after the banns had been read for three weeks running. Marriages performed at night, in secular places like inns or private houses, or in towns or villages remote from the place of residence, would subject the officiating clergyman to serious penalties. The canons also forbade the marriage of persons under twenty-one without the consent of parents or guardians. The catch, however, was that although such marriages were now declared illegal, they were nonetheless valid and binding for life: this was a paradox the laity found hard to understand.

This post-1604 situation resulted in a brisk trade carried on by unscrupulous clergymen, operating in districts which were immune from superior ecclesiastical supervision, who would marry anyone for a fee, no questions asked. This was a commerce which became more and more widespread and scandalous in the late seventeenth and early eighteenth centuries, when parent–child relations on the issue of control of marriage were becoming more and more strained, and more and more children were defying their parents and running away (Plate 1). Shadwell described a clergyman who 'will marry a couple at any time; he defies licence and canonical bann, and all those foolish ceremonies'. If the playwrights are to be believed, some clergymen were even more obliging. Captain Basil in Farquhar's *The Stage Coach* reported: 'We saw a light in the parson's chamber that travelled with me, went up and found him smoking his pipe. He first gave us his blessing, then lent us his bed.' Many London churches, which were by various legal quirks unlicensed or exempt from superior jurisdiction, specialized in quick marriages. Between 1664

31

and 1691 some 40,000 marriages took place in St James's, Duke Place, while 'there's such a coupling at Pancras that they stand behind one another, as 'twere in a country dance'. The most flourishing trade of all was done by decayed clergymen in the vicinity of the Fleet in London, particularly in the first half of the eighteenth century when official weddings were heavily taxed, and those around the Fleet were both legally valid and very cheap. Notice-boards advertised 'Marriages performed within', and touts encouraged passers-by with the invitation 'Sir, will you be pleased to walk in and be married?' For the poor within walking distance of London, Fleet marriages were a financial godsend, but many drunken, hasty and exploitative unions were also sealed in these sordid surroundings, and once performed they could never be dissolved. These venal clergymen were also prepared, for a fee, to back-date a registration to legitimize children already born, or even to supply a man for a woman seeking a husband in a hurry.

It was not until 1753 that Lord Hardwicke's Marriage Act was passed, which at last brought coherence and logic to the laws governing marriage. From 1754 only the church wedding, not the verbal spousals, was legally binding, so that a prior oral contract was no longer a cause for the annulment of a later marriage in church; secondly, all church marriages had to be entered in the parish register and signed by both parties; thirdly, all marriages which occurred at times or in places defined as illegal by the 1604 canons were now also declared invalid; fourthly, no marriage of persons under twenty-one was valid without the consent of parents or guardians; and fifthly, enforcement of the law was transferred from the feeble control of the Church courts to the secular courts, which were empowered to impose up to fourteen years' transportation on clergymen who disobeyed the law. From now on, the only recourse for runaway couples defying their parents was the long and expensive flight to Scotland, especially to Gretna Green, where the new Marriage Act did not apply, and where there sprang up a new trade in commercialized marriage on the spot with no questions asked (Plates 2 and 3).

The debate over the passage of the Bill provides revealing evidence about current attitudes to marriage among the propertied classes. The prime reason for the Bill was frankly stated as being the fact that 'both men and women of the most infamous character had opportunities of ruining the sons and daughters of the greatest families in England, by the convenience of marrying in the Fleet and other unlicensed places; and marrying had become as much a trade as any mechanical profession.' The solution was to deny the validity of the religious ceremony unless it conformed to certain conditions, including parental consent if under twenty-one. This necessarily involved the rejection of the ceremony as a sacrament, an indissoluble union before God. Advocates of the reform complacently declared that 'we have in this age got the better of this as well as a great many other superstitious opinions ...' so as 'to render Christianity consistent with common sense'. Marriage was now regarded as a contract like any other, subject to statutory controls for the public good, for 'this adding of a sanctity to the marriage is inconsistent with the good of every society and with the happiness of mankind in general'. The Bill was thus clearly only made possible by the growing secularization of elite society and by the acceptance of the idea that personal happiness could be achieved by public legislation. Its proponents would have preferred to restrict the clause demanding parental consent to persons of 'fortune and rank', but recognized that 'this is impossible in this country'.

The second object of the Bill was to do away with secret precontracts and secret marriages, which made bigamy all too easy (Plate 4). Public registration of the marriage was now an essential part of the ceremony. It was argued, with some plausibility, that under existing conditions in which marriage could be made by mere verbal contract, by the blessing of a wandering clergyman in an alehouse, by a private chaplain in a private house, or by a commercial clerical marriage-maker in one of the unlicensed London churches, a man could have as many wives as he wished. 'Every man may privately have a wife in every corner of this city, or in every town he has been in, without it being possible for them to know of one another.' Another speaker agreed that 'the crime of polygamy [is] now so frequent'.

At this period there was no divorce permitting remarriage in the Anglican Church. For marriages which broke down, usually because of adultery, there was only separation of bed and board, accompanied by a financial settlement. This was currently called 'divorce', but it did not allow either party to remarry. Moreover the many medieval impediments which could create a nullity were now blocked up. These had been so numerous that a rich man with a good lawyer could probably obtain one, although the records of ecclesiastical courts show that the average man did not use this device. He almost certainly simply divorced himself or ran away without going to law. After the Reformation, an annulment could only be obtained on the three grounds of a pre-contract to someone else, consanguinity within the Levitical degrees, or male impotence over a period of three years – the last not an easy matter to prove. A man or woman whose spouse had left home and had not been heard of for a period of seven years was also free to remarry, on the assumption that the missing spouse was dead. If he or she returned, however, either the first marriage took priority over the second or the woman was permitted to choose which husband she preferred.

For most people in England, therefore, marriage was an indissoluble union, breakable only by death; this point was emphasized by Defoe in 1727, and by that acidulous spinster Miss Weeton in a sarcastic poem in 1808 about a discontented husband:

> 'Come soon, O Death, and Alice take,'
> He loudly groan'd and cry'd;
> Death came – but made a sad mistake,
> For Richard 'twas that died.

Unlike the other Protestant churches, the Anglican Church, largely because of historical accident at its inception, failed to provide for remarriage by the innocent party in cases of separation for extreme cruelty or adultery. This question remained in some doubt throughout Elizabeth's reign, but was finally clarified by number 107 of the canons of 1604, which forbade the remarriage of 'divorced' persons. To the aristocracy this created an intolerable situation, since it meant that a nobleman whose wife committed adultery before producing a son was precluded from marrying again and begetting a legal male heir to carry on the line and inherit the property. It was to circumvent this difficulty that in the late seventeenth century, as the concept of marriage as a sacrament ebbed with the waning of religious enthusiasm, divorce by private Act of Parliament became a possible avenue of escape for wealthy noblemen and others who found themselves in this predicament. But this was a very expensive procedure, and it was almost entirely confined, especially before 1760, to those who had very large properties at stake to be handed on to a male heir by a second marriage. Between 1670 and 1799, there were only 131 such Acts, virtually all instituted by husbands, and only seventeen passed before 1750. Thus in 1715, by a close vote of 49 to 47, the House refused to pass a divorce bill requested by Sir George Downing. In 1701, at the age of fifteen, he had gone through an arranged marriage with a fifteen-year-old girl. They had then immediately parted, Sir George going abroad for four years, and the marriage, by mutual consent, had never been consummated. The bill was rejected on the grounds that both parties had been over the age of consent (fourteen and twelve respectively).

At the other end of the social scale, among the propertyless, there were also alternatives to death as a means of finally dissolving an unsatisfactory marriage. In a society without a national police force, it was all too easy simply to run away and never be heard of again. This must have been a not infrequent occurrence among the poor, to judge by the fact that deserted wives comprised over eight per cent of all the women aged between thirty-one and forty listed in the 1570 census of the indigent poor of the city of Norwich. The second alternative was bigamy, which seems to have been both easy and common. In the eighteenth century, more or less permanent desertion was also regarded as morally dissolving the marriage.

A third alternative for the poor in the eighteenth century was the unofficial folk-custom of divorce by mutual consent by 'wife-sale'. As described in 1772, the husband 'puts a halter about her neck and thereby leads her to the next market place, and there puts her up to auction to be sold to the best bidder, as if she were a brood mare or a milch-cow. A purchaser is generally provided beforehand on these occasions.' This procedure was based closely on that of the sale of cattle. It took place frequently in a cattle-market like Smithfield and was accompanied by the use of a symbolic halter, by which the wife was led to market by the seller, and led away again by the buyer. The transaction sometimes even included the payment of a fee to the clerk of the market. In the popular mind, this elaborate ritual freed the husband of all future responsibility for his wife, and allowed both parties to marry again. Very often, perhaps normally, the bargain was pre-arranged with the full consent of the wife, both purchaser and price being agreed upon beforehand. The latter varied widely, from a few pence to a few guineas.

It appears that this procedure was almost exclusively confined to the lower classes, and was centred mostly in the big towns and the west of England. It had a medieval origin, but evidence for it becomes far more frequent in the late eighteenth century, then dies away in the nineteenth, the last recorded case being 1887. To the labouring classes, this ritualized procedure was clearly regarded as a perfectly legitimate form of full divorce, to be followed by remarriage, despite its illegality in both secular and ecclesiastical courts, and despite increasing condemnation in the public press. Indeed the courts made intermittent and half-hearted attempts to stop it, Lord Mansfield treating it as a criminal offence, a conspiracy to commit adultery.

In the late seventeenth and eighteenth centuries, therefore, full divorce and remarriage were possible by law for the very rich and by folk custom for the very poor, but impossible for the great majority in the middle who could not afford the cost of the one or the social stigma and remote risks of prosecution of the other.

CHAPTER TWO

The Demographic Facts

Birth, copulation and death,
That's all the facts when you come to brass tacks,
Birth, copulation and death.
(T. S. Eliot, *Sweeney Agonistes*)

'Man that is born of Woman is of few days and full of trouble.
He cometh forth like a flower and is cut down. He fleeth also
as a shadow and continueth not.'
(*Emblems of Mortality*, London, 1789, p. 39 (quoting
Job xiv, 1), illustrated in *Early Children's Books and
their Illustration*, ed. G. Gottlieb, Pierpont Morgan Library, New York, 1975, no. 86)

The best way to start an analysis of family structure is to establish
the demographic facts, which inexorably dictated so many of its
basic features, including even such apparently independent variables
as emotional commitment. These facts did not alter very dramatically over time, but they varied from class to class, and it is necessary
to distinguish between the landed, professional and mercantile rich,
the top three to five per cent who dominated the society, and the
plebeians of moderate, modest or marginal wealth who formed the
vast majority.

1. MARRIAGE

Among the landed classes in pre-Reformation England, nuptiality –
the proportion of surviving children who married – was determined
by family strategy. The three objectives of family planning were the
continuity of the male line, the preservation intact of the inherited
property, and the acquisition through marriage of further property or
useful political alliances. Given the very uncertain prospects of survival, the first could only be ensured by the procreation of the largest

possible number of children in the hope that at least one male child would live to marriageable age. The second could only be assured by restricting the claims of the children on the patrimony through primogeniture. This meant excluding younger sons and daughters from the bulk of the inheritance, which delayed their marriage, and in many cases meant depriving them of the opportunity to marry at all. The third could best be achieved by marrying them, and marrying them into wealthy and influential families, which in the case of daughters demanded the provision of large cash portions, and in the case of younger sons required substantial annuities or two-life leases of property. The second objective thus directly clashed with the third, and if the former were given priority, as it often was, it meant the sacrifice of daughters by putting them into nunneries, and the extrusion of younger sons to fend for themselves as military adventurers or clergy or otherwise. The ideal of virginity so valued by the Catholic Church provided the theological and moral justification for the existence of nunneries, which contained considerable numbers of upper-class girls placed there by their fathers in order to get rid of them. Many, but by no means all, of these girls probably found the religious life a satisfying alternative career to an arranged marriage. For those women who sought power, the life of an abbess was clearly preferable even to that of an aristocratic wife.

With the abolition of nunneries in the mid-sixteenth century, this delicate mechanism that made possible vigorous procreation and the avoidance of costly marriages was upset. This abrupt change coincided with a period during which the desire to preserve intact the family patrimony was at its weakest and when it became morally obligatory upon the landed classes to marry off their daughters. The marriage market was flooded with girls who had hitherto been consigned to nunneries, but who now had to be married off, at considerable cost, to their social equals. Despite a heavy and growing drain on the family resources, more than ninety-five per cent of all surviving daughters born in the late sixteenth century to the English nobility eventually married. Among boys from this landed elite, the eldest son and heir at this period almost always married, since his prime duty was to produce a male heir to carry on the line, but about one fifth of the younger sons were obliged to remain bachelors for life.

In the late seventeenth and eighteenth centuries, there was a distinct trend towards bachelordom among owners of medium to large

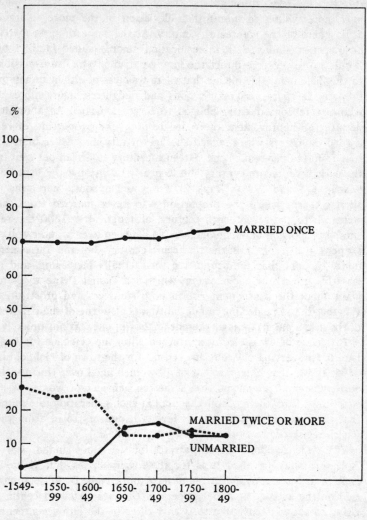

country houses in three sample counties (Graph 1). The cause of this is a mystery, although some may have been homosexual and now more willing to admit their deviation in the more tolerant atmosphere of the eighteenth century. At the same time, property arrangements indicate an intensification among landed families of the desire to preserve intact the family patrimony for transmission to the male heir. This meant that there was less of either money or property to spare for younger sons and daughters, many more of whom were consequently obliged to forgo marriage. As a result, despite the improvement of record-keeping, the proportion of recorded daughters who reached the age of fifty and never married rose from ten per cent in the sixteenth century to fifteen per cent in the early seventeenth century and to nearly twenty-five per cent between 1675 and 1799 (Graph 2). For younger sons, there was a similar sharp rise in the proportion who never married from the sixteenth to the seventeenth century, although after 1600 the recorded proportion of bachelors hovered between twenty and twenty-six per cent (Graph 2). In the eighteenth century contemporaries certainly thought that the proportion was actually increasing, and it was this growth of bachelordom which led Daniel Defoe to complain about the consequent rise in both spinsters and prostitutes. Whether the same decline in nuptiality was also true of the children of the urban patriciate is at present unknown, but it is not unlikely.

For those below the rural and urban elite, the evidence for England is still very patchy, but one census, for the town of Lichfield in 1695, shows that nine per cent of all women aged over thirty were still spinsters. This means that some ten per cent of women were withdrawn from the reproductive pool in each generation, assuming that the illegitimacy rate was as low as it appears to be from the parish registers.

The evidence about age of marriage for the upper landed classes is less satisfactory than it is for the lower classes, but there is enough to be reasonably certain of facts and trends. Daughters married on the average at about twenty in the late sixteenth century, rising to about twenty-two to twenty-three in the late seventeenth and eighteenth. When it comes to boys it is essential to make a clear distinction between the son and heir and his younger brothers, since they followed completely different patterns. The median age at first marriage of heirs for the English squirarchy was about twenty-one in the early sixteenth century, twenty-two in the late sixteenth cen-

GRAPH 2: Proportion of Peers' Children (aged 50 +)
Who Never Married

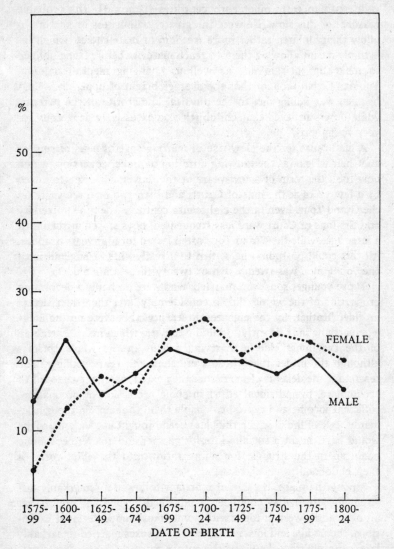

DATE OF BIRTH

tury, twenty-four rising to twenty-six in the seventeenth and early eighteenth centuries, and twenty-seven to twenty-nine in the late eighteenth to early nineteenth centuries (Graph 3). The probable reasons for this slow rise were the greater willingness by parents to allow their children rather more freedom of mate choice, which inevitably meant allowing them to reach maturity before being obliged to make up their minds, as well as changing medical opinion. Thomas Cogan thought that the average height of upper-class Englishmen was falling due to the physical immaturity of the parents, while others believed that childbirth was excessively dangerous for very young girls.

A final cause for the slow rise of marriage age of heirs of squires and their wives was the growing duration of higher education, which now took the form of a few years at the university, often followed by a few years at the Inns of Court, and then two or three years on the Grand Tour. Even in the eighteenth century, when the university and the Inns of Court were less frequented, boys stayed at school to a later age, while the Grand Tour often lasted for four years or more. All this could postpone the return to a settled life in England until the young man was twenty-two or twenty-three years old.

Those younger sons who married, who were probably a decreasing proportion of the whole, did so considerably later than their sisters or elder brother. By the eighteenth century, they were on the average marrying in their early to middle thirties, which makes them one of the two most elderly marrying groups in the whole society, although the brides they chose were some ten years younger. The reason for the delay is clear. Before they could marry they needed to accumulate, by individual effort in some profession or occupation, sufficient income and capital to enable them to maintain the gentlemanly style of life in which they had been brought up. Early marriage would have meant a socially inferior partner and a severe economic handicap in the struggle for reintegration into the elite world of their childhood.

Among the plebs, the age of marriage followed a remarkably different pattern. It has now been established beyond any doubt that all over north-west Europe, with some unexplained regional exceptions, the middle and lower classes of both sexes married remarkably late, certainly from the fifteenth century onward. This created a pattern which was 'unique for all large populations for which data exist or reasonable surmises can be made'. A very large quantity of

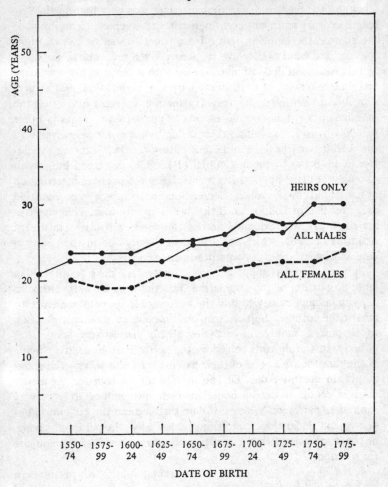

GRAPH 3: Median Age at First Marriage of Peers' Children and Heirs of Squires and Above

evidence for France, some for Italy, and a certain amount for England and America, proves that among small property-owners and labourers the median age of first marriage was very high in the sixteenth century and went even higher in the seventeenth and part of the eighteenth centuries, rising from twenty-seven to twenty-eight for men and from twenty-five to twenty-seven for women.

This custom of delayed marriage for both sexes is an extraordinary and unique feature of north-west European civilization, and at present it lacks a fully satisfactory explanation. It seems likely that the practice of boarding out adolescents as unmarried servants in other people's houses, or binding them as apprentices for seven years in the towns, must have been a contributory factor in causing the delay. In 1556 the Common Council of London, disturbed by growth of poverty caused by 'over-hasty marriages and over-soon setting up of households by the youth', decreed that nobody was to be admitted as a Freeman of London until the age of twenty-four. This effective marriage bar was extended across the country by the Statute of Artificers of 1563, which set a limit of twenty-one in the countryside and twenty-four in corporate towns.

By far the most important cause, however, since it affected a large proportion of the population, was the need to wait, either to save up enough money to buy the necessary household goods, or to inherit the cottage, shop or farm, and so be in an economic position to support a family. In societies where girls marry soon after puberty, this problem is solved by the newly married couple's living in the same house as one of their parents for some years – the stem-family. In north-western Europe, it was the custom for the newly married couple to set up house on their own immediately or very soon after marriage. When and why this became the custom is unknown, but under these conditions, either a lengthy period of saving, or the death or retirement of a parent, was a necessary prerequisite for marriage.

Given the high mortality rates among adults of pre-modern society, and the need for some capital to set up a family, the delayed marriage system makes good economic sense, especially in areas such as England where the father did not normally retire and hand over the farm in return for food and shelter.

It has been argued that post-Reformation Christianity has favoured late marriage, by encouraging asceticism and thrift, and the nuclear family over the kin. It is impossible to prove this suggestion, although there are striking correlations in eastern Europe and the Balkans between Christianity and late marriage, and Islam and early marriage.

There are several consequences which must have followed from the late-marriage pattern, which since the sixteenth century has been normal among the poor and the lower-middle classes, and since the eighteenth century among the professional classes and the younger sons of the landed classes (two categories which to some extent overlap). In view of the low recorded level of illegitimacy it is reasonable to assume that for many young men this delay involved considerable sexual denial at a time of optimum male sexual drive, despite the usual non-procreative outlets. If one follows Freudian theory, this could lead to neuroses of the kind that so regularly shattered the calm of Oxford and Cambridge colleges at this period; it could help to explain the high level of group aggression, which lay behind the extraordinary expansionist violence of western nation states at this time. It could also have been a stimulus to capitalist economic enterprise, by providing a cheap youthful labour force, stimulating saving in order to marry, and generating activist social and economic dynamism. Certainly the delay caused severe problems of social control among the lower classes, which were dealt with by ensuring so far as possible that young people lived in households as family workers, apprentices or servants, rather than in lodgings by themselves.

Secondly, like the relatively low nuptiality rate, late marriage put a severe brake on demographic growth, by withholding sexually mature women from reproduction for some ten of their twenty-five fertile years. This is partly why the demographic growth in England, even in its spurts between 1520 and 1620 and after 1740, was so slow relative to the rates currently experienced by under-developed countries in the late twentieth century.

Thirdly, it means that families tended to be formed consecutively rather than concurrently, marriage taking place as often as not after the death of the father, and in most cases after the death of one parent or another.

If the age of first marriage was very late for all save the male heirs and the daughters of the landed classes, the duration of marriage was generally very short. It is a curious fact that, if one adopts the reasonable criterion of durability, marriages in the mid-twentieth century were more stable than at almost any other time in history, despite the high divorce rate. In the United States in 1955, the average marriage lasted thirty-one years before it was broken either by the death of one or other of the partners or by divorce, the latter accounting for one-third of total dissolutions. In the seventeenth and eighteenth centuries, however, marriages were broken very much earlier by the premature death of one spouse or another, since all pre-modern societies had a fairly high death rate among young adults. In England the only evidence as yet available covers a single village. It suggests that the median duration of first marriages among the poor was about seventeen to nineteen years, rising to twenty-two in the late eighteenth century. For the children of the squirarchy, the median duration of first marriages was twenty-two years in the early seventeenth century, falling to nineteen in the period of high mortality in the late seventeenth century, but rising to thirty as mortality fell in the late eighteenth century (Graph 4). It seems safe to assume that among the bulk of the population the median duration of marriage in Early Modern England was probably somewhere about seventeen to twenty years.

From these facts can be drawn one very firm conclusion about the pre-modern family, namely that it was, statistically speaking, a transient and temporary association, both of husband and wife and of parents and children. Indeed, it looks very much as if modern divorce is little more than a functional substitute for death. The decline of the adult mortality rate after the late eighteenth century, by prolonging the expected duration of marriage to unprecedented lengths, eventually forced Western society to adopt the institutional escape-hatch of divorce. Marriage must, therefore, have lasted longest during the Victorian period, when declining mortality rates had not yet been offset by rising divorce rates.

Secondly, throughout the Early Modern period, a couple marrying had less than fifty per cent statistical probability of life together for more than a year or two after their children had left home. It is only in the twentieth century that the sharp reduction in the age at which the last child is born, coupled with the sharp decline in adult mortality rates, has created the expectation of up to twenty years of life together after the departure of the children.

Thirdly, remarriage was very common, about a quarter of all marriages being a remarriage for the bride or the groom. Among the squirarchy and above, about twenty-five per cent married again in the late sixteenth and seventeenth centuries and about fifteen per

GRAPH 4: Median Duration of First Marriage

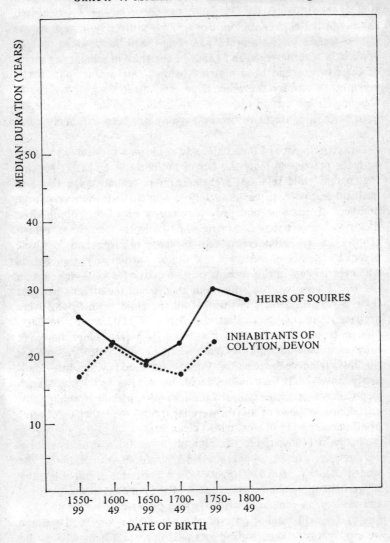

cent in the eighteenth, of whom about five per cent married a third time or more (Graph 1 p. 39). Why the remarriage rate declined so sharply in the eighteenth century remains a mystery, unless it was due to declining adult mortality. Among the plebs the same pattern applies. In Manchester in the 1650s in one third of all marriages one of the partners had been married before. This means that in the seventeenth century the remarriage rate, made possible by death, was not far off that in our own day, made possible by divorce. In both periods, consecutive legal polygamy has been extremely common.

One consequence of high child and adult mortality rates, coupled with the practice of fostering out of the home at an early age, was that parent–child relations were even more tenuous than those of husband and wife. It was a society in which there were very large numbers of orphans, and only a minority of adolescent children had two living parents. Among the sixteenth- and seventeenth-century English aristocracy, one in three children had lost one parent by the age of fourteen, and the proportion among plebeians was even higher. In the records of first marriages in Manchester in the 1650s, over half the brides and almost half the grooms had lost their fathers. In 1696 one third of all the children in Bristol were orphans. It is thus clear that a majority of children in the Early Modern period were bereaved of at least one parent before they were fully adult. How far this created a serious psychological trauma for the child is an open question. What can be said with some confidence, however, is that unions including widows or widowers with step-children of their own, or families which included orphaned or abandoned nephews or nieces, were far from rare. Perhaps a quarter of all families were of this hybrid character.

Finally, it follows from the high adult mortality rate that there were relatively few aged parents to be looked after, even among the landed classes (Graph 5). Gregory King's figures for Lichfield in 1695 suggest that only about five per cent of the population was over the age of sixty, as compared with fourteen per cent in America today. Among the will-making part of the population, bereaved parents were obligatorily looked after by the children. So long as they did not remarry, most widows had a legal right to a room and board, and access to the communal fire, in the house of their eldest child. Widowers also seem to have been 'sojourners' in their sons' houses. It is clear, therefore, that the inexorable consequences of high adult

GRAPH 5: Expectations of Life at 21 of Heirs of Squires and Above

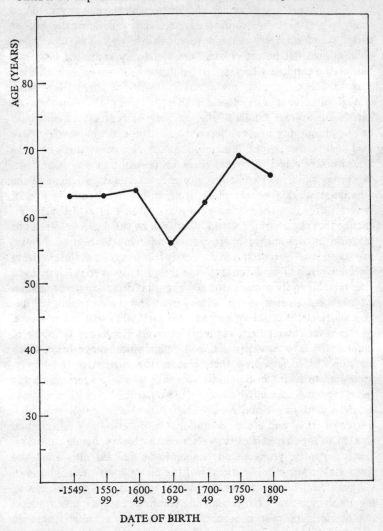

mortality coupled with late marriage was a family structure which was fundamentally different from that to which we are accustomed today. Marriages were contracted late, and were normally broken early; couples rarely survived together for very long after their children had left home; remarriages were very common; less than half of the children who reached adulthood did so while both their parents were alive; and only a small minority of parents lived long enough to become an economic burden on their children in their old age. In the average family of the seventeenth century, a man would be one of four, five or six children, two or three of whom would have died before the age of fifteen. At twenty-six or twenty-seven he would marry a girl of twenty-three or twenty-four and have four, five or six children. Two or three of them would die young, and the remainder would be sent away from home at about the age of twelve. After less than seventeen years there was a fifty per cent chance that the marriage would be broken by the death of himself or his wife. In the Early Modern period this combination of delayed marriage, low life expectation and early fostering out of the surviving children resulted in a conjugal family which was very short-lived and unstable in its composition. Few mutual demands were made on its members, so that it was a low-keyed and undemanding institution which could therefore weather this instability with relative ease.

A final fact about Early Modern marriage that has to be borne in mind is the very limited social and geographical range from which all strata of society drew their brides. The custom of the dowry, according to which brides from all ranks of the propertied classes were expected to contribute a cash sum, together with the great sensitivity to status and rank, meant that there was a very high degree of social and economic endogamy. To give but one example, in Kent in the first half of the seventeenth century, about half of all knights, gentry, yeoman and husbandmen married girls from the same status group, while a third of the clergy married daughters of clergy. Occupational endogamy among artisans and craftsmen was inevitably less close; but among the commoner trades, about one in five of clothiers, tailors, butchers, shoemakers and sailors married daughters of members of their own occupation.

The geographical horizons of marriage were also very limited, although the higher one moves up the social scale, the wider they become. Only with the aristocracy, and only by the early seventeenth century, however, was there a genuinely national marriage market even at this elevated level. The squirarchy, men who carried the title of esquire, knight or baronet, were far more limited in their range, at any rate up to the 1630s, and probably beyond. In the early seventeenth century, sixty per cent of the squirarchy of Lancashire and fifty per cent of that of Dorset married within the county. By about 1700 regional marriage markets were developing for the squirarchy, such as the service performed by the annual fair at Bury St Edmunds. It was attended by 'an infinite number of knights' daughters from Norfolk, Cambridgeshire and Suffolk', and in practice was 'more a market for ladies than merchandises'. In the eighteenth century a national marriage market for the squirarchy also developed at the balls, assemblies and parties that constituted the season at London in the spring and at Bath in the early summer. By the 1740s these were now well-established institutions where the elite young of both sexes from all over the country could freely meet and mingle.

Among squires and above in Northamptonshire, there was a sharp drop from about thirty to forty per cent marrying within the county in the sixteenth century to about twenty per cent thereafter, sinking still further to fifteen per cent in the late eighteenth century. The effect of the development of national marriage markets in London and Bath is very clear.

At the level of agricultural labourers, husbandmen and artisans, studies of several villages, six in Lancashire, and one near York, indicate that as late as 1800 about two thirds of all grooms who married where they were born chose brides from the village itself, about ninety per cent from within ten miles and all but a negligible proportion from within twenty miles. Those who emigrated to towns or elsewhere naturally married further afield, but for those who stayed behind, the limits were set by the distance a suitor was prepared to walk or ride to visit a girl, and by the restricted range which most boys and girls travelled to take up employment as living-in servants.

2. BIRTH

It is commonly supposed that pre-modern homes were swarming with children. This is an illusion derived from a number of striking but in fact exceptional examples. No one who has once read about it will easily forget the family size of the early eighteenth-century

Scottish architect James Smith. Before dying at the age of thirty-seven in 1699 giving birth to twins, his first wife provided him with eighteen children. He then married again and fathered fourteen more, making thirty-two in all, most of whom survived and one of whom he named 'Climacteric Smith', since the child was born in his father's seventieth year.

The normal reality was very different. Since the female age of marriage was commonly between twenty-three and twenty-seven, and the menopause began at about forty, the period during which the average wife could give birth was fairly limited. Moreover, many marriages did not last through the full female reproductive span, owing to the premature death of one spouse or the other. The average number of children born to one wife was therefore only four or less in upper-class England (Graph 6) and six or eight among the yeomen and freeholders in the much healthier conditions of New England.

The interval between births was on the average between twenty-four and thirty months. One explanation for birth intervals of this length is foetal wastage through miscarriages, still-births and possibly induced abortions. The one parish register so far discovered to record still-births shows a very high and rising rate of between four and ten per cent of live births between 1581 and 1710. The rate, which is a bare minimum since it omits unnamed children and possibly others, rose sharply in the late seventeenth century, for reasons which are not at present clear, unless induced abortions were on the increase or maternal nutrition was on the decline.

More important, however, was the contraceptive effect of lactation on most women, and especially those whose diet was insufficient to maintain body-weight. Lactation, which commonly lasted for eighteen months or more, induces amenorrhoea in most cases for about six months for well-fed women and eighteen months for women suffering from malnutrition. It therefore serves as an effective contraceptive, while some women in the more literate classes may have followed medical advice against a lactating woman having sexual intercourse. There is no evidence, however, that there was any superstitious taboo among the poor against intercourse at this time. Finally, birth intervals lengthened very significantly with age, either because of declining female fecundity or male virility, or because of greater incentive to and expertise in contraceptive practices, or some combination of these.

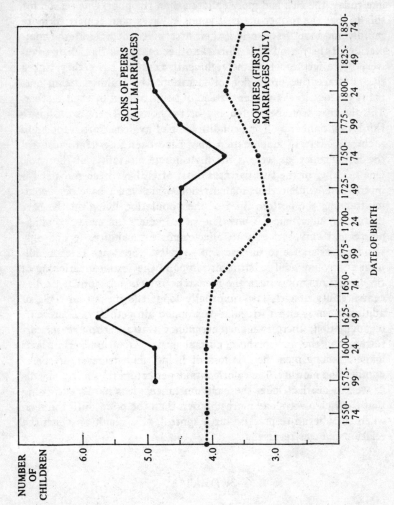

GRAPH 6: Mean Number of Children Born

The other significant fact to notice about family size is that, unlike today, the rich had more children than the poor. One reason for this is that the former married younger wives, and remarried more rapidly and more frequently if their first wives died before the completion of the period of fertility. Another reason is that their wives were more fertile before the eighteenth century, since they lacked the contraceptive protection of lactation, the children being normally put out to wet-nurses instead of being nursed by their mother. Thirdly, they were better fed and better housed. There is reason to think that unhealthy living conditions, bad hygiene, rotten food and a chronic state of malnutrition may have been powerful causes of the low fertility, as well as the high infant mortality, of the poor. One or other of the two partners must often have been too sick for intercourse, while serious malnutrition, which must have been common among the bottom third of the population living on the bare margin of subsistence, is now known to reduce the male sexual appetite and very seriously to affect female fecundity. It not only weakens resistance to disease and so raises the death rate of children and young adults, but it also impairs the sexual functioning of the living. Among women the menarche is delayed; normal adolescent sterility of girls lasts unusually long; the menstrual cycle of adult women is either irregular or stopped altogether, thus preventing ovulation; there is higher pregnancy wastage through miscarriages; and the amenorrhoea normal during lactation period lasts longer. Among men there is loss of libido, and decrease of sperm number and motility. The caloric intake per capita thus affects births as well as deaths. Under these circumstances, it is hardly surprising that the rich always had more children than the poor, until the time when they began to practise birth control, as a result of which the relationship was reversed.

3. DEATH

The most striking feature which distinguished the Early Modern family from that of today does not concern either marriage or birth; it was the constant presence of death. Death was at the centre of life, as the cemetery was at the centre of the village. Death was a normal occurrence in persons of all ages, and was not something that happened mainly to the old. Urban populations were particularly at risk, due to contaminated water supplies, and no early modern city reproduced itself; even to maintain their size, all were dependent on a constant influx from the healthier countryside.

It appears to be a fact that for the last two thirds of the sixteenth century mortality rates declined for a time, during a temporary easing of the ancient threat of bubonic plague and before the ravages of smallpox began. But the relief was only relative, and it did not last into the seventeenth century, when death rates rose again to very high levels. The cause of this rise is unknown, but it was perhaps because the expansion of world commerce carried with it from continent to continent hitherto unknown diseases and new strains of viruses and bacteria, to which local immunity had not been built up by long exposure. In addition, smallpox seems to have become both much more widespread and much more lethal. This would explain why greater general prosperity and cheaper food was accompanied by a higher death rate.

The expectation of life at birth in England in the 1640s was only thirty-two years. Of those born alive, the ones most at risk were new-born infants. The average recorded mortality rate in the first year in France was between fifteen and thirty per cent, with the mean at twenty-one per cent, but the real rate must have been much higher due to unrecorded births of children who died in the first few days or weeks of life.

The recorded death rate of the one-year-olds, which is probably much more accurate, was about eighteen per cent between the ages of one and five, so that prospects of survival were significantly, but not dramatically, improved once the first year was passed. The situation was distinctly better in rural England than in France, so far as we can tell at present, but even so, between a quarter and a third of all children of English peers and peasants were dead before they reached the age of fifteen (Graph 7).

There is growing reason to suspect that a proportion of the infant deaths of the poor were due to culpable neglect. Infants in the Early Modern period were exposed to lack of attention by the mother in the first critical weeks; premature weaning; accidental smothering in bed with their parents; the transfer of the infant to the care of a wet-nurse (with the high probability of death by neglect); abandonment in doorways; or deposit in parish workhouses or foundling hospitals, which were often almost equally lethal if less offensive to the public than the spectacle of dead babies littering the streets.

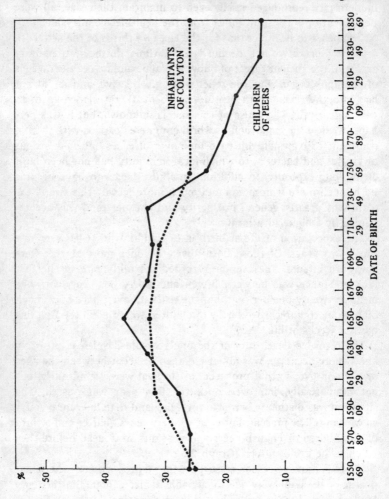

Even if mortality rates in England were lower than those of France, this will not alter the fact that to preserve their mental stability, parents were obliged to limit the degree of their psychological involvement with their infant children. Even when children were genuinely wanted and not regarded as economically crippling nuisances, it was very rash for parents to get too emotionally concerned about creatures whose expectation of life was so very low. Nothing better illustrates the resigned acceptance of the expendability of children than the medieval practice of giving the same name to two living siblings in the expectation that only one would survive. The sixteenth-, seventeenth- and early eighteenth-century practice of giving a new-born child the same name as one who had recently died indicates a lack of sense that the child was a unique being, with its own name.

As late as the 1770s Mrs Thrale, who in some respects was a devotedly child-oriented mother, was nonetheless unmoved by the sickly appearance or early death of her infant children, although she took the death of the older children very hard indeed. When in 1770 Susanna Arabella was born two months prematurely, her mother never expected her to live, and took an instant dislike to her, since 'she is so very poor a creature I can scarce bear to look on her'. When two years later another daughter, Penelope, died within ten hours of birth, her mother commented coolly, 'one cannot grieve after her much, and I have just now other things to think of.'

The high mortality rates of the Early Modern period did not only affect children, and therefore the attitude of parents to children. They also radically affected young adults, who continued to die at a rapid rate in the prime of life, between the ages of twenty and fifty. The modern association of death with the aged bears no relation to reality at any earlier period, when relatively few died at a ripe old age.

It should be pointed out, however, that members of the rural elite – wealthy squires and above – who survived to twenty-one could expect to live into the early sixties at all times except the lethal late seventeenth century, and to the late sixties after 1750 (Graph 5, p, 49). The incidence of death was highly class-specific, and those who lived in comfort, lived mainly away from cities, and could flee epidemics, had far better chances of survival than town dwellers or their social inferiors. Even they, however, were at the mercy of chance, and their hold on life was a perpetual gamble. The lucky

GRAPH 8: Expectation of Life at Birth of Sons of Peers

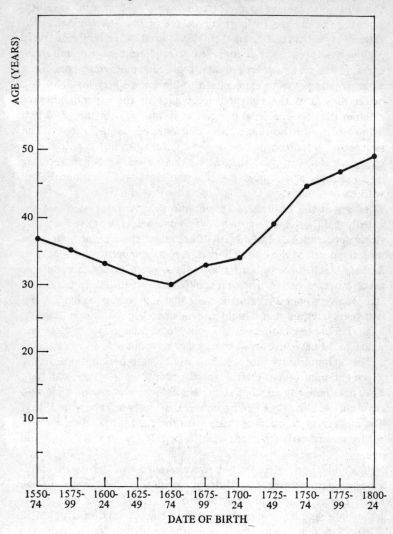

AGE (YEARS)

DATE OF BIRTH

survivors were treated with great respect, since they were so few, compared with the multitude who were born and fell by the way-side.

It was not until after 1750 that in England the level of infant and child mortality began to fall, and the expectation of life at birth to rise (Graphs 7 and 8). The reasons for this remarkable change are not at all clear. One possibility is an improvement in the under-standing of obstetrics. The medical profession at last began to take the problem seriously, and male midwives appeared, who possessed stronger hands and who pioneered two extremely important tech-nical advances, which were widely spread between 1730 and 1770. The first was version, or the turning of the infant's body in the womb so that if it did not come out head first, it at least emerged breech first. The second was the slow development of efficient forceps, the use of which would extract the infant without killing it in the pro-cess. This was an enormous improvement on the previous resort to hooked instruments, which certainly killed the infant and were quite likely to tear into the mother's uterus as well.

Both developments were the product of the growing profession of male midwives, whose rise in numbers and popularity was looked upon with deep suspicion both by the ignorant female midwives, whose livelihoods were threatened by their advent, and also by their professional medical colleagues, who associated the trade with that of abortionists. The first male midwife to achieve knighthood was Sir David Hamilton in 1703 – an event that so outraged a conservative colleague that he spread the couplet:

'Rise up, Sir David,' said the Queen
The first cunt-knight that e'er was seen.

Another suggestion for the post-1770 decline in infant mortality is that it was caused by the increase in the supply of cow's milk to urban areas, which saved many infant lives. Better personal hygiene, facilitated by the spread of easily washable cotton clothing, may have helped. The greater opportunities for child employment during the early phases of industrialization may also have provided poor parents with a greater incentive to preserve their children, and a greater ability to feed them and keep them alive. The decline in child mortality was probably due, to a significant extent, to the effectiveness of inoculation against smallpox, which became normal among the elite in the latter half of the eighteenth century. How widespread the practice was lower down the social scale is still a matter for dispute.

The psychological and practical effects upon family life of the high mortality rates of Early Modern England can easily be judged by looking at almost any tomb of the period. For example, at Yarnton, in Oxfordshire, there is a memorial to Sir Thomas Spencer and his family. Sir Thomas died aged forty-six in 1685, while his widow survived him for twenty-seven years. But he lived to bury not only two infant sons (called successively Thomas) and two infant daughters, but also his only surviving son and heir, William, who died aged twenty-six. The tomb shows Sir Thomas flanked by his dead heir, his widow and his four surviving daughters and co-heiresses.

Similar evidence of high mortality can be culled from the genealogy of any well-documented family of the period. The story of the upper squirarchy family of the Verneys of Middle Claydon in Buckinghamshire during the middle and late seventeenth century will serve as well as any. In 1625 the mayor of Abingdon and his wife both died of the plague, leaving a seven-year-old orphan girl, Mary. Relatives bought her wardship from the Crown and sold her at the age of thirteen to Sir Edmund Verney, to be married to his sixteen-year-old son and heir, Ralph. Ralph lived on to the age of eighty-three but Mary died at thirty-four, having given birth to six children. Of the six, two died in infancy and two when aged four and eight. Seven of Ralph's eleven brothers and sisters lived to the age of fifty and over (one died at eighty-eight and another at ninety-two) and six were married, and yet between them they produced only two sons who survived to maturity. Ralph's eldest son, Edmund, married at twenty-six a girl who turned out to be a life-long and incurable melancholic, but who managed to produce three children. Their eldest son died unmarried of a fever at the age of twenty in the lifetime of his father (who died aged fifty-two); the second son died unmarried of a fever at the age of twenty-two four years later; and the surviving daughter died in childbirth at the age of twenty-one, the infant also dying a month later. With the death of all three children, the direct line thus came to an end.

Ralph's second son, John, had been a Turkey merchant and married very late, after he had first made a fortune in Aleppo. Six years after his return to London, at the age of forty, he married a sixteen-year-old girl. She bore him four children (who all lived) and then died six years later, at the age of twenty-two. Six years later still, now aged fifty-two, John married the thirty-one-year-old daughter of a baronet to serve as a stepmother to his four young motherless children. She produced a child who died almost immediately, and a year later, once again pregnant, she succumbed to smallpox and died after only two years of marriage. So he tried again and married a twenty-five-year-old girl, who lived, but failed to produce a child.

In many respects these stories are largely typical of the life experiences of any family in the seventeenth century. On the other hand, it has to be emphasized that the wives in this case were exceptionally fertile, and also that this seems to have been a particularly unhealthy period. It was not until 1665 that the great scourge of England, bubonic plague, which had a death rate among its victims of about seventy per cent, finally and mysteriously died away after half a century of particularly severe recrudescence, with major outbreaks in London in 1603, 1625, 1636 and 1665, and many even more lethal outbreaks in country towns. One of the things that made the plague so psychologically shattering was that fear of contagion destroyed the bonds of family solidarity: 'then all friends leave us, then man or woman sits and lies alone and is a stranger to the breath of his own relations ...' since not even his nearest and dearest dared approach him.

Second only to the plague was the newer and now extremely common disease of smallpox, which if it did not so frequently kill, yet left many of the survivors either blinded altogether or pockmarked and disfigured for life. It seems likely that in the early eighteenth century smallpox was an all but universal disease, with a death rate among its victims of about sixteen per cent. There is mounting evidence of a peculiarly high mortality rate in the late seventeenth and early eighteenth centuries, and it seems likely that one cause was this new scourge of smallpox, not yet brought under control by inoculation.

Physical isolation was no insurance against smallpox. Alice Thornton first had a mild infection at the age of six in 1631, and contracted it a second time at the age of sixteen, when she nearly died. The disease also ravaged her surviving children. Both her daughters, Alice and Katherine, contracted it in 1666–7, losing all their hair and ruining their complexions as a result. The third surviving child, Robert, also went down with it, although with rather less devastating results: 'he never recovered his sweet beautiful favour and pure colour in his cheeks; but his face grew longish; his hair did not fall off.' As Oliver Goldsmith put it in 1760:

> Lo, the smallpox with horrid glare
> Levelled its terrors at the fair;
> And, rifling every youthful grace,
> Left but the remnant of a face.

So terrifying was this disease that it was sometimes difficult to find a clergyman willing to bury anyone who had died of it, and after the 1760s no prudent family would hire a servant who had not already had it or been inoculated against it. In 1766 Tom Watts of Bletchley had himself inoculated 'as he has a design to go to London for a place', and he knew that this was an essential requirement for employment in a genteel household. By the end of the century, it was recognized as a parental duty to have all one's children inoculated 'to alleviate the frightful disease'.

Apart from endemic diseases like smallpox, small children were exposed to a host of other dangers. According to Dr William Cadogan in 1748, the most common causes of infantile mortality were fever at teething time, and intestinal worms. Other causes were inadequate milk supply from mother or wet-nurse; poisoning from pewter dishes and lead nipple-shields; lack of fresh air; and excessive swaddling. Inadequate diet in infancy deformed many children by rickets, while the unbalanced diet of the rich made more than one in twelve of the late sixteenth- and early seventeenth-century peers the victims of years of agony from stones in the kidney or the bladder.

The almost total ignorance of both personal and public hygiene meant that contaminated food and water was a constant hazard. Personal standards of hygiene were no better at the very top of the social pyramid than at the bottom. In 1665 the court of Charles II fled from the great plague in London, and took refuge in the Oxford colleges. They did not go back to London until early the next year, 'leaving at their departure their excrements in every corner, in chimneys, studies, coal-houses, cellars'. In the same year Samuel Pepys, when one night he was sleeping in a strange house and found that the maid had forgotten to provide a chamber-pot, did not light a candle and fumble his way to the privy, but simply deposited his excrement – twice – in the fireplace.

In towns in the eighteenth century, the city ditches, now often filled with stagnant water, were commonly used as latrines; butchers killed animals in their shops and threw the offal of the carcasses into the streets; dead animals were left to decay and fester where they lay; latrine pits were dug close to wells, thus contaminating the water supply. Decomposing bodies of the rich in burial vaults beneath the church often stank out parson and congregation; urban cemeteries became overcrowded as the population grew, and the decaying bodies, constantly disturbed to make way for others, began to pollute the air of the neighbourhood. A special problem in London in the early eighteenth century was the 'poor's holes', large, deep, open pits in which were laid the bodies of the poor, side by side, row upon row. Only when the pit was filled with bodies was it finally covered over with earth. 'How noisesome the stench is that arises from these holes so stowed with dead bodies, especially in sultry seasons and after rain.'

In 1742 Dr Johnson described London as a city 'which abounds with such heaps of filth as a savage would look on with amazement'. There is corroborative evidence that indeed great quantities of human excrement were 'cast into the streets at night time when the inhabitants shut up their houses'. It was then dumped on the surrounding highways and ditches so that visitors to or from the city 'are forced to stop their noses to avoid the ill smell occasioned by it'. It was not until the 1750s that local regulations for sewage disposal and paving and lighting Acts at last improved the sanitary conditions of London. Even so, in the 1780s in the big slum tenement houses, there was a single inside privy shared by many families, so that 'there was always a reservoir of putrid matter in the lower part of the house ... But few houses were drained from the basement.' It was not until the very end of the eighteenth century that the English began to feel boastful about the state of their national sanitation, even though in fact it only applied to the rich. A caricature of 1796 illustrated 'National Conveniences' – the English water-closet, the Scotch bucket, the French latrine, and the Dutch lake.

The result of these primitive sanitary conditions was constant outbursts of bacterial stomach infections, the most fearful of all being dysentery, which swept away many victims of both sexes and of all ages within a few hours or days. Stomach disorders of one kind or another were chronic, due to poorly balanced diet among the rich, and the consumption of rotten and insufficient food among the poor. The prevalence of intestinal worms was the one scientific justification for the current medical practice of regular violent purges and emetics to empty the bowels and colon. A Mr Evans, 'the famous man for curing worms at Knightsbridge', had a very active practice indeed among the rich in the late eighteenth century. Sometimes recourse to him was too late, as in the case of Mr Carter's son, as 'the creatures had eaten into the intestines and the boy died'. On other occasions, his cures were ineffective, as in the case of Mrs Thrale's eldest daughter, who was 'grievously tormented with worms' in 1771 when she was taken to Mr Evans, and still 'mightily tormented' with them ten years later. Worms were a slow, disgusting and debilitating disease that caused a vast amount of human misery and ill health in the eighteenth century. Some of the remedies also were extremely dangerous, often consisting of swallowing pills of mercury or tin.

In the many poorly drained marshy areas, recurrent malarial fevers were common and debilitating diseases, while everyone was at the mercy of a miscellany of swift and incurable bacterial and viral infections which carried off young and old at a few days' notice. Perhaps even more heartbreaking was the slow, inexorable, destructive power of tuberculosis, or 'consumption' as it was then called, which seems to have been one of the commonest causes of death at this time, especially among children and adolescents. James Boswell's wife endured eleven years of spitting blood and slow physical deterioration before the disease finally killed her.

For women, childbirth was a very dangerous experience, for midwives were ignorant and ill-trained, and often horribly botched the job, while the lack of hygienic precautions meant that puerperal fever was a frequent sequel. All too common were such stories as one recorded succinctly by Oliver Heywood in 1684; 'Mistress Earnshaw of York was in sore labour, had her child pulled from her by piecemeal, died at last, left a sad husband.' Because of this high mortality from childbirth, at all periods from the sixteenth to the nineteenth century, in three out of four cases of all first marriages among the squirarchy that were broken by death within ten years, the cause was the death of the wife (Plate 5).

Finally, there was the constant threat of accidental death from neglect or carelessness or association with animals like horses – which seem to have been at least as dangerous as automobiles – or elements like water. From the series of accidents and diseases experienced by Simonds D'Ewes, the son of a wealthy lawyer in the early seventeenth century, it is hardly surprising that, after surviving so many hazards, he became convinced that he was one of the Elect of God.

The medical profession was almost entirely helpless to deal with human disease, since the scientific theory upon which treatment was based was disastrously wrong, and since virtually nothing was known about the importance of personal and public hygiene. The standard treatment was to aid nature by the forcible evacuation of evil 'humours' through bloodletting, induced vomiting, and the constant application of purges and enemas to clean out the stomach and bowels. No single disease had been properly diagnosed, except bubonic plague and smallpox, and there was no proper system of classification. Many of the remedies prescribed by reputable doctors hardly differed from the magical formulas of the witch doctors: for example, for apoplexy, swallow a glass of urine of a healthy person, mixed with salt, to induce vomiting; for gout, apply live earthworms to the affected part until they begin to smell. London virtuosi and members of the Royal Society were as helpless and credulous as any rural practitioner. Robert Boyle advised blowing dried and powdered human excrement into the eye as a remedy for cataract, while Robert Hooke took medicines made up of powdered human skull, among other ingredients.

The last cause of infant and child death was the indifference and neglect of many parents. The rich sent their children away to wet-nurses for the first year, despite the known negligence of nurses, which resulted in a death rate double that of maternally fed babies. The poor were sometimes obliged to leave their children tied up in swaddling-clothes for hours to wallow in their own excrement while they went out to work; poverty also obliged them to put the infants with them in their own beds, where they occasionally rolled over and smothered them in their sleep; like the parents, the infants were fed badly and irregularly; and if things got desperate, the parents might simply abandon the infants in the street rather than watch them starve. Part of the very high infant mortality must have been due to this neglect, itself the product of poverty and ignorance. But at the same time the neglect was caused in part by the high mortality rate, since there was small reward from lavishing time and care on such ephemeral objects as small babies. It was a vicious circle.

4. CONCLUSION

Under existing social and technological conditions, the availability of land and food set limits to the numerical size at which a population could be supported, which was effectively controlled by natural, social and cultural practices, affecting both birth and death.

The result was a population of which about half was under twenty and only a handful over sixty; in which marriage was delayed longer than in any other known society; in which so many infants died that they could only be regarded as expendable; and in which the family itself was a loose association of transients, constantly broken up by death of parents or children or the early departure of children from the home. It is impossible to stress too heavily the impermanence of the Early Modern family, whether from the point of view of husbands and wives, or parents and children. None could reasonably expect to remain together for very long, a fact which fundamentally affected all human relationships. Death was a part of life, and was realistically treated as such.

It would be foolish, however, to adopt a reductionist position that there is a simple and direct correlation between the level of mortality and the amount and degree of affect at any given moment in history. Mortality in England was abnormally high in the fifteenth century, abnormally low in the sixteenth, high again in the late seventeenth and early eighteenth, and began a prolonged secular fall in about the middle of the eighteenth century. This see-saw oscillation does not coincide with what little we know about affective relationships, which seem to have begun to improve when mortality was at a peculiarly high level, between 1650 and 1750. There is clearly an important intervening variable: the cultural norms and expectations of society. On the other hand, it is fairly clear that the relative lack of concern for small infants was closely tied to their poor expectation of survival and that there is on the average a rough secular correlation between high mortality and low gradient affect. The high gradient affect characteristic of modern Western societies is unlikely to develop on a mass scale before child and young adult mortality have declined and before child numbers have been reduced by contraception.

PART TWO

The Open Lineage Family
1450–1630

CHAPTER THREE

Family Characteristics

'The intent of matrimony is not for man and his wife to be always taken up with each other, but jointly to discharge the duties of civil society, to govern their families with prudence, and educate their children with discretion.'
(Restatement of the traditional position in *The Lady's Magazine*, V, 1774, p. 240)

1. STRUCTURE AND VALUES

The most striking characteristic of the late medieval and early sixteenth-century family, at all social levels, was the degree to which it was open to external influences, a porosity that is in contrast to the more sealed off and private nuclear family type that was to develop in the seventeenth and eighteenth centuries. Not only its individual members, but the nuclear family itself was strongly other-directed. The principal external agencies varied from class to class: among the landed elite being mainly the kin and the 'good lord'; and among the peasantry, artisans and labourers being mainly the neighbours. In both cases the nuclear family had only weak boundaries to separate it from wider definitions of social space.

In the late middle ages the nuclear family of the landed elite was no more than a loose core at the centre of a dense network of lineage and kin relationships. The degree to which the kin interacted with the nuclear core depended on social rank. It was dominant among the great aristocracy, very influential among the squirarchy, and still important among the parish gentry. The reason for this is the preoccupation with the preservation, increase and transmission through inheritance and marriage of the property and status of the lineage, of the generations of ancestors stretching back into the remote past. The larger the property and status, and the more ancient the family on its ancestral acres, the more intense was the preoccupation with the lineage, and thus the greater the participation of the kin in the formation and daily life of the conjugal family. A great many of the functions now performed by the nuclear family, and a great many of the emotions now focused upon it, were then shared with the kin. The family at this period cannot, therefore, be looked at in isolation, since at every turn it was being affected by and interacting with kin relatives. Since the kin formed a community, marriage meant not so much intimate association with an individual as entry into a new world of the spouse's relatives, uncles, nephews and distant cousins: 'I was married into my husband's family,' recalled Mary, Countess of Warwick, as late as the early seventeenth century, in a revealing phrase.

To understand the moral premises upon which such a society is based, it is necessary to rid ourselves of three modern Western culture-bound preconceptions. The first is that there is a clear dichotomy between marriage for interest, meaning money, status or power, and marriage for affect, meaning love, friendship or sexual attraction; and that the first is morally reprehensible. In practice in the sixteenth century, no such distinction existed; and if it did, affect was of secondary importance to interest, while romantic love and lust were strongly condemned as ephemeral and irrational grounds for marriage. The second modern preconception is that sexual intercourse unaccompanied by an emotional relationship is immoral, and that marriage for interest is therefore a form of prostitution. The third is that personal autonomy, the pursuit by the individual of his or her own happiness, is paramount, a claim justified by the theory that it in fact contributes to the well-being of the group. To an Elizabethan audience the tragedy of Romeo and Juliet, like that of Othello, lay not so much in their ill-starred romance as in the way they brought destruction upon themselves by violating the norms of the society in which they lived, which in the former case meant strict filial obedience and loyalty to the traditional friendships and enemies of the lineage. An Elizabethan courtier would be familiar enough with the bewitching passion of love to feel some sympathy with the young couple, but he would see clearly enough where duty lay.

Marriage among the property-owning classes in sixteenth-century England was, therefore, a collective decision of family and kin, not an individual one. Past lineage associations, political patronage, extension of lineage connections, and property preservation and accumulation were the principal considerations. Property and power were the predominant issues which governed negotiations for marriage, while the greatest fear in a society so acutely conscious of status and hierarchy was of social derogation in marriage, of alliance with a family of lower estate or degree than one's own. In the late middle ages, the current head of one of the larger landed families was regarded as no more than a temporary custodian of the family estates, which were the permanent assets of the lineage and were tied up in unbreakable entails, under which the bulk of them passed to the eldest son by the convention of primogeniture. The other children, both daughters and younger sons, were at the economic mercy of their father or elder brother, who could allocate to them as much or as little as he chose of the personal estate in cash or two-life leases. He could also grant them parts of the unentailed estates, and often did so, but was unable to give them any share of the entailed landed property.

The prime factor affecting all families which owned property was therefore the principle of primogeniture, for the preservation and protection of which the entail was designed. No study of the English landed family makes any sense unless the principle and practice of primogeniture is constantly borne in mind. It was something which went far to determine the behaviour and character of both parents and children, and to govern the relationship between siblings. Owing to the demographic insecurity which threatened all families, a father tried to see to it that the heir to the estate was married fairly early. This was the most important strategic decision of a generation, and it was made by the father and the family council of elders, negotiating directly with equivalent representatives of the family of the bride.

Under such a system, both the elder and the younger children suffered. The latter normally inherited neither title nor estate, unless one of them happened to be heir to his mother's property, and they were therefore inevitably downwardly mobile, until they had made their own fortunes in some profession or occupation. Some were kept hanging around on or near the estate, as a kind of walking sperm-bank in case the elder son died childless and had to be replaced. As for the elder sons, their entrepreneurial drive was sapped by the certainty of the inheritance to come, until which time they were condemned to live a kind of shadow existence waiting for their father to die, when they would at last come into their own. James Boswell, who for years was in just this situation, once talked bitterly about his 'narrow and dependent state'. Both heirs and younger sons were thus willy-nilly forced into the Micawberish situation of waiting for something to turn up, namely an early death of father or brother.

The third inter-related factor, along with entails and primogeniture, which governed the structure of the English family at all levels of the propertied classes from the sixteenth century on through the nineteenth century, was the dowry system. In England, brides who were not landed heiresses were unable, because of primogeniture, to provide landed property, but were expected instead to bring with them as a dowry a substantial cash sum, called a 'portion'. In the sixteenth and early seventeenth centuries, this money went directly to the father of the groom, who often used it himself as a dowry in marrying off one of his own daughters. In return, the father of the groom guaranteed the bride an annuity, called a 'jointure', if she survived her husband as a widow. Marriage, therefore, always involved a transfer of a significant amount of real or personal property from the family of the bride to that of the groom, with a reverse commitment in the future of a significant proportion of annual income.

Several important consequences followed from this. The first was that there was a high probability of strong class endogamy, that women would tend to marry spouses from a similar economic bracket, since only they were suitable recipients of the cash portion and were able to guarantee the appropriate jointure in return. Secondly, the system gave great power to the head of the family in controlling the marriages of his children, since he alone could provide the necessary portions for his daughters and guarantee the necessary jointures for his sons' widows. Not only the male heir and the daughters, but also the younger sons, were at his mercy. Thirdly, under such conditions marriages tended to be arranged by parents rather than by the children themselves. Fourthly, rich wives were valuable – and widows more valuable still (especially widows past the childbearing age) – as prizes to be fought for. To obtain likely brides, a sixteenth-century family often relied on a marriage broker to make the first suggestions and contacts, and the financial preliminaries were often settled between the parents before the pair had even set eyes on each other. Conversely, the dowry system, and the cultural obligation to marry off the girls, meant that daughters were a serious economic drain on the family finances, though they were useful in cementing political connections. Under these conditions, personal factors entered into the strategy of marriage only in so far as it was important to ensure a healthy genetic strain for breeding.

It should be emphasized that lineage and kinship was only one of three foci of loyalty for the greater and lesser landowners of the fifteenth and early sixteenth centuries. The second highly prized value was that of 'good lordship' – a reciprocal exchange of patronage, support and hospitality in return for attendance, deference, respect, advice and loyalty. This 'lordship' embraced not only the wider ramifications of the kin, but also the household retainers and servants, the client gentry, and the tenants on the estates, all comprising a collective 'affinity'. The kin was, therefore, merely one component of this larger whole, under which all the others were subsumed. Its physical manifestation was the great house with its open hospitality, its lack of privacy, and its constant crowds of attendants, retainers, servants, clients and suitors. Its psychological manifestation was a particularist system of values, by which personalized loyalty and lordship was the highest and most prized of qualities, taking precedence over those of obedience to the Ten Commandments, of submission to the impersonal dictates of the law, and of deference to the personal authority of the King. It was a bounded, localized, highly personal world, which had yet to be affected by wider notions of loyalty to more universalistic codes and ideals.

Not only was this network of patronage the cement that held sixteenth-century society together; it also determined the life-chances of every individual in it. For this was a society run by what Weber defined as a 'patrimonial bureaucracy', in which offices, favours and rewards were all distributed not according to merit or need, but according to partiality. Primogeniture and patriarchy meant that power tended to drift into the hands of the oldest males, and that in every family, village and county, and even at court, there was a constant struggle to win the approval of, or establish some reciprocal claim upon, some individual – often an old man – who controlled the levers of power. In such a society marriage, with its attendant family settlement, was a critical ingredient for the extension of the network of patronage connections, and was therefore strictly controlled by the elders of both families.

The third highly prized value was not collective, like lineage or lordship, but personal: that of honour. Honour was itself in part, of course, derived from lineage and from lordship, but there was more to it than that. A relic of late medieval ideas about chivalry, it demanded public recognition of individual worth, a high reputation in the peer-group world of gentlemen as a person deserving respect and 'worship'. This honour was best achieved and maintained by vigorous, even combative, self-assertion, military glory in the field, a scrupulous maintenance of good faith, backed by good lineage origins and good marriage conditions. One's honour was something worth fighting for and even dying for to protect, which explains the code of the duel. It was a value that was to persist into the eighteenth century, when it merged with the new sense of individualism. As a result, many gentlemen would continue to fight duels over 'giving the lie'.

Because they served such important social, economic and political functions, it follows that lineage loyalties, kin networks, and the ties of 'good lordship' will persist longest where the alternative support system, namely the state and the law, are weakest, and that they will tend to revive and expand in times of national political or economic crisis. It is not surprising, therefore, that it was in the turbulent and weakly governed upland areas of the north of England that a lineage and lordship culture flourished most strongly in the early sixteenth century, centred around the great and ancient 'houses' of the Nevilles, the Percys, the Cliffords, and the Dacres. In 1569 a Dacre follower told Leonard Dacre that 'the poor people ... favour you and your house, and cry and call for you and your blood to rule them'. He added that Dacre's brother was willing 'to suffer death patiently ... so that ... you and your blood in name might continue with your ancestor's living'. But in that year the final showdown occurred between this old particularist lineage and lordship culture and the new universalistic culture of the nation state. The Rebellion of the Northern Earls proved conclusively that the old culture was already hollow, and no longer able to sustain the challenge of outright rebellion against the sovereign.

Those classes below the nobility and gentry, who for convenience may be subsumed under the status category of 'plebs', comprised the vast bulk of the population, most of whom were resident in villages or small towns. One would suppose that those who owned land, however small, planned their marriages and inheritance strategies to preserve the property and extend the influence of the lineage. They were presumably also open to similar pressures from the kin as the rich, but to a lesser extent since personal contact involving travel and hospitality was restricted by poverty, and communication in writing was restricted by lack of literacy.

But until there has been carried out in England a comprehensive study of inheritance customs among the peasantry, we do not know the extent to which primogeniture was practised among the English peasantry of the sixteenth century and before. To the extent that it was, the principle had very important effects. It tended to produce low nuptiality, since many younger sons could not afford to marry; late marriage for those who did marry since the eldest sons were often dependent on their fathers' death or retirement to be able to afford it, while the younger sons had first to make their own way in the world; much migration to the towns or new lands, since only one son could remain on the home farm; low population density, since farms remained large; and relatively high fertility within marriage, since there was no very strong incentive to keep down the number of children. At the peasant level, the key issue was whether the father was willing to retire from work and hand the farm over to a son or son-in-law in return for stipulated pension rights for the lifetime of himself and his wife. This was a common practice in central Europe, but apparently less normal in Early Modern England.

The one detailed study available, based on wills in the late sixteenth and early seventeenth centuries in Cambridgeshire, suggests that these fathers were exercising great latitude in their dispositions. Primogeniture prevailed, but there was a general tendency to carve off small tenements to provide a livelihood for younger sons. This fragmentation process weakened the economic strength of the smallholder and helped to force him into liquidation in crisis periods of harvest failures, which came in the early seventeenth century. If these findings are confirmed elsewhere, the decline of the small landowner in England was due as much to cultural patterns of inheritance as to economic pressure from the nobility and gentry.

Below the peasantry, the propertyless poor lacked any sense of lineage or of status, and possessed neither the house room nor the surplus food to be able to shelter and feed a relative in a crisis. Control over the marriage of children was weak, since they mostly left home somewhere between the ages of seven and fourteen to go into domestic or agricultural service as living-in servants, or to serve out a term of apprenticeship, also living in the master's house. They were therefore removed at an early age from the direct control of their natural parents, and when they came to marry, some ten or fifteen years after they left home, they were inevitably free to choose a spouse for themselves. In any case, the family and kin interest in the marriage of the propertyless was low since no money or land changed hands, and the incentive to interfere was consequently limited. Marriage among the poor, we must assume, was far more a personal than a family and kin affair. Kin were very useful, on the other hand, for economic advancement and job placement, and the role of uncles in the life of the poor should not be underestimated. Among the propertied peasants and artisans, moreover, marriage control remained strong owing to the need to share out the property in order to give the young married pair a start in life.

Interference in the affairs of the nuclear family among the plebs, however, came mainly not from the kin but from the neighbours in the village community. The economic life of every open-field village was strictly controlled by community decisions in the manorial court, while the laws of copyhold tenure often interfered with the freedom of a widow to remarry while retaining her plot of land. All aspects of the economic planning of the family – who could plough when, who could sow or reap what and where, how many cattle of what type could be permitted to graze where – came under collective control in the open-field system.

Secondly, domestic life in the village was unable to develop so long as it was overshadowed by the luxuriant growth of neighbourly activity and scrutiny. During the late sixteenth and early seventeenth centuries, this intrusive scrutiny actually intensified due to the rise of ethical Puritanism and the increased activity of the Church courts in controlling personal morality. Everyone gossiped freely about the most intimate details of domestic relations, and did not hesitate to denounce violations of community norms to an archdeacon's visitation inquiry, so that people were constantly testifying in court about the alleged peccadilloes of their neighbours.

2. AFFECTIVE RELATIONSHIPS

i. *The Society*

Any discussion of emotional relationships in general is inevitably a most hazardous undertaking, since the evidence is so scanty, ambiguous and divergent that the stock historical methodology of demonstration by example is even less convincing than usual. What follows is, therefore, no more than a highly impressionistic account of what could and should be the subject of a much more intensive investigation.

Such personal correspondence and diaries as survive suggest that social relations from the fifteenth to the seventeenth centuries tended to be cool, even unfriendly. The extraordinary amount of casual inter-personal physical and verbal violence, as recorded in legal and other records, shows clearly that at all levels men and women were extremely short-tempered. The most trivial disagreements tended to lead rapidly to blows, and most people carried a potential weapon, if only a knife to cut their meat, As a result, the law courts were clogged with cases of assault and battery. The correspondence of the day was filled with accounts of brutal assault at the dinner-table or in taverns, often leading to death. Among the upper classes, duelling, which spread to England in the late sixteenth century, was kept more or less in check by the joint pressure of the Puritans and the King before 1640, but became a serious social menace after the Restoration. Friends and acquaintances felt honour bound to challenge and kill each other for the slightest affront, however unintentional or spoken in the careless heat of passion or drink. Casual violence from strangers was also a daily threat. Brutal and unprovoked assaults by gangs of idle youths from respectable families, such as the Mohawks, were a frequent occurrence in eighteenth-century London streets; and the first thing young John Knyveton was advised to do when he came to the fashionable western suburbs of London in 1750 was to buy himself a cudgel or a small sword, and to carry it for self-defence, especially after dark.

It is significant that the one large-scale study of crime in medieval England, in the early fourteenth century, shows that violence was far more frequently directed outside the family than within it. Only eight per cent of homicides, for example, were within the family, compared with over fifty per cent in England today. What is so striking, however, is that the family was more a unit for the perpetration of crime – a third of all group crimes were by family members – than a focus for crime. It is tempting to argue that the family that slayed together, stayed together. One conclusion one can draw from this evidence is that familial emotive ties were so weak that they did not generate the passions which lead to intra-familial murder and mayhem. Neither Othello nor Oedipus nor Cain were familiar figures in fourteenth-century England, any more than they were, so far as is known, in the sixteenth century.

Habits of casual violence are not incompatible with habits of casual friendliness and hospitality, and it is the relative absence of evidence of the latter which is perhaps more revealing about the inner dynamics of the society. The violence of everyday life seems to have been accompanied by much mutual suspicion and a low general level of emotional interaction and commitment. Alienation and distrust of one's fellow man are the predominant features of the Elizabethan and early Stuart view of human character and conduct. A not untypical, if a little extreme, example of this attitude is provided by Sir William Wentworth's 'Advice' to his son Thomas, the future Earl of Stafford, written in 1607. The basic assumption is that no one is to be trusted, since anyone and everyone – wife, servants, children, friends, neighbours, or patrons – are only kept loyal by self-interest, and may, therefore, at any moment turn out to be enemies. The only safe way to manoeuvre through the world is by the exercise of extreme self-control, outward reserve, secrecy, and even duplicity. 'Be very careful to govern your tongue, and never speak in open places all you think ... But to your wife, if she can keep council (as few women can) or to a private faithful friend, or some old servant that hath all his living and credit under you, you may be more open.' Judges, juries, under-sheriffs, and men of influence are to be courted both with flattery and with judicious gifts; but 'give little or nothing beforehand' in case the recipient pockets it for himself. As for noblemen, 'be careful not to make them hate you'. 'He that will be honoured and feared in his country must bear countenance and authority, for people are servile, not generous, and do reverence men for fear, not for love of their virtues.' 'Nothing but fear of revenge or suits can hold men back from doing wrong.' Even kinsmen, 'if any of all these have lands or goods joining with you, in no case trust them too much'. 'Ever fear the worst.' 'Whosoever comes to speak with you comes premeditate for his advantage.' 'In any case, be suspicious of the conscience of any that seems more saintlike than others and smooth like oil.' 'Never persuade yourself that any man is honest', without long experience of dealing with him. As for servants, 'trust them not more than you need must in matters that may greatly concern your danger'. To keep a hold on servants, never reward them with fixed annuities, but always with things that can be revoked, like tenancies at will. Be suspicious of the advice of lawyers 'who live by the suits and contentions of others'. Tenants 'notwithstanding all their fawning and flattery ... seldom love their landlord in their hearts'. Therefore, give no long leases but keep them as tenants at will. Even a wife is to be subjected to the same treatment, being assured a small fixed jointure for her widowhood and kept in line with promises of more on condition of continual good behaviour. All this reflects a thoroughly cynical view of the human condition and social relationships, including those with wives, kinsfolk and friends.

This general approach to life can be duplicated in many other examples of this genre of 'Advices', even if the somewhat paranoid overtones are peculiar to William Wentworth. The use of the word 'friend' in the sixteenth and early seventeenth centuries does much to illuminate this climate of opinion. Used in the singular, the word did indeed often mean a loved one, as when in 1628 Sir Fulke Greville arranged that the inscription on his tombstone should record that he had been 'friend of Sir Philip Sidney'. It certainly had this meaning if qualified for clarity as 'a choice special friend', 'my dear friend', etc. But it was also frequently used to mean not a person to whom one had some emotional attachment, but someone who could help one on in life, with whom one could safely do business, or upon whom one was in some way dependent. Significantly enough, it was not until the mid-eighteenth century that the word unambiguously took on its original and its modern meaning, being defined by Dr Johnson as 'one who supports you and comforts you while others do not', someone 'with whom to compare minds and cherish private virtues'.

Used in the plural, as 'my friends', the word before the eighteenth century always meant no more than 'my advisors, associates and backers'. This category often indicated a relative, particularly a parent or an uncle by blood or marriage. But it could also include a member of the household, such as a steward, chaplain or tutor; or a neighbour; or a political associate sharing a common party affiliation; or a person of high status and influence with whom there was acquaintance and from whom there was hope of patronage. As late as the 1820s, in the full romantic period, Lady Louisa Stuart commented that 'a young man's *friends*, in this sense meaning parents, guardians, old uncles and the like, are rarely propitious to love'. Indeed they were not, but the survival of the phrase in the nineteenth century to mean no more than conservative and hard-boiled matrimonial councillors is evidence of how long the old usage persisted, long after 'friend' in the singular had taken on its modern meaning.

What is being postulated for the sixteenth and early seventeenth centuries is a society in which a majority of the individuals who composed it found it very difficult to establish close emotional ties to any person. Children were often neglected, brutally treated, and even killed; many adults treated each other with suspicion and hostility; affect was low, and hard to find. To an anthropologist, there would be nothing very surprising about such a society, which closely resembles the Mundugumor in New Guinea in the twentieth century, as described by Margaret Mead. The lack of a unique mother figure in the first two years of life, the constant loss of close relatives, siblings, parents, nurses and friends through premature death, the physical imprisonment of the infant in tight swaddling-clothes in early months, and the deliberate breaking of the child's will all contributed to a 'psychic numbing' which created many adults whose primary responses to others were at best a calculating indifference and at worst a mixture of suspicion and hostility, tyranny and submission, alienation and rage.

It is not being claimed that everyone in the sixteenth and early seventeenth centuries suffered from this psychic numbing, for this would be both ridiculous and untrue. There were certainly plenty of cheerful and affectionate Wives of Windsor in real life as well as in the works of Shakespeare. But it is remarkable how difficult it is to find in the correspondence and memoirs of that period that ease and warmth which is so apparent in the eighteenth century. So far as the surviving evidence goes, England between 1500 and 1660 was relatively cold, suspicious, and violence-prone. It should be emphasized that this is a comparative judgement, not an absolute one, and it may be skewed by the relative paucity of evidence before 1640, the relative dominance of that evidence by the Puritans, and the relative clumsiness and unfamiliarity with the use of the written word to express emotions. But enough legal and other evidence survives to indicate that the difference between periods is a reality, not merely a product of distorted evidence.

ii. *The Family*

In the sixteenth century, relations between spouses in rich families were often fairly remote. Living in big houses, each with his or her own bedroom and servants, husband and wife were primarily members of a functioning social universe of a large household and were rarely in private together. It has been seen that their marriage was usually arranged rather than consensual, in essence the outcome of an economic deal or a political alliance between two families. The transaction was sealed by the wedding and by the physical union of two individuals, while the emotional ties were left to develop at a later date. If they did not take place, and if the husband could find sexual alternatives through casual liaisons, the emotional outlet through marriage was largely non-existent for either husband or wife.

In any case, the expectations of felicity from marriage were pragmatically low, and there were many reasons why disappointment was minimal. The first is that the pair did not need to see very much of one another, either in elite circles, where they could go their own way, or among plebs, where leisure activities were segregated, with the men resorting to the ale-house, and the women to each other's houses.

One reason why such a system was so readily accepted was the high adult mortality rates, which severely reduced the companionship element in marriage and increased its purely reproductive and nurturance functions. There was a less than fifty-fifty chance that the husband and wife would both remain alive more than a year or two after the departure from the home of the last child, so that friendship was hardly necessary. William Stout's comment on a marriage in 1699 could stand as an epitaph for many sixteenth- and seventeenth-century couples: 'they lived very disagreeably but had many children.'

This rather pessimistic view of a society with little love and generally low and widely diffused affect needs to be modified in two ways if it is accurately to reflect the truth. Romantic love and sexual intrigue was certainly the subject of much poetry of the sixteenth and early seventeenth centuries, and of many of Shakespeare's plays. It was also a reality which existed in one very restricted social group: the one in which it had always existed since the twelfth century, that is the households of the prince and the great nobles. Here, and here alone, well-born young persons of both sexes were thrown together away from parental supervision and in a situation of considerable freedom as they performed their duties as courtiers, ladies and gentlemen in waiting, tutors and governesses to the children. They also had a great deal of leisure, and in the enclosed hot-house atmosphere of these great houses, love intrigues flourished as nowhere else. These were the circles in which the content of the love poetry and theatre of the Elizabethan period was fully understandable, since it formed the background to their lives.

The second modification of the pessimistic general description of affective relations concerns a far wider group, including many who were subjected to the loveless arranged marriage, which was normal among the propertied classes. It is clear from correspondence and wills that in a considerable number of cases, some degree of affection, or at least a good working partnership, developed after the marriage. In practice, as anthropologists have everywhere discovered, the arranged marriage works far less badly than those educated in a romantic culture would suppose, partly because the expectations of happiness from it are not set unrealistically high, and partly because it is a fact that sentiment can fairly easily adapt to social command. In any case, love is rarely blind, in the sense that it tends to be channelled along socially acceptable lines, towards persons of the other sex of similar background. This greatly increases the probability that an arranged marriage, provided it is not undertaken purely for mercenary considerations and that there is not too great a discrepancy in age, physical attractiveness or temperament, may well work out not too badly. This is especially the case where leisure is segregated, so that the pair are not thrown together too much, and where both have a multitude of outside interests and companions to divert them. In a 'low affect' society, a 'low affect' marriage is often perfectly satisfactory.

Between upper-class parents and children, relations in the sixteenth century were also usually fairly remote. One reason for this was the very high infant and child mortality rates, which made it folly to invest too much emotional capital in such ephemeral beings. As a result, in the sixteenth and early seventeenth century very many fathers seem to have looked on their infant children with much the same degree of affection which men today bestow on domestic pets, like cats and dogs. Montaigne commented: 'I have lost two or three children in infancy, not without regret, but without great sorrow.'

The phrase 'two or three' indicates a degree of indifference and casual concern which would be inconceivable today.

The longer a child lived, the more likely it was that an affective bond would develop between it and its parents. Thus when in 1636 the wealthy antiquary Simonds D'Ewes and his wife lost their only son at the age of twenty-one months, after having already lost three sons who only lived a matter of days or weeks, he commented on the difference in the quality of their response. Part of the reaction was admittedly generated by D'Ewes's passionate desire to have a male heir to carry on the name and line, his fear that this child was his last chance, and his very articulate expression of his feelings, but part of it went deeper: 'We both found the sorrow for the loss of this child, on whom we had bestowed so much care and affection, and whose delicate favour and bright grey eye was so deeply imprinted on our heart, far to surpass our grief for the decease of his three elder brothers, who dying almost as soon as they were born, were not so endeared to us as this was.' Quite apart from the powerful disincentive to psychological involvement caused by the high infant mortality rate, most upper-class parents, and many middle- and lower-class ones, saw relatively little of their children because of the common practice of 'fostering out'. In the upper classes, babies were put out to wet-nurse at birth, usually away from home, for between twelve and eighteen months. In his *Civile Conversation* of 1581, Stephen Guazzo tells a story of a child saying bitterly to its mother: 'You bore me but nine months in your belly, but my nurse kept me with her teats the space of two years ... So soon as I was born, you deprived me of your company, and banished me your presence.'

One of the reasons for this system of sending new-born infants out to mercenary wet-nurses for the first year or more was that it made the appalling level of infant mortality much easier to bear. Admittedly the death rate of infants fed by hired wet-nurses seems to have been about twice that of infants fed by their mothers, but at least the parents did not see them or know about them. The child thus only entered the home and his parents only began to get acquainted with him after he had survived the first extremely dangerous months of life elsewhere.

Not only were the infants of the landed, upper-bourgeois and professional classes in the sixteenth and seventeenth centuries sent out to hired wet-nurses for the first twelve to eighteen months, but thereafter they were brought up mainly by nurses, governesses and tutors. Moreover they seem normally to have left home very young, some time between the ages of seven and thirteen, with about ten as the commonest age, in order to go to boarding-school. Lower down the social scale they also left home at between ten and seventeen to begin work as domestic servants, labourers or apprentices, but in all cases living in their masters' houses rather than at home or in lodgings. What one sees at these middle- and lower middle-class levels is a vast system of exchange by which parents sent their own children away from home – usually not very far – and the richer families took in the children of others as servants and labourers. As a result of this custom, some very fragmentary census data suggests that from just before puberty until they married some ten years later, about two out of every three boys and three out of every four girls were living away from home. Nearly one half of all husbandman households and nearly one quarter of craftsman and tradesman households contained living-in servants or apprentices. The reason for this mass exchange of adolescent children, which seems to have been peculiar to England, is far from clear. All we do know is that this was a medieval practice.

There are important consequences to the 'exporting' families of this widespread process of adolescent 'fostering out'. Firstly, it greatly reduced the oedipal and other tensions which inevitably arise between parents and adolescent children struggling to assert their independence and master the problems of their budding sexuality. As a result, the choice of a marriage partner was the one major issue of conflict between parents and children at this time. Secondly, it reduced the danger of incest in the classes of society where housing was poor and there were insufficient bedrooms. Thirdly, it meant that neither upper-class nor labouring- and artisan-class parents saw very much of their children, since the latter spent so short a time within the confines of the home, possibly no more than between the ages of two, when they returned from the wet-nurse, and somewhere between ten and seventeen. When a child married, even if his or her spouse had been chosen by the parents, the pair normally set up house independently, often at some distance. A fourth result of this practice of fostering out was the strong contemporary consciousness of adolescence (then called 'youth'), as a distinct stage of life between sexual maturity at about fifteen and marriage at about twenty-six.

The autobiography of Sir Simonds D'Ewes provides a revealing account of childhood in an upper-class kin-oriented patriarchal family in the early seventeenth century. His father was Paul D'Ewes, a successful Middle Temple lawyer and later holder of the lucrative office of one of the Six Clerks in Chancery, and his mother was Cecilia, daughter of Richard Simonds, a wealthy Dorset landowner. Cecilia was an heiress worth £10,000, and her marriage with Paul D'Ewes in 1594, when she was only fourteen, had been arranged between her father and her future husband, with financial considerations uppermost on both sides. Owing to the extinction of collateral lines, a male heir to the marriage would be the only surviving representative of both the D'Ewes and the Simonds families and was, therefore, desperately wanted by both the parents and the maternal grandparents. Teenage women in the seventeenth century seem to have been relatively infertile, and it is not surprising that it was not until six years later that a child was conceived of the marriage, during a visit in March 1602 to Cecilia's parents' house of Coxden in Chardstock, Dorset. Paul then returned to London to his law practice and did not return until midsummer, while Cecilia remained with her parents. When he arrived, she told him that 'her father intended to take that child ... because it had been begotten and was now likely to be born in his house, and so he claimed it for his own'. The child, named Simonds after the surname of his maternal grandfather, was born in December after a difficult and bungled delivery which so damaged his right eye that he could never use it for reading. His first months were spent at Coxden, where his mother nursed him herself and his father visited them during the legal vacations. His father was worried about the management of his own house and estate in Suffolk and was determined to move his wife back there to look after the property. So when Simonds was five months old they set out over rough country roads in a poorly sprung coach; the jolting so affected the child that he nearly died after the first twenty miles to Dorchester. Since the child could clearly not be moved again, a wet-nurse was found in the town, and after seeing him settled in for a couple of weeks, his mother left him and proceeded on to Suffolk. After some months with the wet-nurse, Simonds moved back to his grandfather's house at Coxden, where he remained for the next seven years, during which time his parents only visited him twice. His grandfather spent a lot of time in London on law business, his grandmother was old and sick, and he was mostly thrown into the company of ill-disciplined servants who taught him drinking, swearing and 'corrupt discourses'. Part of the time he spent as a boarder with the local clergyman, who ran a small school and taught him to read and write English and study the Bible.

When he was eight years old his grandfather, much to his dismay, returned him to his parents, whom he hardly knew. Although his mother screeched for joy when she saw her child again, she in fact saw very little of him since he was immediately sent off to boarding-school at Lavenham. Within eight months, both his maternal grandparents had died, leaving Simonds as the heir to a great estate, with his father as trustee on his behalf. The boy was suddenly removed from school to attend the funeral of his grandfather at Coxden. Since this was the country he knew and loved and since he still hardly knew his parents, he persuaded them to let him stay there and go to school with another local clergyman, where he remained for three years learning Latin. His mother left his father in London, and spent six months at Coxden to be near him, during which time he saw enough of her to become deeply attached to her and to be converted to her own brand of intense Puritan faith. Three years later, he left the west country and returned to London, where he entered yet another school as a boarder for two years. But being dissatisfied with the master's erudition, he got his parents to move him to the grammar school at Bury, near the new family country seat of Stow Hall, where he spent his vacations. In 1619, at the age of sixteen, he left school and went up to St John's College, Cambridge. Soon after he arrived there, however, he was suddenly summoned home to attend the death-bed of his mother, who was the only one of his parents to whom he had any deep attachment, and whose premature death at thirty-eight he took very hard indeed.

It cannot be pretended that Simonds D'Ewes was typical of his age. For one thing, he was rare in being the sole male heir to both his father's and his maternal grandfather's estates, so that two families were competing for him. All the same, it is a story that could only have occurred in the early seventeeth century, and there are several interesting conclusions to be drawn from it. As a child, his principal attachments had been to his maternal grandparents rather than to his parents, and he neither saw much of his father nor cared much for him. Almost all his childhood and adolescence was spent away from home, at the house of his wet-nurse, with his grandparents, at five different boarding-schools, and finally at university. It was a fragmented and peripatetic existence, lacking any stable geographical or affective base, and as such is probably not too unlike the childhood experiences of many upper-class children in the sixteenth and early seventeenth centuries. When he came to write his autobiography, he displayed both the all-pervasive influence of his Puritan beliefs and a great sensitivity to the nuances of domestic relations. He was a transitional figure, half-way between the kin-oriented anonymity of the past and the affective individualism of the future.

Younger sons, and particularly daughters, were often unwanted and might be regarded as no more than a tiresome drain on the economic resources of the family. The attitude towards his daughters of William Blundell, an impoverished Lancashire Catholic gentleman of the mid-seventeenth century, provides an illuminating example of parental attitudes. In 1653 he reported with sardonic malice the birth and almost immediate death of his sixth daughter and ninth child: 'My wife has much disappointed my hopes in bringing forth a daughter, which, finding herself not so welcome in this world as a son, hath made already a discreet choice of a better.' When his surviving daughters grew up in the 1670s, he shipped two of them off to nunneries abroad, without informing their mother of his plans, at the cut-rate cost of £10 and £15 each a year for life. When they complained from their foreign nunneries that they almost never got letters from home, he retorted coldly that 'When business requires no more, your mother or I do commonly write to our children once (and seldom oftener) in little less than a year. We hope they will be pleased with this, for we have too much business and too much charge in the world to comply with all our dear relations according to the measure of our love.'

As for the relations between siblings among the upper classes, primogeniture inevitably created a gulf between the eldest son and heir and his younger brothers who, by accident of birth order, were destined to be thrown out into the world and would probably become downwardly mobile. In the mid-seventeenth century Sir Christopher Guise commented on 'the malice of cadets, who are often the most unnatural enemies of their own house, upon no stronger provocation than what nature and their own melancholy thoughts present them'. Between brother and sister, however, this embittered sense of envy did not exist, and there is evidence of the frequent development of very close ties indeed. Since upper-class boys were often kept at home with a private tutor until they went off to university at sixteen or seventeen, there was time for these relationships to mature and deepen. When John Wandesford got smallpox in 1642, his sixteen-year-old sister Alice was so attached to him that she broke the strict quarantine enforced by her parents by exchanging messages tied round the neck of the family dog, as a result of which she also contracted the disease. And when eleven years later her eldest brother George was accidentally drowned in crossing the river Swale, she nearly died of grief.

3. CONCLUSION

About all that can be said with confidence on the matter of emotional relations within the sixteenth- and early seventeenth-century family at all social levels is that there was a general psychological atmosphere of distance, manipulation and deference; that high mortality rates made deep relationships very imprudent; that marriages were arranged by parents and kin for economic and social reasons with minimal consultation of the children; that evidence of close bonding between parents and children is hard, but not impossible, to document; and that evidence of close affection between husband and wife is both ambiguous and rare. Moreover, belief in the immortality of the soul and the prospect of salvation was a powerful factor in damping down such grief as might be aroused by the loss of a child, spouse or parent.

Family relationships were characterized by interchangeability, so that substitution of another wife or another child was easy, and by conformity to external rules of conduct. The family group was held together by shared economic status and political interests, and by the norms and values of authority and deference. This was a family type which was entirely appropriate to the social and economic world of the sixteenth century, in which property was the only security against total destitution, in which connections and patronage were the keys to success, in which power flowed to the oldest males under the system of primogeniture, and in which the only career opening for women was in marriage. In these circumstances the family structure was characterized by its hierarchical distribution of power, the arranged marriage and the fostering out of children. It was a structure held together not by affective bonds but by mutual economic interests.

It was, moreover, an institution that lacked firm boundaries. It was part of a wider network of relationships, linked to the kin by ties of dependence, loyalty, reciprocity and mutual aid, and to the patron by the network of allegiance to the principles of 'good lordship'. The significance of these factors was at its maximum at the highest levels of society, among the aristocracy and greater gentry, and diminished the lower one descends in the social scale. But they applied to all owners of property down to the lower-middle class of small freeholders, artisans and shopkeepers, and were irrelevant only to the very poor lacking either property or influence.

Finally, it should be stressed that no modern value judgements are involved in this description of a now vanished familial world. The central theme of this book is the extraordinary changes in attitudes towards the individual and towards emotion that occurred between 1660 and 1800, and if the sixteenth century seems somewhat bleak and impersonal, it is by contrast with the warmth and autonomy of the eighteenth century. This change is partly, of course, a change of verbal style and of cultural expression, but there are sufficient concrete changes, which cannot be disposed of by these arguments, to prove that it is also an historical reality.

PART THREE

The Restricted Patriarchal Nuclear Family 1550–1700

CHAPTER FOUR

The Decline of Kinship, Clientage and Community

'The attachment of relatives to one another was warmer, and the duties founded on consanguinity were extended to a wider circle. Even distant relationship was considered as constituting an obligation to reciprocity of love and good offices. To keep alive the bond of union, relatives in all circumstances addressed one another by their kindred names, as "uncle", "aunt", "niece", "cousin".'

(T. Somerville, reflecting on eighteenth-century Scotland – which changed well over a century later than England – in *My Own Life and Times 1741–1814*, Edinburgh, 1861, p. 368)

1. INTRODUCTION

Between about 1500 and 1700 the English family structure at the upper levels began a slow process of evolution in two related ways. Firstly, the importance of the nuclear core increased, not as a unit of habitation but as a state of mind: as its boundaries became more clearly defined, so the influence of the kin and clientage correspondingly declined. Secondly, the importance of affective bonds to tie the conjugal unit together began to increase. These two changes were the product of three concurrent and interrelated changes: the decline of kinship and clientage as the main organizing principles of landed society; the rise of the powers and claims of the state, encouraged by the Protestant reformers, both taking over some of the economic and social functions previously carried out by the family, the kin and the clientage, and subordinating kin and client loyalties to the higher obligations of patriotism and obedience to the sovereign; and the missionary success of Protestantism, especially its Puritan wing, in bringing Christian morality to a majority of homes, especially among the gentry and urban bourgeoisie, both in sanctifying holy matrimony and in making the family serve as a partial substitute for the parish.

At the same time, these and other forces were at work to bring about a third important development: the reinforcement for a time among these same social groups of the pre-existing patriarchal aspects of internal power relationships within the family. This occurred partly because the nuclear family became more free from interference by the kin, especially the wife's kin, and partly because of wider religious, legal and political changes which enhanced the powers of the head of the household.

The period is, therefore, one in which two overlapping family types can be seen to coexist among the upper and middle ranks, each slowly but imperfectly replacing the other.

2. THE LANDED CLASSES: THE DECLINE OF KINSHIP AND CLIENTAGE

Between 1500 and 1750 it is clear that there was a decline in the role played in landed society by both kinship and clientage. One indication is that claims to cousinhood ties in the subscription of letters occur far less frequently in the late seventeenth and eighteenth centuries than in the sixteenth or early seventeenth, presumably because it was no longer so useful in creating a favourable predisposition in the recipient. It would, for example, be hard to find a parallel in the eighteenth century for the claim to cousinhood advanced in the early seventeenth century by Thomas Wentworth in a letter to Sir Henry Slingsby. The connection was indeed there, but there were no fewer than seven links in the genealogical chain which joined the two, three of them by marriage through the female line. Kinship connections certainly continued to be important for many purposes, especially economic aid and job placement, but they were increasingly limited to the closer relatives. Uncles and aunts, fathers-in-law, brothers-in-law and sons-in-law were still called upon to serve surrogate or interchangeable roles with members of the nuclear family.

Another significant pointer to a change in both kinship and clientage relations is the decay of 'hospitality' among the aristocracy and greater gentry, which was a common burden of complaint in the seventeenth century. When in the late sixteenth century Lord Burghley advised his son, 'Let thy kindred and allies be welcome to thy table, grace them with thy countenance and ever further them in all honest actions,' he was giving advice that was already becoming out of date. The practice of open-handed hospitality was something about which one boasted on one's tombstone. There was, of course, more to this ideal than personal honour defined by generosity demonstrated by open-handed support of kin relatives, clients and allies, for it extended to a whole way of life, including the retaining of hordes of largely idle servants and the keeping of an open table for all comers. The decline of these habits in the late sixteenth and early seventeenth centuries involved a major reorientation of consumption patterns, caused by the growth of a more inward-looking, more private and more urbanized life-style for the aristocratic family. It was characterized by the withdrawal of the family from the great hall to the private dining-room and by the increasing habit of residing for long periods in London to enjoy the 'season'.

The decay of the gigantic and fantastically expensive funeral ritual attended by literally hundreds of kindred, cousins, retainers, domestic servants and poor was another symbol of the same shedding by the social elite of outer layers of familial and extra-familial client ties, and a slow withdrawal to a more private domestic existence. The decline of these late feudal practices represented primarily a decline of traditional good lordship, of the function of a great household as a centre of patronage for kin, clients, retainers, servants and tenants. But this decline of good lordship carried with it a weakening of ties to the kin, and a narrowing of the focus of concern down to the interests and pleasures of the nuclear core.

More concrete evidence than these indicators of a decline of expenditure on, and attention paid to, the ramifications of the kin and clientage network is provided by the very clear decline in the concept of kin responsibility for individual crimes and actions. In the early and mid-sixteenth century, at any rate in the Highland zone of the north and west, the royal writ and the royal law courts were less important as law enforcement agencies than the blood feud and the vendetta. Under the vendetta there is collective kin responsibility for individual action, as opposed to the legal theory of individual responsibility: the law will punish the individual criminal but no one else; the vendetta is perfectly satisfied by the punishment of the criminal's brother, father, uncle or nephew, which is a classic example of the principle of interchangeability. By the end of the sixteenth century, this custom had virtually died out in England. Henry VIII was the last English king to punish whole families, such as the De La Poles, for the treason of one member.

The degree to which kinship, clientage and even family loyalties had become subordinated to the principle of autonomy of choice of political and religious ideology became clear during the English Revolution of the 1640s, when one aristocratic family in seven was divided father against child or brother against brother. If the divisions within the nuclear core were so frequent, it is obvious that the cousinhood was even more hopelessly fragmented, and that clientage was equally weak.

At the end of the seventeenth century, the English political nation was bitterly divided into two parties, going under the labels of Whigs and Tories. In binding together these political groupings, there were four main elements: clientage, meaning dependence on a political patron; kinship; professional ties; and personal friendship. Kinship was certainly a help, and was used by politicians to increase their influence. But for every family connection which carried clear political associations, there were three or four about which nothing is known. There may have been no connection, or the kin may in fact have been split down the middle. Thus of the ten MPs and candidates of the Bertie kin in the reign of Queen Anne, seven were Tories, two Whigs, and one a Whiggish waverer. Kinship often remained useful in the formation of the Whig factions in the eighteenth century, such as the Walpole group, the Pelham Whigs or Rockingham Whigs, but it was no more than one element among several, and not necessarily the most important or the most durable one.

In local affairs, kin ties undoubtedly continued to be important well into the eighteenth century. As the English elite was fissured down religious lines in the late sixteenth and seventeenth centuries, fairly strict religious endogamy developed among Catholics and Puritans, but in this case the lines of kinship followed and reinforced the ties of religion, not vice versa. After the middle of the seventeenth century, the amount of social mobility shrank significantly, so that relatively little new blood was coming into the squirarchy to keep the system fluid. Meanwhile in each county for century after century the squires had been intermarrying with one another, until the web of cross-cousinhood became so dense and so universal that it lost its meaning. If everybody is everyone else's cousin, the connection does not matter any more, which is why the recent discovery that Charles

I was a remote cousin of John Hampden does nothing to advance our understanding of the English Revolution of the seventeenth century.

Another test of the declining role of kinship is the moral legitimacy accorded to nepotism as a factor in recruitment to state and private offices. It is, of course, a truism that ties of blood and clientage remained very important and respectable elements in appointments in Church and state well into the middle of the nineteenth century. Generation after generation of younger or illegitimate sons were found comfortable berths in the public service, either at home or in the colonies. But each time there had to be a struggle, and each time there was competition to the ties of blood or marriage from the alternative principles of money and merit. Moreover, the influence was primarily exercised by fathers for sons, or sometimes uncles for nephews, and only rarely for more distant members of the kin. It was thus a product of the bonding of the nuclear family rather than of the lineage.

To conclude, everything points to a very slow erosion of the significance of kinship ties among the landed classes, but there is also good reason to suppose that they persisted and continued to play a part in family strategy and local and national politics well into the nineteenth century. A slow trend should not be mistaken for radical change. Moreover, with the decline of ideological passion in national politics after 1720, there was a positive revival of the power of patronage networks and clientage, until ideological conflict rose again towards the end of the century.

3. THE MIDDLE RANKS:
THE MODIFICATION OF KINSHIP

Lower down the social scale, changes in the ties of kinship are more difficult to determine. On the one hand, the same factors as were affecting the elite – especially religious loyalties – were also influencing the middle ranks of society. Just as with the elite, there is plenty of evidence that the closer kin relatives, particularly paternal and maternal uncles, continued to play a large part in family decisions, especially when the parents died and the children had to be found jobs or husbands. In 1637–40 a young Cambridge graduate, the Reverend Ralph Josselin, used one uncle's credit to borrow money to tide him over, stayed with another when he was unemployed, and found his first church living by the good offices of the first uncle, who in fact paid £10 of his £44-a-year income. On the other hand, Josselin's links to more distant kin relatives, such as cousins, were very remote and casual. Of his thirty-odd first cousins, his elaborate diary over a period of forty-two years mentions only three of them more than five times, and only fourteen even once.

Among the peasantry, the same pattern seems to have prevailed. In one Leicestershire village in the sixteenth and seventeenth centuries, peasant wills show that it was only those who had no nuclear family obligations, or who had already fulfilled them by other means, who left real or personal property to members of the kin. This evidence is supported by an examination of wills in a Worcestershire village between 1676 and 1775, which shows over half of the testators making bequests to the nuclear family, and only a quarter to kin relatives. By this test, the economic role of the kin among small property-owners in the village was now very limited.

Certain groups, however, continued to lay considerable stress on kin ties for social, political or economic purposes. Intermarriage was very commonly used as social bonding among parish gentry families within the county in the early seventeenth century. It was also used for economic bonding among the recently mobile mercantile elites in London and the major cities. In these latter circles, economic circumstances – the need for capital and for reliable business associates – stimulated the search for marriage and kinship connections, which were more carefully cherished than among other social groups. They were particularly common among successful wealthy bourgeoisie without ambitions to transform their children into gentlemen. These upwardly mobile groups might cut the ties of blood which bound them to their humbler relatives back home, but would cement business connections with their economic peers or superiors by a new set of kinship relations. Much joint investment with, and much borrowing from, kin relatives continued to take place throughout the eighteenth century, although the growth of country banks and joint stock companies provided increasingly important alternatives.

A few examples will serve to illustrate this point. An extraordinarily tight web of family ties linked the twenty-eight men who in 1580 formed the Court of Aldermen, the ruling elite of the City of London. Of these twenty-eight, three were sons of aldermen, nine sons-in-law, two brothers, six brothers-in-law, and one had married an alderman's widow. Many of them were also linked to other aldermanic families by marriages of their children. There were some fifteen cluster families whose connections by blood or marriage in one way or another embraced two thirds of the sixty-four men who held office as Lord Mayor and served as aldermen throughout the whole Elizabethan period. What is most significant, however, is that these clusters did not form coherent groups in terms of trading interests, wealth or political connections, so that this evidence for family linkage in the higher echelons of the London business elite should not be pushed too far. Nor was it a closed world by any means, for the cluster families did not dominate the scene, and outsiders could fight their way in. But family ties, mostly fairly close ones, certainly helped to cement pre-existing bonds of friendship and mutual economic and political interests, and also helped to ease the access of outsiders into this elite world. Newcomers were easily co-opted and absorbed through marriage.

This use of marriage ties to develop or to cement commercial alliances among urban patriciates was a practice which flourished in the sixteenth and seventeenth centuries and only began to weaken in the eighteenth. Among the eighteenth-century merchants of Leeds and Hull, the family firm predominated, and Robert Pease could explain 'we keep entirely together to help one another'. In Hull, however, there is clear evidence that by the late eighteenth century more and more partnerships, loans, etc., were being contracted outside the family. Even among the urban patriciates, the bonds of kinship were on the decline.

4. THE CAUSES OF CHANGE

The modern state is a natural enemy to the values of the clan, of kinship, and of good lordship and clientage links among the upper classes, for at this social and political level they are a direct threat to the state's own claim to prior loyalty. Aristocratic kinship and clientage lead to faction and rebellion, such as the Wars of the Roses or the Fronde, to the use of kin loyalty and client empires by entrenched local potentates to create independent centres of power, and to make the working of the jury system of justice impossible by the subordination of objective judgement to ties of blood or local loyalty. In the sixteenth century, the state in England increasingly assumed monopoly powers of justice and punishment, military protection, welfare, and the regulation of property. This takeover was accompanied by a massive propaganda campaign for loyalty, inculcating the view that the first duty of every citizen is obedience to the sovereign, that man's highest obligation is to his country, involving the subordination of all other considerations and loyalties, even life itself.

This fundamental shift in human values and in the social arrangements that went with them in the period from 1560 to 1640 has been well described by one historian as a shift from a 'lineage society', characterized by bounded horizons and particularized modes of thought, to the more universalistic standard of values of a 'civil society'. The causes of this vast change are clear enough: the Reformation with its powerful drive for the christianization of society and its claim to overriding moral allegiance through the preaching of the Word; grammar school and university education in the rhetoric of Humanism with its stress on loyalty to the prince; Inns of Court education in respect for an abstraction, the common law, as superior to any private or local loyalties to individuals; the growth of more commercialized relationships between man and man; the rise of 'possessive market individualism' that was slowly beginning to erode old communal affiliations. Finally there was the institutional expansion of the nation state: the growth of its bureaucratic size, organization and powers, as literacy and record-keeping expanded and were taken over by the laity; the extension of its claims to universal obedience to the sovereign; and the persistent and progressive intrusion by the central authorities into local government, local jurisdiction and local patronage networks. These were not autonomous processes, but were driven forward by the massive transformation of popular and elite ideas about where prior loyalty lay. Fuelled initially by a general desire for security, the expansion of the bureaucratic nation state soon took on an independent life of its own. The consequent decline of kinship and clientage was a major cause of the rise of the nuclear family.

This shift of emphasis towards the nuclear family was given powerful support by Reformation theology and practice. The medieval Catholic ideal of chastity, as a legal obligation for priests, monks and nuns and as an ideal for all members of the community to aspire to, was replaced by the ideal of conjugal affection. The married state now became the ethical norm for the virtuous Christian, its purpose being more than what Milton described contemptuously, referring to the Pauline view, as 'the prescribed satisfaction of an irrational heat . . ., the promiscuous draining of a carnal rage'. The great Puritan preacher William Perkins now described marriage as 'a state in itself far more excellent than the condition of a single life' – a clear contrast to the contemporary Catholic view of Cardinal Bellarmine that 'marriage is a thing humane, virginity is angelical' – in other words that it is no more than an unfortunate necessity to cope with human frailty. This sanctification of marriage – 'holy matrimony' – was a constant theme of Protestant sermons of the sixteenth century, which were directed to all classes in the society, and is to be found in both Puritan and Anglican moral theology of the early seventeenth century from William Gouge to Jeremy Taylor.

It was Archbishop Cranmer who in England first officially added a third to those two ancient reasons for marriage, the avoidance of fornication and the procreation of legitimate children. In his Prayer Book of 1549 he added the motive of 'mutual society, help and comfort, that the one ought to have of the other, both in prosperity and in adversity'. Later on in the sixteenth century Robert Cawdrey, as revised by Cleaver and Dod, and then Thomas Gataker, William Perkins and William Gouge, authors of the most popular family handbooks of their day, also emphasized that the purposes of marriage included spiritual intimacy.

Having beaten back efforts to legalize divorce with remarriage by the innocent party for the adultery or desertion of the wife, which was recognized by most Reformed churches abroad, the Tudor Protestants had no alternative but to urge the importance of affective ties as a necessity for marriage, in addition to the old Pauline arguments. Although they were as respectful as ever of the need for social equality and economic security as prime factors in mate selection, they were nonetheless obliged to oppose the strongly commercial attitude to marriage which had been prevalent in the late middle ages and the early sixteenth century, by which bride and groom had been bartered by their parents without their consent. Since the Puritan moral theologians were equally insistent upon the need for filial obedience to parents, the result was often to place the dutiful child in an impossible conflict of role models. They had to try to reconcile the often incompatible demands for obedience to parental wishes on the one hand and expectations of affection in marriage on the other. Puritans solved this dilemma by arguing that affection could and would develop after marriage, provided that no violent antipathy manifested itself at a first brief interview.

In England in the 1630s this new attitude to marriage gave rise to some extravagant hyperbole, used by both laity and Anglican theologians. In 1638 Robert Crosse spoke of marriage as 'an earthly paradise of happiness', though he added the conventional warnings against 'an oversottish and doting affection' and 'unlawful and raging lusts'. In 1642 Daniel Rogers thought that 'husbands and wives should be as two sweet friends' and Jeremy Taylor declared that 'the marital love is a thing pure as light, sacred as a temple, lasting as the world'. It is no accident that Charles I and Henrietta Maria were 'the first English royal couple to be glorified as husband and wife in the domestic sense', even if this development owed as much to the rarefied cult of neo-Platonic love in court circles as it did to the attitude of the contemporary Anglican moral theologians.

It should be noted that hardly any of these Protestant or Puritan writers were willing to carry their ideas about the spiritual nature of the marital union to the point of giving it priority over all other considerations. It was left to Milton, tormented by his own unhappy marriage and influenced partly by Renaissance thought and partly by previous Puritan theologians, to demote all other ends to marriage – the procreation of children, sexual control, the public interest in law and order, and the clerical interest in an ecclesiastically blessed *rite de passage*. For him the prime object of marriage was 'the apt and cheerful conversation of man with woman, to comfort and refresh him against the solitary life'. The logical conclusion to this step was to advocate – as Milton did, three hundred years ahead of his time and with almost no contemporary support – divorce and remarriage in cases of hopeless temperamental incompatibility. The argument was very simple, based on the proposition that 'Where love cannot be, there can be nothing left of wedlock but the empty husk of outside matrimony.' By minimizing the sexual and procreative functions of marriage, he easily came to the conclusion that 'natural hatred is a greater evil in marriage than the accident of adultery'. On the other hand, Milton had very strong views about the subordinate function of women – 'Who can be ignorant that woman was created for man, and not man for woman?' – and he therefore demanded divorce only when the 'unfitness' lay with the

102

wife, not the husband. It could be demanded by both parties or by the husband alone, but not by the wife alone. Milton thus carried the Protestant concept of holy matrimony about as far as it could go without abandoning the sexual superiority of the male. The roots of affective individualism in seventeenth-century Puritan sectarianism are clearly demonstrated in these writings.

The intensification of married love brought about by the stress on holy matrimony played a part in the shift from a kin-oriented to a nuclear family. In the open lineage family, where affect was low and widely diffused, the lack of privacy and the self-interest of the kin put a damper on intensive marital emotional bonding. But with the churches now ringing with sermons encouraging such bonding, the influence of the kin tended to decline, as the married couple presented a more unified front towards the external world. The rise of married love and the decline of kin influence were therefore mutually reinforcing trends. The former also was important in helping to detach the couple psychologically from their parents. This major shift in moral allegiances was well understood by the preachers who advocated married love, one of whom frankly stated that 'it is a less offence for a man to forsake father and mother and to leave them succourless ... than it is for him to do the like towards his lawful married wife'. The opposition of parents and kin to the principle and practice of married love was based on a perceived threat to their power and interests.

There were also more profound, although less easily demonstrable, effects on the family of the change from pre-Reformation Catholicism to Anglican Protestantism. Sometimes slowly, more often quickly and violently, the Reformation destroyed the social and psychological supports upon which both the community and the individual had depended for comfort and to give symbolic meaning to their existence. Miracle-working images and relics were defaced and destroyed, chantries endowed for masses for the dead were suppressed, the priests dispersed and the property nationalized. Purgatory was declared inoperative. Confession to priests was forbidden, and their power to remit sins declared a pious fraud. May Day festivities, church-ales, religious processions, the celebration of saints' days were all denounced as mere relics of pagan superstition, to be suppressed along with the physical cult objects – the maypole or the sacred images – around which they had been organized. Man now stood alone before his Maker, with nothing but his conscience, the Bible and the preachers to guide him, deprived of all the old psychological props, collective rituals, and opportunities for blowing off steam.

There were only two beneficiaries of this drastic elimination of sacred ritual by the Protestant zealots. The first was the nation state which now laid claim to those loyalties which had hitherto gone to the community, the city, the parish or the confraternity. The second was the household and its head, which filled the vacuum left by the decline of the Church and its priests as the central institution for moral and religious instruction.

Attendance at service in church remained a formal Sunday obligation, but devotional piety shifted to the daily attendance at family prayers; moral control by the priest was partially replaced by moral direction by the head of the household; and Church catechisms were partially replaced by catechisms for the household, about a hundred of which were published between 1550 and 1600 alone. Edward Dering's popular *Catechism* was described by its author as 'very needful to be known to all householders whereby they may better teach and instruct their families in such points of Christian religion as is most meet'. John Stalham, a Puritan minister, urged the readers of his *Catechism for Children*, in 1644, to make 'all your households as so many little churches'. Marriage sermons stressed the need for the bridal couple 'never to neglect family prayer'. In the more pious households, husbands and wives would confess their sins to each other at home, instead of to the priest in church. In many other cases the private diary was the substitute for the confessional, although the forgiveness of the latter is much easier on human frailty than the self-torture of the former. In towns in southern England by the early seventeenth century, the Bible was available in most upper and middle and even lower-middle-class homes, and daily public readings from it by the head of the household, fortified by a rousing sermon in the church on Sunday, replaced the ritual of the sacrament as the main vehicle of religious expression.

Whether in Anglican or Puritan households, there was, in varying degrees, a new emphasis on the home and on domestic virtues, and this was perhaps the most far-reaching consequence of the Reformation in England. The household was the inheritor of many of the responsibilities of the parish and the Church; the family head was the inheritor of much of the authority and many of the powers of the priest. Thus the Word of God was to some degree removed from the parish church and transferred to the private home: the Holy Spirit was partly domesticated.

5. PEASANTS, ARTISANS AND THE POOR: THE DECLINE OF COMMUNITY

Although the evidence is fragmentary in the extreme, it is fairly clear that neither kinship nor clientage had played anything like the same role among peasants, artisans and poor as they did among their betters. At this social level, it was the community of neighbours whose influence on and control over family life had been of the greatest importance. This influence and control increased or became more institutionalized in some areas, weakened and all but disappeared in others. One in which there was a positive intensification of public interference in family life was the field of morals. The steady advance of Christianity throughout the century, and the growing censoriousness about sin which accompanied it, led to growing interference by Church authorities, supported by neighbours and parish officials, to make all inhabitants conform to the new community norms. Domestic life in the village was conducted in a blaze of publicity.

The clergy struggled to persuade the lower classes to abandon altogether the traditional habit of consensual unions unblessed by the church. There was an earnest effort to ensure that all sexual unions, whether of clergy and their pre-Reformation 'housekeepers' or of the poor, should now be recognized and sanctified by a formal Christian sacrament. Some tentative evidence of the success of this pressure upon the lower classes is the apparent decline in illegitimacy rates in the backward north and north-west from about four per cent in the 1590s, before educated Protestant ministers first became available in large numbers in these areas, to about one and a half per cent in the mid-seventeenth century when the Puritan supremacy was at its height.

A powerful means of enforcing public standards of morality on family life was through denunciations to the archdeacons' courts, however ineffectual the latter may have been in punishing transgressors. Neither fornication nor adultery was easy in so public an arena as a village, although of course there was plenty of both. Neighbours gossiped about the most intimate details of family relationships, and were quick to complain to the ecclesiastical courts of anything that violated local mores. Reputed seducers of maidens were duly reported on the basis of hearsay only. They thought it wrong that a boy over seventeen should continue to sleep in the same bed as his mother. They were very suspicious about the household of husband and wife, one manservant and one maid, which only contained two beds, so that the husband slept in a bed with both his wife and the maid. They even knew about, and complained of, unusually enthusiastic or deviant sexual behaviour between man and wife. They complained when a husband turned a blind eye to the adultery of his wife, and were quick to denounce cases of bigamy or trigamy. They lurked about to catch the curate in bed with a girl. While approving of a husband's power to discipline an unruly wife, they objected to noisy and excessive brutality or use of foul language which disturbed the peace of the village, as much as they objected to the female propensity to scolding and slander.

An alternative to the archdeacons' courts, whose powers were limited to the more or less voluntary compliance with shame punishments such as standing in church in a white sheet during a service, was enforcement of the moral code by the local secular authorities. In the late Elizabethan period, any constable was empowered to break into any house in which he suspected fornication or adultery to be in progress and, if his suspicions were confirmed, to carry the offenders to jail or before a Justice of the Peace. This was a power that was used up to about 1660, but died out after the Restoration, although it remained in the standard handbook on local justice. Convicted offenders were often ordered to be whipped in the sixteenth and early seventeenth centuries.

Among the poor the principal area in which the function of peasant kinship can be shown to have been on the decline in the seventeenth century is that of aid and welfare for the helpless, the sick and the indigent. In traditional societies these problems are handled by the conjugal family, the kin and the neighbours, with some minor help from the church. In sixteenth-century England, rapid demographic growth in the villages, urban immigration, the impoverishment of the towns, and the ravages of price inflation meant that support from the extended network of the kin and from neighbours in the community became inadequate for large numbers of orphans, widows, cripples, sick, and aged, while structural unemployment of the able-bodied first became a problem. During the century, welfare for those unable to support themselves had perforce to be progressively taken over by public bodies. In the early sixteenth century, some towns were obliged to organize their own poor relief system, paid out of taxes, and in the second half of the century the practice spread to the countryside on a voluntary and emergency basis only. In about 1600 a nationwide system based on local compulsory taxation and expenditure was instituted, and during the seventeenth century it became a fully functioning organization run by the parish, which effectively relieved the kin, the conjugal family and the neighbours of their previous sense of obligation to provide relief to the sick and the indigent to save them from starvation. In addition to these public arrangements, private legacies from the wealthy built and endowed a significant number of orphanages, hospitals and almshouses for the old, and set up supplementary funds for poor relief in a fair number of villages. A rather similar transfer of responsibility occurred, over a long period of time, in the socialization of the child, part of which was slowly shifted from the family to the school.

To sum up, among the plebs the degree of community control over the family in some respects decreased and in others increased between 1540 and 1640. At the higher level of the social elite, the trend is unambiguous; there was a clear decline in allegiance to kinship and clientage, with a corollary growth of loyalty outward to the state and the religion and inward to the family. The effects on family life of this withdrawal of the kin may not have been altogether for the good. Wives maltreated by their husbands were now less able to turn to their kin for support and defence. Intervention by the elders of the kin to settle marital quarrels was now less easy and less welcome. The kin could no longer so readily serve as mediators between the parents and the children in the case of a direct clash between the two on the issue of the choice of a spouse. The partial withdrawal of external support and intervention thus made family life more liable to explosive conflict between husband and wife, and parents and children. On the other hand, the partial withdrawal of the kin was an essential preliminary step to clear the way for the subsequent development of the domesticated family and the selection of spouses by the choice of the individuals on the basis of prior affection. But this would not occur for a long time, until the late seventeenth and the eighteenth centuries. Kinship ties did not disappear overnight, but merely slowly, if irregularly, receded over several centuries as they became less desirable and less necessary. Thus, when the gentleman merchant John Verney was considering marriage in 1671, one of his options was a Miss Edwards. Her father took care to tell John that the girl 'brought in no kindred with her, neither of great persons to be a charge by way of entertainment, nor of mean to be a charge by way of charity and their neediness'. Kinship was clearly now regarded more as a potential burden than a potential opportunity.

CHAPTER FIVE

The Reinforcement of Patriarchy

'If ever thou purpose to be a good wife, and to live comfortably, set down this with thyself: mine husband is my superior, my better; he hath authority and rule over me; nature hath given it to him . . . God hath given it to him.'

(W. Whately, *The Bride Bush*, London, 1617, p. 36)

1. GENERAL CAUSES

The enhancement of the importance of the conjugal family and the household relative to the kinship and clientage at the upper levels of society was accompanied by a positive reinforcement of the despotic authority of husband and father – that is to say, of patriarchy. Both Church and state provided powerful new theoretical and practical support, while two external checks on patriarchal power declined as kinship ties and clientage weakened. At the same time, a new interest in children, coupled with the Calvinist premise of Original Sin, gave fathers an added incentive to ensure the internalized submissiveness of their children. It cannot be proved conclusively that in reality the powers of fathers over children and of husbands over wives in the upper and middle ranks most exposed to this propaganda became greater than they had been in the middle ages. But this seems a plausible hypothesis, given the fact that patriarchy for its effective exercise depends not so much on raw power or legal authority, as on a recognition by all concerned of its legitimacy, hallowed by ancient tradition, moral theology and political theory. It survives and flourishes only so long as it is not questioned and challenged, so long as both the patriarchs and their subordinates fully accept the natural justice of the relationship and of the norms within which it is exercised. Willing acceptance of the legitimacy of the authority, together with a weakness of competing foci of power, are the keys to the whole system.

The growth of patriarchy was deliberately encouraged by the new Renaissance state on the traditional grounds that the subordination of the family to its head is analogous to, and also a direct contributory cause of, subordination of subjects to the sovereign. In 1609 James I informed his somewhat dubious subjects that 'The state of monarchy is the supremest thing upon earth', one of his arguments being that 'Kings are compared to fathers in families: for a King is truly *parens patriae*, the politic father of his people.' When some twenty-five years later Robert Filmer argued the case for absolute monarchy, he used exactly the same logic: 'We find in the Decalogue that the law which enjoins obedience to Kings is delivered in the terms of: "Honour thy Father".' (As a strong anti-feminist, he discreetly omits 'and Mother'.)

In 1618 Richard Mocket published a book, *God and the King*, in which he made the connection even clearer. All subjects were the children of the King, and bound by the Fifth Commandment to honour and obey him. James I was so delighted with this book that he ordered it to be studied in schools and universities and bought by all householders, thus ensuring it a very wide sale. Both the products of the printing press and homilies and catechisms in church were harnessed to the task of spreading the message.

There are good reasons to think that the support given by the state to the principle of patriarchy paid off in generating an internalized sense of obligation of obedience to the absolute king as the father of his people. Despite Charles I's long record of duplicity and illegal actions, very many individuals were in the last resort unable to shake off the ideological chains with which they had so long been bound. Men like Hyde were exasperated enough to destroy the machinery of royal government in 1640–41, but not enough to take up arms against the king in 1642. Even more striking is the response of the vast crowd in Whitehall in 1649, when Charles I's head was severed from his body. Seventy years later, an old woman could still recall with horror the 'dismal groan' that she heard from the crowd as a child, while a boy remembered as long as he lived 'such a groan as I never heard before, and desire I may never hear again'. This mass response to a public execution must surely have been a reflection of a feeling by the crowd that it had witnessed an act of national patricide: the father of his people had been publicly murdered.

What seems to have happened is that a diffuse concept of patriarchy inherited from the middle ages that took the form of 'good lordship' – meaning dominance over kin and clientage – was vigorously attacked by the state as a threat to its own authority. Patriarchy was now reinforced by the state, however, in the much modified form of authoritarian dominance by the husband and father over the woman and children within the nuclear family. What had previously been a real threat to political order was thus neatly transformed into a formidable buttress to it.

In 1528 Luther himself boasted of bringing order, discipline and obedience to the family, as well as to society as a whole. 'Among us', he wrote, there was now knowledge of the Scriptures and also of 'marriage, civil obedience, the duties of father and mother, father and son, master and servant'. The triumphant emphasis on patriarchy as one of the benefits of the Lutheran Reformation is here unmistakable. All the magisterial Reformed Churches stressed the subordination of wives to husbands, summed up in John Milton's terse description of sex-typed obligations: 'He for God only, she for God in him.' Nor was this all. The shift to Protestantism meant the loss by the wife of control over the domestic rituals of religious fasting and feasting on the appropriate days. Lastly, the doctrine of the priesthood of all believers meant in practice that the husband and father became the spiritual as well as the secular head of the household. The aggrieved or oppressed wife could no longer rely on the priest to provide a counterpoise to potential domestic tyranny arising from this new authority thrust upon her husband.

Not all heads of households were capable of fulfilling these heavy responsibilities, nor were all wives willing so abjectly to subordinate their wills. Moreover, the identity of the husband and father with the family religious confessor placed severe strains on many wives and children, who found themselves trapped in a situation where they had no one to turn to for escape or alternative counsel. In many pious upper-class households in the seventeenth century, the power of the head of the household was oppressive in its completeness. Sir George Sondes certainly made his family and servants attend church services twice on Sundays. But 'all the week after, it was my constant course to pray with my family, once if not twice every day; and if I had not a [chaplain] in my house, I performed the office myself'. As for Sir Nathaniel Barnardiston, 'towards his children he executed his office of an heavenly father to their souls ... and many times he would take them into his closet and there pray over them and for them'. In the 1630s the Kentish Puritan gentleman Thomas

Scott spent 'the evening with my wife, children and family in hearing prayers'. Supper was prefaced by a reading from the Bible, and after it 'my wife reads Dr Preston's sixth sermon. My daughter-in-law reads line by line, and she and all the rest of my family . . . sing Psalm 5.' These family exercises were by no means confined to Puritans, and in the high Anglican household of Sir Christopher Wandesford, apparently in the 1630s when he was Master of the Rolls in Ireland, there were family prayers three times a day, at 6 a.m., 10 a.m. and 9 p.m. After his death, his widow would assemble her children every day before breakfast to pray together and read or repeat psalms and chapters of the Bible, after which the children knelt to receive their mother's blessing. In this all-enveloping atmosphere of domestic piety, in many gentry and bourgeois homes not only had the household replaced the parish, but the father had replaced the priest. The link between Protestant religion and family patriarchy was made by the Presbyterian Thomas Edwards in 1646, when he vigorously opposed the granting of religious toleration on the grounds that 'they should never have peace in their families more, or ever after have command of wives, children, servants'.

A change in legal arrangements for the inheritance of property, which in origin probably had nothing to do with the motives of either Church or state, nonetheless powerfully reinforced the trend to patriarchy within the nuclear family. During the middle ages control over landed property through entail meant that the head of the family was no more than a life tenant of most of the estates, with little freedom to dispose of them at his pleasure. In the late fifteenth century, the lawyers found a way to break entails without too much difficulty, and some confusing legislation of the 1530s had the result of still further widening the breach. This greatly strengthened the ability of the current head of the family to dispose of the property as he chose, although it also greatly weakened his capacity to prevent his heir from doing the same thing. He could now quite easily either sell land to meet current needs or split it up amongst his children as he thought fit. The increase in this freedom of action of the current owner meant an increase in his capacity to punish or reward his children or siblings. Thus it meant the further subordination of the children, including the heir, to the father, and of younger sons and daughters to their elder brother if he inherited the estate before they married. The current owner of the estates could now not only bribe his children with promises of more; he could threaten them with total exclusion from the inheritance. He possessed the power to manipulate the distribution of his property, either to serve his own selfish interests or to preserve and increase in perpetuity the family status and property through primogeniture, or to control and direct his children in making the two most critical decisions of their lives: choice of a spouse and choice of a career. Only later did this power come to be seen as a temptation to dissipate the estates which was a danger to the patrimony, as well as harmful to the interests of daughters and younger sons, who were entirely at the mercy of their father or elder brother.

Among the poor, the common practice of fostering out, and the high level of geographical mobility caused by this social custom and by economic dislocations, meant that the control of the father over his children was limited to the relatively short period before they left home. After that point, patriarchal authority over them was exercised not by their natural father, but by the master whose living-in servants or apprentices they became. Thus, among the lower classes the patriarchal principle and practice remained powerful, but was exercised mainly upon the children of other people after they had reached the age of about ten to seventeen.

2. PARENTS AND CHILDREN

i. *Areas of Permissiveness*

All the evidence we have suggests that infants were fed on demand, and were not weaned until a year or eighteen months, often fairly slowly. Among the more prosperous classes it was normal before the mid-eighteenth century to send the children out to mercenary wet-nurses, who may or may not have given the infants the milk and the attention that they needed. It is very uncertain, therefore, to what extent children at this period suffered the oral trauma of weaning to anything like the degree that Freudian theory would suggest.

It also seems fairly certain that children throughout the Early Modern period were not subjected to early and severe toilet training, which has become so marked a feature of nineteenth- and twentieth-century child-rearing. This was a time when personal and public hygiene was largely disregarded. Men and women rarely, if ever, washed their bodies, and they lived in the constant sight and smell of human faeces and human urine. Many houses, even palaces, lacked latrines, while public conveniences in the streets or public places were largely nonexistent. When in 1667 Mrs Pepys was seized with diarrhoea in the theatre, she had no option but to go off to a corner of Lincoln's Inn walks, where 'she did her business'. Close-stools and chamber pots were scattered around the wealthier houses and used when convenient, then emptied directly into the street. Samuel Pepys was a wealthy man, whose house in Seething Lane in London in the 1660s had a privy which drained into a vat in the cellar. From time to time the vat had to be emptied by night-soil men with buckets which they carried through the kitchen to a cart outside the door, a process which Pepys found nauseating. But Pepys himself and his rich friends were far from fastidious. One day he suddenly opened the door of his dining-room to find the wife of his patron, the Countess of Sandwich, 'doing something upon the pot'.

In such a society, the toilet training of infants could obviously not be a matter of serious concern. The total lack of references to this problem in child-rearing manuals of the time strongly reinforces the hypothesis that children were left to control their sphincters more or less at their own pace. Bed-wetting at a late age, however, was severely punished by flogging or worse, since it seriously inconvenienced the adults. When Eugene, one of William Byrd's servants, wetted his bed twice in a week, his master made him drink a pint of urine each time. Eugene never did it again. The principal interference with the infantile bowels, in those classes which could afford the harmful ministrations of doctors, was the constant application of purges and suppositories and enemas to ensure their forcible evacuation.

Passage through the oral and anal stages of infantile development was thus probably relatively easy, with milk on demand, late weaning and late toilet training. It may well be that the genital stage of childhood was equally free from repression, and that the main problem in this area was premature over-stimulation. There is some little evidence to suggest that adults found the genital stage of childhood sexuality amusing rather than horrifying. This encouragement of sexual play may have been no more than one aspect of a general tendency to treat children from about two to seven as amusing pets to entertain the grown-ups. It was the one period in a child's life when his parents and other adults treated him other than harshly or with indifference.

It should be emphasized that none of this historical evidence from the Early Modern period disproves Freud's theory about how at different stages of infantile development different erogenous zones become the foci of sexual stimulation, thus providing a logical explanation for the later relationship between oral, anal and genital pleasure. Nor does the historical record do anything to belittle the importance of sublimation, or of the unconscious operating with a secret dynamism of its own. What it does, however, is to cast very great doubt upon the assumption that the particular kinds of infantile traumas upon which Freud laid so much stress have been suffered by the whole of the human race at all times and in all places. It is now fairly clear that four of the main traumas (oral, anal, genital and oedipal) which Freud looked for among his patients and therefore assumed to be universal, are dependent on experiences which were peculiar to the late Victorian European middle-class society from which his patients came. As we shall see, children in the Early Modern period suffered a different, and perhaps even more psychologically disturbing, process of traumatic experiences.

ii. *Areas of Repression*

If children were weaned very late and were not severely toilet trained in the seventeenth century, and if there was no great emphasis on the repression of infant sexuality, in other ways they were treated with the utmost severity. For one thing, their physical mobility was severely reduced. For the first four months or so after birth, they were tightly bound in bandages so that they were unable to move either head or limbs. They were completely immobilized (Plate 6). Only after about four months did they gain the use of their arms, but not their legs. The medical reasons behind this practice of swaddling were that 'for tenderness the limbs of a child may easily and soon bow and bend and take diverse shapes'. There was also a widespread popular fear that unless restrained the infant might tear off its ears, scratch out its eyes or break its legs. Finally, it was extremely convenient for the adults, since modern investigation shows that swaddling in fact slows down the infant's heartbeat and induces far longer sleep and less crying. Swaddling also allowed the infant to be moved about like a parcel and left unattended in odd corners or hung on a peg on a wall without danger to life or limb and without overt protest.

Once removed from the swaddling bandages, the boys were left free, but the girls were encased in bodices and corsets reinforced with iron and whalebone to ensure that their bodies were moulded to the prevailing adult fashion. Dressed in miniature adult clothes, they were expected to conform to the ideal adult feminine shape and carriage, and in particular to maintain an upright posture and to walk slowly and gracefully. The contraptions used to achieve these ends often frustrated them, leading instead to the distortion or displacement of the organs, and sometimes even death. When in 1665 George Evelyn's two-year-old daughter Elizabeth died, the doctor told him that 'her iron bodice was her pain, and had hindered the lungs to grow'; the surgeon who examined the body 'found her breast bone pressed very deeply inwardly, and he said two of her ribs were broken, and the straightness of the bodice upon the vitals occasioned this difficulty of breathing and her death'.

During the period from 1540 to 1660 there is a great deal of evidence, especially from Puritans, of a fierce determination to break the will of the child, and to enforce his utter subjection to the authority of his elders and superiors, and most especially of his parents. John Robinson, the first pastor of the Pilgrim Fathers in Holland, was only reflecting current ideas when he observed that 'surely there is in all children ... a stubbornness, and stoutness of mind arising from natural pride, which must in the first place be broken and beaten down'. 'Children should not know, if it could be kept from them, that they have a will in their own, but in their parents' keeping.' In the seventeenth century the early training of children was directly equated with the bating of hawks or the breaking-in of young horses or hunting dogs. These were all animals which were highly valued and cherished in the society of that period, and it was only natural that exactly the same principle should be applied to the education of children, especially now that parents began to care more about them.

In the middle ages, schools had used physical punishment to enforce discipline, and the characteristic equipment of a schoolmaster was not so much a book as a rod or a bundle of birch twigs. The emblem of *Grammar* on Chartres Cathedral porch is a master threatening two children with a scourge; at Oxford University the conferring of the degree of Master of Grammar was accompanied by presentation of a birch as symbol of office and by the ceremonial flogging of a whipping-boy by the new Master.

In the early sixteenth century, there were a number of significant

116

changes; firstly flogging became the standard routine method of punishment for academic lapses for all schoolchildren, regardless of rank or age; secondly a far larger proportion of the population began to go to school, and therefore became liable to this discipline; thirdly, as education changed from a minority privilege to a widespread social obligation, many more schoolboys were poorly motivated to learn, and therefore created disciplinary problems most easily solved by the use of force. As a result corporal punishment at school became a standard practice applied to rich and poor, old and young, regardless of rank. In the late sixteenth and seventeenth centuries it was normal for the social elite to send boys to school rather than to have them taught at home by a private tutor. The argument in favour of elite boys going to public schools was that by mingling with other boys of all kinds, rich and poor, virtuous and vicious, friends and enemies, 'they learn the pratique of the world', as Roger North put it.

There can be no doubt, therefore, that more children were being beaten in the sixteenth and early seventeenth centuries, over a longer age span, than ever before. It looks as if the greater evidence of brutality in the sixteenth-century home and school is a reflection of a harsher reality, not merely of a larger and more revealing body of written records. Whipping was now so normal a part of a child's experience that when a seventeenth-century moral theologian wished to convey to children some idea of Hell, the best way he could think of describing it was as 'a terrible place, that is worse a thousand times than whipping'. As for Heaven, it was a place where children 'would never be beat any more'.

Scholastic punishments normally took two forms. The first and most common was to lay the child over a bench, or alternatively to horse him on the back of a companion, and to flog his naked buttocks with a bundle of birches until the blood flowed. The second was to strike his hand or mouth with a ferula, a flat piece of wood which expanded at the end into a pear-shape with a hole in the middle. One blow with this instrument was enough to raise a most painful blister.

There can be no doubt whatever that severe flogging was a normal and daily occurrence in the sixteenth- and seventeenth-century grammar school, and some of the most famous headmasters of the most elitist schools of their day, like Dr Busby of Westminster School or Dr Gill of St Paul's, were notorious for their savagery.

Indeed, some of them seem to have been pathological sadists, and John Aubrey's account of Dr Gill's 'whipping-fits' suggests a man who had become the slave of a perverted sexual obsession. Other schoolmasters had even more bizarre habits. At the Free School at Witney in 1725 the master 'had some indiscretions, such as making boys whip one another round the school, and when he whipped them himself, of taking a turn round the school between every lash'. But what is significant is that elite parents were willing to give such men a free hand over their sons without censure or restraint, since flogging was then regarded as the only reliable method of controlling both children and adults. In 1622 Henry Peacham reported that scholars were 'pulled by the ears, lashed over the face, beaten about the head with the great end of the rod, smitten upon the lips for every slight offence with the ferula'. Peacham deplored these sadistic excesses but explained them by the fact that schoolmasters believed that 'there is no other method of making a scholar but by beating him'. The routine normality of the practice allowed Ben Jonson to describe a schoolmaster as a man accustomed to 'sweeping his living from the posteriors of little children'.

The extension of flogging even reached into university education. During the late sixteenth century the colleges of Oxford and Cambridge had received for the first time a huge influx of sons of the wealthy laity, to house whom they had greatly enlarged their accommodation. The key feature of the sixteenth-century college was the application to lay children of the strict, prison-like conditions previously applied to regular clergy in monasteries and colleges. This was the time when the college assumed its now familiar function of acting *in loco parentis*, with all the aids of high walls, gates closed at 9 p.m., and strict internal surveillance by the tutors. This was also the time, between 1450 and 1660, when the colleges freely used physical punishments on their younger students, normally, but not always, under the age of eighteen, either by public whippings in the hall or over a barrel in the buttery, or else by putting them in the stocks in the hall. By the medieval statutes of Balliol and Lincoln Colleges, the college head had powers of physical punishment, but in the sixteenth century this authority was greatly extended, and delegated to deans and even tutors. Aubrey, who entered Oxford in 1642, noted that there 'the rod was frequently used by the tutors and deans on his pupils, till Bachelors of Arts'.

It should be emphasized that this widespread and constant use of flogging as the prime method of spreading a knowledge of the classics was the last thing that the Humanist educational reformers had in mind when they pressed for a classical training of the European elite. From Guarino to Vives to Erasmus, and from Elyot to Ascham to Mulcaster, they were to a man opposed to the indiscriminate use of severe physical punishments. They all advised that to spare the rod was to spoil the child, but they also believed that children could and should be enticed into the classics, not driven like cattle, and should be punished only for moral failures such as obstinacy or idleness, not for stupidity. What happened in practice was that a man like Mulcaster, successively headmaster of Merchant Taylors' and St Paul's in the reign of Elizabeth, practised what he preached and ran his schools on model humanist lines. But the majority of lazier and less dedicated schoolmasters extended the medieval tradition of flogging on an ever-increasing scale as classical education spread, since it was the easiest and least troubleso ne means of drilling Latin grammar into large numbers of thick or resistant skulls. Renaissance school practice thus eventually came to bear little relation to Renaissance educational theory: the subject matter was more grammatical, the method of learning more by rote memorizing, the discipline more brutal. In practice, post-Renaissance education, because of its insufferably tedious content and method of instruction, demanded effective repression of the will, the imagination, the emotions, and even intellectual curiosity. In part, at least, the increased use of physical punishment was therefore a natural accompaniment of the spread of this degenerate kind of classical learning as a subject of study in school and home. This connection was suggested by Locke, who asked, 'Why ... does the learning of Latin and Greek need the rod, when French and Italian needs it not? Children learn to dance and fence without whipping; nay arithmetic, drawing, etc., they apply themselves well enough to without beating.'

In the very early sixteenth century, when Humanism was still riding high, some families in their domestic discipline in the home followed a different drummer. The Humanist Sir Thomas More reminded his children that 'I never could endure to hear you cry. You know, for example, how often I kissed you, how seldom I whipped you. My whip was invariably a peacock's tail. Even this I wielded hesitantly and gently, so that sorry welts might not disfigure your tender seats. Brutal and unworthy to be called father is he who does not himself weep at the tears of his child.' But More was an exceptional man, as he himself hinted. His fellow Humanist, the Spaniard Vives, recalled that 'there was nobody I did more flee, or was more loath to come nigh, than my mother when I was a child', and he himself advised parents that 'cherishing marreth sons, but it utterly destroyeth daughters'. This severity was powerfully reinforced by the first wave of Protestantism, and by her own account her pious parents led Lady Jane Grey a miserable life in the 1530s and 1540s. 'When I am in presence either of father or mother, whether I speak, keep silence, sit, stand or go, eat, drink, be merry or sad, be sewing, playing, dancing, or doing anything else, I must do it, as it were, in such weight, measure, and number, even so perfectly as God made the world, else I am so sharply taunted, so cruelly threatened, yea presently sometimes with pinches, nips and bobs, and some ways I will not name for the honour I bear them, so without measure misordered that I think myself in Hell.'

The fostering-out system by which children were sent away from home at an early age to act as servants or living-in apprentices in someone else's house meant that perhaps two out of every three households contained a resident adolescent who was not of the family. Apprentices were usually indentured at the age of fourteen for seven years, and in London were sufficiently numerous to form a distinct adolescent subculture of their own. They were exposed to almost limitless sadism from their masters, mitigated only by the fact that the bolder spirits among them could, and sometimes did, sue their torturers for assault. These law suits reveal a female apprentice who was stripped naked, strung up by her thumbs and given twenty-one lashes; a boy who was beaten so severely that he could not stand upright and who spat blood for a fortnight; another who was flogged, salted and then held naked to a fire; another who was beaten so severely with a boat-hook that his hip was broken; and so on.

Only psychotic parents treated their own children with such calculated ferocity, but whipping was the normal method of discipline in a sixteenth- or seventeenth-century home, mitigated and compensated for, no doubt, by a good deal of fondling when the child was docile and obedient. Both rewards and punishments took physical rather than psychological forms. Up to the age of seven, the children were mostly left in the care of women, primarily their mother, nurse, and governess. Many of these women were demonstratively affectionate, but they all believed in the current doctrine of the need to crush the will. Roger North, a son of Dudley, fourth Lord North, recalled in old age that his upbringing in the mid-seventeenth century 'was in general severe but tender'. If the children were disobedient, their mother 'would reduce us to tears by the smart of correction; and which was more grievous, would force us to leave crying and condescend to the abject pitch of thanking the good rail [i.e. the rod], which she said was to break our spirits, which it did effectively'. As a successful product of the system, Roger North believed in it, and thought that the relaxation of discipline he perceived in his old age at the end of the century was leading to profligacy and debauchery.

But not all children reacted so positively, and it is hardly surprising that this treatment meant that many children grew up with a fear and even hatred of their parents, particularly in the seventeenth century, when the ideological underpinnings of repression were breaking down. Gilbert Burnet, who was born in 1630, recalled in his old age that he was subjected to 'much severe correction; ... the fear of that brought me under too great an uneasiness, and sometimes even to a hatred of my father. The sense of this may have perhaps carried me in the education of my children to the other extreme of too much indulgence.' Richard Norwood had a regular nightmare of parental rejection: 'Usually in my dreams I methought I saw my father always grievously angry with me.' Joseph Lister was regularly beaten by his mother, while Thomas Raymond recalled bitterly about his father: 'upon all occasions felt the effects of his choler, which was of great mischief unto me, being of a soft and timorous complexion'. Robert Boyle recalled that his father had 'a perfect aversion for fondness' to or from his children, while John Aubrey, who was inclined to exaggeration, claimed that in his youth, parents 'were as severe to their children as their schoolmasters; and their schoolmasters as masters of the House of Correction'. 'Fathers and mothers slashed their daughters ... when they were perfect women.' As a result, 'the child perfectly loathed the sight of his parents as the slave his torture'. Aubrey is clearly not to be taken literally, and his remarks are significant primarily since he, like North and Burnet, was contrasting conditions before 1640 with the more amiable parent–child relations that he thought prevailed when he was writing in the late seventeenth century. All three claimed to have lived through a period of marked change in the treatment of children.

As one might expect, there were even examples in the early seventeenth century of what is known today as the 'battered child syndrome', in which maternal or paternal hatred of the child reaches pathological proportions. Lady Abergavenny 'in a passion killed her own child about seven years old. She having been a great while whipping it, my Lord being grieved to hear it cry so terribly, went into the room to plead for it, and she threw it with such force on the ground she broke the skull; the girl lived but four hours after it.'

This extension of the use of physical punishment throughout the whole educational system at home and in school merely reflected a growing use of this method of social control throughout the society, including naturally the home. A late sixteenth-century Dutchman, appropriately enough called Batty, who was rapidly translated into English, developed the theory that the providence and wisdom of God had especially formed the human buttocks so that they could be severely beaten without incurring serious bodily injury. The late sixteenth and early seventeenth centuries were for England the great flogging age: every town and every village had its whipping-post, which was in constant use as a means of preserving social order.

This stress on domestic discipline and the utter subordination of the child found expression in extraordinary outward marks of deference which English children were expected to pay to their parents in the sixteenth and early seventeenth centuries. It was customary for them when at home to kneel before their parents to ask their blessing every morning, and even as adults on arrival at and departure from the home. This was a symbolic gesture of submission which John Donne believed to be unique in Europe. The children of the widowed Lady Alice Wandesford in the 1640s knelt daily to ask her blessing, and in 1651 her twenty-eight-year-old eldest son knelt for her blessing before leaving on a journey. Even when grown up, sons were expected to keep their hats off in their parents' presence, while daughters were expected to remain kneeling or standing in their mother's presence. 'Gentlemen of thirty and forty years old', recalled Aubrey, 'were to stand like mutes and fools bareheaded before their parents; and the daughters (grown women) were to stand at the cupboard-side during the whole time of their proud mother's visit, unless (as the fashion was) leave was desired, forsooth, that a cushion should be given to them to kneel upon, ... after they had done sufficient penance in standing.' Well into his middle age Sir Dudley North 'would never put on his hat or sit down before his father, unless enjoined to it'. Elizabeth, Countess of Falkland, always knelt in her mother's presence, sometimes for an hour at a time, despite the fact that she had married above her parents into the peerage, and that she was 'but an ill kneeler and worse riser'. In the first half of the seventeenth century a son, even when grown up, would commonly address his father in a letter as 'sir', and sign himself 'your humble obedient son', 'your son in continuance of all obedience', or 'your most obedient and loving son'. In the 1680s Edmund Verney as an undergraduate at Oxford cautiously began his letters home 'Most honoured father', while those he received began with the peremptory word 'Child'.

This pattern of extreme deference to parents in the home was in full conformity with behaviour norms of the society at large. Thus the doffing of the hat, the bowing, and the respectful forms of address to superiors were all part of the disciplinary rules of late sixteenth- and early seventeenth-century colleges. The Oxford University Statutes of 1636 prescribed that 'the juniors shall show due and suitable reverence to their seniors both in public and private, that is, undergraduates to Bachelors, Bachelors of Arts to Masters, and in like manner Masters to Doctors; that is, by yielding to them the best places at meetings, by giving way when they meet, and by uncovering the head at a suitable distance and by a reverent greeting and address'.

It would be quite wrong to suppose that in the sixteenth and early seventeenth centuries conformity to these behaviour patterns aroused widespread resentment. Human beings – and especially children – can adapt fairly easily to a very wide range of expectations, from the repressive to the permissive, so long as the rules are clearly understood and generally accepted. Under conditions in which everyone knows and accepts his place, the deferential system provides a comfortable framework for all social relationships, at least as comfortable as the egalitarian norms of American society today. They only cease to work harmoniously when the premises on which they are based come under challenge. The prescriptions, therefore, represented ideals congruent to a particular phase of English development, both in the family and in society generally, which was confined to the sixteenth and early seventeenth centuries. The full significance of these symbolic gestures and use of words to indicate filial deference becomes apparent only when they are contrasted with the very different modes of the late seventeenth and eighteenth centuries.

One of the most effective methods used to socialize children in the seventeenth century was to teach them, at a very early age, to be afraid of death and of the possibility of eternal damnation. It was standard advice in the sixteenth and seventeenth centuries to tell them to think much about death; and since it was then so likely a prospect for a child, it was reasonable that they should be well prepared. One example from the diary of Samuel Sewall of Boston, who was an enlightened and loving parent, will serve to illustrate the use of this very common psychological control device, employed especially by Puritans on both sides of the Atlantic. When in 1690 a little boy aged nine died of smallpox, Sewall took the opportunity to tell his eight-year-old son Samuel about it, and to warn him 'what need he had to prepare for death'. Sam seemed not to be impressed at the time, but later that day 'he burst out into a bitter cry and said he was afraid he should die'. Nervous children could be temporarily driven hysterical by this treatment. One afternoon in 1696, Sewall's fifteen-year-old daughter Betty 'a little after dinner burst out in an amazing cry, which caused all the family to cry too'. She explained that 'she was afraid she should go to Hell, her sins were not pardoned', a conclusion she reached from a sermon her father read to her and from her own reading of Cotton Mather. Five weeks later she was still distraught and came to her father as soon as he was awake, to tell him that she 'was afraid [she] should go to Hell, like Spira, not Elected'. Ten weeks later she was still in the same profound melancholia, and could hardly read her prescribed chapter of the Bible for weeping. Six months later, she was still not cured, and was a prey to fits of passionate weeping, saying that she 'was a reprobate, loves not God's people as she should'.

This evidence all suggests strict subordination of children to parents and a high degree of severity adopted in their upbringing in the sixteenth century. Paradoxically enough, this was the first result of a greater interest in children. So long as no one cared about them very much, they could be left to run wild, or in the hands of nurses, servants and tutors. But the Reformation — and in Catholic Europe the Counter-Reformation — drive for moral regeneration brought with it an increasing concern to suppress the sinfulness of children. A pedagogic movement, which had begun a century earlier with the Italian Renaissance as a glorification of the purity and innocence of the child, was twisted in its late sixteenth- and early seventeenth-century northern religious transplantation into a deadly fear of the liability of children to corruption and sin, particularly those cardinal sins of pride and disobedience. The threat of religious, intellectual and political chaos triggered off by the Reformation induced moral theologians — who were the most articulate leaders of educated opinion — to agree that the only hope of preserving social order was to concentrate on the right disciplining and education of children. This accounts in large measure for the sudden access of interest in pedagogy in the second and third decades of the sixteenth century, and the swamping of the more gentle and affectionate ideas of the Humanists.

The doctrine of Original Sin strongly encouraged the stress on repression rather than encouragement as the core of educational theory. 'If thou smite him with the rod, thou shalt deliver his soul from Hell' was a quotation from the Bible that Protestants took very seriously indeed. Oliver Heywood recollected that his mother 'though she was very indulgent to us, yet she was severe and sharp against sin'. Many late sixteenth- and seventeenth-century mothers were both caring and repressive at the same time, for the simple reason that the two went together. Puritans in particular were profoundly concerned about their children, loved them, cherished them, prayed over them and subjected them to endless moral pressure. At the same time they feared and even hated them as agents of sin within the household, and therefore beat them mercilessly. Even the gentle John Bunyan was severe with children.

Not only were most of the most popular child-rearing handbooks written by Puritans, but Puritans seem to have been exceptionally prominent among authors of books for children published before 1700. Of those authors whose religious opinions can be identified, twice as many were Puritans or Dissenters as were conformist Anglicans, despite the enormous preponderance of the latter in the population both before 1640 and after 1660. This may be partly because nonconformists are better recorded and more easily identified than Anglicans, but even so the discrepancy is both striking and persuasive: Puritans were abnormally concerned about children and their upbringing because it was only by the mass conversion of the younger generation that they could hope to create or perpetuate the godly society to which they aspired.

Another reason for the severity of the treatment accorded to children at this time is the rapid spread of knowledge of the Bible, and Protestant treatment of the book as an authoritative source on all subjects. The *Apocrypha* and *Proverbs* contain some extremely harsh instructions about how to bring up children. Sirach in the *Apocrypha* was particularly severe, and yet his advice struck a congenial chord among sixteenth-century parents. 'If thou play with him, he shall bring thee to heaviness. Laugh not with him lest thou weep with him also, and lest thy teeth be set on edge at last . . .' The advice is to keep a psychological distance. No hint of tenderness is to be permitted, since this would undermine authority and destroy deference. In the newly sanctified conjugal marriage, the duty of the wife and mother was to assist her husband in the task of the repression of their children. She 'holds not his hand from due strokes, but bares their skins with delight to his fatherly stripes'. The last factor to be born in mind is that immature children were regarded as mere animals lacking the capacity to reason, and therefore to be broken in just as one would break in a puppy, a foal or a hawk.

The psychological coolness and physical severity that characterized the upbringing of children in late sixteenth- and early seventeenth-century England can thus be explained in terms of specific factors peculiar to the time. They were part of the traditional cultural baggage of the age, a set of values which were deeply internalized and were congruent with the social organization. They were probably accepted by children as part of the natural order of things, just as the harshly hierarchical and authoritarian character of the society as a whole was accepted by the adults. By putting the treatment of children in the sixteenth century into this broader context, it becomes intelligible and even reasonable.

A rather different theory has it that the deferential society is itself a reflection of the defence mechanism of the ego when it discovers a basic conflict between its own impulses to autonomy and the strict canons of obedience ruthlessly enforced by its parents. Thus the deferential behaviour of the children is a defensive response to ego repression, as the only way to survive, while the authoritarian and remote behaviour of the parents is an expression of the original desire for autonomy, which now at last finds an outlet in the bullying of their own children. This thesis also makes good sense, and could also be applied to explain the persistence for so long of the traditional experience of an English public school, where in the first year the boy is a virtual slave at the mercy of the older boys and in the last he turns the tables and in his turn acts as a cruel and arbitrary tyrant towards his juniors.

iii. *Control of Occupation and Marriage*

Paternal absolutism in the family was not only the basis for order in the society at large. It also had specific ends in view within the family system of the age, for obedience which began in little things was expected to lead to obedience in big ones. The practical benefit to be gained by parents from the extraordinary measures taken to break the child's will at an early stage was that later on he would accept with passive resignation their decisions in the two most important choices of his life, that of an occupation, and that of a marriage partner.

The choice of a career did not affect girls, for whom the only option was marriage. But it was the parents who decided, with the interests of the family primarily in mind, whether a boy was to be prepared to fulfil the duties of a country gentleman or to be given specialized training for the Church, the law, trade, or some other occupation.

By the seventeenth century education was already dictating career-choice, which is why parents were so angry when their children balked. In 1685 Edmund Verney wrote furiously to his nineteen-year-old eldest son, Ralph: 'I hear you hate learning and your mind hankers after travelling. I will not be taught by my cradle how to breed it up; it is insolence and impudence in any child to presume so much as to offer it.' The memory of this mild act of insubordination still rankled some months later, when young Ralph died suddenly of a fever. His father saw the hand of God in the tragedy and hastened to press the moral home to his second, and now only, son: 'I . . . exhort you to be wholly ruled and guided by me, and to be perfectly obedient to me in all things according to your bounden duty . . . For should you do otherwise and contrary in the least, . . . I am afraid that you will be in that evil circumstance snatched away by death in your youth, as your poor brother was last week.' One wonders whether Edmund remembered this warning when the boy died four years later.

The choice of marriage partner concerned both boys and girls and was especially important in a society where there were large financial and political stakes in marriage and where divorce was virtually impossible. Almost all children until the end of the sixteenth century were so conditioned by their upbringing and so financially helpless that they acquiesced without much objection in the matches contrived for them by their parents. The moral justification for parental control was derived, as has been seen, from the social values of the society and from the Fifth Commandment. 'Honour thy father and mother' was a sacred precept reiterated by both Protestant preachers and state propagandists, and interpreted to mean strict obedience. When this argument began to fail after the middle of the seventeenth century, one defender of traditional behaviour tried in 1663 to base filial obedience on the sanctity of private property: 'Children are so much the goods, the possessions of their parent, that they cannot, without a kind of theft, give away themselves without the allowance of those that have the right in them.' This was an ingenious attempt to shore up ancient but decaying patterns of authority by using new economic theories, but it was not very convincing.

A pragmatic calculation of family interest was the accepted viewpoint of the sixteenth century, and the one upon which the approach to marriage in real life was normally based. The elite, however, were also subjected by the poets and playwrights to propaganda for an entirely antithetical ideal of romantic love, as expressed for example in Shakespeare's *Sonnets* and plays. Until romanticism temporarily triumphed in the late eighteenth century, there was thus a clear conflict of values between the idealization of love by some poets, playwrights and the authors of romances on the one hand, and its rejection as a form of imprudent folly and even madness by all theologians, moralists, authors of manuals of conduct, and parents and adults in general. Everyone knew about it, some experienced it, but only a minority of young courtiers made it a way of life, and even they did not necessarily regard it as a suitable basis for life-long marriage.

The accepted wisdom of the age was that marriage based on personal selection, and thus inevitably influenced by such ephemeral factors as sexual attraction or romantic love, was if anything less likely to produce lasting happiness than one arranged by more prudent and more mature heads. This view finds confirmation in anthropological studies of the many societies where love has not been regarded as a sound basis for marriage, and where one girl is as good as another, provided that she is a good housekeeper, a breeder, and a willing sexual playmate. Dr Johnson was not merely being a cranky eccentric when he persisted in taking this now outmoded view in the late eighteenth century. He argued that 'marriages would in general be as happy, and often more so, if they were all made by the Lord Chancellor, upon a due consideration of the characters and circumstances, without the parties having any choice in the matter'. In 1734 Lord Hervey was only repeating traditional wisdom when he told Queen Caroline not to worry about the repellent aspect of her daughter's husband: 'Lord, Madame, in half a year all persons are alike. The figure of the body one is married to . . . grows so familiar to one's eye that one looks at it mechanically, without regarding either the beauties or deformities that strike a stranger.' In the early sixteenth century, these were views which would not have excited any comment or controversy.

In any case, most children inevitably took the same calculating attitude towards marriage as their parents, so that intergenerational conflict was reduced because they shared the same objectives. In 1639 Christopher Guise was the twenty-two-year-old son and heir of a moderately wealthy Gloucestershire gentry family, living on an allowance of £80 a year. He was unwilling to get married, 'having observed some young married couples to live in a very narrow compass'. Three years later, however, at the urging of his parents, he married the daughter of Sir Lawrence Washington, who was clearly a good financial catch. He did it merely in order to get the family estate firmly settled on him, and to extract from his father £400 a year as present maintenance (and future jointure for his widow). 'I was at last content to make all sure, at the loss of my loved liberty.' He was not held in marriage bonds very long, however, since his wife died within seven weeks 'and left me again at liberty', although a little melancholy. Back from the Civil War in 1645, and overwhelmed with debt, 'I found myself in a manner enforced to look after another match', and finally managed to capture the daughter of a wealthy Londoner. When she too died in 1659 he took back to live with him an ex-mistress from earlier days, who looked after him until he died eleven years later, and in return was rewarded with a substantial cash sum, a life annuity of £100 a year for herself, and another of £50 a year for her son, who was presumably an illegitimate child of Sir Christopher. It is a revealing story of the benefits and defects of the mercenary marriage system, and the role of mistresses as an emotional escape-hatch.

It is significant that up to 1640 the landed classes continued to endure, although with increasing discontent, the practice of wardship, by which the marriages of young fatherless heirs and heiresses of landed property were put up for sale by the Crown. The Court of Wards was tolerated as long as the society upon which it levied its tribute had itself little respect for individual freedom of choice, and treated its own children with as little consideration for personal feelings as did the Court itself. Thus in 1567 the first Lord Rich made provision in his will for his illegitimate son Richard. He directed his executors to purchase from the Crown 'one woman ward or some other woman' with an estate of £200 a year clear 'for a marriage ... to the said Richard'. If Richard were to refuse the girl, he lost all his inheritance, for the executors were then 'to sell the said ward ... to the uttermost advantage'. The possibility that the girl ward might refuse Richard clearly did not cross Lord Rich's mind. It was not until a century later, at the Restoration, that the Court of Wards was finally abolished, in part at least due to a growth of novel ideas about personal autonomy, and in part in order to restore control of marriage to the family, and to remove this form of inheritance tax upon the elite.

Only a handful of children resisted parental dictation before the end of the sixteenth century, and their rebellion was soon crushed. In the mid-fifteenth century, Elizabeth, daughter of Agnes Paston, obstinately insisted on choosing her own husband. To bring her to heel, her mother put her in virtual solitary confinement, forbidden to speak either to visitors or to male servants. In addition, 'she hath since Easter the most part been beaten once in the week or twice, and sometimes twice on a day, and her head broken in two or three places'. It is hardly surprising that few children had the strength of will to resist such treatment.

In the sixteenth century, violence was less necessary since the duty of filial obedience had been more successfully internalized. On the rare occasions when children threatened to marry to suit themselves, parents were quick to emphasize the traditional need to consider the interests of the lineage and the obligation to obey one's parents. In 1658 the fourth Lord Mountgarret's eldest son, Richard Butler, fell in love with Emilia Blundell, the daughter of an impoverished gentleman. When he learned what was in the wind, his lordship wrote a stern fatherly letter to his son.

I am informed that you are so miserably blinded as to incline to marry, and so with one wretched act to undo both the gentlewoman and yourself, and (as much as in you lies) to dash all my designs which concern my self and house. Son, I charge you by the bond of nature and duty which you owe me, that you presume not to proceed in so desperate a purpose, as a thing which I detest and abhor. And therefore lay these words close in to your heart, and read in them as high indignation of mine, as if they were far more sharper ... Be not you wanting in the obedience of a son in a matter of so great importance as this to me and my family: but let this ... suffice to keep you from plunging yourself into ruin ... If it do not, I shall take order that the blow smart there where in justice it should.

This firm reminder of where morality and family duty lay, coupled with the final ominous threat, was sufficient to break off the match.

Authoritarian control by parents over the marriages of their children inevitably lasted longeest in the richest and most aristocratic circles, where the property, power and status stakes were highest. When in 1719 the son and heir of the Duke of Richmond was married to the immature daughter of Lord Cadogan,

the marriage was made to cancel a gambling debt; the young people's consent having been the last thing thought of: the Earl of March was sent for from school, and the young lady from the nursery; a clergyman was in attendance and they were told that they were immediately to become man and wife. The young lady is not reported to have uttered a word; the gentleman exclaimed 'They are surely not going to marry me to that dowdy.'

But the marriage took place, and the pair immediately parted, the groom to set off with his tutor for some years on the Grand Tour, the bride to go home to her mother. By now, however, the circumstances seem to have been sufficiently unusual to arouse comment. It is also true that, entirely by serendipity, the marriage eventually turned out to be a fairy-tale success. The young man returned from the Grand Tour some years later, noticed a beautiful young woman sitting near him at the theatre, and found that it was his own wife. According to the story, they lived happily ever after. But this was a subsequent bonus of the gods, bestowed upon what had been a ruthlessly arranged, purely mercenary marriage of the most old-fashioned kind.

Lower down in the social scale, among the squires and wealthy lawyers of the early seventeenth century, patriarchal authority had to struggle to maintain itself. A typical example of the new complexities is provided by the account Simonds D'Ewes gives of his own marriage. In 1626 he was twenty-four years old, a Middle Temple lawyer, and already more or less financially independent in his own right as the co-heir to his late maternal grandfather's estate. He was, therefore, economically free to marry, so long as he was not seeking an heiress, in which case he was dependent on a firm property settlement from his father. But Simonds was a genealogical snob, who wished to marry into ancient stock, and also aspired to ally himself to a landed heiress. He therefore needed his father's consent to a settlement which would provide a suitable jointure for the bride after his own death, and would settle the D'Ewes estate upon him in reversion. His father, on the other hand, was a greedy man who wanted not a landed heiress but a bride with a large cash portion, which under current arrangements would go to himself and not to his son.

Simonds first proposed to his father two co-heiresses of ancient family, but in each case the negotiations never got off the ground. His father then made some proposals for daughters of great City merchants with large cash portions, whom Simonds rejected. Then her uncle made an opening proposal for a match with Anne, the daughter and heiress of the late Sir William Clopton, of an ancient and wealthy Suffolk family. This led to tedious and complex negotiations between Simonds's father on the one hand and Anne's grandmother and guardian on the other. Everything seemed settled, when his father suddenly broke off negotiations, having heard of an alternative offer bringing a cash portion of £5,000. Simonds learned who the girl was and told his father that he had seen her, but 'finding her face rough and unpleasant, I could upon no terms affect her'. His father then gave way, and the draft financial arrangements with the Cloptons were finally concluded.

At this point, Simonds had not yet met the prospective bride, who was anyway only thirteen-and-a-half years old. He had seen her two or three times seven years before when she was only a child, but not since. He therefore had a preliminary interview with Anne to inspect her physical appearance, 'whose person gave me absolute and full content as soon as I had seriously viewed it'. She was a reasonably pretty girl and he was satisfied; she presumably raised no objection to him (after all she was only a child still), and the marriage contract was, therefore, finally signed.

Thereafter, he saw more and more of Anne, who rapidly became devoted to him, while his own affection to his child bride also deepened. But her grandmother was unwilling to agree to an immediate marriage, allegedly for two reasons. The first was that the girl was too young for sexual intercourse, which might stunt her growth and endanger her health. Secondly, she was afraid that the child's 'good will and affections was no solid or real love grounded on judgement, and might thereafter alter and lessen again after marriage'. Here was the traditional fear of love as a temporary fever. However, Simonds, who was afraid that either his father or her grandmother might at any moment change their minds if a better offer presented itself, finally overcame their objections by promising to remain chaste for a period after the marriage, which he in fact did for eight months. He was soon as devoted to his young wife as she was to him, and he persuaded her to participate in his private fasting and prayers, seeking assurances that she as well as he could be counted among the Elect.

This is a complicated story, with many different strands of cultural behaviour involved in it. It shows the continuing control of parents over the marriage, even of grown-up sons, well into the early seventeenth century, as well as the way they bartered heiresses while they were still mere children and not even sexually mature. On the other hand it also shows a son exercising the right of refusal on grounds of dislike of the physical appearance of a bride proposed by his father, an argument the latter accepted. It also shows that after all the financial negotiations had been concluded, the contract was not actually signed until the groom had inspected the bride and found her physically satisfactory. The mutual love and affection, cemented by common Calvinist zeal, which subsequently developed between the bride and groom was an accident, which merely aroused the suspicion of the bride's grandmother, who had no faith in the enduring quality of such emotions. The story thus perfectly illustrates the transitional pattern of marriage among the early seventeenth-century English landed classes as they moved uneasily between one set of values based on kin interest and marriage arranged by others with a view to financial advantage, and another set based on allowing children a right of veto in order to provide a better chance of marital harmony. The result was an awkward interplay of forces, which in this particular case turned out to everyone's satisfaction.

These illustrations of marriage arrangements show very clearly how things were slowly changing. At first, in the early sixteenth century, children were bought and sold like cattle for breeding, and no one thought that the parties concerned had any right to complain. But Protestant moral theology, with its stress on 'holy matrimony' slowly forced a modification of this 'extreme position, which was only maintained in its pure state through the seventeenth century in the highest ranks of the aristocracy where the stakes of property and power were largest. To retain 'holy matrimony', which the theologians thought desirable in itself, as well as being a way to reduce adultery, it was necessary that the couple should be able to develop some affection for each other. It was therefore thought necessary to concede to the children the right of veto, the right to reject a spouse chosen by the parents on the grounds that the antipathy aroused by a single interview was too great to permit the possibility of the future development of affection. This right of veto could only be used with caution and probably only once, or at most twice, while for women there was always the risk that its exercise might condemn them to spinsterhood, if their parents failed to provide another suitor.

Popular attitudes on such fundamental issues changed with glacial slowness, varying from family to family, as well as from class to class, while the law was naturally even slower to change. In 1706 a gentleman died leaving a will which entirely disinherited his son, on the grounds that the latter had married against his wishes. Although the son contested the will, the jury voted to uphold it. There was clearly a very long period of conflict between elite parents and children, lasting right through the seventeenth century before the old patriarchal attitudes to marriage were finally discredited.

Because the key to the system of controlled marriage was the exchange of property, it theoretically follows that children lower down the economic scale would enjoy greater freedom of choice. Whether this is so is not at present known for certain. Harrington thought that the arranged marriage system did not press 'so heavy on the lower sort, being better able to shift for themselves, as upon the nobility and gentry'. On the other hand, a large proportion of the population owned some property, and there is plenty of evidence for arranged marriages among the yeomanry in the sixteenth century. For example, in 1514 a Lancashire girl was forced by her uncle and her 'friends', under threat of losing her inheritance in land, to marry a man she actively disliked. She fled from him a month later after a severe beating, and sued for a separation, explaining that 'but only for the fear of loss of my land I would never be with him an hour'. In his will of 1599 William Shaftoe curtly decreed: 'To my daughter Margery, 60 sheep, and I bestow her in marriage upon Edward, son of Reynold Shaftoe of Thockerington.' When in 1632 the eldest son of Adam Martindale's artisan father came to marry, his father expected him to marry a girl with a portion of at least £120, and was furious when he chose one with only £40. The case-books of Richard Napier suggest that the choice of marriage partner was the principal issue which divided parents and children at all social levels above that of the absolute poor in the early seventeenth century.

Among the propertyless at the bottom of society, however, children even in the sixteenth century were probably very much freer to choose a spouse than their superiors, as they certainly were in the eighteenth century. In the first place, their parents had little economic leverage over them since they had little or nothing to give or bequeath them. In the second place, most of the children left home at the age of ten to seventeen in order to become apprentices, domestic servants, or living-in labourers in other people's houses. This very large floating population of adolescents living away from home were thus free from parental supervision and could, therefore, make their own choice of marriage partners as soon as they were out of apprenticeship. The only thing that held them back was the need to accumulate sufficient capital to set up house and to start a shop or trade, which was the principal cause for the long delay in marriage into the middle twenties.

The fact that the children of the poor were freer to make their own choices than the children of the rich did not mean, however, that affective considerations weighed more than the same prudential ones that would govern choice if made for them by their parents. The diary in the 1660s of Roger Lowe, an impoverished apprentice to a small shopkeeper, indicates great freedom of communication between the sexes, and great freedom of choice, based on both affective and prudential considerations. One detailed study of marriage in an Early Modern European peasant society, based on a careful study of all the evidence, has concluded that 'in a peasant society, an engagement of marriage may have nothing of the character of an intimate, private understanding between two lovers. In a peasant marriage contract, the economic unit, with its human and material requirements, is the dominant consideration. Personal preferences have a lower priority.' Very little information is at present available for England, but there is no reason to suppose that attitudes there were at all different before the nineteenth century.

3. HUSBAND AND WIFE

i. *Subordination of Wives*

There is evidence to suggest that a trend towards greater patriarchy in husband–wife relations was also developing in the sixteenth century. But, just as with patriarchal power over children, strong countervailing forces began to operate towards the end of that century and in the seventeenth century, so that the picture is by no means clear. For a considerable period, two conflicting trends were at work at the same time, and the growing authority of the husband can only be seen in a relatively pure form during the first half of the sixteenth century.

At this time a woman's legal right to hold and dispose of her own property was limited to what she could specifically lay claim to in a marriage contract. By marriage, the husband and wife became one person in law – and that person was the husband. He acquired absolute control of all his wife's personal property, which he could sell at will. By a judicial interpretation, a husband's debts became by law a prior charge on his wife's jewels and other personal property, although it is fair to add that the husband also became responsible for his wife's debts. A husband always had full rights during his lifetime over his wife's real estate, and by an act of 1540 he was empowered to make long leases for three lives or twenty-one years and to pocket the fines.

As Widow Blackacre put it in Wycherley's *Plain Dealer*, 'matrimony to a woman [is] worse than excommunication in depriving her of the benefit of the law'. Defoe's *Roxana* was even more critical of the legal impotence of a wife: 'the very nature of the marriage contract was ... nothing but giving up liberty, estate, authority and everything to a man, and the woman was indeed a mere woman ever after – that is to say a slave'.

In the sixteenth century a widow's rights over real estate were in practice weakened by the rise of the legal device of the use to feoffees, which could bar her from her dower; moreover, until the end of the seventeenth century, her medieval common-law right to a share of the personal estate was effective only in Wales, the province of York and the city of London. If women entered the agricultural and servicing labour market, as they did in considerable numbers in the sixteenth and seventeenth centuries, they were everywhere paid at a rate which was at most only one half of that of men: the differential may even have widened.

In some ways the status of wives, as well as their legal rights, seems to have been on the decline in the sixteenth century, despite the genealogical accident by which so many women became queens at that period. Some Elizabethans revived the Platonic doubts whether a woman could be considered as a reasoning creature; others questioned whether she had a soul. Despite a century-long trickle of books in praise of women, many lay commentators in the late sixteenth and seventeenth centuries remained thoroughly ambivalent in their attitude towards them. In a sermon before Queen Elizabeth, Bishop Aylmer trod cautiously between the two poles of opinion:

> Women are of two sorts: some of them are wiser, better learned, discreeter, and more constant than a number of men; but another and worse sort of them are fond, foolish, wanton, flibbergibs, tattlers, triflers, wavering, witless, without council, feeble, careless, rash, proud, dainty, talebearers, eavesdroppers, rumour-raisers, evil-tongued, worse-minded, and in everyway doltified with the dregs of the devil's dunghill.

From the baroque richness of the vocabulary in the latter section, there can be little doubt about what the bishop really thought of women, despite his care to mollify his highly sensitive queen. Others were less tactful in expressing their feelings. John Smith of Nibley recorded a local Gloucestershire saying, 'a woman, a spaniel and a walnut tree, the more they are beaten, better they be', but added doubtfully 'sed quaere de hoc'. Others relapsed into total cynicism. In a play by George Wilkins, Ilford advised that 'women are the purgatory of men's purses, the paradise of their bodies, and the hell of their minds: marry none of them'. It is highly significant of popular attitudes towards women in the early seventeenth century that Joseph Swetman's *The Arraignment of Lewd, Idle, Froward and Unconstant Women*, a savage anti-feminist piece of polemic, went

137

through no less than ten editions between its first publication in 1616 and 1634, although it also generated some fierce rebuttals.

The Protestant preachers and moral theologians were as zealous as the laity in advocating the total subordination of wives. In Matthew's Bible of 1537 there was an ominous gloss to 1 Peter 3, noting that a husband, if his wife is 'not obedient and helpful to him, endeavoureth to beat the fear of God into her head, and that thereby she may be compelled to learn her duty and do it'. William Gouge, in his popular manual *Of Domesticall Duties* of 1622 and 1634, argued that 'though an husband in regard of evil qualities may carry the image of the devil, yet in regard to his place and office, he beareth the image of God'. The old arguments from the Bible were dredged up and repeated to support this position. 'We cannot but think that the woman was made before the Fall that the man might rule over her.' There was good reason 'that she who first drew man into sin should now be subject to him, lest by the like womanish weakness she fall again'. Even when advocating married love, Robert Cawdrey never forgot the need for male mastery: 'we would that the man when he loveth should remember his superiority'.

Of greatest impact, in the sense that it must have reached the widest audience, over the longest period of time, was the Homily on Marriage, which was the eighteenth of the many from which all parsons were ordered by the Crown to read in church every Sunday from 1562 onwards. It left the audience in no doubt about the inferior status, rights and character of a wife: 'the woman is a weak creature not endued with like strength and constancy of mind; therefore, they be the sooner disquieted, and they be the more prone to all weak affections and dispositions of mind, more than men be; and lighter they be, and more vain in their fantasies and opinions'. For the sake of domestic peace, however, the husband is advised not to beat his wife, as is his right, but to take account of the psychological fact that a woman is 'the weaker vessell, of a frail heart, inconstant, and with a word soon stirred to wrath'. The ideal woman in the sixteenth and seventeenth centuries was weak, submissive, charitable, virtuous and modest, like the wife of the Massachusetts minister in the 1630s whom he publicly praised for her 'incomparable meekness of spirit, towards myself especially'. Her function was housekeeping, and the breeding and rearing of children. In her behaviour she was silent in church and in the home, and at all times submissive to men. As contemporaries were well aware, modes of

address are significant indicators of social realities. Women habitually signed letters to their husbands 'your faithful and obedient
wife'. In 1622 the Puritan moral theologian William Gouge was
insistent that wives should address their spouses respectfully as
'Husband', and to avoid such demeaning endearments as 'sweet,
sweeting, heart, sweetheart, love, joy, dear, duck, chick or pigsnie',
as well as such egalitarian modes as the first name. Some women
were clearly using familiar modes of address, and some of this male
chauvinist propaganda may have been designed to hold back the
trend. On the other hand, eighteenth- and early nineteenth-century
evidence from all over Europe shows peasant wives addressing
their husbands in deferential terms, never sitting down at the table
at which the men and boys were eating, and always walking a step
or two behind their husbands. These are concrete symbols of patriarchy in the family which were presumably also normal in sixteenth-
and seventeenth-century England, even if contemporary evidence is
at present lacking.

But it would, of course, be absurd to claim that the private reality
fully matched the public rhetoric, and there are plenty of examples
of Elizabethan women who dominated their husbands. Their monopoly of certain work responsibilities, their capacity to give or withhold sexual favours, their control over the children, their ability to
scold, all gave them useful potential levers of power within the
home. All that is here claimed is that the theoretical and legal doctrines of the time were especially insistent upon the subordination
of women to men in general, and to their husbands in particular, and
that many women accepted these ideas. Defoe's Roxana grimly reflected that 'a wife is looked upon as but an upper servant'. The
treatment of wives by their husbands naturally differed widely from
individual to individual, but one gets the impression that the casual
insouciance expressed in the diary of the small Lancashire gentleman Nicholas Blundell on 24 September 1706 was far from uncommon in the seventeenth century: 'My wife felt the pains of labour
coming upon her. Captain Robert Fazakerley and I went a-coursing.'

The subordination of wives to husbands certainly applied to the
upper and upper-middle classes, but the situation is less clear among
artisans, shopkeepers, smallholders and unskilled labourers. In these
classes at any period of pre-industrial society, husband, wife and
children tended to form a single economic unit, like the crew of a
ship, in which the role of the wife was critical. When the husband

was away, she looked after his affairs for him. On a smallholding, she had limited but very clearly defined duties over which she had full control: she managed the dairy and poultry side of the business, and marketed the produce. If there was cottage industry, she was in charge of spinning the yarn, knitting, glove-stitching and lace-making. If her husband was a day labourer, on the other hand, she and her children were likely to do no more than assist him in the back-breaking work in the fields. She might also set up an ale-house in the home, or sell perishable goods from door to door. In the cloth-manufacturing areas, the family was even more a wholly inter-dependent economic unit, since the putting-out system prevailed and spinning was exclusively done by women and children. In the early eighteenth century, Defoe observed that in the wool-manufacturing areas of the West Riding of Yorkshire, cloth was made in every house, 'women and children carding and spinning; all employed from the youngest to the oldest, scarce anything above four years old but its hands were sufficient for its own support'. Later on in the eighteenth century similar conditions prevailed in the first stages of the development of the cotton industry round Manchester. In the towns, the wife helped to manage the shop, or helped the craftsman at his trade. She also added a critical element to the family budget by sewing, dressmaking or lace-making. At the lowest levels, she would take in laundry or act as a charwoman, carter, street-cleaner, prostitute, beggar or thief. At any rate in the eighteenth and early nineteenth centuries, when our evidence is ample, the lower-class wife managed the domestic economy, being responsible for the spending of the pooled family income. In such circumstances, re-gardless of the current legal or moral theories, and regardless of how her husband treated her in terms of status or deference, she was at least an important economic asset.

This does not mean, however, that the economic contribution of the wife to the family budget necessarily gave her higher status and greater power, and that her progressive removal from the labour force as capitalism spread prosperity slowly downward was the cause of her social degradation. This was a theory of Engels, but the historical evidence suggests that it is untrue. The lot of a working wife was probably like that of many women today in underdeveloped countries, and as described by an early nineteenth-century visitor to the Scottish Highlands. 'Here, as in all semi-barbarous countries, the woman seems to be regarded rather as the drudge than the companion of the man ... I wish you but saw with what patience these poor females continue thus dumbly employed, for the greater part of a long summer's day.' As a result of their work load, 'I scarcely saw a Gairlock woman of the humbler class turned of thirty, who was not thin, sallow and prematurely old.' Poverty is an acid that erodes both physical beauty and affective relations.

A test of the sense of independence displayed by women in the late sixteenth century, when many were gainfully employed, is whether or not the crimes they committed were similar in scale and type to those of men. The evidence suggests, on the contrary, that married and unmarried women were as submissive and as dependent as the conduct books suggested that they ought to be. They had a minimal share in crimes of theft, commercial fraud and violence, and when violence took place they were usually aiding their menfolk. They were prominent only in defamation, especially accusations against other women of sexual incontinence. The only two areas where they showed a spirit of independence was in leading food riots, and in adhering to dissident religious opinions, whether Puritan or Catholic, but in both cases they were relying on the higher moralities of the just price and the true faith to spur them to defy the law.

The reasons for the apparent positive decline in the status and rights of wives in the sixteenth and early seventeenth centuries are not entirely clear. One obvious cause was the decline of kinship, which left wives exposed to exploitation by their husbands, since they lost the continuing protection of their own kin. Secondly, the end of Catholicism involved the elimination of the female religious cult of the Virgin Mary, the disappearance of celibate priests, who through the confession box had hitherto been so very supportive of women in their domestic difficulties, and the closing-off of the career option of life in a nunnery. Puritanism was unable to fill the same role for more than a tiny minority of educated female zealots who attached themselves to charismatic preachers, while post-Reformation English society had nothing but contempt for spinsters. A third important factor was the emphasis placed by the state and the law on the subordination of the wife to the head of the household as the main guarantee of law and order in the body politic.

Finally it could be argued that the Protestant sanctification of marriage and the demand for married love itself facilitated the subordination of wives. Women were now expected to love and cherish their husbands after marriage and were taught that it was their sacred duty to do so. This love, in those cases where it in fact became internalized and real, made it easier for wives to accept that position of submission to the will of their husbands upon which the preachers were also insisting. By a paradoxical twist, one of the first results of the doctrine of holy matrimony was a strengthening of the authority of the husband over the wife, and an increased readiness of the latter to submit herself to the dictates of the former. Sir Kenelm Digby complacently remarked in the late 1630s that one should be careful to choose an obedient wife, 'which none can promise to himself ... whose will is not wholly in his power by love'. This is similar to the paradox by which the first result of an increased concern for children was a greater determination to crush their sinful wills by whipping them.

ii. *The Education of Women*

There is one socially very restricted, short-lived and paradoxical exception to the rule that literacy and classical education widened the gap between the sexes. For a brief period, during the middle third of the sixteenth century, there was a vigorous drive for female classical education by Renaissance Humanists like Vives and Erasmus. Perhaps encouraged by Queen Catherine of Aragon, no fewer than seven ambitious treatises on this theme appeared in England between 1523 and 1538. Sir Thomas More was merely repeating the standard arguments of this school when he wrote 'if the female soil be in its nature stubborn, and more productive of weeds than fruit, it ought, in my opinion, to be more diligently cultivated with learning and good instruction'. 'I do not see why learning ... may not equally agree with both sexes.'

As a result of this active propaganda by influential English Humanist educators, there appeared for a short time a handful of aristocratic women who were as expert as men in classical grammar and language: women like Lady Jane Grey, the daughters of Sir Anthony Cooke, and Queen Elizabeth, who were thoroughly familiar with, and read and spoke easily, Latin, Greek, French and Italian. In 1580 the schoolmaster Richard Mulcaster could still boast:

Do we not see in our country some of that sex so excellently well trained and so rarely qualified in regard both to the tongues themselves and to the subject-matter contained in them, that they may be placed along with, or even above, the most vaunted paragons of Greece or Rome?

Though he did not know it, Mulcaster was writing the swan-song of the movement. This period when a learned education was given to aristocratic women did not last much longer than forty years, from about 1520 to 1560. In 1561 there appeared in translation Castiglione's *The Courtier*, which put forward a different ideal of womanhood, one who had a sprinkling of letters, but whose prime qualities were now the social graces — skill in music, painting, drawing, dancing and needlework. This new courtly ideal, and the Protestant, especially Puritan, ideal of the woman as the docile housewife, the diligent upholder of holy matrimony in a subservient role to the husband, spelt the end of the learned lady. In 1694 William Wotton summed up the change. In the sixteenth century, learning 'was so very modish that the fair sex seemed to believe that Greek and Latin added to their charms; and Plato and Aristotle, untranslated, were frequent ornaments of their closets'. But in the seventeenth century 'this humour in both sexes abated by degrees'. To the late seventeenth-century playwrights, would-be learned ladies like the Duchess of Newcastle became figures of fun, to be satirized and ridiculed for their pedantic and unattractive folly. 'Plato in petticoats' was not a popular figure in Restoration drama or Restoration society.

During the seventeenth century, this masculine literary education for noble and gentle women was replaced by the traditional feminine accomplishments and graces needed to catch a husband, such as music, singing, dancing, needlework and embroidery, and no more than the basic elements of reading and writing in English and also French. Perhaps the most striking feature of upper-class English women's education for several centuries was to be their fluency in French. In 1652 Sir Ralph Verney advised his twelve-year-old goddaughter: 'In French you cannot be too cunning, for that language affords many admirable books fit for you, as romances, plays, poetry, stories of illustrious not learned women ... and in brief all manner of good housewifery.' To her father he wrote: 'Let not your girl learn Latin nor shorthand; the difficulty of the first may keep her from that vice, for so I must esteem it in a woman.' His objection to shorthand was that 'the pride of taking sermon notes had made multitudes of women most unfortunate', a reference, presumably, to the current enthusiasm of many women for extremist religious preachers.

Even women agreed with these lowered educational aspirations, and in 1662 Mrs Elizabeth Josceline, before the birth of her first child, told her husband how she wanted the child educated if it were a daughter and if she herself should die in childbirth (both mother and child in fact died within nine days): 'I desire her bringing up may be learning the Bible as my sisters do, good housewifery, writing and good work; other learning a woman need not.' When in 1682 the eight-year-old Molly Verney was sent away to school in Chelsea to learn dancing and other social graces and asked for permission to learn the expensive art of japanning boxes, her father readily agreed, with the comment that 'I admire all accomplishments that will render you considerable and lovely in the sight of God and man.' His programme for her further education was to train her in behaviour in the household of a lady of quality, in preparation for marriage to a country squire of substantial but moderate means. A kindly and affectionate father, as Edmund Verney undoubtedly was towards Molly, could think of no more appropriate goal for a girl to aspire to, nor a better way to achieve it than the acquisition of such elegant but unintellectual accomplishments.

If this was the case among upper-class women in the seventeenth century, it is not difficult to imagine conditions lower down the social scale. The education of the daughters of yeomen was confined to a very little reading and writing, barely enough for religious and functional use, together with sewing and the management of domestic affairs. In this class reading and writing were barely necessary; many were in the condition of the wife of Edward Duffield, a Suffolk yeoman, who 'could not write or read a written hand'. Among the population in general, only one woman in three could even sign her name in a marriage register in 1754, which was not much more than half the proportion of men, and there is every reason to suppose that the proportion was if anything worse in the seventeenth century. Women at all levels of society were an educationally deprived group compared with men.

4. CONCLUSION

During the sixteenth and seventeenth centuries there took place a series of important changes in the structure of the English middle- and upper-class family, in its social and economic functions, and in affective relationships within it and towards the groups outside it. Under pressure from the state and from Protestant moral theology, it shifted from a predominantly open structure to a more restrictedly nuclear one. The functions of this nuclear family were now more and more confined to the nurture and socialization of the infant and young child, and the economic, emotional and sexual satisfaction of the husband and wife. Within this nuclear core with its more limited and more specialized functions, power flowed increasingly to the husband over the wife and to the father over the children. Although it cannot be proved that the power of the husband and father was more authoritarian and patriarchal than it had been in the late middle ages, there are certainly theoretical reasons why this should have been so. He was now less hampered by interference from the kin, either his own or that of his wife, both Church and state were unanimous in reinforcing his authority and pressing new duties on him, and he was now more concerned about the right education of his children, and therefore more likely to interfere with their free-dom from a very early age.

There were a variety of causes for the reinforcement of the authority of the father and husband within the family. There was the pressure of state propaganda for an authoritarian state and there-fore an authoritarian family; Protestant Reformation emphasis on the role of the household rather than the Church as the agency for moral and religious control; Calvinist views about Original Sin and the need for severe measures towards children to defeat the Devil and punish wickedness; the spread of classical education which ex-posed more and more children to flogging in school; legal changes in women's rights over property, and the capacity of the family head to dispose of his estates as he wished; the critical need to be able to control a child's choice of marriage partner, education and career; the urge to break the will of one's child because one's own will had also been broken in childhood.

All these are true and necessary causes but they are not, perhaps, entirely sufficient. There is some deeper underlying force at work in the society, both in Protestant and in Catholic areas. Sixteenth- and early seventeenth-century Europe saw a breakdown of old values and sense of order. The unity of Christendom had been irreparably shattered by the Reformation, and the pieces were never put together again. The result was that from henceforth there were various options in terms of religious ideology, faith and practice, and no one could be completely certain which was right and which was wrong. The first result of this uncertainty was extreme fanaticism. Internal doubts could only be appeased by the most ferocious treatment of those who disagreed. The authoritarian family and the authoritarian nation state were the solutions to an intolerable sense of anxiety, and a deep yearning for order.

Having made this general statement about the growth of patriarchy in the home, one caveat must be entered. In any familial relationship, the degree of affective bonding and the distribution of power over decision-making will, in the last resort, depend on the personal characters of the husband and the wife. All that is here being claimed is that at this particular period in history, law, custom, state propaganda, moral theology and family tradition all conspired to create a set of internalized values and expectations. These values stressed the nuclear family against the kin, maintained coolness and distance in interpersonal relations within the nuclear core, and created expectations of authority and respect by the husband and father, and of submission, obedience and deference by the wife and the children. This being the case, it is reasonable to suppose that in a majority of cases reality conformed, to some degree, to the ideal.

PART FOUR

The Closed Domesticated Nuclear Family 1640–1800

CHAPTER SIX

The Growth of Affective Individualism

'To every individual in nature is given an individual property by nature, not to be invaded or usurped by any: for everyone as he is himself, so he hath a self propriety, else he could not be himself ... For by natural birth all men are equally and alike born to like propriety, liberty and freedom.'

> (R. Overton, *An Arrow against all Tyrants*, London, 1646, in G. E. Aylmer (ed.), *The Levellers in the English Revolution*, London, 1975, pp. 68–9.)

'All men are naturally in ... a state of perfect freedom to order their actions and dispose of their possessions and persons as they think fit, within the bounds of the law of nature, without asking leave or depending upon the will of any other man.'

> (J. Locke, *Two Treatises of Government*, London, 1689, Second Treatise, sect. 4.)

1. INTRODUCTION

The sixteenth-century trend towards increasingly authoritarian relationships within the middle- and upper-class family was progressively overtaken in the late seventeenth and eighteenth centuries by an opposite trend towards greater freedom for children and a rather more equal partnership between spouses. It was a development that was accompanied by a further walling-off of the nuclear family from either interference or support from the kin, and a further withdrawal from the community. Thirdly, there developed much warmer affective relations between husband and wife and between parents and children, which was itself a powerful reason for the declining influence of kin and community. A fourth feature was the identification of children as a special status group, distinct from adults, with its

149

own special institutions, such as schools, and its own information circuits, from which adults now increasingly tried to exclude knowledge about sex and death.

Another development, which emerged only among the landed elite and hardly affected the bourgeois and professional classes, was the increasingly open recognition and acceptance of sensuality. One result was the open inclusion of eroticism in marital relations as well as in the extra-marital liaisons to which it had previously been, in theory and perhaps also in practice, largely confined. Further discussion of this fourth feature, however, will be postponed until the problem of sexuality is taken up in Part Five of this volume.

Apart from eroticism, these trends first became prominent in wealthy merchant and professional households in the city in the last third of the seventeenth century. From there they spread to the upper landed classes, gathering strength rapidly in the early eighteenth century, and reaching a climax towards 1800.

These changes in human relations within the microcosm of the family cannot be explained except in terms of changes in the macrocosm of the total cultural system, a major reorientation of meaning among those sectors of society which experienced these changes. This being so, the search for explanation must carry us to areas far removed from the family itself, since what is involved is a change in how the individual regarded himself in relation to society (the growth of individualism) and how he behaved and felt towards other human beings, particularly his wife and children on the one hand, and parents and kin on the other (the growth of affect). Before beginning a discussion of this very difficult subject, it should be clearly understood that what is being put under the microscope is a secondary, but highly significant, tendency at work within what still remained at all levels a deferential society based, although to a diminishing extent, on the time-honoured principles of hierarchy and obedience. These principles found open expression in the elaborate rituals of doffing of hats in the presence of superiors; the giving of the wall when passing in the street; the meticulous ordering of official processions such as funerals, by which every rank was allotted his appropriate place; the socially graded arrangements for seating in churches. The array of huge family tombs which filled the chancels of so many English parish churches in the sixteenth and seventeenth centuries were, like the elaborate genealogies so lovingly drawn up by the heralds, evidence of a widespread and cultivated ancestor-worship, which supported the authority of the elders in the family over the younger members of it.

These elaborate rituals and symbols had profound psychological significance, their purpose being to buttress the social order and protect it from the chaos threatened by the Reformation and re-distribution of church property and the growing inequalities of wealth and poverty. In the long run, these efforts were successful in containing the threat of social disintegration, and by the early eighteenth century a period of calm began. The 'quality' were once more reunited on basic issues.

It was precisely because of this underlying unity of the elites, and of the largely unquestioning habits of deference by those below, that the state apparatus could remain so relatively weak in eighteenth-century England without a total collapse of social order. It was a close thing, anarchy lay only just below the surface, and the authority of the elite was tempered by the fear and reality of a mob riot. But authority held, for, as Burke pointed out, political liberty was – and is – bought at the price of internalized respect for social discipline. Individual autonomy – contemporaries called it 'freedom' or 'liberty' – therefore, was a new luxury which could now safely be indulged in by the well-to-do, and which modified and mitigated the rigidities of a society whose fundamental cohesion was preserved by habits of obedience to legitimate authority, two of the most im-portant aspects of which were the subordination of children to parents, and of women to men.

Individualism is a very slippery concept to handle. Here what is meant is two rather distinct things: firstly, a growing introspection and interest in the individual personality; and secondly, a demand for personal autonomy and a corresponding respect for the indi-vidual's right to privacy, to self-expression, and to the free exercise of his will within limits set by the need for social cohesion: a recog-nition that it is morally wrong to make exaggerated demands for obedience, or to manipulate or coerce the individual beyond a cer-tain point in order to achieve social or political ends. Because these are now such familiar tenets of Western society, they should not be taken for granted. They are culturally determined values, which most societies in world history have despised or deplored, and which most still do. Normally, individualism is equated with narcissism and ego-centricity, a selfish desire to put one's personal convenience above the needs of the society as a whole, or those of sub-units such as the kin or the family. The emergence in late seventeenth- and eighteenth-century England of a different set of values, which placed the individual above the kin, the family, the society and even, in some eighteenth-century judicial pronouncements, the state, is therefore a very unusual phenomenon, which requires very careful demonstration and explanation.

It should be noted that the development of personal introspection and the growth of toleration for other individuals stem from what are in some ways antithetical psychological impulses. The most powerful influence behind the first was the overpowering sense of sin and the preoccupation with individual salvation that was the hallmark of the Puritan personality in the seventeenth century, and was greatly stimulated by literacy and the habit of private reading and meditation. The interest in the self sprang from the urgent need to discipline the self – the 'sphincter morality' as the Freudians describe it. Puritanism, introspection, literacy and privacy form a single affinity group of characteristics. They do not, however, necessarily lead to a willingness to respect the liberty or privacy of others. On the contrary, both in England and in New England, they led directly to the creation of a suspicious and inquisitorial society, constantly on the watch to spy out the sins of others and to suppress all deviations from the true way.

The spirit of toleration for the autonomy of others derives as much from indifference as from principle. With its stress on the liberation of other individuals and their freedom in the pursuit of personal goals, it is a feature of the opposite personality type, extrovert, easy-going, and willing to tolerate diversity, if only for the sake of peace. What seems to have happened was this. In the late sixteenth and early seventeenth centuries, two different world views, the Puritanically ascetic and the secularly sensual, were competing for the allegiance of the ruling classes. Between 1640 and 1660 the former won, abused its victory by attempting to impose its values by force, and then collapsed. The result was a strong reaction to hedonism, while Puritanism persisted as a viewpoint adhered to by a minority.

There was thus a major oscillation between two predominant personality types in England in the seventeenth century. Both types, in their different ways, made their contribution, the first to the growth of introspection and the second to the growth of respect for the autonomy of others. Puritanism in its death throes left behind it

certain critically important legacies. Despite its authoritarian inclinations, it also emphasized the importance of the individual
conscience and of private prayer to God, and in defeat after 1660 it
had no option but to plead for religious toleration from the majority.
Moreover its stress on the importance of holy matrimony – meaning
marriage bound by mutual affection – helped to undermine its contrary emphasis on the need for strict filial obedience to parents. But
it was the post-1660 cultural supremacy of the anti-Puritan character
type which built on this foundation decisively to change attitudes
towards authority, affection and sex within the middle and upper
ranks of society.

2. AFFECTIVE INDIVIDUALISM IN SOCIETY

In the seventeenth century there is clear iconographic and literary
evidence for a new interest in the self, and for recognition of the
uniqueness of the individual. This is a development common to
Europe, and which apparently has its origins in two different strands
of thought: the secular Renaissance ideal of the individual hero as
expressed in the autobiography of Cellini or the essays of Montaigne; and religious introspection arising from the Calvinist sense
of guilt and anxiety about salvation. In England, both influences
were at work, although the second seems to have been the most important, at any rate before 1660.

Changes in the predominant type of funerary memorials of the
wealthy provide a significant clue to changes in attitudes. In the
sixteenth and early seventeenth centuries tombs were nearly all de-
personalized family monuments. The contracts specified a featureless
stock effigy representing the deceased, to be set within an elaborate
architectural framework chiefly noticeable for the display of brightly
painted coats of arms that emphasized the antiquity and status
connections of the family (Plate 7). It was a display of family pomp
and position, not a memorial to the individuality of the dead. In the
1620s portraiture was introduced from abroad by Nicholas Stone,
and in the late seventeenth century the most common type thereafter became a personalized bust, based on personal sittings or a
death mask, although still surrounded by a formal architectural setting with family coats of arms (Plate 8). Thus the contract for a late
seventeenth-century tomb of the Earl of Dorset specifies that the

images should be likenesses passed as satisfactory by the court painter, Lely. A similar development was the personal portrait in oils or watercolours, first around the court by Hilliard, Van Dyck, Dobson and Lely, and later spreading into the country through visits by itinerant painters from London. It is true, of course, that this change is in part due to a long-delayed spread of Renaissance artistic styles and fashions, but the fact that these styles laid such emphasis on the individual is nonetheless significant. Those who commissioned these monuments and portraits now wished to commemorate for posterity a personalized image, not a faceless item on a genealogical tree.

At the same time, there developed a series of almost wholly new genres of writing, the intimately self-revelatory diary, the auto-biography and the love letter. Partly, of course, these products were the result of a shift from an oral to a written culture among the laity. Literacy is probably a necessary pre-condition for the growth of introspection. But there is more to it than this. In the first place, writing and reading, unlike the telling of tales by the fireside, are inherently lonely occupations. Unless he is reading aloud, which often happened in the seventeenth and eighteenth centuries, the individual is carrying on an interview between himself and the writing on the page, and this inanimate object, this page of paper covered with lines in ink, provided the essential means of communication for the new sensibility. The growth of literacy, moreover, created a literature of self-exploration, from the novel to the love letter. Secondly, there is overwhelming evidence that a desire to investigate the self was greatly stimulated by Calvinist theology and morality. Most of the English diaries and autobiographies written before 1700 were religious in inspiration, their numbers were far larger than those found in Catholic countries, and a disproportionately large proportion of them were the work of Puritans. The Puritan was constantly searching his soul, performing a moral and spiritual stock-taking to discover whether or not he was among the Elect of God. If literacy and Calvinist predestinarian theology were the driving forces, the emergence of these new, intensely personal, literary modes signifies the consequent development of a new, more inner-directed personality.

The first of the new genres of writing was the diary. As David Riesman has put it, 'the diary-keeping that is so significant a symptom of the new type of character may be viewed as a kind of inner time-and-motion study by which the individual records and judges his output day by day. It is evidence of the separation between the behaving and the recording self.'

The second new type of document was the introspective autobiography. 'I write not my gests, but myself and my essence,' explained Montaigne. This particular form first appeared in England in 1576 with the autobiography of Thomas Wythorne, just a year before the first self-portrait, by Nicholas Hilliard. The motives behind these productions were mixed. The vast majority of the late sixteenth- and seventeenth-century autobiographies were inspired by a desire to record a profound religious experience, and therefore were mainly written by Puritan nonconformists, many of them Quakers: over two hundred and twenty of this type (many written by women) have survived for the period before 1725. It was not until the late seventeenth century that the autobiography commonly became both secular and introspective, a record of personal emotions rather than of external events or religious experiences. Lady Halkett is the first English woman whose autobiography is primarily the story of her chequered love-life, and it is at just this time that there is a quantum jump in the number of love letters, like those of Dorothy Osborne to William Temple.

These are all signs of the spirit of secular individualism emerging out of the ashes of religious enthusiasm after 1660, and it would be difficult to exaggerate the significance and novelty of this widespread evidence of a desire for personal self-expression in the late seventeenth and the eighteenth centuries. It demonstrates a wholly new scale and intensity of interest in the self. It is no longer a matter of isolated works written centuries apart by exceptional men of religious genius like St Augustine or Luther; from the seventeenth century onwards there bursts on to paper a torrent of words about intimate thoughts and feelings set down by large numbers of quite ordinary English men and women, most of them now increasingly secular in orientation. There are known to have survived over three hundred and sixty English diaries and over two hundred autobiographies, all written before 1700. Since only twelve of these autobiographies were written before 1660, only one of which was the personal type, it is evident that the genre was a seventeenth-century phenomenon, gathering popularity and becoming less religious in motivation and content in the eighteenth.

Undoubtedly a great stimulus to these developments was provided by the disruptions of the Civil Wars, and their aftermath of exile for the defeated. These events tore many families apart, and the only lifeline that bound them was the letter. Many women found themselves not only suddenly saddled with unusual responsibilities, but also dependent on the art of writing to hold their families together.

These same trends inevitably were reflected in the imaginative literature of the day, and were indeed partly responsible for the evolution of the novel from a surface tale of picaresque adventure, like *Robinson Crusoe,* to a deep probe into personal psychology, like *Wuthering Heights.* This was a process which took a long time to develop and it was only with Richardson in the middle of the eighteenth century that the novel became primarily preoccupied with feelings. Richardson was a pioneer, and had to cast his novels in the form of a series of letters, for lack of a better technical way of conveying his message. But the interest in self-expression was evident long before, for example in Defoe's *Roxana,* and the late eighteenth century sees the full development of the romantic novel, whose central theme was the struggle of love and personal autonomy against family interest and parental control.

This change in the content of novels coincided with a change in quantity. There was an explosion of novels published in the late eighteenth century, stimulated by a reduction in book costs made possible by cheaper paper and larger sales. The latter were made possible because of the new demand provided by the growing army of educated and leisured women, whose needs were met by the invention and spread of the circulating subscription library. The first such library was set up in Bath in 1725, the next was in London in 1739, and by the 1780s they were to be found in all the major market towns of England. These libraries were by then buying some four hundred copies of an average printing of about one thousand. As one heroine of a novel said in 1786: 'I subscribed to a circulating library and read, or rather devoured ... from ten to fourteen novels a week.'

The second aspect of individualism was the rising demand for autonomy, which found practical expression in growing resistance to attempts to put extreme pressure on the individual's body and soul. The rise of the sovereign nation state and the religious divisions of the Reformation in the early sixteenth century had increased both the scale and the intensity of those pressures, so that there eventually developed a head-on clash between two systems of values: the one demanded total conformity in deeds and words and even in secret thoughts to the collective will as expressed by the state and the official Church; the other insisted on the right of the individual to a certain freedom of action and inner belief. In the sixteenth century, the first trend was visible all over Europe, as dissidents and deviants were interrogated, tortured and often killed. Treason laws were extended to the spoken word without action, and heresy laws demanded inner agreement with official dogmas which not only changed from year to year, but were concerned with issues, like the real presence in the sacrament, which could not be decided by reason alone. England and Holland were the two countries where opposition to such excessive demands for conformity of belief first officially developed, although they were certainly opposed to the 'Radical Reformation' of Anabaptists and other sects, which were ferociously crushed out of existence by the authorities everywhere, both Catholic and Protestant.

The first clear sign of the new attitude in official circles occurred in the late sixteenth century when Lord Burghley protested against Archbishop Whitgift's inquisitory procedures to investigate private religious opinions, on the grounds that they were making 'windows into men's souls', which he regarded as an illegitimate intrusion into personal privacy. In the middle of the seventeenth century, the English state was headed for a time by Oliver Cromwell, a man who genuinely believed in the virtue of granting 'liberty to tender consciences'. During the heady revolutionary atmosphere of the late 1640s, radicals were busy denouncing all infringements on the freedom of the individual to think as he pleased about religion. 'Why should we hate and destroy one another?' asked the Leveller Richard Overton, 'Are we not all the creatures of one God, redeemed by one Lord Jesus Christ?' Persecution 'is the utter enemy of all spiritual knowledge, a hinderer of its increase and growth'.

These and other libertarian ideas of the Levellers of the late 1640s derived partly from religious sectarianism and its stress on the individual conscience, now extended to a contract theory according to which submission to authority is based exclusively on prior voluntary agreement; partly to secular ideas about natural law and the proprietary right every individual had in himself which could not justly be violated by anyone else; partly from ideas about the common law, based on a misunderstanding of the meaning of

Magna Carta; and partly from an interpretation of English history based on the false theory of 'the Norman yoke', according to which there had been a golden age of primitive popular democracy in the Anglo-Saxon period, before kings, lords and all the apparatus of tyranny were fastened on England by the Norman Conquest of 1066.

The Levellers were crushed, but some trace of their belief in religious toleration lived on as a minority opinion, as did Milton's bold plea for the abolition of political and religious censorship: 'Let truth and falsehood grapple. Whoever knew truth put to the worse in a free and open encounter?' Moreover, their ideas about an individual's natural property right in himself, and the consequent contractual basis for the state, were eventually incorporated into conventional political thinking, and became a part of standard Whig orthodoxy in the eighteenth century.

More important in this respect, however, was almost certainly the deep-rooted 'country' ideology of fidelity to an ancient 'balanced constitution' that protected the personal and property rights of men of substance from intrusion by the state. First coherently formulated in the parliamentary battle over the Petition of Right in 1628, in the crucible of Civil War and in the political struggles from 1600 to 1720, this ideology took powerful hold of the country squires, and was the inspiration for their political behaviour throughout the eighteenth century. In its fully developed form, it ran something like this: 'The Country consists of men of property: all others are servants. The business of Parliament is to preserve the independence of property, on which is founded all human liberty and human excellence. The business of government is to govern, and that is a legitimate authority; but to govern is to wield power, and power has a natural tendency to encroach. It is more important to supervise government than to support it, because the preservation of independence is the ultimate political good.'

Although passed through Parliament and accepted by the social elite largely for pragmatic reasons of political necessity rather than idealistic conviction, the fact remains that by 1689 a limited religious toleration was the law of the land, the sovereign powers of the executive were strictly limited, and a few years later political censorship of newspapers and pamphlets was allowed to lapse. Finally, between 1688 and 1714 large numbers of Tory preachers and politicians were obliged to eat their words and to renounce very quickly two generations of fervent subscription to the doctrines of the

Divine Right of Kings and of Non-Resistance to the will of an anointed King. The fact that the change took place so swiftly, and with such relatively little moral soul-searching, suggests that the rhetoric was already something of a hollow façade concealing a void. By 1741, a Tory, David Hume, could say that 'to talk of a King as God's Viceregent on earth, would but excite laughter in everyone.' What had been an accepted political truism in 1540 and 1640 had become a mere joke in 1740. The new scale of values placed personal morality above religious dogma, as expressed in Pope's famous couplet of 1733:

> For modes of faith let graceless zealots fight
> He can't be wrong whose life is in the right.

The very title of Joseph Trapp's anti-Methodist treatise in 1739 is itself sufficient indication of the change of mood away from the fanaticism of the early and mid-seventeenth century: *The Nature, Folly, Sin and Danger of being Righteous Overmuch* – a message visually reinforced by Hogarth in about 1760 with a popular print entitled *Enthusiasm Delineated*.

At the root of all the most significant changes of the late seventeenth and eighteenth centuries lies a progressive reorientation of culture towards the pursuit of pleasure in this world, rather than postponement of gratification until the next. One aspect was a growing confidence in man's capacity to master the environment and to turn it to his use and benefit. This reorientation of human goals was made possible by the shift away from an attitude of passive resignation before disease, exploitation, poverty and misery, as being the will of God, relieved only by the promise of reward after death. Man was now freed to seek his own personal pleasure here and now, no longer hedged in by the narrow boundaries laid down by moral theology or traditional custom. This new attitude could lead to anything, from the experimental breeding of specialized dogs and horses and cattle, to the use of sex for pleasure rather than procreation by taking contraceptive measures, and to challenging the wishes of one's parents over the choice of a spouse.

The evidence of rational, this-worldly secularization is too well known to need recapitulation here. What is significant in religion is not so much the growth of Deism and atheism as the growth of an attitude of indifference towards the authority of the clergy, the scriptures and moral theology. One suggestive piece of evidence of this change is the slump between 1650 and 1740 of the number of editions of the Bible published in England, despite the continued spread of literacy. This is not to say that the Bible – and *The Pilgrim's Progress* – were not still the staple diet of all literate Englishmen, but they had now to compete with novels and with a flood of textbooks on all aspects of nature and the physical world.

It was in the late seventeenth century that English physical scientists and astronomers destroyed traditional ideas about the hierarchically organized universe. Although many scientists, like Leibniz, strongly denied that their finds were subversive of the hierarchical principle, in fact their work tended to cast doubt upon the theory of the Great Chain of Being, which bound every man, woman and child in a web of dependency and subordination to the will of others and ultimately of the universe. Newton may have been 'the last of the Magi', a superstitious crank, but he was also undoubtedly (if unintentionally), a great liberator of the human mind. In his clockwork universe, Man was now an isolated atomized individual, set free to act as he chose. More important, however, in its influence on society at large, was probably the diffusion through the Royal Society of the Baconian hope that science would supply the technology which would enable man to master nature. Once there was hope of escape from unpredictable catastrophe, it became possible and reasonable to assert one's right to determine and plan one's own future. The first medical breakthrough that gave families some confidence that this might be true was the great success of smallpox inoculation in saving many children's lives, sight and beauty. This suggested that passive acceptance of one's fate was no longer the only, or even the best, response to the problems of life on earth. But there is no direct one-to-one relationship between needs and cognitive systems, so that this argument should not be pressed too hard. It should also be remembered that Protestantism was a very practically oriented religion, so that, for example, the leading Puritan minister in early eighteenth-century Boston, Cotton Mather, was also the first to introduce the smallpox inoculation. The roots of eighteenth-century self-help lie in religion as well as science.

This sense of control over the environment, and particularly over animal breeding, inevitably led men to choose their wives as one would choose a brood mare, with a great care for their personal genetic inheritance, and to train their children with the same patience and attention as they had long devoted to their horses, dogs or hawks. Often men of infinite leisure, they had plenty of time on their hands which in the eighteenth century could be spent in educating their children in the home. The Lockean model of the child as a plain sheet of paper exactly conformed to current scientific views of the effects of careful nurture in the improvement of domesticated animals.

Other influences were at work to encourage the growth of possessive individualism in economic affairs. Commercial, industrial and agricultural expansion, with individual entrepreneurs using new technologies to increase production, were all powerful motors for cultural change. Evidence of a growing acceptance of the idea of possessive individualism is to be found in the emphasis placed both by the eighteenth-century common law and by political theorists like John Locke on the sanctity of private property; in the new, more favourable attitude adopted towards enclosures of common lands and open fields; and in the abandonment of many of those safeguards against untrammelled and amoral free enterprise which had been erected, by both Anglicans and Puritans, to enforce traditional ideas about the just price, the wickedness of usury, etc.

One of the most important intellectual innovations of the late seventeenth and eighteenth centuries was to place the selfish pursuit of pleasure in this world at the centre of human psychological motivation. When in the Declaration of Independence of 1776 Thomas Jefferson substituted 'Life, Liberty and the Pursuit of Happiness' for the previous trio of 'Life, Liberty and Property' as the three inalienable rights of man which it was the function of the state to preserve and encourage, he was thinking of happiness as defined by Locke in 1690 as the basis of liberty, and in contradiction to the theologians like Pascal and Butler for whom this world was a vale of tears and misery, and for whom happiness could only be looked for in the next. Eighteenth-century English and American theologians were modifying their former stress on austerity, and the Stoic and Epicurean classics were enjoying a new vogue. The idea was spreading that selfish individual pursuit of happiness, which meant moral happiness but could be interpreted to include all forms of pleasure, was itself a contribution to public welfare and virtue. The argument was exactly similar to that of Adam Smith for economics, who proclaimed that the individual lust for gain, if left to itself, produced a self-regulating market economy that would maximize collective economic benefit. 'The greatest good of the greatest number' was defined as an objective of the political order as early as 1725, long before it was adopted by Bentham and the Utilitarians.

Another broad philosophical movement, which gathered strength throughout the mid- and late eighteenth century, was a growing antipathy to cruelty. The origins of this sentiment may be traced back to some obscure zone of English Puritan thought, since its first clear expression is to be found in *The Liberties of the Massachusetts Colony*, adopted by the General Court in 1641. This document placed strict limits on the use of judicial torture to extract information, and forbade husbands to beat their wives or maltreat their servants or apprentices. It even, for the first time in history, legislated to protect domestic animals: 'No man shall exercise any tyranny or cruelty towards any brute creatures which are usually to be kept for man's use.' Since 1641 was the last year in which the English state formally ordered the use of torture on a political prisoner, the same motives must have been working in England to place restraint on the treatment of prisoners by the Parliamentary leaders and Oliver Cromwell, despite the hatreds generated by a bitter civil war.

Late seventeenth-century evidence for this trend of Puritan thought is hard to find, and the spread of revulsion against cruelty in the eighteenth century seems to have been concurrent with, and related to, the spread of Enlightenment ideas throughout Europe. Even then, it was at all times a state of mind confined to a relatively small part of the population. But it was a highly articulate and ultimately very influential part which slowly learned to employ all the devices of mass persuasion available in what was increasingly an educationally literate and politically open society. Organized in societies formed for the purpose of promoting this or that change, the reformers used the spreading bulk of newspapers, as well as pamphlets, sermons, novels, cartoons and prints, to influence a wider public and then mobilized that public through the machinery of the mass petition to bring pressure on Parliament. They were responsible in the end for such things as the abolition of the slave trade, the suppression of most cruel sports, prison reform, and reform in the treatment of the mentally sick. It is too facile to point out that the most successful of these endeavours affected others than the reformers themselves, and that it was therefore only too easy for the English elite to incorporate the concept of benevolence into their set of cultural imperatives. The movement was a genuinely moral one involving the upsurge of new attitudes and emotions, which acquired an enormous stimulus thanks to the development in the mid-eighteenth century of a new ideal type, namely the Man of Sentiment, or the Man of Feeling, the prototype of the late eighteenth-century Romantic. Conformity to this new ideal positively reinforced the legitimacy of the ruling class.

The connection between maltreatment of animals and maltreatment (and murder) of human beings was the theme of Hogarth's popular set of openly propagandist prints, *The Four Stages of Cruelty*, published in 1751. Years later, Hogarth remarked that he thought 'the publication of them has checked the diabolical spirit of barbarity to the brute creation, which, I am sorry to say, was once so prevalent in this country'. Ten years later there was published a most successful book for young teenagers, *The Newtonian System of Philosophy adapted to the Capacities of young Gentlemen and Ladies ... by Tom Telescope*. This work inculcated into the young the same distaste for cruelty to animals, and extended the moral to include slaves and others. 'Kindness to animals, yes, but greater kindness to human beings is the burden of Tom's final lecture.'

This moralizing was often wrapped up in a package which to modern tastes seems nauseously sentimental, but the message was new and clear. One has to steel oneself to read such boring, moralistic and sentimental contemporary best-sellers as Richardson's *Pamela*, or the archetype of the new trend, Henry Mackenzie's *The Man of Feeling* of 1770, in which there is an outburst of weeping (by either sex) on average every ten-and-a-half pages. But behind the flow of tears lies a new attitude towards man's inhumanity to man. For about half a century, from 1770 to 1820, it was fashionable to express emotional anguish concerning cruelty, a distress which finally opened the way to remedial legislation and institutional reform.

In its effect on family life, the connection between hostility to cruelty to animals and to cruelty to children is clear enough, while both slaves and women were ultimately beneficiaries, along with felons and madmen, of the drive for legal protection for the helpless. At the same time, the Romantic movement encouraged a more openly emotional involvement in family relationships. Thus some of the improvements in the treatment of wives and children of the middle and upper classes, particularly in the latter half of the eighteenth century, were spin-offs from this growing desire to ameliorate the human lot and to reduce the amount of sheer physical cruelty in the world. Why this movement should have emerged with such power at this particular moment in history remains a mystery, but its success undoubtedly owes much to the evangelistic enthusiasm of its leading protagonists and their skilful use of the new media of mass communications that had only recently become available.

3. AFFECTIVE INDIVIDUALISM IN THE FAMILY

i. *Attacks on Patriarchy*

The most direct and explicit link between political theory and family life occurs in John Locke's *Two Treatises of Government*, published in 1689, but written a decade earlier. The first Treatise attacked Robert Filmer's *Patriarcha*, which had based the authority of the king in the state on the analogy of the authority of the father in the family, and in the process it redefined the latter as well as the former. Marriage was stated to be a mere contractual relationship giving 'common interest and property', but not, for example, the power of life and death over a wife. It was argued that the power of the father over his children is merely a utilitarian by-product of his duty to nourish them until they can look after themselves. It is thus only a limited and temporary authority, which automatically ends when the child grows up. In any case, parental authority is irrelevant to the authority of a king, to which adults voluntarily submit on condition that he acts for their own good. The practical need to remodel the political theory of state power in the late seventeenth century thus brought with it a severe modification of theories about patriarchal power within the family and the rights of the individual.

The issue had already been debated on the stage in 1697, when in Vanbrugh's play *The Provoked Wife* Lady Brute applies Locke's breakable contract theory of the state to her own situation: 'The argument's good between the King and the people, why not between the husband and wife?' In 1701 Mary Chudleigh also criticized men because

> Passive Obedience you've transferred to us
> . . . .
> That antiquated doctrine you disown,
> 'Tis now your scorn, and fit for us alone.

In 1706 Mary Astell asked 'If absolute sovereignty be not necessary in a state, how comes it to be so in a family? Or if in a family, why not in a state? ... Is it not then partial in men to the last degree to contend for and practise that arbitrary dominion in their families which they abhor and exclaim against in the state? ... If all men are born free, how is it that all women are born slaves?'

The incompatibility of domestic patriarchy with the political theory of contractual obligation became so glaring that the moral theologians were forced to modify their position. In 1705 Bishop Fleetwood set out the new doctrine, which in effect undermined the traditional absolute authority of the father and husband. 'There is no relation in the world, either natural or civil and agreed upon, but there is a reciprocal duty obliging each party ... I only mention this to make it very evident that the obligation of children to love, honour, respect and obey their parents is founded originally upon the parents' love and care of them.' Marriage was now similarly a contract, with mutual rights and obligations, whose nature could be debated endlessly. It was still the duty of wives to be 'submissive, subject and obedient to their husbands', but it was also the duty of husbands to 'love their wives', a duty which carried obligations of affection, fidelity and care.

Another philosophical trend, towards the pursuit of individual happiness as an ideal, also had profound repercussions on ideas about power relationships within the family. Under this new scale of values, marriage ceased to be mainly an artificial but necessary constraint placed upon man's otherwise unbridled lust, and became instead a prime source of personal pleasure, both emotional and sexual. Those who wished to reduce the amount of adultery were concerned to make marriage a companionate bond freely entered into, so that sexual passion could be more comfortably confined to the marriage bed. This new pragmatism planned to make the individual's selfish desire for happiness contribute to the common good. As such, it was a potent force eroding the legitimacy of patriarchal control of marriage arrangements among the propertied classes. It is symptomatic of how this new attitude had penetrated the thinking of the landed classes that when the clause in Lord Hardwicke's Marriage Bill, making parental consent obligatory for all under twenty-one, was being debated in Parliament in 1753, there was opposition to it on ethical as well as self-interested grounds. It was said that the clause involved 'controlling all the emotions of love and genuine affection in youth by the frigid maxims of avarice and ambition imbibed by age'. The result would be to enforce 'a splendid and wretched state of legal prostitution in which the happiness of the party was sacrificed to the pride of family'. Behind the rhetoric there clearly lies a passion for individual welfare as opposed to family interest, which would never have found wide acceptance at an earlier period. The contrast with Lord Halifax's cynical and pessimistic *Advice to a Daughter* of 1688 could hardly be greater. The opinions of Romeo and Juliet were now emerging from the mouths of their parents.

Another way this criticism of patriarchy made itself felt was in the establishment of new property arrangements among wealthy landowners. It will be remembered that between 1500 and 1660, the current owner was relatively free to dispose of his estates as he wished, which gave him a formidable weapon to help impose his will upon his children. The threat of partial or even complete disinheritance as a penalty for disobedience was a very real one. During the early seventeenth century, progressive attempts were made by current owners to tighten up the legal arrangements again so as to preserve the family patrimony, and to reduce the freedom of their successors to alienate it. These efforts culminated in the development in the middle of the century of a legal device called the 'strict settlement'. Under its provisions, the powers of the current owner were once again reduced to those of a life trustee, since he had willed away his rights to his unborn children in a settlement drawn up before his marriage.

This resulted in a third set of family property arrangements, by which the owner was again no more than a life tenant, but careful provisions were now made for the settlement of annuities or marriage portions on all children before they were born. The owner could thus neither alienate the property nor deprive any of his children of their arranged inheritances. He could reward favourites by giving them more, but he could not punish those who displeased him by giving them less. The rights of each member of the family were thus clearly defined and carefully preserved against encroachment by any other member. The difference that the strict settlement made was not in changing the distribution of property among the children so much as in reducing the arbitrary control of the father over that distribution and therefore his power to enforce his own will upon them over such critical issues as marriage. That this was the issue at stake was clearly seen at the time, and in 1715 Defoe described 'the mischievous consequence of leaving estates to children entirely independent of their parents' as 'a fatal obstruction to parental authority'. This was an exaggeration, but not an unreasonable distortion of the new reality of a decline in patriarchy within the family. More enlightened parents, however, came to regard it as morally wrong to manipulate their children by the exercise of economic blackmail. Thus in 1775 Mrs Hester Thrale, who was by temperament a dictatorial and authoritarian parent, was given power by her husband to settle her own inherited estate on her children in any manner she wished. Her lawyer pointed out to her that 'I had a right to leave it to whichever of my children I pleased, or to keep such a right in reserve for the greater encouragement of them to duty and attention. But I scorned to create such paltry dependencies and resolved to entail it according to birth alone, that there might be no temptation in me to practise, or in them to suspect, so mean partiality.'

Another feature of late seventeenth- and eighteenth-century marriage settlements was that far greater care was taken to protect the property rights of the wife. Not only was an allowance of pocket-money – 'pin money' – specified in the marriage contract, but increasingly she was managing to keep more of her own property under her personal control. Partly, this was due to a series of judicial decisions in the law courts, which went a long way towards protecting married women's property. Partly, also, it was because an increasing number of women, especially widows, were taking the precaution of vesting their property in separate trustees before marriage, so that their husbands could not touch it. Men who found their powers hampered in this way often took it very badly. When Sir John Guise made his second marriage in 1710, it was under the novel system of the separation of estates and goods. He found it most unsatisfactory, causing him eight years of hell, and he advised his posterity, 'Let all men and women, I say, avoid these things.'

At first sight this reaffirmation of the principle of primogeniture to preserve in perpetuity the family estates appears to run contrary to the spirit of individualism, which might seem to argue for partible inheritance. In fact, however, the careful provisions for younger sons, daughters and widows secured the rights of all parties, and thus undermined the principle of patriarchal power. By this means, primogeniture was successfully harmonized with individualism, although admittedly it preserved a highly inegalitarian distribution of family resources.

Less tangible indications of the same underlying trend of thought can be seen in attitudes towards family prayers, and towards personal and bodily privacy.

ii. *Decline of Family Prayers*

The general decline in religious enthusiasm in the late seventeenth and eighteenth centuries carried away with it the role of the husband and father as the religious head of the household, symbolized by the regular assembly of all members, often twice a day, to hear him lead the family in prayer and obtain his blessing. The corrosive influence of the individual religious conscience bred of sectarian radical ideas in destroying this traditional hierarchical custom is well brought out in the autobiography of the later Ranter, Laurence Clarkson. His religious career began in his teens in the 1630s by defiance of the views of his cautiously conformist Arminian father. He found himself unable to accept the Book of Common Prayer and, therefore, was driven to reject his father.

> The next thing I scrupled was asking my parents' blessing; that oftentimes in the winter mornings, after I have been out of my bed, I have stood freezing above, and durst not come down till my father was gone abroad. And the reason, I was satisfied the blessing or prayers of a wicked man God would not hear, and so should offend God to ask him blessing. For either of these two ways I must down on my knees and say 'Father, pray to God to bless me', or 'Give me your blessing, for God's sake', either of which I durst not use with my lips.

This appeal to the individual conscience generated by religious radicalism was one factor in the undermining of family prayers, but far more important was the general decline of religious enthusiasm and religious practice in the reaction against the rule of the Puritans after the Restoration. In the 1660s, Samuel Pepys, who seems to have been fairly average in his respect for religious observance, only held a family service once a week, on Sunday evenings, when the maid read a passage from the Bible and Pepys led the family prayers. In 1692 John Dunton in the *Athenian Mercury* urged his numerous bourgeois readers to keep up the old practice of family prayers in the home, one reason being that it 'conciliates respect and reverence to the head of it' – a frank confession of its function in reinforcing patriarchy. An anonymous pamphleteer of about 1700 and Defoe in 1715 reiterated the complaint that family worship and religious instruction were dying. Three-quarters of a century later it was a rarity: in 1778 James Boswell lamented 'that there is no appearance of family religion today, not even reading of chapters. How different from what was the usage in my grandfather's day, or my mother's time.'

It is no coincidence that this formal ritual of regular, daily, collective family prayers developed in the sixteenth century, along with patriarchalism; declined in the eighteenth century as a more egalitarian, individualistic and companionate family type developed; revived again in the nineteenth century along with the Victorian patriarchal family; and died out once again in the twentieth century with the revival of the more egalitarian and permissive family type. The rise and fall of family prayers coincided not only with the rise and fall of religious enthusiasm, but also with the rise and fall of patriarchy in the family.

iii. *Personal and Bodily Privacy*

The most striking change in the life-style of the upper classes in the seventeenth and eighteenth centuries was the increasing stress laid upon personal privacy. The great houses of the fifteenth and sixteenth centuries had been constructed of interlocking suites of rooms without corridors, so that the only way of moving about was by passing through other people's chambers. In the late seventeenth and the eighteenth centuries, however, house plans allocated space to corridors, which now allowed access without intruding upon privacy. Inventories of goods show a decline in the practice of putting truckle beds here, there and everywhere. Most bedrooms were transferred upstairs, leaving the ground floor for living-quarters. Although public rooms remained large, there was a proliferation of smaller rooms where daily life was increasingly led.

The motive was partly to obtain privacy for individual members of the family, but more especially to provide the family itself with some escape from the prying eyes and ears of the ubiquitous domestic servants, who were a necessary evil in every middle- and upper-class household. Many years later Dr Johnson warned acidly:

They first invade your table then your breast,
Explore your secrets with insidious art,
Watch the weak hour and ransack all the hearts,
Then soon your ill-paid confidence repay,
Commence your lords, and govern or betray.

That Dr Johnson was speaking no more than the truth was amply proven at the trials for noble adultery of the eighteenth century. The key witnesses in these trials were always servants, whose prying curiosity clearly made sexual privacy almost impossible for anyone of standing who wished to conduct a discreet affair in his or her own home. Always, at all times of day or night, servants were spying through cracks in the wainscoting, peering through keyholes, listening at doors to hear the rhythmic creaking of beds, and carefully inspecting the bed-linen for tell-tale stains. The architectural innovations of the eighteenth century were a help, but they offered inadequate protection from such watchful and prurient curiosity. These trends to architectural privacy mainly affected the wealthy, but in the seventeenth and eighteenth centuries the housing of all classes down to that of yeoman and tradesman became more varied, more subdivided and more specialized in function, and thus afforded greater privacy.

One piece of evidence that farmers, shopkeepers and artisans now wanted more privacy in the home was that apprentices and unmarried wage labourers were increasingly removed from the households of their masters. As a result, paternal control of employers over their adolescent labour force declined, and the non-monetary component of rewards – free food and free lodging – were replaced by wages in money. This in turn signified the cultural erosion of paternalism in the relations of employers and employees, and the increasing isolation of the domestic nuclear household. So far as can be seen, this was not a development fought for by servants seeking personal freedom in the teeth of paternalist opposition from masters, but was one that for different reasons suited the new ideas about domestic life of both parties. The change brought greater liberty for the servants and greater privacy for the masters.

As for the poor, who constituted the majority of the population, they continued well into the nineteenth century to live in one- or two-roomed houses. Under these conditions, privacy was neither a practical possibility nor, one imagines, even a theoretical aspiration. As George Crabbe delicately, but firmly put it in 1897:

See! Crowded beds in those contiguous rooms,
Beds but ill parted by a paltry screen
Of paper'd lath or curtain dropp'd between.
Daughters and sons to yon compartments creep
And parents here beside their children sleep.
Ye who have power, these thoughtless people part,
Nor let the ear be first to taint the heart.

One aspect of this trend to individualism and privacy was an out-growth of the Renaissance Humanist stress on 'civility', defined as a set of external behaviour traits which distinguished the civilized from the uncivilized. Spreading outwards and downwards from the princely courts of Europe, this aspect of Renaissance thought was particularly stressed by Erasmus. One of the features of this new 'civility' was the physical withdrawal of the individual body and its waste products from contact with others. It is no coincidence that the fork, the handkerchief and the nightdress arrived more or less together and spread slowly together in the late seventeenth and early eighteenth centuries. A plentiful supply of plates, knives, forks, and spoons were now provided by the host, to be changed at each course. They were meant for personal use only, and were no longer to be dipped in the communal dish after being put in the mouth. There was no longer any chance of a mingling of the salivas of different persons around a dinner-table. Another aspect of the same trend was the rise of personal cleanliness. Spitting was frowned upon. Shaving the head and using wigs, which became common among the elite in the late seventeenth century, though no doubt mainly adopted to stay in fashion, was one way to keep down lice. Finally, the habit of washing the body, and the introduction of wash-basins and portable bathtubs into the bedroom began to spread among wealthy households in the late eighteenth century.

The motive behind all these refinements of manners is clear enough. It was a desire to separate one's body and its juices and odours from contact with other people, to achieve privacy in many aspects of one's personal activities, and generally to avoid giving offence to the 'delicacy' of others. The essence of this movement was to create a culture in which the elite, the gentleman and the lady, were clearly distinguished by a whole set of immediately recognizable external behaviour traits. Even their language now began to divide on status lines. In the sixteenth century the prime characteristics of language were local dialect rather than national status patterns, but by the eighteenth century there was a fashionable language taught at school and used in the upper-class home, which overrode the provincial dialects of the uneducated. A new word was invented for this elite: 'the quality', a word whose significance is clear enough.

4. CONCLUSION: THE CAUSES OF CHANGE

In the sixteenth century and earlier, the standard world view was that all individuals in society are bound together in the Great Chain of Being, and all are interchangeable with each other. One wife or one child could substitute for another, like soldiers in an army. The purpose in life was to assure the continuity of the family, the clan, the village or the state, not to maximize the well-being of the individual. Personal preference, ambition and greed should always be subordinated to the common good. The second view, which developed in the sixteenth and seventeenth centuries, was that each individual thinks of himself as unique, and strives to impose his own will on others for his selfish ends. The result is a Hobbesian state of nature, the war of all against all, which can only be brought under control by the imposition of stern patriarchal power in both the family and the state. The third view, which developed in the late seventeenth and early eighteenth centuries, was that all human beings are unique. It is right and proper for each to pursue his own happiness, provided that he also respects the right of others to pursue theirs. With this important proviso, egotism becomes synonymous with the public good.

The causes of the evolution of this third view have been spelt out at length. They involve a complex of semi-independent developments spread out over more than a century, each evolving at its own tempo. The result was not, however, a mere intersection of curving lines, but the shift of a whole system of values, which dominated the thinking of substantial numbers of the English elite.

It is not difficult to list economic changes that were helping to create greater personal and familial autonomy, and a relaxation of community discipline. Progressive enclosure of the common fields was destroying co-operative village farming; guild and corporation controls of production and distribution in the towns were weakening; the growth of a market economy was encouraging new economic strata and new economic organizations, particularly the family trading or artisanal shop, and the free wage labourer; population pressures and the gigantic growth of London were generating geographical mobility and giving an increasing proportion of the society some experience of the quality of life in a big city, where earned income mattered more than ascribed status, production more than consumption, and where the principal ties were with one's workmates in the shop; new attitudes to property were developing, by which men now had economic rights divorced from social obligations; human relationships were increasingly seen in economic terms, governed by the rules of the free market. All these trends helped to stimulate the growth of 'possessive individualism' as appiled to economic behaviour. Novel ideas about the elasticity of demand, due to man's infinite desire for more and new goods, were based on the identical psychological principle. Man was egotistical, vain, envious, greedy, luxurious and ambitious. His main desire was to differentiate himself from his neighbours in some way or another. As Nicholas Barbon put it in 1690, 'The wants of the mind are infinite. Man naturally aspires, and as his mind is elevated, his senses grow more refined and more capable of delight. His desires are enlarged, and his wants increase with his wishes, which is for everything which is rare, can gratify his senses, adorn his body, and promote ease, pleasure, and pomp of life.'

How far this theory of pleasure-seeking economic individualism in turn stimulated individualism in other spheres of life cannot, of course, be proved one way or the other. But it seems plausible to suppose that there was some carry-over. Dr Johnson was undoubtedly correct when he pointed out to Boswell the corrosive influence of a monetary market economy on feudal dependencies and kinship networks. The cultural lag between Scotland and England is sufficient proof of the critical importance of this basic economic factor. Boswell

talked of the little attachment which subsisted between near relations in London. Sir, said Johnson, in a country so commercial as ours, where every man can do for himself, there is not much occasion for that attachment. No man is thought the worse of here whose brother was hanged. In uncommercial countries many of the branches of a family must depend on the stock; so, in order to make the head of the family take care of them, they are represented as connected with his reputation, that, self-love being interested, he may exert himself to promote their interest. You have first large circles, or clans; as commerce increases, the connection is confined to families. By degrees, that too goes off, as having become unnecessary and there being few opportunities of intercourse.

One critical development was the emergence to a position of economic, and to a limited extent political and social, eminence of a wealthy entrepreneurial bourgeoisie. There are many reasons why persons from this background are likely to be more receptive than others to the principle of affective individualism. First, their whole way of life is based on a strict code of personal behaviour, emphasizing thrift, hard work and moral self-righteousness. The association of so many of this class with nonconformity in the late seventeenth century and with Evangelicalism in the late eighteenth and early nineteenth centuries is no coincidence, since there is a psychological congruity between these religious beliefs and the day-to-day achievement-oriented behaviour of an economically upwardly mobile social group. In their striving to achieve respectability, they are particularly likely to be affected by popular didactic works of religious or secular morality, especially in the area of home life. Cast adrift by their economic and professional success from the cultural moorings of the class from which they have emerged, they adopt whatever doctrine seems most appropriate to their new condition of life. Because of their high level of literacy and their sense of moral purpose, they are avid readers of current didactic literature. Upwardly mobile themselves, they care for their children and are anxious to give them the benefits of the elite education which they themselves may have lacked. Often deeply religious, in the seventeenth century they were strongly affected by the current stress on holy matrimony and marital affection. Their business experience makes them value autonomy and self-reliance as the way to succeed in this world. They are therefore the first to shed the ties to their own kin (although they use marriage ties to cement business connections), to stress merit and the sanctity of contracts, to develop close affective relations within the home, and to lavish care and attention upon their children.

The second social fact of central importance is the predominance – politically, socially and culturally – of the squirarchy in England, resulting from its consolidation of control over local government, and its near monopoly of high prestige and status. It was in the interests of this landed elite, in loose alliance with the commercial and professional upper bourgeoisie, that there were invented the new ideas about a limited contract state, religious toleration, and a Bill of Rights. Stimulated and sustained by the 'country' ideology, it was the concept and reality of individual liberties and individual property rights among this group which was so carefully nurtured and protected in the eighteenth century by the common law and by cultural convention. The political events of the seventeenth century were crucial in this respect.

Thanks to the extraordinary homogeneity of English elite society, and the ease of cultural and social connections between the landed classes and the wealthy bourgeoisie from the late seventeenth century, the latter's ideas about domestic behaviour soon spread to the squirarchy, with Locke's *Some Thoughts upon Education* and Addison's *Spectator* as the key instruments of their propagation. Together, the upper bourgeoisie and the squirarchy thus formed the elite which not only dominated political, social and economic life in the eighteenth century, but which served as the carrier of these new cultural values in personal and family life. There had been bourgeois cultures before and elsewhere, but nowhere else had they spread their values through the landed elite as well.

These purely economic and social changes provide a necessary, but certainly not a sufficient, cause for the rise of individualism, and on another occasion in 1778 Dr Johnson admitted that something else was involved. He recognized the obvious fact of the general decline of social deference.

Subordination is sadly broken down in this age. No man now has the same authority which his father had – except a gaoler. No man has it over his servants; it is diminished in our colleges, nay in our grammar schools ... There are many causes the chief of which is, I think, the great increase of money ... Gold and silver destroy feudal subordination. But besides there is a general relaxation of reverence. No son now depends upon his father as in former times. Paternity used to be considered as of itself a great thing which had a right to many claims. That is, in general, reduced to very small bonds.

Dr Johnson made no attempt to explain this change, nor to relate it to the complex but convergent set of ideas, some of them inherited from the egalitarian and individualistic movements thrown up by the English Revolution, which were current from the late seventeenth century.

The most important underlying trend which allowed vent to this desire for autonomy in the late seventeenth century was the recovery of psychological balance, the dying away of the siege mentality of the late sixteenth and early seventeenth centuries, which saw everywhere a conspiracy of evil, planning the satanic capture of the world. In this more relaxed atmosphere, the pressure for unquestioning obedience and conformity within the family, as within the society, naturally declined.

In the late seventeenth century, this psychological relaxation and the failure of the great Puritan experiment at moral regeneration from 1640 to 1660 led to the (temporary) collapse of Puritanism as a major religious and moral force in English life. As it withdrew into isolated nonconformity, however, Puritanism bequeathed a number of essential – if unintended – legacies to the more secularized society that succeeded it. The 'Puritan ethic' of thrift, sobriety and hard work survived the decline of Puritanism to find its finest exponents in Benjamin Franklin and Samuel Smiles, and was internalized in the eighteenth-century bourgeois family. Secondly, respect for the individual conscience directed by God was one element of Puritanism (which, in many other ways, was repressive and authoritarian) that survived to help create not only the desire to provide religious toleration for 'tender consciences', but also to induce a respect for personal autonomy in other aspects of life. Thirdly the stress by the Puritans on the need for holy matrimony was ultimately incompatible with the patriarchal authority which they also extolled. How could paternal control over the choice of a marriage partner be maintained, if the pair were now to be bound by ties of love and affection? The concession of some element of choice was an inevitable by-product of such thinking, and it is no accident that it was the late seventeenth-century nonconformists who led the way in demanding freedom for children in the choice of spouse.

Other religious views also led to wholly unforeseen consequences. Slowly, the Protestant church began to place mutual comfort as one of the main – sometimes even *the* main – purposes of marital sex, no longer viewed as an instinct mainly limited to the purpose of procreation. This immediately cast doubt on the previous hostility to sex during pregnancy since it could not lead to procreation. A related area where the moral theologians led the laity into unforeseen problems was the dilemma over paid wet-nursing. There was general medical agreement, supported by modern statistics about contemporary conditions, that wet-nursing was far more dangerous for

176

the child than nursing by the mother. It was also held that sexual excitement in a nursing mother spoiled her milk, while if by chance she should become pregnant, the milk would dry up altogether and the suckling child would therefore die. Since nursing normally lasted a year to eighteen months, the moral theologians, with their concern for holy matrimony and the avoidance of 'unnatural practices' and of adultery, were forced to choose between advising the resumption of sexual relations with a nursing mother – thus endangering the life of the child – or forbidding it – thus risking adultery by the sex-starved husband. When in doubt they tended to prefer the former.

A final important development, which seems to have been an accidental by-product of Puritan theology, and its accompanying haunting sense of guilt, was the growth of self-awareness. This is shown by the fact that the bulk of diaries and autobiographies of the seventeenth century come from the pens of Puritans.

Thus the effective christianization in the late sixteenth and early seventeenth centuries, for the first time, of large sectors of the population had profound effects on family life which lasted long after religious enthusiasm had ebbed, and hardly any of which were either intended or anticipated. It was the reaction to the excesses of Puritanism, however, which provided other important contributions to the trend towards individual autonomy. One was the eighteenth-century hostility to 'enthusiasm' of all kinds and the consequent growth of a willingness to tolerate most forms of Christian sectarianism provided they did not disturb the public peace. When toleration at last became a positive virtue, a great step had been taken in the direction of autonomy. Without in any way meaning to do so, the march of natural science in the late seventeenth century greatly aided the rise of latitudinarianism and eventually even of Deism, and thus contributed to this mood of sceptical toleration. 'This is, I believe, the first age that has scorned a pretence to religion,' remarked a woman in Henry Fielding's *The Modern Husband* in 1732.

Another result of the decline of Puritanism was the rejection of the concept of Original Sin, of the infant child as being born an agent of the Devil. For this pessimistic theory was substituted the idea, given immense publicity by Locke's *Some Thoughts on Education* of 1693, that an infant is a *tabula rasa*, a blank sheet upon which the adults can imprint either good or evil. This did not do much to mitigate the desire to mould the child, but it did a lot to stimulate a show of love and affection in the home, and to reduce physical brutality in the schools.

The connection between the decline of absolute monarchy in the state and the decline of patriarchal authoritarianism in the family was made very explicit in the debate between Robert Filmer and John Locke in the 1680s. After forty years of inconclusive wrestling with this inconvenient theoretical problem by the defenders of limited monarchy and by Republicans, Locke at last cleared the way in the first of his *Two Treatises of Government*. He realized that he had to destroy the ancient argument, so forcibly restated by Filmer in his *Patriarcha*, at last published in 1680, that the authority of a king and that of a father were directly linked by scriptural authority and the natural laws of hierarchy. He therefore abandoned scripture, and relied solely on natural law, which was now becoming the normal basis for philosophical discussion. He argued that conjugal society was formed by voluntary contract for the purpose of begetting and rearing children. There was no need for absolute sovereignty in marriage to achieve these limited ends, but merely leadership by the stronger and wiser of the two, namely the man. The marriage contract could therefore include a wide variety of dispositions about a wife's property, and in logic could be dissolved at will once its purpose was fulfilled, that is when the children left home.

It was in the atmosphere created by this relaxation of psychological tension, this decline in religious enthusiasm, and this new political theory that in the mid-eighteenth century some of the ideas of the Enlightenment were enabled to take root. Thus family relationships were powerfully affected by the concept that the pursuit of individual happiness is one of the basic laws of nature, and also by the growing movement to put some check on man's inhumanity to man or animals which is so prominent a feature of eighteenth-century intellectual and political life.

By the early eighteenth century, complete identification had been made between the pursuit of gratification by the individual and the welfare of the public. In 1733 Alexander Pope concluded one section of his *Essay on Man* with the words: 'Thus God and Nature link'd the general frame/And bade self-love and social be the same.' He then went even further, concluding the next section with the claim 'That reason, passion answer one great aim/That true self-love and social are the same.' In these two couplets Pope drags in God,

Nature, Reason and Passion to support a proposition which can only be described as a transformation of human consciousness. For the first time, some men were beginning to believe – with very little justification – that the egocentric pursuit of self-interest contributed to the public good rather than to its destruction. Secondly, Pope's identification of passion and reason as working to the same end rather than as polar opposites harmonized emotion and logic. It thus prepared the way for the rise of romantic love as a respectable component of marital strategy and married life.

In order to answer the subsidiary question, not why individualism grew in this period, but why England took the lead over continental Europe, it is necessary to separate developments which were peculiar to England from those which were common throughout the whole of western Europe.

This-worldly secularism, literacy, the pursuit of happiness, humanitarianism, physical and bodily privacy, were common to the whole of Western culture. But it was the high development of the market economy in England that made possible and necessary the theory of economic individualism; the legacies from Puritanism of respect for the individual conscience, the ideal of holy matrimony, and the admission by Protestant theology that sex could be for purposes other than procreation were also ideas very limited in their geographical scope; the development of a large, wealthy, powerful and cultivated upper bourgeoisie was confined to Holland, England and France; the seizure of power by the gentry after a bloody civil war and the creation of a state based on the theory of a mutual contract between sovereign and people were purely English; the strong sense of cautious pragmatism engendered by such an historical experience and so delicately balanced a polity was very English; the cultural homogeneity of upper bourgeoisie and gentry, which allowed ideas to flow freely from the one to the other, was also peculiarly English, as was the absence of censorship and the creation of a large unified market of 'the quality' for literary production of all kinds; the role of London as the only political, economic and cultural centre of the country was unique; the development of the novel of sensibility, and the enormous growth of novel-reading thanks to the generalized institution of circulating libraries, were especially English phenomena. One can thus identify some specifically English features over and above those shared by all of Europe, which adequately explain the wide and early diffusion of new familial ideals and practices throughout the middle and upper ranks of English society. As a result, nowhere else, so far as we know, did the landed classes accept so readily the wide ramifications of the ideology of individualism, the notion that self-interest coincided with the public welfare.

The abandonment of the principle of human interchangeability and the rise of the concept that each person is unique, and cannot be exactly replicated or replaced, is adequately explained by these convergent forces. The rise of affect, however, is only partly a product of individualism, and seems to have its roots also in a basic personality change. In the sixteenth and early seventeenth centuries there predominated a personality type with 'low gradient' affect, whose capacity for warm relationships was generally limited, and who diffused what there was of it widely among family, kin, and neighbours. In the eighteenth century there predominated among the upper bourgeoisie and squirarchy a personality type with 'steep gradient' affect, whose general capacity for intimate personal relationships was much greater, and whose emotional ties were now far more closely concentrated on spouse and children. The cause of this personality change is not known, but it seems plausible to suggest that it may have been associated not only with the broad social and intellectual changes of the period, but also with a series of changes in child rearing, which created among adults a sense of trust instead of one of distrust. There were also two ideas which helped to stimulate affect in the eighteenth century. The first was the new confidence that the pursuit of happiness, best achieved by domestic affection, was the prime legitimate goal in life. The second was the new ideal of the 'Man of Sentiment' who was easily moved to outbursts of indignation by cruelty and to tears of sympathy by benevolence. Finally there was the slow structural shift that first weakened the power of the kin, and then that of the parents. With this shift in power went a change in concepts of duty and obligation.

These two trends towards individualism and towards affect came together to form affective individualism, the development of which in bourgeois and squirarchy family life in the late seventeenth and eighteenth centuries is the theme of the next three chapters.

CHAPTER SEVEN

Mating Arrangements

'Who marrieth for love without money hath good nights and
sorry days.'
> (J. Ray, *A Collection of English Proverbs*, Cambridge,
> 1670, p. 17)

'There is a certain trifle not much thought of in modern marriages called love.'
> (D. Defoe, *Review*, 1704 (Fascimile edn, ed. A. W.
> Secord), Vol. III, *Supplementary Journal*, No. 1, p. 9)

'Parents require in the man fortune and honour, which are requisite to make the married state comfortable and honourable. The young lady may require personal accomplishments
and complaisance, which are requisite to render a union
agreeable.'
> (*The Lady's Magazine*, V. 1774, p. 82)

1. THEORY

Changes in mating arrangements among classes owning substantial
amounts of property depend on changes in two theoretically distinct,
but practically interrelated, issues. The first is the distribution of
power over decision-making between the parents and the children;
and the second is the distribution of weight attached to various factors in making the choice.

In terms of power to make a match, four basic options are available in a society. The first is that the choice is made entirely by parents, kin, and family 'friends', without the advice or consent of the
bride or groom. The second option is that the choice is made as before, but the children are granted a right of veto, to be exercised on
the basis of one or two formal interviews which take place after the
two sets of parents and kin have agreed on the match. It is a right
which can only be exercised once or twice, and tends to be more

181

readily conceded to the groom than to the bride. The principle that underlies this concession is that mutual compatibility is desirable to hold a marriage together, and that this will slowly develop between any couple who do not exhibit an immediate antipathy towards each other on first sight. In a deferential society, this is a reasonable assumption. The third option, made necessary by the rise of individualism, is that choice is made by the children themselves, on the understanding that it will be made from a family of more or less equal financial and status position, with the parents retaining the right of veto. The fourth option, which has only emerged in this century, is that the children make their own choice, and merely inform their parents of what they have decided.

Within this range of options, the richer and more well-born the family, the greater is the power likely to be exercised by parents. Furthermore, at that time eldest sons were particularly exposed to parental pressure, since under primogeniture they inherited the bulk of the estate and their marriage was therefore critical to the future of the family. Daughters were also in a weak position since their only viable future lay in marriage. It was not much use for a critic to complain in 1703 that 'a woman . . . has been taught to think marriage her only preferment, the sum total of her endeavours, the completion of all her hopes'. The teaching merely conformed to reality. This being the case, the most free were younger sons.

Just as there are only four basic options concerning the distribution of decision-making, so there are only four basic options in the motives of choice. The first and most traditional motive for marriage is the economic or social or political consolidation or aggrandizement of the family. If these are the objectives, marriage is primarily a contract between two families for the exchange of concrete benefits, not so much for the married couple as for their parents and kin – considerations subsumed by contemporaries under the single rubric of 'interest'. This tended to be the predominant motive at the top and also towards the bottom of the social scale. In 1786 Mary Wollstonecraft correctly pointed out that 'in many respects the great and little vulgar resemble, and in none more than the motives which induce them to marry'.

The second motive is personal affection, companionship and friendship, a well-balanced and calculated assessment of the chances of long-term compatibility, based on the fullest possible knowledge of the moral, intellectual and psychological qualities of the prospective spouse, tested by a lengthy period of courtship. The third is physical attraction, stimulated by some degree of mutual experimentation before marriage, a possibility on the whole only open to young people of high rank away from home, in attendance in noble households or the royal court, or people of low rank among whom physically intimate courting was customary. The result could be a narrowly focused lust, a physical obsession with the body of a particular person. The eighteenth century described men affected by this powerful emotion as 'cunt-struck'. Mostly, however, this was assumed to be a force operating outside the bounds of marriage, something for which the man in its grip was prepared to abandon all other obligations, responsibilities and interests – work, home, children, friends, reputation, everything. The fourth possible personal motive was romantic love as portrayed in fiction and on the stage, a disturbance in the mental equilibrium resulting in an obsessive concentration upon the virtues of another person, a blindness to all his or her possible defects, and a rejection of all other options or considerations, especially such mundane matters as money.

By 1660 the shift from the first to the second option in the distribution of power over decision-making had already taken place in all but the highest ranks of the aristocracy: it had been conceded, in the interests of 'holy matrimony', that children of both sexes should be given the right of veto over a future spouse proposed to them by their parents. Between 1660 and 1800, however, there took place the far more radical shift from the second to the third option, with the children now normally making their own choices, and the parents being left with no more than the right of veto over socially or economically unsuitable candidates. At the same time there was inevitably a marked shift of emphasis on motives away from family interest and towards well-tried personal affection. Almost everyone agreed, however, that both physical desire and romantic love were unsafe bases for an enduring marriage, since both were violent mental disturbances which would inevitably be of only short duration. It was observed in 1703 that 'there is no great odds between his marrying for the love of money or for the love of beauty; the man does not act in accordance with reason in either case'. It is obvious that at the root of these changes in the power to make decisions about marriage, and in the motives that guided these decisions, there lie a deep shift of consciousness, a new recognition of the need for personal autonomy, and a new respect for the individual pursuit of happiness.

Besides this shift in basic attitude from deference to autonomy, there are also three sociological conditions required for the development of relatively free individual mate selection based on psychological compatibility. The first is that the nuclear family has become relatively independent of the kin, so that decisions about marriage are no longer made by a grand family council of elders, whose main concern is necessarily to defend and advance the interests of the clan rather than to gratify the personal wishes of the individuals, although usually they will genuinely seek to find a compatible mate. The second is that close parent–child bonding has developed, so that parents are reasonably satisfied that their own values have been internalized in their children and the latter will therefore make their selection from within the socially appropriate group. Thirdly, parents must be willing to grant adolescents considerable freedom to meet on neutral ground with members of the other sex and to develop their own courting rituals of conversation, dancing, etc.

The principal early evidence for this shift of consciousness and these sociological changes comes from the wealthy bourgeois and professional classes towards the end of the seventeenth century. There was, however, an earlier trend of thought in the same direction among the Arminian clergy and the Cavalier poets around the court in the 1630s, especially in the entourage of Queen Henrietta Maria where a cult of neo-platonic love flourished. Shortly afterwards, in 1645, Lord North was the first in English history to take the extreme radical position, publicly urging 'parents to leave their children full freedom with their consent in so important a case'. By 1700 Sir Richard Newdigate abandoned all but his financial interest in his son's marriage: 'let him marry whom he will, so I have the portion.' It is clear, therefore, that there is a rather thin stream of aristocratic and gentry opinion in favour of giving children freedom of choice in marriage and of placing companionship above interest that ran strongly in the 1630s and 1640s and thereafter fell away to a trickle. But its existence probably does much to explain why, when similar bourgeois ideas were propounded to the landed classes in the early eighteenth century by Addison and others, they took to them so readily. They had already been softened up to receive them.

When in 1706 Mary Astell complained that 'a woman, indeed, can't properly be said to choose, all that is allowed her is to refuse or accept what is offered', she did not seem to realize what an advance this was on the situation two or three generations before. The only motive for marriage that she would admit was settled and well-reasoned affection. She rejected the influence of both money and beauty since 'the man does not act in accordance to reason in either case, but is governed by irregular appetites.' In the first decade of the eighteenth century, that archetypal bourgeois propagandist Daniel Defoe expressed the most advanced male position: 'the limit of a parent's authority in this case of matrimony either with son or daughter, I think, stands thus: the negative, I think, is theirs, especially with a daughter; but I think, the positive is in the children's.' This is a very tentative statement peppered with deprecatory 'I thinks', but it was nonetheless a revolutionary position to adopt. When dealing with marriage for money, both Defoe and *The Spectator* dropped all hesitation, denouncing 'family marriage for the preserving of estates in the lines and blood of houses, keeping up names and relations and the like precedent ends', as the equivalent of violent rape, since the women are always forced to comply. 'Forcing to marry is, in the plain consequences, not only forcing to crime, but furnishing an excuse to crime.' Defoe's reasons for adopting this position were also very clear. 'As marriage is a state of life in which so much of humane felicity is really placed ... it seems to me the most rational thing in the world that the parties concerned, and them alone, should give the last strokes to its conclusion; that they only should be left to determine it, and that with all possible freedom.' For 'to say love is not essential to a form of marriage is true; but to say it is not essential to the felicity of the married state ... is not true.'

Addison in *The Spectator* hammered home the same point to the squirarchy: 'Those marriages generally abound most with love and constancy that are preceded by a long courtship. The passion should strike root and gather strength before marriage be grafted on to it.' He was clearly in full agreement with one of his correspondents who angrily rejected the advice of the conservatives, which he described as: 'Marry first and love will come after, or pigs love by lying together.' Steele took the same line in *The Tatler*, asserting cautiously but clearly that 'a generous and constant passion in an agreeable lover, where there is not too great a disparity in other circumstances, is the greatest happiness that can befall the person beloved'. All now agreed that all a parent might lawfully do was to 'command her not to marry this or that person'. In other words, the power of veto, which had already been conceded to the child, was now all that was left of parental authority, the positive choice passing to the children themselves.

In 1673 the heroine in Ravenscroft's *The Careless Lover* frankly declared her independence: 'But Uncle, it is not now as it was in your young days. Women then were poor, sneaking, sheepish creatures. But in our age we know our own strength and have wit enough to make use of our talents.' In Colley Cibber's *Non-Juror* of 1717, the heroine asked bluntly: 'Do you think a man has any more charms for me for my father's liking him? No, sir . . .'

For over half a century, from the 1680s to the 1740s, the arranged marriage exclusively for interest, as practised by the aristocracy, also came under growing assault from the fashionable playwrights and artists of the day. 'Oh how fatal are forced marriages!' lamented Lady Fulbank in *The Lucky Chance* of 1686, 'How many ruins one such match pulls on.' Half a century later, in Garrick's *Lethe* of 1740, Lord Chalkstone remarks: 'I married for a fortune; she for a title. When we had both got what we wanted, the sooner we parted the better.' The possible tragic consequences and the mutual frustration of the schemes of both parents who planned such mercenary matches were brought vividly before a mass public of all walks of life by the publication in 1745 of the six prints of Hogarth's *Marriage à la Mode*. The continued, though declining, obsession with property among the landed classes explains why in 1701 even so ardent a champion of women's rights as Mary Astell was claiming no more for a girl than the right of veto of a clearly incompatible partner, a position already conceded, even to girls, by more advanced parents for at least half a century: 'Modesty requiring that a woman should not love before marriage, but only make choice of one whom she can love hereafter; she who has none but innocent affections being easily able to fix them where duty requires.'

It is also significant that Lord Halifax's *Advice to a Daughter*, which was first published in 1688 and represented the traditional view of marriage arrangements, was continually republished throughout the eighteenth century, running to seventeen editions in English before 1791, besides several in French translation. He explained to his daughter the bitter truth of her situation.

It is one of the disadvantages belonging to your sex, that young women are seldom permitted to make their own choice; their friends' care and experience are thought safer guides to them than their own fancies, and their modesty often forbiddeth them to refuse when their parents recommend, though their inward consent may not entirely go along with it. In this case there remaineth nothing for them to do but to endeavour to make that easy which falleth to their lot, and by a wise use of everything they may dislike in a husband, turn that by degrees to be very supportable, which, if neglected, might in time beget an aversion.

You must first lay it down for a foundation in general, that there is inequality in the sexes, and that for the better economy of the world, the men, who were to be the law-givers, had the larger share of reason bestowed upon them, by which means your sex is the better prepared for the compliance that is necessary for the better performance of those duties which seem to be most properly assigned to it.

He told her that a separation from a hated husband involved a sordid washing of dirty linen and should be avoided if possible. He explained the reason for the double sexual standard, to prevent doubts about the legitimacy of offspring and their right of inheritance, and advised her to look the other way if her husband should embark on extra-marital liaisons. 'To expostulate in these cases looketh like declaring war and preparing reprisals.' Anyway, 'an indecent complaint makes a wife much more ridiculous than the injury that provoketh her to it'. If he turns out to be an alcoholic, 'it will be no new thing if you should have a drunkard for a husband', and the drink may make him more affectionate and tolerant. If he is short-tempered, he needs to be handled with extreme tact and discretion. If he is mean, he needs to be cajoled to spend more generously ... and so on. These are counsels of resignation and despair, and yet they were widely read and approved of in aristocratic circles until nearly the end of the eighteenth century.

In *Tom Jones*, published in 1749, Henry Fielding set out the two views of marriage, the old and the new. Her aunt, Mrs Western, advised Sophia that 'the alliance between the families is the principal matter. You ought to have a greater regard for the honour of your family than for your own person.' She also told her that marriage was 'a fund in which prudent women deposit their fortunes to the best advantage'. Her father, Squire Western, who had treated her mother like 'a faithful upper-servant all the time of their marriage', locked Sophia in her room until she would agree to marry the man of his choice, who would be 'one of the richest men in the county'. By way of contrast, there was Squire Allworthy, who 'thought love the only foundation of happiness in a married state, as it can only produce that high and tender friendship which should always be the cement of this union.' He therefore would tolerate neither any use of parental compulsion, nor marriage motivated by lust for a beautiful person or by avarice for a great fortune or by snobbery for a noble title. Sophia herself took the same position, promising that she would not marry without her father's consent, but obstinately refusing to marry a man chosen by him and not by herself. In this novel Fielding presents somewhat ideal stereotypes of the two extremes in attitudes to marriage, and the plot revolves around the clash between the two.

It is the current intense interest in this conflict of ideals that explains the enormous popularity of Richardson's novel *Clarissa Harlowe* in the middle of the eighteenth century, especially, it is said, among the bourgeoisie. The heroine of the novel, who comes from an aspiring gentry family, after much moral heart-searching finally refuses a purely mercenary match with the disagreeable Mr Solmes, which had been arranged for her by her parents. She elopes instead with a dissolute squire, who rapes her when under the influence of drugs. She then dies, consumed with guilt, but as morally pure as when the story began. This literary evidence shows that there was a prolonged public argument during the late seventeenth and eighteenth centuries about a child's freedom of choice of a marriage partner, with more liberal views slowly but steadily becoming more common among authors catering both to the middling ranks of commercial and professional people, and also to the wealthy landed classes.

A concurrent prolonged argument was also proceeding about the respective weight of 'interest' and love as motives for marriage. In 1704 a wealthy man in love with a poor lady, who reciprocated the love, put his dilemma to Defoe in *The Review*: 'If I marry her, I am ruined; if I lie with her, she is.' Defoe's reply was without equivocation. By his own admission the man could afford to marry, and 'mutual love [is] the essence of matrimony and makes it a heavenly life'. On the other hand, evidence of hostility to sexual desire as a basis for choice of a marriage partner can be found in every commentator of the seventeenth and eighteenth centuries, and it would be merely wearisome to stack up a pile of quotations to prove so uncontested and unchanging a point. Even Defoe, who has already been shown to be a pioneering 'liberal' on the marriage issue, thought that marriage for lust 'brings madness, desperation, ruin of families, disgrace, self-murders, killing of bastards, etc.'

There can be no doubt that at all times a few young people at all levels of society have defied the conventional wisdom of the day which condemned such mental disturbances, and have fallen head over heels in love. But given the hostility towards socially or financially unbalanced matches, and given the great influence over choice of partners still exercised by parents, 'friends', and masters, it is hardly surprising that these love affairs often failed to end in a happy marriage. The waiting-room of a popular psychological practitioner like the Reverend Richard Napier in the early seventeenth century saw not a few victims of unrequited or unfulfilled love. How commonly passionate pre-marital love developed in defiance of the wisdom of the day it is impossible to say, but it is fairly certain that it happened to no more than a minority of either men or woman. Ever since the twelfth century it had been familiar to court and aristocratic households, and Shakespeare's comedies were built around the theme of love, often, but not always, ending in marriage. In the early seventeenth century, the melancholia induced by unrequited love was an increasingly familiar theme both to dramatists and to scholars like Robert Burton. It seems likely, therefore, that love before marriage, however rare it may have been in the sixteenth century, may have been on the increase in the early seventeenth century and after. Ralph Josselin, a clergyman and the son of a small farmer, himself described the classic case of love at first sight, which struck him suddenly when as a poor curate he preached his first sermon in 1639: 'the first Lord's day, being October 6, my eye fixed with love upon a maid, and her's upon me, who afterwards proved my wife.' In 1723 Swift was still taking the traditional view that love was 'a ridiculous passion which hath no being but in plays and romances'. Even in the middle of the eighteenth century, most influential men and women were still firmly opposed to the idea, but by then they were fighting a losing battle against the mounting flood of romantic novels and poems. In 1773 a writer in *The Lady's Magazine* complained that 'there is scarce a young lady in the kingdom who has not read with avidity a great number of romances and novels, which tend to vitiate the taste'. By the end of the century, the rise of the circulating library had greatly stimulated both output and consumption, and in 1799 a (fictitious) mother complained to *The Lady's Monthy Museum* that her daughter reads nothing in the world but novels – nothing but novels, Madam, from morning to night ... The maid is generally dispatched to the library two or three times in the day, to change books. One week she will read in the following order: *Excessive Sensibility, Refined Delicacy, Disinterested Love, Sentimental Beauty*, etc.

The mother believed, not unreasonably, that 'a continued repetition of such reading seems, by infusing false and romantic notions, to injure, rather than to improve, the natural feelings of sensibility'.

Despite these valid objections, after 1780 romantic love and the romantic novel grew together, and the problem of cause and effect is one that is impossible to resolve. All that can be said is that for the first time in history romantic love became a respectable motive for marriage among the propertied classes, and that at the same time there was a rising flood of novels filling the shelves of the circulating libraries, devoted to the same theme. An extraordinarily large number of these novels were now written not merely for women, but also by women. As *The Times* remarked satirically in 1796, 'four thousand and seventy-three novels are now in the press from the pens of young ladies of fashion'. The results of massive exposure to this pulp literature were clear enough to contemporaries. Thanks to notions imbibed from this reading, young people fell head-long into the arms of whoever took their fancy, and, if their parents raised objections, they ran away to Scotland to get married in a hurry. 'Of all the arrows which Cupid has shot at youthful hearts,' remarked *The Universal Magazine* as early as 1772, '[the modern novel] is the keenest. There is no resisting it. It is the literary opium that lulls every sense into delicious rapture ... In contempt of the Marriage Act [demanding parental consent if under twenty-one] post-chaises and young couples run smoothly on the North Road.' (Plate 2.) In 1792 *The Bon Ton Magazine* warned its female readers that under the influence of romanticism, 'women of little experience are apt to mistake the urgency of bodily wants with the violence of a delicate passion'. In short, they were likely to mistake male lust for the emotion they read about in novels (Plate 9). Both Dr Johnson and Mary Wollstonecraft regarded them as the same thing, romantic love being no more than a purely artificial emotion invented by novelists and adopted by men as a cover for sexual desire. The latter argued that 'in the choice of a husband, [women] should not be led astray by the qualities of a lover, for a lover the husband ... cannot long remain'. She went so far as to claim that 'love and friendship cannot subsist in the same bosom', then backed off to concede that women should 'be contented to love but once in their lives; and after marriage, calmly let passion subside into friendship'.

Anthropological studies of the many societies in which sentiment is unknown tend to support La Rochefoucauld's observation that 'people would never fall in love if they had not heard of love talked about'. It is a product, that is, of learned cultural expectations, which became fashionable in the late eighteenth century thanks largely to the spread of novel-reading. It took even so clear-sighted a woman as Mrs Cappe quite a long time to realize that 'the heroine of the novel is not exactly fitted for the exemplary wife', and that passion based on external appearance 'may consist with very great defects of temper and moral character'. Not all young men or girls were, or are, so practical and sensible, and the romantic novel of the late eighteenth and early nineteenth centuries has much to answer for in the way of disastrous love affairs and of imprudent and unhappy marriages.

It is not so much the fact that romantic love existed, for that is nothing new: it is the radically different attitude towards it which is so striking in the mid- and late eighteenth century. By becoming fashionable, it inevitably also became much more common, and the response to its frustration more extreme. In 1794 Dorothea Herbert fell deeply in love with a man who eventually abandoned her. Years later, she was still in profound and bitter despair. 'What could induce the specious rogue to seduce my affections, betray me to lingering torments, and then desert me for ever, is a problem I never could solve. Ah, my poor heart, what cruelties did it suffer. What more than Hell-born woe when the monster struck his last blow and left me forever benighted in intolerable despair.' It was stories like this that made William Cobbett remark in 1829 that 'few people are entitled to more compassion than young men thus affected [by love]; it is a species of insanity that assails them, and it produces self-destruction in England more frequently than in all other countries put together.' Whether or not his statistics on suicide for thwarted love are correct, he was certainly expressing the standard view when he advised young men to choose their brides for such enduring companionate qualities as chastity, sobriety, industry, frugality, cleanliness, knowledge of domestic affairs, good temper and beauty – in that order.

2. PRACTICE

The extent to which the new values were put into practice by the readers of these plays, novels and didactic treatises is very hard indeed to determine. In a period of flux, some families opted for one pattern of marriage and some for another. Moreover there were very considerable differences in the responses at different social and economic levels in the society, so that very careful distinctions have to be made. One social group, the lower-middle class, seems to have accepted one aspect of the new ideas, namely that the choice should lie with the children, but rejected the other, that prior affection rather than financial gain and prudential calculation should be the basis of the choice. Another social group, namely the gentry and squirarchy, accepted the need for affection, but the parents still continued to exert a good deal of influence. The picture is therefore a very confused one, which can best be described by giving a series of real-life examples, beginning with the middling ranks of society, moving down to the lower-middle class, then up to the squirarchy, and finishing with the high aristocracy.

A very ambiguous story about parental attitudes among the middling ranks concerns Catherine, the daughter of Admiral Yeo. She was secretly wooed by a naval surgeon, Mr B, but he not only had nothing but the lieutenant's salary to live on, but also was the son of a personal enemy of her father. To put a stop to the courtship, her father 'locked me up for two months, during which space I never saw a creature but the person who brought me victuals. I was suffered neither pen, ink or paper.' Her release only came when Mr B's ship sailed, not to return for four years. On her release she was courted by the son of a rich tradesman, but she did not like either his person or his Presbyterian religion. The next suitor was an old lecher, to escape from whose attentions she went into the country to stay with a farmer. There she was courted by an apparently rich mercer, Mr Jemmat, who professed to have a fortune of £3,000. Catherine agreed to marry him 'not for love indeed, but to avoid the persecutions of a too rigid father, whose behaviour was insupportable'. But she jumped out of the frying-pan into the fire. Mr Jemmat turned out to be insanely jealous, an habitual drunkard, and on the verge of financial ruin. Within three years he was bankrupt. What is interesting about this story is that Admiral Yeo was only trying to exercise a right of veto, admittedly enforced by incarceration, and that Miss Yeo herself chose Mr Jemmat, so that she had only herself to blame for her misfortunes. At any period in history a father who believes that his cherished son and heir is throwing himself away on a worthless girl, and by doing so is endangering a promising career, is bound to be resentful and hostile. What was new about the eighteenth century was that this hostility was no longer effective in stopping children marrying to suit themselves.

There can be no doubt that public opinion in landed and bourgeois circles in the late eighteenth century was turning decisively against parental dictation of a marriage partner. The silversmith Joseph Brasbridge tells the story of an attorney at Banbury, a Mr Aplin, who took on as his articled clerk a poor but bright young boy of humble origins, Richard Bignell. Bignell and Aplin's daughter, who also worked in her father's office, fell in love and when the period of his clerkship was expired, Bignell asked Aplin for his daughter's hand, only to be rejected 'with the utmost scorn'. When he later discovered that the young couple had secretly married, Mr Aplin turned his daughter out of doors and refused to have anything more to do with her. What is so interesting is the reaction of the attorney's middle-class and gentry clientele in Banbury to this traditional treatment of disobedient children. 'The people in the town and neighbourhood, condemning the father's harshness and, willing to encourage the young man's industry, gradually withdrew their business from Mr Aplin and transferred it to Mr Bignell.' It would be hard to find a more convincing demonstration of the new attitude to parental control over marriage among provincial townspeople and county gentry at the end of the eighteenth century.

In the eighteenth century the importance of money was far less generally accepted as a crucial factor in marriage than it had been in the seventeenth. In the late seventeenth century the two motives were jostling for priority within the mind of a single suitor, like the successful Turkey merchant John Verney, who in the 1670s was looking around for a wife. He came from upper gentry stock, but was by profession a member of the commercial bourgeoisie, so that the origin of his system of values is a little obscure. When he first came back from Aleppo in 1674, he embarked on a cold-blooded search for a mercenary marriage. He was soon approached by a sixty-year-old wealthy London citizen anxious to marry off his nineteen-year-old daughter. Although Mr Edwards promised a good estate to go with her and that she was 'a good housewife', he was very reluctant to allow John Verney even to take a look at the girl before the financial details were ironed out. But at last he agreed to stage an 'accidental' meeting in the street, so that the prospective groom could assure himself that there was 'nothing disgustful' about the girl. During the meeting, the girl (who was totally ignorant of what was afoot) did not exchange a single word with John Verney, but the sight of her allowed him to report coolly to his father that 'though her beauty is not like to prefer her to the title of a duchess, yet she is a very passable woman and well-shaped'. He was content to pursue the negotiations on the grounds that 'the gentlewoman is a passable handsome woman and her father able, if he be but willing, to give her money enough'. In the end the financial negotiations broke down, but it is clear that on both sides of this match there was no suggestion of consulting the feelings of the prospective bride, who was not even told that she was under consideration, much less of the need for prior affection by either the bride or the groom.

When John Verney tried again six years later in 1680, however, he fell in love with a fifteen-year-old girl long before the marriage negotiations were concluded. At a point when her father was raising impossible obstacles and he thought the match had fallen through, he wrote asking for a 'lock of your delicate hair' as a keepsake. After everything had been straightened out and the marriage had taken place, he and his young bride remained devoted to each other. When she left for a visit soon after the birth of their first child, he wrote letters to her headed 'Dearest dear' or 'Dearest Heart', thanking her for 'tender expressions' and giving details of the growth of 'pretty precious'. Some years later, after the birth of two children and when a third was *in utero*, he concluded a letter with a phrase revealing the depth of his domestic felicity. He sent her 'everything that the lovingest of husbands can express to the best of wives, and love to the little ones, not forgetting the kicker in the dark'.

These matrimonial ventures by a man who was both the younger son of a baronet and a Turkey merchant in the 1670s and 1680s show very clearly the way in which two very different attitudes towards marriage were in sharp competition in these circles at that time, affecting all three elements in the situation: the degree to which property and money should be the prime considerations in marriage; the degree to which marriage should be arranged by the parents without much consideration for the wishes of the prospective groom or bride; and the degree to which prior love should serve as an essential basis for a stable and successful marriage. Between 1674 and 1680 the mind of John Verney seems to have moved from one position to another on all three issues. In the end, he and his wife provided an early model of the new domesticated affective nuclear family, but he could equally easily have married Miss Edwards for her money, and experienced the most conventional of arranged marriages.

The story of how the barrister Mr Elers found his bride in the 1740s shows that more old-fashioned seventeenth-century styles still persisted into the eighteenth century. His friend and client Mr Grosvenor fell heavily into debt due to gambling losses and sought to recoup by a wealthy marriage. And so when his friend Mr Hungerford offered him the hand of his only daughter and heiress, Mr Grosvenor accepted her unseen. As a precaution, he took Mr Elers down with him to the Hungerford house in the country in order to examine the title deeds and draw up the necessary conveyances. When they arrived, they found that Miss Hungerford 'had not much beauty, grace or dignity; she was a plump, good-natured, unfashioned girl with little knowledge of any sort and with no accomplishments'. Mr Grosvenor confided in Mr Elers that 'the girl is a sad encumbrance on the estate'. When Mr Elers mildly disagreed, Grosvenor said, 'Suppose you were to take the whole bargain off my hands?' 'Most willingly,' replied Elers. Mr Hungerford readily agreed to the change of the prospective bridegroom; 'the young lady ... submitted with blushes and becoming filial duty to the wishes of her parents', and Elers gained a landed fortune of £800 a year. As a result, he gave up his London practice and retired to live the life of a country gentleman. But he had no talent for estate management, disliked field sports, and found the conversation of the neighbouring squires a bore. He became idle and apathetic. His wife was tiresomely fertile and kept producing healthy children who were very expensive to look after; and so he eventually got into difficulties. It is a story with several morals.

Among the lower-middle class, where the economic leverage of parents was weak since they did not have much to give as a bribe or to withhold as a threat, and in which their social control was weak since the children had already left home, patriarchal authority seems to have been in full decay by the late seventeenth century, if not earlier. A further reason for this is that the very late age of marriage, which was customary in these circles, meant that in many cases the parents were already dead and so unable to control the marriage, and that in all cases the spouses were fully adult men and women, who could not easily be controlled, least of all from a distance. It seems inevitable that parental control of marriage among the lower classes must have been severely limited by all these factors. Only those with expectations of inheritance of a little property, such as a peasant son who was waiting to inherit a yardland or so from his father, or an artisan or shopkeeper's son with hopes of inheriting the tools, the shop and the goodwill, could be expected to pay much attention to parental directions or advice, if they did not coincide with his own inclinations.

This advice, however, was increasingly falling on deaf ears. As early as the middle of the seventeenth century, the Reverend Ralph Josselin was struggling vainly to control the marriage of his children. Various prospective suitors were brought to stay in the house and were carefully inspected, but it was the children who had chosen them, and not the parents. Away in service in London, the daughters found their own potential husbands. Josselin was distressed when his son John married without his knowledge, but merely commented resignedly: 'God pardon his errors.' The patriarchal authority that Josselin perhaps wished to exercise over the choice of marriage partner for his children was clearly neither very resolutely attempted nor very successfully enforced. He was normally consulted, the family opinion carried great weight, but the initiative lay with the absent children, both girls and boys, who themselves first selected their potential mates for submission to inspection by their parents.

In the eighteenth century, the opinion of the parents was often ignored. The diary of James Frelwell, a Yorkshire yeoman in the 1720s and 1730s, records many cases of children marrying by free choice without the advice or consent of parents. His cousin's only daughter married at the age of seventeen 'without her parents' knowledge, much less with their consent', but they were forced to accept the situation and teach the young man the family trade of tanning. Both James's sisters married against the wishes of their parents or brothers, and indeed without their knowledge. It was a situation which Frelwell seems to have accepted with philosophical resignation.

In lower-middle-class circles, where capital was a critical factor in getting a start in life by buying a shop or starting a business, it was inevitable that financial considerations should continue to play a very large part in marriage plans, even though the decisions were left to the children themselves. Defoe's Moll Flanders, who moved in these circles, soon came to the sad conclusion that 'marriages are here the consequence of politic schemes, for forming interests, carrying on business', and that love had no share or very little in the matter. After a bitter experience she decided that 'money only made a woman agreeable ... the money was the thing'. In other words, in terms of marriage, a woman in the late seventeenth and eighteenth centuries was still regarded in these circles less as a companion or a sex object than as property, and to some extent also as a status object.

The ambiguities of the motives for lower-middle-class marriage in the late eighteenth century are well revealed by the correspondence of the Cumberland brothers in the late 1770s, when both were in their middle twenties. Richard was a parson in Gloucestershire, and George a clerk in the Exchange Assurance Office in London. George thought that Richard ought to get married and they engaged in a debate about the qualities desirable in a wife. Richard declared himself 'proof against beauty', thinking 'neatness and good nature everything in a wife'. He would accept someone whom he found attractive with no more money than 'just enough to pay fees and preliminaries'; failing that he would settle for 'one of the common run' with money enough 'to make amends for trifling deficiencies, and of an amiable temper – supposing a probability of our making each other as happy as the generality of married people'. Richard's expectations were clearly not high. Indeed he was soon congratulating himself 'on having escaped a most dangerous temptation, that of connecting myself with a partner for life, for the sake perhaps of a few hundreds to begin with, a very common case with young men in my situation'. George, on the other hand, was seriously courting a Miss Townshend and Richard wrote advising discretion. He conceded that 'she is a woman of honour, taste and spirit', but questioned whether she also possessed such virtues as 'economy, prudence, a love of home and domestic amusements'. But the key issue was financial: 'The question is, will your united incomes, added to any reasonable expectancies you may have, enable you to enter the state of matrimony without experiencing any of those self-denials which I suspect you are neither disposed to submit to?' Not surprisingly, the brothers remained bachelors.

Among the lower-middle ranks and the more respectable elements of the poor there is statistical evidence to indicate a trend towards a later marriage age, due to a prudent desire to accumulate the necessary economic resources before embarking on such an expensive undertaking. In 1778 George Crabbe, then an unsuccessful and unqualified surgeon, fell in love. But the girl 'was too prudent to marry where there seemed to be no chance of a competent livelihood; and he, instead of being in a position to maintain a family, could hardly by labour which he abhorred earn daily bread for himself'. The match was therefore postponed for the time being. It is not surprising, therefore, to find Crabbe in 1807 giving warm approval to those of the rural poor who had the prudence to delay marriage until they had the economic means to support a family.

> Reuben and Rachel, though as fond as doves,
> Were yet discreet and cautious in their loves;
> Nor would attend to Cupid's wild commands,
> Till cool reflection bade them join their hands.
> When both were poor, they thought it argued ill
> Of hasty love to make them poorer still;
> Year after year, with savings long laid by,
> They brought the future dwelling's full supply;
> Her frugal fancy cull'd the smaller ware,
> The weightier purchase ask'd her Reuben's care;
> Together then their last year's gain they threw,
> And lo! an auction'd bed, with curtains neat and new.
> Thus both, as prudence counsell'd, wisely stay'd
> And cheerful then the calls of Love obey'd.

Others, however, no doubt influenced by novel-reading, were cheerfully putting love before prudence, as Crabbe was well aware. In 1751, that hard-boiled and highly sophisticated young surgeon John Knyveton, who was then working in a London hospital, tells of a young woman patient who had to have a leg amputated after an injury to her knee. She was a country girl from Norfolk who had fallen in love with a farmer's son, but had been packed off to London by her guardian who disapproved of the connection. One day the farmer's son appeared in the hospital ward, having finally discovered where she was. Despite her maimed condition, their love was renewed and they were married the next day at the bedside. In his professional capacity Knyveton learned from this episode that, as the head surgeon told him, 'there be no medicine like love'. He also meditated that 'this strange, intoxicating distemper of love, which I have heard described as a disease ... [is] surely one affection above all others that one would pray to be inoculated with'. These sentiments were apparently shared by all the other patients in the ward, who observed the scene 'half of them in tears, and the other half unwonted quiet, according to their several temperaments'. This is a true story of nature imitating art.

Among the wealthier landed classes, the two issues of power and motive are too inextricably mixed to be usefully disentangled. The most fruitful way of examining conflict and change in these classes is therefore to examine the conduct of marriage negotiations from the point of view first of men and then of women.

A typical but particularly well-documented example of late seventeenth-century marriage arrangements, as conducted in conservative aristocratic and courtly circles, concerns those in 1665 for the union of Jemima, a daughter of the first Earl of Sandwich, and Philip, the eldest son of Sir George Carteret. The idea of a match was first broached by her mother to the family client Samuel Pepys in February, and in June the Sandwich parents decided to go ahead with the plans and authorized Pepys to make the first moves. The object was partly financial but more to cement a politico-administrative alliance, since both fathers were now very high officials in the Admiralty. Pepys, therefore, approached a Carteret client, Dr Clerk, who approved the match on the egotistical grounds that 'being both men relating to the sea, under a kind aspect of His Majesty, already good friends, and both virtuous and good families, their alliance might be of good use to us'. In other words, the two clients hoped to benefit from a cementing of the alliance of their influential patrons. The financial details were rapidly worked out – a marriage portion of £5,000 from Sandwich and a jointure for Jemima, if she were widowed, of £800 a year from Carteret; the approval of the King and of the Duke of York was secured; and the contract was signed and sealed on 5 July. It was not until this moment that Jemima was sent for from the country to be informed what fate her parents had decided for her. The only person at all bothered by this procedure was her mother, Lady Sandwich, who confided in Pepys her doubts 'whether her daughter will like of it or no, and how troubled she is for fear of it, which I do not fear at all'. Her anxiety seems to have arisen not from doubts about her daughter's happiness, but from

the fear of the political damage that would be done if she un-
expectedly turned recalcitrant.

By 15 July Jemima had arrived, the trousseau had been bought,
and the time had come to introduce the couple to one another.
Pepys was put in charge of taking the young Philip Carteret down to
meet his bride. As a man of the world himself, with a winning way
with women, whom he was constantly pawing and kissing, he was
irritated to discover that he had on his hands a most bashful and
tongue-tied young man. So shy was Philip that he did not speak to
Jemima or touch her at the introduction or all through dinner. Lord
Sandwich suggested leaving the pair alone after dinner for a while,
but Pepys advised against it; 'lest the lady might be too much surprised'. He was afraid of the effect of Philip's clumsy bashfulness.
When he took Philip off to bed, he asked him how he liked his bride.
The young man expressed approval 'but in the dullest, insipid manner that ever lover did'. Next day was Sunday, and Pepys instructed
Philip to take Jemima by the hand and lead her as they came and
went to and from church, but he was still too shy even to approach
her. Later on that day, the pair were deliberately left alone for two
periods of about an hour each in order to get acquainted as best they
could. Pepys then took Jemima aside and asked her 'how she liked
the gentleman and whether she was under any difficulty concerning
him. She blushed and hid her face awhile, but at last I forced her to
tell me. She answered that she could readily obey what her father
and mother had done, which was all she could say, or I expect.' It
was indeed all she *could* say, seeing that both sets of parents were
determined on the match; it already had the approval of the King
and his brother; the contract was already signed and sealed; and the
trousseau had already been purchased. Jemima was trapped, as indeed was Philip also, and the effort to ascertain her feelings was
clearly merely perfunctory. Over the next few days, Jemima remained
solemn and discreet, Philip as shy and tongue-tied as ever. Meanwhile Jemima had to have minor surgical attention, to prepare her
for the marriage. On 31 July the pair were married with due pomp
and ceremony, although Pepys found 'the young lady mighty sad',
and the wedding dinner a stiff and joyless affair. Later he attended
Philip into the bridal chamber, kissed Jemima, drew the curtains
around the four-poster, and withdrew. The next day he found the
pair 'pleased this morning with their night's lodging', although
whether they were really pleased or not, indeed whether the match

was in fact consummated that night, is far from clear. At all events, Jemima did not become pregnant until fifteen months later. History does not relate how they got on with each other for the rest of their short married life, which lasted until Philip was killed at the battle of Solebay seven years later, leaving his widow with three children.

The story which best epitomizes the transitional position from one mode of behaviour to another in the early eighteenth century is that of the negotiations in 1710–11 to marry Mary, the daughter of a very wealthy self-made Sheffield attorney, Joseph Banks of Scofton, to the son and heir of Colonel Talbot of Thornton-le-Street in Yorkshire. Himself now a substantial landowner and accustomed in his business to act as agent for dukes and landed gentry, Banks had adopted the traditional marriage habits of the class to which he aspired. On the other hand, as a professional man of bourgeois origins, he also brought with him the idea that the personal choice of the two individuals was paramount. A few months before the story opens, Banks had burned his fingers in abortive negotiations for Mary's marriage to another landed son and heir, in which he thought he had been financially double-crossed. This time, negotiations were carried on via two intermediaries, that for Banks being a cousin, the Reverend William Steer of Sheffield, who first proposed the match. Throughout June, July, August and September 1710, the fathers exchanged financial information and offers in an atmosphere of total secrecy, neither the two young people nor even Banks's wife being informed of what was going on. There were considerable financial problems, for the Talbots turned out to be far less wealthy than Banks had expected and Colonel Talbot demanded an excessively large marriage portion, half of which was to go to himself. However, by the end of September these matters had been straightened out, and 'Mally' at last knew what was going on. The two fathers met on neutral ground and agreed on the financial terms. Banks then stipulated and the Colonel agreed 'that the young people should have an interview, and if they liked one another the matter was done, but if otherwise there was to be an end'. Inquiries about young Roger Talbot turned up nothing derogatory, except 'his loving a pot', or an inclination to drink to excess. After the visit, Steer reported optimistically on 11 October that Mary 'looks on him (as far as she can learn by their short acquaintance) to be so good humoured that she can reasonably propose to live happily with him'. This seemed good enough for Steer, who was of the old school and thought that 'they seldom fail to be happy that marry into an honest family', and therefore that family standing was more important than personal inclination.

But Mary was, in fact, very uncertain; other visits may have followed, and Mary was now writing to her mother in a much more discouraging tone. In January Joseph Banks wrote to Mary, placing the final decision fairly and squarely on her. 'I leave it to thyself. But after I have gone so far, without more reasons than I knew, to go off would not look well.' On the other hand, Mary was still young (only twenty), and she could probably do better for herself financially. 'Pray God direct thee. I leave it to thyself.' Encouraged by this letter, Mary wrote Steer a firm refusal of the offer. 'I cannot for my life think him agreeable . . . and I think that man and woman must run a great hazard of living miserably all their lives where there is not a mutual inclination beforehand . . . My Papa has left me entirely to choose which way I please in this affair.' The fact of the matter was that Mary had heard that Roger had got dead drunk at Pontefract on the way home from his visit, and decided not to tie herself to a life-long alcoholic. Her father himself agreed: 'I . . . cannot blame her, for the apprehension of want of government that way must be very dreadful.'

So far as it goes, this story is one of a perfect compromise between old-fashioned economic horse-trading between the fathers and the new rules of granting total freedom of choice to the young people, in this case exercised entirely on the principle of the need for prior affection. On the other hand, this veto power exercised by Mary was a card which could hardly be played more than once, at most twice, and the records do not tell us whether there was any more enthusiasm on her part some time later, when she made the far more socially and financially advantageous marriage to a local notable, Sir Francis Whichcote, third Baronet. It is, however, reasonable to suppose that her father's choice was then more prudent, and that, in view of the good will she had shown the first time, she may have been consulted at an earlier stage of the negotiations.

Later on in the eighteenth century, the motives for marriage among the aristocracy were still confused, but all sides were beginning to recognize the need for prior affection. In the 1780s the Earl of Pembroke was heavily in debt and therefore urged his heir Lord Herbert to find a bride 'as beautiful as you please, and as rich as Croesus . . . *ou nous sommes tous . . . foutus*'. The latter first made an offer to Caroline, daughter of the Duke of Marlborough, but was rejected. Her brother explained that 'she has not that kind of liking for you, without which she is determined not to marry any man ... She likes you very well, but not as a lover.' This was now thought, on all sides, to be a sufficient reason for refusal. Lord Herbert also made some very half-hearted overtures to the only daughter and heiress of Sir Richard Child of Osterley, the fabulously wealthy banker. In this he seems to have been following up an earlier suggestion of his governor and friend Major Floyd, who asked him: 'have you ever seen her, and do you think you could bring yourself to lay your chaste leg over her for the dirty consideration of two or three hundred thousand pounds?' But nothing came of this, and a year later, Lord Herbert got himself engaged to a penniless cousin, Elizabeth Beauclerk, and had to ask his father not only for his blessing but for an extra £1,000 a year with which to set up house. His father's philosophical acceptance of the *fait accompli* was highly illuminating about the new scale of values. He pointed out 'how very much the situation of our affairs stand in need of at least thirty thousand pounds ... It would have been lucky for us had you found a thirty thousand pounder as agreeable to you as Elizabeth.' Having made the point, however, Pembroke dropped it, and gave his approval of the match without further argument, on the grounds that 'the greatest pleasure I can feel is to know that you are happy. If you are happy my dearest George, I must be so ... *N'en parlons plus*.'

A detailed and absorbing example from a woman's point of view of the confusion of values existing among the upper classes in the mid-seventeenth century is provided by the autobiography of Lady Anne Halkett, which is one of the first in England to be mainly the history of a chequered love-life. She was a woman strongly influenced by her sense of religious duty, which had been instilled into her at an early age. As the daughter of Thomas Murray, a court official and Provost of Eton, she had been brought up in a strict Anglican tradition, in many ways as austere as that practised by the Puritans. This piety was the main driving force in her life, and as a result she had difficulty in accommodating to her complicated emotional entanglements. She also believed in the traditional view about obedience to at least a parental veto in marriage: 'I ever looked upon marrying without consent of parents as the highest act of ingratitude and disobedience that children could commit, and I resolved never to be guilty of it.' On the other hand, she was modern enough to refuse to allow a parent or anyone else to dictate her feelings or tell her whom to marry, an attitude which infuriated her mother. Her situation was further complicated by the chaos and disorder of civil war and revolution, particularly since she and her friends and relatives were all on the losing side and were constantly in hiding or on the move.

Her story opens in 1644, when Lord Howard of Escrick, an impoverished royalist nobleman in exile, sent his eldest son and heir, Thomas, to stay in her sister's household. Lord Howard's intention was 'to marry him to some rich match that might improve his fortune', and in particular 'to marry a rich citizen's daughter that his father had designed for him'. But instead the young man fell head over heels in love with the twenty-one-year-old Anne, although she did her best to discourage him, knowing well the opposition of both his father and her mother (her father had died twenty years before). She was nevertheless very fond of him, and even in the face of violent parental opposition arranged a secret meeting with him (with her sister present as chaperone). When the young man nearly fainted with emotion, Anne sat on his knee to comfort him, but she remained resolute in her determination to obey her mother. The next day Thomas Howard departed 'and left me to the severities of my offended mother, whom nothing could pacify'. Her mother threatened that if Anne ever saw Thomas Howard again, she would 'turn me out of her doors and never own me again', an order that Anne ingeniously frustrated by agreeing to another secret meeting with the young man, but with her eyes blindfolded. She reiterated her refusal to marry him without parental consent, but vowed to be faithful to him, while he exchanged many similar vows of his undying devotion to her. When she got to hear of this further meeting, her mother was naturally even more enraged and demanded again that Anne cease to think about Thomas Howard, a demand for thought-control that Anne obstinately refused to give. About two years later, however, in 1646, Thomas married – willingly or not is unknown – a daughter of the Earl of Peterborough, and this episode, therefore, came to an end.

Soon after the death of her mother in 1647 or 1648, Anne went to live in her brother's house in London, where she met an Irish royalist colonel, Joseph Bampfield, who was then engaged on a series of secret missions for the imprisoned king. Excited by the conspiratorial activities of the colonel and her devotion to the royalist cause, she took a prominent and dangerous part in helping Bampfield to smuggle the king's younger son James, Duke of York (the future James II) out of the country. The colonel had not seen his wife for over a year, a fact which he explained away to Anne's satisfaction by the fact that she and her friends were all Parliamentarians. The intimacy throve on royalist plotting, and soon afterwards in 1649 he announced one day that his wife was dead and asked Anne to marry him. Anne by then had convinced herself that she was in love with this romantic secret agent, and she engaged herself to marry him as soon as the political situation made it possible. But he was in hiding, and she had to leave London in a hurry to avoid arrest for her complicity in the plot to smuggle out the Duke of York. She therefore took refuge at Naworth Castle with her friend Lady Howard and her husband Sir Charles. There she heard, almost simultaneously, two shattering pieces of news. The first was the arrest of the colonel and his grave danger of execution, and the second (from her brother and sister) that the colonel was a rogue and a liar and that his wife was in fact still alive. On hearing this news 'I fell so extremely sick that none expected life for me.' But the colonel made a daring and successful escape from prison; and she persuaded herself that the story about the wife was false. She indignantly repudiated rumours that she 'designed to marry a man that had a wife'. Meanwhile her brother-in-law had accidentally met Colonel Bampfield in a boat going to Flanders and had abruptly challenged him to a duel for trifling with the affections of his sister-in-law while he was a married man. The colonel denied the accusation but fought the duel, very badly wounding Anne's brother-in-law in the hand.

By now she had moved on to Edinburgh, where the ubiquitous colonel turned up and asked for an interview, which threw her into another hysterical collapse. 'The conflict betwixt love and honour was so great and prevalent that neither would yield to other, and betwixt both I was brought into so great a distemper that I expected now an end to all my misfortunes.'

The colonel was busy plotting for a rising in Scotland on behalf of Charles II, and among his fellow conspirators was Sir James Halkett, an elderly widower with four children, some of whom were nearly grown-up. Sir James saw more and more of Anne, and eventually asked her to marry him. She refused on the grounds of her prior engagement to Colonel Bampfield, whose protestations about his wife's death she continued more or less to believe. She told Sir James that 'nothing but the death of Colonel Bampfield could make me ever think of another'. Meanwhile, there took place the invasion of Scotland by Charles II and the crushing defeat of the Scottish royal army by Cromwell at Dunbar. Anne fled with the royalist nobility into the Highlands.

A year later in 1653 confirmation that Mrs Bampfield was alive and well caused a further psychological collapse. When she recovered, Sir James revived his suit, which she eventually accepted, and she agreed to marry him as soon as she had fully cleared up her financial affairs. Anne returned to London for this purpose in 1654, when the colonel, who was now (entirely unknown to her) acting as a double agent for both Charles II and Cromwell, turned up for the last time. He asked her flatly whether or not she was married to Sir James Halkett, because if she was he would not bother her again. 'I hated lying, and I saw there might be some inconvenience to tell the truth, and (Lord pardon the equivocation) I said "I am" out loud, and secretly said "not".' Thus she was finally freed from a nine-year involvement with the colonel, which was clearly the most passionate emotional experience of her life, and in 1656, at the age of thirty-three, she married her patient elderly suitor, Sir James Halkett.

This is a story which could only have happened in the seventeenth century. The extreme piety which dominated her life was typical of her age, as was that reverence for parental wishes which prevented her from giving herself to either of her first two lovers, and the code of the duel which drove her brother-in-law to risk his life in a challenge on her behalf but against her wishes. Both fornication and bigamy were unthinkable for her, and on delicate occasions she took a chaperone with her to interviews with her suitor. At the same time the civil wars and their aftermath caused constant interruptions of relations and the impossibility of establishing even such a simple fact as whether or not the wife of a prominent gentleman were still alive. These separations not only stimulated literacy, since writing was now a prime means of keeping in touch, they also stimulated a strong, if ephemeral, sense of independence among many women who suddenly found responsibility thrust upon them. One instance of Anne's new-found spirit of independence was her adoption of the practice of going to plays and amusement gardens with female friends, each paying her own way, after she overheard some gentleman complaining about the cost of taking a lady to the theatre. Her emotional attachment to the colonel was also a product of war, being stimulated by his glamorous role as a secret royalist agent. But once he was shown up as a liar and a fraud, and once the upheavals of war were over, she made a practical prosaic match of the most traditional kind, and settled down once more in the subordinate role of dutiful wife and mother. She was a woman who moved uncertainly between two worlds: the one, in which she had been brought up and in which she was to live out her last decades, was based on female subordination to men, and marriage for interest not attraction; the other, which boiled up for a while in the crucible of war, was one of excitement, glamour, intrigue, love and feminine independence, literacy and responsibility. Her conflict between love and honour is characteristic of the plots of contemporary classical drama.

The autobiography of Mary Granville (later Mrs Delany) reveals similar conflicts at a later period but at a similar social level. Mary was born in 1700, the daughter of a younger son of a Groom of the Bedchamber and with close aristocratic and court connections. Her parents and relatives were staunch Tories and were driven from court and office by the Hanoverian succession in 1714. She therefore grew up a well-connected, lively and intelligent girl, but without a fortune. Judging by her story, however, she must have been extremely attractive to men. Her first suitor was a Mr Twyford, who paid court to her at the early age of fifteen and asked her to marry him. Mary's father 'told him I had no fortune, and it was very probable, for this reason, his friends would not approve of his choice'. When Mr Twyford found that his parents, especially his mother, flatly refused their consent, he asked Mary to marry him privately, a step she refused to take. Some three years later, after she was married, she learned that this rebuff and her marriage had driven Mr Twyford into an hysterical collapse:

His mother's cruel treatment of him and absolute refusal of her consent for his marrying me affected him so deeply as to throw him into a dead palsy. He lost the use of his speech, though not of his senses, and when he strove to speak, he could not utter above a word or two, but he used to write perpetually and I was the only subject of his pen. He lived in this wretched state about a year after I was married. When he was dead, they found under his pillow a piece of cut paper, which he had stolen out of my closet.

At the age of seventeen, Mary was invited to stay with her uncle Lord Lansdowne at Longleat, where she was thrown in the company of a Mr Alexander Pendarves, a very wealthy Cornish Tory landowner. He found Mary very attractive, and Lord Lansdowne, who probably planned the whole thing in advance, saw an opportunity of providing his impoverished niece with a rich husband, while at the same time consolidating his own Tory political influence in Cornwall. Neither Lord and Lady Lansdowne nor her other aunt Lady Stanley regarded the personal feelings of this seventeen-year-old girl towards her sixty-year-old suitor as of the slightest importance. Indeed, they easily convinced themselves that she would see things their way, and called her 'childish, ignorant and silly' to raise objections to a marriage which was so clearly in her own best interests.

The trouble was that Mary could not abide her suitor's 'large, unwieldly person and his crimson face'. 'I thought him ugly and disagreeable; he was fat, much afflicted with gout, and often sat in a sullen mood, which I concluded was from the gloominess of his temper.' For two months Mr Pendarves followed Mary about the enormous house, and Mary fled from him in apprehension and disgust. He was anxious to declare his intentions, but was deterred by Mary's attitude, and was only provoked into action by jealousy of a young man who was staying in the houses, a younger son of Edward Villiers, Earl of Jersey, whose attentions Mary clearly found far more acceptable than his own. He therefore approached Lord Lansdowne, who 'readily embraced the offer and engaged for my compliance; he might have said obedience, for I was not entreated but commanded'. Seizing a suitable opportunity, Lord Lansdowne summoned her to a talk. He

took me by the hand, and after a very pathetic speech of his love and care of me and of my father's unhappy circumstances, my own want of fortune, and the little prospect I had of being happy if I disobliged those friends that were desirous of serving me, he told me of [Pendarves'] passion for me, and his offer of settling his whole estate on me; he then, with great art and eloquence, told me all his good qualities and vast merit, and how despicable I should be if I could refuse him because he was not young and handsome.

In a state of shock, Mary stammered out her willingness to obey his commands, excused herself, and fled to her room, where she wept for two hours until ordered to come down to supper. But she was trapped.

I had nobody to advise with; every one of the family had persuaded themselves that this would be an advantageous match for me – no one considered the sentiments of my heart; to be settled in the world, and ease my friends of an expense and care, they urged that it was my duty to submit, and that I ought to sacrifice everything to that one point.

Her one hope was that her parents would support her, but instead they were delighted at so rich a catch as Mr Pendarves. To Mary, however, he was repellent. In the first place, he was sixty years old, forty-three years older than herself.

As to his person he was excessively fat, of a brown complexion, negligent in his dress, and took a vast quantity of snuff, which gave him a dirty look: his eyes were black, small, lively and sensible; he had an honest countenance, but altogether a person rather disgusting than engaging. He was good-natured and friendly, but so strong a 'party man' [i.e., a Tory], that he made himself many enemies . . . He was very sober for two years after we married, but then he fell in with a set of old acquaintance, a society famed for excess in wine, and to his ruin and my misery was hardly ever sober. This course of life soured his temper, which was naturally good, and the days he did not drink were spent in a gloomy sullen way, which was infinitely worse to me than his drinking; for I did not know how to please or entertain him, and yet no one ever heard him say a snappish or cross thing to me.

In this character sketch, Mary does her best to be fair to poor Mr Pendarves, but, as we shall see, she does not ask herself to what extent her dislike of him might have been responsible for his moroseness and his drinking.

So married they were 'with great pomp' early in 1717, after which they progressed slowly back to the family seat at Roscrow in Cornwall, accompanied by the blessings of Mary's aunt Lady Stanley, 'wishing you and Mr Pendarves all happiness together, riches, honour and length of days' – as if this was all that was needed for happiness. On arrival at Roscrow, Mary found to her horror that it was a gloomy and dilapidated old structure, which had not been lived in for thirty years. At this point, for the first time, she collapsed in a fit of weeping. However, Mr Pendarves, whom even Mary admitted was a kindly and affectionate old gentleman, gave her a free hand in restoring the house, which cheered her up for a time.

Whether Mr Pendarves attempted sexual relations with her and whether she submitted with frigidity and loathing or openly rebuffed him is naturally not stated in her autobiography. But inevitably he was jealous of his pretty young wife, who was pursued by a succession of hopeful men. There was Mr Pendarves' nephew Mr Basset of

Tehidy, a man of gallantry, married to a very dull wife, whose attentions to Mary caused poor Mr Pendarves to sulk. There was a dear young friend of Mr Pendarves who left his wife and stayed in the house for months on end. He finally avowed his love for Mary, was rebuffed, and threatened suicide. He was got rid of by the simple expedient of telling him that the Pendarves were moving back to London.

Soon afterwards Mr Pendarves, worried by debts and also, one may suspect, by his failure to win the affection of his wife, took to alcohol in order to drown his pain. His drinking bouts were only interrupted by violent attacks of gout, when he was confined to bed. 'As soon as he was able to go abroad, he returned to his society, never came home sober, and has frequently been led between two servants to bed at six and seven o'clock in the morning. Unhappy cruel state! How many tears have I shed ...' One may suspect that for Mr Pendarves, this may have been one solution to the torment of sleeping in the same bed as an attractive young woman for whom he had great affection, but who found him physically revolting.

Meanwhile, Mary was besieged by suitors. There was the Earl of Clare (married to Mary's aunt) who once wrote her a letter when Pendarves was laid up with gout, in which he deplored 'my unhappy situation in being nurse to an old man and declared most passionately his admiration for me'. Another admirer was the young Herminius, Lord Baltimore, a handsome and well-bred young man, whom Mary clearly found most attractive. But Mary remained faithful to her husband for seven years until finally in 1726 she woke up one morning to find herself lying beside a dead man with a blackened face. The initial shock was great, but the new state of widowhood was, as she frankly admitted, 'not unwelcome', although Mr Pendarves had not signed his will, so that she was not the great heiress she had anticipated. Moreover, honesty forced her to admit that Mr Pendarves had been 'very obliging in his behaviour to me, and I have often reproached myself bitterly for my ingratitude (if it can be so called) in not loving a man who had so true an affection for me'.

Three years after the death of Mr Pendarves, Lord Baltimore met her one Saturday at the opera and blurted out that he 'had been in love with me for five years'. She put him off for the moment, and they parted in order to think things over. Since she was a widow, and he had already succeeded to his estate, they had no one to please but themselves. Two days later he came to visit her and declared that he was 'determined never to marry unless he was well assured of the affection of the person he married. My reply was "can you have stronger proof (if the person is at her own disposal) than her consenting to marry you?" He replied that was not sufficient. I said he was unreasonable, upon which he started up and said, "I find, Madam, this is a point in which we shall never agree",' and promptly left, never to return. Not so long afterwards, he married the daughter of the enormously wealthy Sir Theodore Janssen, upon the news of which Mary fell very ill indeed. She turned violently against the whole male sex, declaring her distaste for men as a species: 'everyday my dislike strengthens; some few I will except, but very few, they have so despicable an opinion of women and treat them by their words and actions so ungenerously and inhumanly.'

On the other hand, there are two interpretations which can be put on this last episode. The first is that Lord Baltimore meant what he said, that he fully believed in the ideal of positive prior affection before marriage, and demanded a reciprocal statement from Mary of affection (and perhaps consent to sleep together), which she refused to give because she preferred flirtation to commitment, being basically frigid. The other is that in the forty-eight hours since his first declaration, he had had second thoughts, had decided after all to look for a richer wife, and had used the demand for a declaration of love, and maybe consent to fornication, as an excuse to get out of a difficult situation.

The whole story of Mary Granville illustrates the see-saw battle between family wishes and personal choice, between interest, money and affection, that was waged in the hearts and minds of the English elite in the early eighteenth century. Mary's marriage to Mr Pendarves was a classic case of an arranged marriage purely for money and influence. Mr Twyford's love for Mary and his paralysis and death, apparently caused by his parents' refusal to allow him to marry, illustrate the opposite pole of pure romantic love. The constant attempts on her virtue made by married relatives and acquaintances show the way the arranged marriage positively encouraged adulterous attempts on the chastity of married women, while Mary's refusal of her suitors, and her subsequent attitude to men may well have been caused by frigidity induced by cohabitation with the odious Mr Pendarves. The case of Lord Baltimore shows a young man torn between love and money, unable to make up his mind as to which came first, but apparently opting in the end for money, possibly because he could not obtain reciprocal affection.

Among the high aristocracy as late as the 1780s, some girls still allowed themselves to be guided by their parents into more or less blind marriages. There were, however, two critical differences from the old-style arranged marriage. In the first place the parental motive, at least ostensibly, was the future happiness of the daughter, not the best financial or political interests of the family at large. Secondly, the means employed to obtain compliance was love and not authority. The new affectionate parent–child relations were now used with great effect, especially by mothers, to get their daughters to do what they wanted. Thus, when in the 1780s Harriet Spencer, daughter of Lord Spencer, became engaged to Lord Duncannon, the son and heir of the Earl of Bessborough, she told a friend that 'I had not the least guess about it till the day papa told me ... I wish I could have known him a little better first, but my dear papa and mama say that it will make them the happiest of creatures, and what would I not do to see them happy?' Everything she could learn about the young man was in his favour, so that she concluded that 'I have a better chance of being reasonably happy with him than with most people I know.' On these terms she accepted him, and indeed the marriage turned out reasonably well.

It is clear that the eighteenth-century aristocracy and squirarchy were hopelessly torn in their sense of priorities and values in matrimonial projects and that no single or simple pattern will serve to explain the complex reality. Choices varied from person to person; the pressures varied from parent to parent. The only certain facts which emerge are that the least free were the heirs and heiresses to great fortunes, unless their parents were dead and they had obtained full financial control; that even if they were free, young people might well opt for money rather than love or lust; that the loveless marriage was now generally regarded as a direct encouragement to adultery by both parties; that marriage at the free choice of bride and groom and based on solid emotional attachment was increasingly common by the end of the century; and that some noble and gentry parents were using the ties of affection that now bound their children to them in order to direct their choice. One can make the theoretical assumption that it is only in circles where the cult of individualism and privacy has taken hold that well tested affection is either generally sought after by young people, or is necessarily a better way of handling a decision of critical importance, which is always largely a gamble, however and by whom it is decided. Another theoretical assumption is that freedom of choice can most easily be conceded by parents in closely integrated groups with internalized norms, where there is little chance that the children will come into close contact with members of a lower social class; where the property at stake in the marriage is not too great; where the risk of seduction by penniless adventurers is small; and where the age of marriage is postponed at least to the mid-twenties, when a sensible choice is more likely to be made than in the late teens.

Finally the society must have devised means by which young people can mix freely and test out each other's character and temperament, so as to be in a position to make a rational choice based on settled affection. This was not permitted before the end of the seventeenth century, when at last there developed a series of institutions by which the courting process could go on among the elite. The balls, card parties and assemblies in the country town, particularly at the two assizes or at the major annual fairs or horse-racing events, were important mechanisms for the new style of local matchmaking. The building of assembly rooms in town after town during the eighteenth century is evidence of its importance. On the national level, the development of the London season, lasting from early in the New Year to June, and the subsequent season at a major watering place like Bath, provided the necessary facilities for the development of acquaintances across county boundaries. By the middle of the eighteenth century, there were both a series of county marriage markets, centred on the facilities of the county towns, and a national marriage market, centred on London and Bath. After Lord Hardwicke's Marriage Act came into force in 1754, parents could allow a child to associate with others rather more freely, since they were at least certain that he or she could no longer contract a secret but binding engagement with an unsuitable person, and could only make a clandestine marriage by travelling all the way to Scotland.

This development of a national marriage market in London and Bath greatly widened the pool of potentially satisfactory spouses, from the parental point of view. So long as the gentry were confined to marrying within their own class and within their own county, the number of suitable spouses was so restricted that direct parental choice of a specific individual made good sense. The national marriage market of the eighteenth century greatly reduced the need to be so specific, for there were now a larger number of potential spouses who would meet the necessary financial and social qualifications. With internalized parental norms and the availability of a wide range of socially acceptable potential mates, children could safely be allowed greater freedom of access to members of the other sex, and greater freedom of choice, without threatening the long-term interests of the family in the making of a 'suitable' marriage.

Despite this evidence of a very ambiguous situation, which varied widely from family to family and generation to generation, foreign visitors in the mid- and late eighteenth century were unanimous in their conviction that the English enjoyed greater freedom of choice of a marriage partner and greater companionship in marriage than was the case on the Continent. As early as 1741 Baron de Pollnitz was struck by the greater liberty English women enjoyed than those in his own country, and forty-seven years later the Duc de la Roche-foucauld had the same reactions: 'the English have much more opportunity of getting to know each other before marriage, for young folk are in society from an early age; they go with their parents everywhere. Young girls mix with the company and talk and enjoy themselves with as much freedom as if they were married.' The explanation for this practice of free and lengthy courtship he ascribed directly to the rise of the companionate marriage, which he also thought was peculiar to England, alleging that 'three marriages out of four are based on affection', and that subsequent relations remained far closer than in France.

I am not sure whether the obligation to live constantly with one's wife does not make it necessary to marry at a later age, but I am inclined to think so. To have a wife who is not agreeable to you must, in England, make life a misery. Accordingly the Englishman makes more effort to get to know his bride before marriage; she has a similar desire, and I suppose it is on this account that marriage before the age of twenty-five or twenty-eight is rare.

There is statistical evidence to show that the median age of first marriage among the elite had risen sharply by the eighteenth century, to about twenty-four for women and twenty-eight to twenty-nine for men (Graph 3, p. 43). By that age, young people know better what they are about, their identity is more firmly established, their experience of the world is larger, and their judgement more mature. Companionship *plus* economic security were the prime goals of mar-

GRAPH 9: Proportion of Sons of Peers Who Married Heiresses

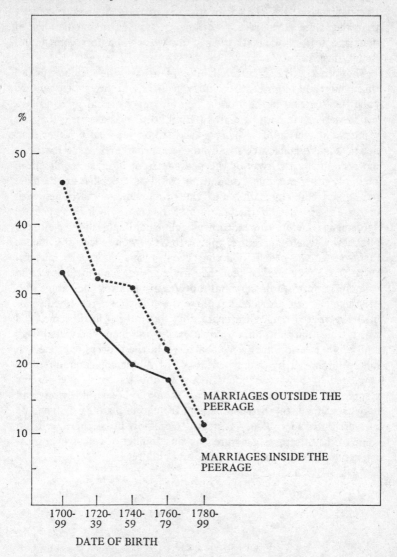

%

50

40

30

20

10

MARRIAGES OUTSIDE THE
PEERAGE

MARRIAGES INSIDE THE
PEERAGE

1700-   1720-   1740-   1760-   1780-
99   39   59   79   99

DATE OF BIRTH

riage; young people of the English elite were, therefore, more likely to make satisfactory choices of mate in the late eighteenth century than they were in the seventeenth century, when the median age of marriage was only about twenty to twenty-one for women and twenty-five for men.

The other piece of statistical evidence is the prolonged fall throughout the eighteenth century from about forty per cent to about ten per cent in the proportion of all marriages of sons of peers which were made with heiresses (Graph 9). If it is assumed that the principal attraction of an heiress tends to be her wealth rather than her personal qualities, this fall indicates a marked shift in marriage motives among the sons of the peerage from interest to affection. The only other possible explanation could be a decline in the male infant and child mortality. But the proportion of marriages with heiresses was halved in the first half of the century, which by general agreement is before this mortality decline could possibly have taken effect. This would, therefore, appear to be a strong piece of evidence in favour of the proposition that even at this exalted social level there was a very marked tendency for a preference shift away from economic and towards personal motives in dictating the choice of a marriage partner, provided of course that the choice remained within the restricted range of acceptability by status. All the same, this was a transition that did not come easily, and many individual lives and family relationships were shattered in the process. No one can fail to be moved by that masterpiece of Augustan understatement employed by Edward Gibbon in his autobiography to register his response when he was obliged by his family to break off the one and only attachment to a woman he ever formed in his life: 'I sighed as a lover; I obeyed as a son.' Beneath the stately prose there wells up some of the bitterness generated by this conflict of values over mating arrangements between parents and children.

1. Elopement from boarding-
   school, 1798.

2. Flight to Gretna Green,
   pursued by the father. By T.
   Rowlandson, 1785.

3. A wedding at Gretna Green.
   By T. Rowlandson, 1811.

4. The bigamist, 1787.

5. Death takes a wife and child: tomb of Lady Margaret Leigh and her infant, both dead in childbirth. Fulham, Middlesex, *c.* 1605.

6. The swaddled child. Infant of Sir John St John Lydiard Tregoze, Wiltshire, *c.* 1634.

7. The stock heraldic figure:
   Sir Richard Knightley.
   Fawsley, Northamptonshire,
   c. 1535.

8. Realistic portraiture:
   Elizabeth, wife of Sir Moyle
   Finch. Eastwell, Kent (now in
   the Victoria and Albert
   Museum), 1623–8.

9. The formalities of courtship, 1785.

10. Marital discord. By John Collett, 1782.

11. The middle-class companionate family, *c*. 1780.

12. Sexual segregation after dinner: the men, 1814.

13. Sexual segregation after dinner: the women, 1814.

14. The accomplished wife and the bored husband, 1789.

WILL WANDER'S WALK,
With both his Companions
And all of their Talk.

Says Will to his Sister
My Dog here proposes,
To take a nice Walk
And just follow our noses.

London Published by J Aldis, N.ºgº Pavement, Moorfield & August 9, 1806.

15. Children's books for amusement: Will Wander's Walk, 1806.

16. The educated upper-middle-class child: Mrs Hester Thrale and her daughter Queeney. By Sir Joshua Reynolds, 1781.

17. The educated lower-middle-class child: Farmer Giles and his daughter, 1809.

18. The spoiled child. By T. Rowlandson, 1808.

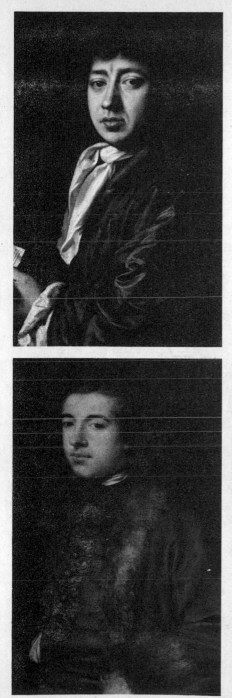

19. Samuel Pepys. By John
    Hayls, 1667.

20. James Boswell. By G.
    Willison, 1765.

21. Margaret Boswell. *c.* 1769.

22. Seductive fashions: the topless style and the cult of maternal breast-feeding, 1796.

23. Venereal disease and its treatment by mercury, 1784.

24. The late eighteenth-century sexual scene: the objects for sale, besides women, include condoms, birches, pornographic books, pills and surgical instruments for VD, and aphrodisiacs. By T. Rowlandson, 1786.

25. Sexual deviations: flagellation, 1752.

26. Pornography. By T. Rowlandson, c. 1812.

27. A brothel for the upper classes. By T. Rowlandson, 1781.

28. A brothel for the lower classes, 1807.

29. Pre-nuptial pregnancy: a shot-gun wedding, 1778.

30. Pre-nuptial pregnancy: a paternity claim, 1800.

CHAPTER EIGHT

The Companionate Marriage

> 'I know or fancy that there are qualities and *compositions of qualities* (to talk in musical metaphor) which in the course of our lives appear to me in her [Mrs Boswell], that please me more than what I have perceived in any other woman, and which I cannot separate from her identity.'
> (James Boswell in *Boswell: The Ominous Years, 1774–1776*, ed. C. Ryscamp and F. A. Pottle, New York, 1963, p. 290)

1. THE RISE OF THE COMPANIONATE MARRIAGE

The many legal, political and educational changes that took place in the late seventeenth and eighteenth centuries were largely consequences of changes in ideas about the nature of marital relations. The increasing stress laid by the early seventeenth-century preachers on the need for companionship in marriage in the long run tended to undercut their own arguments in favour of the maintenance of strict wifely subjection and obedience. Once it was doubted that affection could and would naturally develop after marriage, decision-making power had to be transferred to the future spouses themselves, and more and more of them in the eighteenth century began to put the prospects of emotional satisfaction before the ambition for increased income or status. This in turn also had its effect in equalizing relationships between husband and wife.

In 1727, Daniel Defoe complained that still in his own time 'the money and the maidenhead is the subject of our meditations', the result being 'how much marriage, how little friendship'. But he believed that 'matrimony without love is the cart before the horse'. He recognized that this demand for love as the basis of marriage involved a fundamental change in power relations within the family. 'I don't take the state of matrimony to be designed ... that the wife is to be used as an upper servant in the house ... Love knows no superior or inferior, no imperious command on the one hand, no reluctant subjection on the other.' He made the point that 'persons of a lower station are, generally speaking, much more happy in their marriages than Princes and persons of distinction. So I take much of it, if not all, to consist in the advantage they have to choose and refuse.' Defoe and others saw very clearly how a shift of control of marital choice from parents to children would have important effects upon marital relations thereafter.

It is significant of changing attitudes that one of the principal themes of George Farquhar's very successful play *The Beaux' Strata-gem*, first produced in 1707, is that of the miseries of an unhappy marriage, in which the husband neglects his wife and spends all his time tippling with male companions. He makes Mrs Sullen give an inimitable description of her intolerable life, buried deep in the countryside with Squire Sullen, who never even speaks to her. 'He came home this morning at his usual hour of four, wakened me out of a sweet dream of something else by tumbling over the tea table, which he broke all to pieces. After his man and he had rolled about the room, like sick passengers in a storm, he comes flounce into bed, dead as a salmon into a fishmonger's basket, his feet cold as ice, his breath hot as a furnace, and his hands and face as greasy as his flannel night cap. O matrimony!' Deprived of friendship, conversa-tion, companionship, sex and sleep by her sottish husband, her suc-cessful formal separation at the end of the play, with the enforced return by Squire Sullen of her marriage portion of £10,000, is clearly regarded as no more than moral justice.

For the English middle and upper classes in the middle of the eighteenth century, Mrs Hester Chapone summed up the prevailing opinion about the ideal relationship between husband and wife: 'I believe that a husband has a divine right to the absolute obedience of his wife in all cases where the first duties do not interfere.' On the other hand, 'I believe it . . . absolutely necessary to conjugal hap-piness that the husband have such an opinion of his wife's under-standing, principles and integrity of heart as would induce him to exalt her to the rank of his *first and dearest friend*.' In 1740 Weten-hall Wilkes published *A Letter of Genteel and Moral Advice to a Young Lady*, which ran to eight editions in the next twenty-six years. In it he further developed the view of the married state as an arena of domestic happiness. 'This state, with the affection suitable to it, is the completest image of heaven we can receive in this life; the greatest pleasures we can enjoy on earth are the freedoms of conversation with a bosom friend ... When two have chosen each other, out of all the species, with a design to be each other's mutual comfort and entertainment, ... all the satisfactions of the one must be doubled because the other partakes in them.' Despite this high-flown and idealistic rhetoric, Wilkes took great care to spell out the limits of what was to be expected. 'The utmost happiness we can hope for in this world is contentment, and if we aim at anything higher, we shall meet with nothing but grief and disappointments.' He advised his readers to seek in a husband such qualities as 'a virtuous disposition, a good understanding, an even temper, an easy fortune, and an agreeable person'. He warned against marriage for money or title, stressed that the key quality was 'the temper', and advised that 'the conversation of a married couple cannot be agreeable for years together without an earnest endeavour to please on both sides'. On the whole, the advice Wilkes offered was prudent and sensible, and except for the fact that he avoids altogether the problem of compatibility of sexual tastes and demands, his book does not differ greatly from a modern marriage manual. Its success was symbolic of the new era in family relationships. In 1762 Dr John Gregory, in an equally popular treatise, wrote that 'I have always considered your sex, not as domestic drudges, or as the slaves of our pleasures, but as our companions and equals.' This was an uncompromising statement of the now conventional ideal of wifely status, the contemporary literary apotheosis of which is to be found in Oliver Goldsmith's *Vicar of Wakefield* of 1776. An early example of this new ideology among the landed elite is the monumental inscription at Yarnton, in Oxfordshire, to Catherine, wife of the Honourable George Mordaunt, who died in 1714. Her husband had inscribed on the slab a statement of his feelings recorded in marble for all time:

> With unavailing tears he mourns her end,
> Losing his double comfort, wife and friend.

Foreign observers had no doubt that by the second half of the eighteenth century there was a clear trend to companionate marriages, particularly in the upper and the lowest levels of society. Sophie von La Roche, who visited London in 1786, regarded it as a well-known fact that 'so many love-marriages are made in England', and was not at all surprised to learn at the lunatic asylum of Bedlam

that most of the young female inmates had been unhinged by
thwarted love. This comment about the poor was supported by
others about the rich. The Duc de La Rochefoucauld noted with surprise in 1784 that:

> Husband and wife are always together and share the same society. It
> is the rarest thing to meet the one without the other. The very richest
> people do not keep more than four or six carriage-horses, since they pay
> all their visits together. It would be more ridiculous to do otherwise in
> England than it would be to go everywhere with your wife in Paris. They
> always give the appearance of perfect harmony, and the wife in particular
> has an air of contentment which always gives me pleasure.

He observed that newly married couples immediately set up house
on their own, often in a different town away from their parents, and
concluded that 'the Englishman would rather have the love of the
woman he loves than the love of his parents'.

More concrete evidence of change is provided by the abandonment in many circles of the formal seventeenth-century modes of
address between husband and wife of 'Sir' and 'Madam', and the
adoption of first names and terms of endearment. When Dorothy
Osborne was writing her love letters to William Temple in the middle
of the seventeenth century, she began by addressing him as 'Sir', and
then later got around the problem by dropping any opening at
all once they were formally engaged. At no time did she address
him as 'William'. In 1707, immediately after his marriage, Richard
Steele addressed his wife as 'Madam', but soon slid into 'Dear
creature', 'My loved creature', 'My dear'. Within a few months, however, he was writing to her as 'Dear Prue'. In 1699 the conservative
John Sprint objected to the practice of women calling their husbands
by their first names, 'as if they esteemed them at no higher rates
than their very servants', since it signified a lack of that deference
and respect he was so anxious to preserve. His female opponent defended the practice as no more than 'the effect of tenderness and
freedom which will banish all the names of haughty distance and servile subjection'. Around 1700 this issue of what to call a husband
was clearly a widely debated issue, the conservatives realizing the
egalitarian and anti-patriarchal implications of a change to the use
of the first name by a wife to a husband.

During this transitional period of the early eighteenth century, the
mode of address can be deceptive and may be a poor index of the

true relationship between man and wife. In 1732 Catherine Banks ended her letters to her husband Joseph with 'I am, dear Mr Banks, your most affectionate C. Banks'. Two years later, however, when her husband was in Bath for his health, we find him writing to his 'dear Kitty' six days a week, and when in the same year she gave birth to a boy, he declared 'I ... hope we three shall make each others' days happier.' The pursuit of personal happiness through domestic intimacy was clearly uppermost in the mind of her husband, despite the continued use on his wife's part of the old formal mode of address. By the end of the century this formality had gone, and in 1797 Thomas Gisborne noted with satisfaction that 'the stiffness, the proud and artificial reserve, which in former ages infected even the intercourse of private life, are happily discarded'. It was, however, to return later.

The hardest evidence for a decline in the near-absolute authority of the husband over the wife among the propertied classes is an admittedly limited series of changes in the power of the former to control the latter's estate and income. The seventeenth century saw a sharp rise in the size of marriage portions paid by the bride's parents to the groom's parents. This rise meant an increase in the economic stakes in marriage, and so enhanced the position of the wife. By her marriage portion she was now making a major economic contribution to her husband's finances. This was because in the eighteenth century the portion was normally invested in land to be settled on the young couple, whereas in earlier centuries it had gone straight into the pocket of the groom's father. Moreover the introduction of the practice of inserting into the marriage contract a clause about pin money now guaranteed the wife an independent fixed income at her exclusive disposal. The property of widows and heiresses was also now more carefully safeguarded against seizure and exploitation by the future husband. After 1620 the Court of Chancery intervened to enforce marriage contracts, and over the next fifty years, by judicial interpretation and practice, it virtually succeeded in creating the legal doctrine of the wife's separate estate. For the commercial classes this was a welcome development, since it provided some protection against total loss from bankruptcy proceedings.

It must be emphasized that these improvements in the legal position of married women only affected those restricted social groups whose marriages were accompanied by a legal settlement, and who could, if necessary, afford the cost of launching a suit in the Court of Chancery. Even so, the financial position of some of the highest women in the country was very precarious. Georgiana Duchess of Devonshire could secretly run up huge debts for which her husband would be responsible, but she owned nothing of her own. When she wrote her will in 1792 she had to ask the Duke's permission to bequeath a few trinkets to personal friends to remember her by, since 'everything I have is yours'.

For the vast majority of the population, including all the poor, the limited safeguards offered to wealthy women were unknown. As Blackstone put it bluntly, 'the husband and wife are one, and the husband is that one'. As late as 1869 John Stuart Mill could accurately describe the legal position of most women in England as one of total dependence on their husbands. In terms of property, they could acquire nothing which did not automatically become their husbands'. 'The absorption of all rights, all property, as well as all freedom of action is complete. The two are called "one person in law", for the purpose of inferring that whatever is hers is his.' Similarly, by law the children belonged solely to the husband, and even after his death the widow had no rights over them, unless she was made their guardian in his will. If she should desert him, however severe the provocation, she could take nothing with her, neither her children nor her property. Her husband could, if he chose, compel her to return. Or he could at any time seize any income she might earn, or any means of support given to her by others. Only a legal separation, the cost of which put it beyond the reach of the majority, gave any protection to the deserting or deserted wife, and even then, before a change in the law in 1839, she had no claim upon her children unless her husband wanted to get rid of them. Moreover, in other ways the wife remained in a legally inferior status. A man convicted of murdering his wife would be hanged, but a woman convicted of murdering her husband would by law be burned alive. This barbarous penalty was in practice disappearing in the eighteenth century, but a woman was burned alive at Tyburn for this crime as late as 1725.

Although statistical proof is lacking, one gets a distinct impression that wives married to impossible husbands in the upper classes were increasingly seeking formal separations, accompanied by adequate financial provisions which allowed them to continue to live active and satisfying social lives. Formal separations certainly became more common, and in January 1766 the newspaper gossip alleged – as usual with exaggeration – that seventeen couples in the world of fashion were on the point of breaking up. Paradoxically enough, the rise of separations in the eighteenth century, like the rise of divorces in the twentieth, is an indication of rising emotional expectations from marriage. In periods when expectations are low, frustrations will also be low. Nor were separations always taken too seriously by high society when they did occur. In the 1760s Lady Sarah Lennox reported that 'The Duke and Duchess of Grafton are absolutely parted; he allows her £3,000 a year. She has the girl and the youngest boy with her, and they say that the reason of their parting is only that their tempers don't suit.' The extremely generous terms of the separation, with the mother keeping the girl and the youngest child and so handsome an allowance, led Lady Sarah to think 'they would soon be friends again'.

One revealing indication of the rise of the concept of privacy and the rise of companionate and sexually bonded marriage is the new definition of the old word 'honeymoon'. Previously taken to mean no more than the month after marriage, characterized by goodwill and perhaps sexual passion, it was now re-defined as a period during which the newly married couple were expected to go away together and to be left totally alone in order to explore each other's bodies and minds without outside support or interference. In upper- and middle-class society where so much stress was laid on pre-marital virginity, the bridal night in the sixteenth and seventeenth centuries had been surrounded with ritual, much of it public. The pair were brought to the bedroom in state by the relatives and friends, often accompanied with horse-play and ribald jests, and were only left alone (perhaps for the first time in their lives) once the curtains of the four-poster bed were closed and the last wedding guest and maid had withdrawn. Even then the ritual continued, for it was apparently customary on this occasion for the bride to go to bed in gloves. When in 1708 a protesting girl sent a letter to the correspondence column of *The British Apollo*, she was told that 'since it is the custom and fashion to go into the bridal bed with gloves on, we think it not genteel to go to bed without'. One assumes that the gloves were subsequently removed, to symbolize the loss of virginity. The details of that loss were something about which the pair could often expect to be closely questioned the next morning. The concept of the honeymoon as a period of holiday travel certainly existed by the end of the eighteenth century, but it is far less certain that there was general recognition of the importance of privacy and isolation, which is central to modern ideas about this experience. An early example occurred in the middle of the eighteenth century, when Mr West told Mrs Elizabeth Montagu how William Pitt and his new wife were living privately by themselves at Wickham for a few weeks for 'the free course of those pleasures which for a time at least possess the whole mind, and are most relished when most private'.

In some wealthy and near-wealthy aristocratic circles, however, marriage and its aftermath in the eighteenth century were as much a public affair as they had ever been. In 1756 John Spencer, the wealthy heir to the Spencer barony, married Margaret Georgiana Poyntz, and the groom's mother insisted on the most extravagant display. After the wedding, the party set out from Althorp for London in three six-horse coaches accompanied by two hundred horsemen. So alarming was the cavalcade that villagers on the road assumed that it was a French invasion, and either turned out with pitchforks to fight the enemy, or barricaded themselves in their houses. It is significant, however, that all this publicity was 'quite disagreeable to both the young people'.

All this was a far cry from the very private wedding of Mary Thackeray to Mr Pryme of Cambridge in 1813, followed by a lengthy, solitary honeymoon in hotels in London, Brighton and Worthing. But even then this isolation was unusual, and a chaperone was common. When Elizabeth Robinson married Edward Montagu in 1742, they were accompanied on their honeymoon tour by her sister Sarah, and late eighteenth-century novelists confirm the persistence of this pattern in wealthy circles. Thus Jane Austen in *Mansfield Park* makes Mr and Mrs Rushworth go to Brighton for some weeks after their marriage, the latter being accompanied by her sister Julia, 'each of them exceedingly glad to be with the other at such a time'. The need for supportive female assistance in this time of psychological and physiological crisis shows how strong was the social attraction of each sex for its own company, even in those days of the companionate marriage. It was not until 1846 that an upper-class marriage manual commented, as a relative novelty, that 'the young couple take their journey, as is now the fashion, in a tête-à-tête'.

2. EARLY FEMINIST MOVEMENTS

The companionate marriage demanded a reassessment of power relations between the sexes since it depended on a greater sense of equality and sharing. Consequently, the early feminist movements have a place in this story, even if one concludes in the end that they were largely abortive and without much influence in changing public attitudes.

During the Civil War of the 1640s, women played a very prominent role in the host of radical sects which based themselves on the extreme interpretation of the doctrine of Grace. In these independent churches, women were at last allowed to debate, to vote, to prophesy when moved by the Spirit, and even to preach. Many left the former family church without the consent of their husbands, and some even abandoned their unregenerate spouses and chose new mates who shared their new-found faith. Their opponents saw these developments as a threat to family subordination, claiming that they were demanding sexual equality of rights:

> We will not be wives
> And tie up our lives
> To villanous slavery.

What is more remarkable, however, is the way the breakdown of royal government in 1640, the prolonged political crisis between King and parliament of 1640–42, the Civil Wars of 1642–8, and the emergence of many extremist independent sects and of a genuinely radical political party, stimulated the women of London and elsewhere to unprecedented political activity. On 31 January and 1 and 4 February 1642, women, operating without help from fathers, husbands or other males, took independent political action on the national level as women, for the first time in English history: they petitioned the Houses of Lords and Commons for a change of public policy. They numbered some four hundred or more, and were apparently composed of working women, artisans, shop-girls and labourers, who were suffering severe financial hardship as a result of the decay of trade. When the outraged Duke of Richmond cried 'Away with these women, we were best have a Parliament of women', the petitioners attacked him physically and broke his staff of office.

Another crisis came in April and May 1649 when very severe economic hardship coincided with a political showdown between the army and Parliament and the London-based lower-middle-class radical movement of the Levellers. Once again masses of women assembled at Westminster, complaining of the economic crisis and demanding the release of the Leveller leaders who had been imprisoned. This time the House responded with disdain, telling the women that they were petitioning about matters above their heads, that Parliament had given an answer to their husbands, who legally represented them, and that they should 'go home and look after your own business and meddle with your housewifery'.

By now, however, the women were not satisfied with these patronizing replies and were making statements which revealed the development of a wholly new level of feminine consciousness. 'The lusty lasses of the Levelling party' were now claiming equal participation with men in the political process, and were backing up their claims with petitions signed, so they said, by up to ten thousand women. In 1642 the petitioners had humbly emphasized that women were not 'seeking to equal ourselves with men, either in authority or wisdom', but merely 'following the example of the men which have gone ... before us'; moreover, they frankly admitted that their intervention 'may be thought strange and unbeseeming our sex.' By 1649, however, they were rejecting the idea that they were represented by their husbands: 'we are no whit satisfied with the answer you gave unto our husbands'. They coolly faced a barrage of criticism that they were claiming to 'wear the breeches', and that 'it can never be a good world when women meddle in state's matters ... their husbands are to blame, that they have no fitter employment for them'. In reply the women quoted the example of Esther from the Bible and even rewrote history to argue that 'by the British women the land was delivered from the tyranny of the Danes ... and the overthrow of episcopal tyranny in Scotland was first begun by the women of that nation'. They claimed an equal share with men in the right ordering of the Church 'because in the free enjoying of Christ in his own laws, and a flourishing estate in the Church ... consisteth the happiness of women as well as men'. This principle they then extended to the state: 'we have an equal share and interest with men in the Commonwealth', a claim which logically led to a demand for female voting rights. But 1649 was the apogee of this movement towards women's political liberation, and it is very noticeable that even the Leveller leaders always excluded women from their proposals for a greatly enlarged suffrage. This feminine agitation at a time of temporary breakdown of law and order should, therefore, best be seen as a symptom rather than as a cause. The episode is significant as the first emergence on a mass level of feminist ideas among an artisan urban population, but it was a movement without a future.

New claims concerning the status and rights of women were set in motion by the repudiation of monarchical patriarchy in the state in 1688, and were publicized by a handful of zealous feminists at the end of the seventeenth century. Most notable among them were Hannah Woolley, Aphra Behn, Mary Astell and Lady Chudleigh.

Few were as savage as the last, in her poem of 1703 addressed 'To the Ladies':

> Wife and servant are the same,
> But only differ in the name
>
> . . . .
>
> When she the word 'obey' has said,
> And man by law supreme has made,
>
> . . . .
>
> Fierce as an Eastern Prince he grows
> And all his innate rigor shows.
>
> . . . .
>
> Then shun, oh shun that wretched state
> And all the fawning flatterers hate.
> Value yourselves and men despise:
> You must be proud if you'll be wise.

The rise of the blue-stockings a century later as leaders of salons which included the most distinguished intellects and wits of London is proof of how at any rate some women were now forcing themselves upon male society and holding their own there. At the same time, inspired first by the American and then by the French Revolution, there emerged a new wave of feminists far more radical in their demands, their personal behaviour and their religious attitudes than their predecessors had been a century earlier. The most prominent among them was Mary Wollstonecraft, who probably did the cause of women's rights positive harm, for her passionate claim to sexual equality, together with her sympathy for the French Revolution and her irregular personal life, merely alienated the support of all but the most tolerant of men. It was this combination of radicalism in both national and sexual politics that drove Horace Walpole to describe her as 'that hyena in petticoats'.

It is hard to see that any of these feminist movements of the seventeenth and late eighteenth centuries had much effect in changing attitudes towards relations between the sexes. Consciousness of the problem of sexual equality was certainly aroused by them, but the fears engendered in men by these indignant women may have inhibited change rather than speeded it up.

3. THE EDUCATION OF WOMEN

In view of the greater degree of companionship in marriage that was developing in the eighteenth century, it is not surprising that considerable, and in the long run successful, efforts were made to improve the quality and quantity of female education among the upper classes.

When serious pressure for a better education for women began in about 1675, it was led by a group of middle-class women, with a little male help from John Locke, William Law and Jonathan Swift addressing the gentry and from John Dunton and Daniel Defoe addressing the bourgeoisie. Mrs Woolley, who had herself been the mistress of a school, a governess, and the wife of a free-school usher, expressed her feelings on this subject in a bitter pamphlet in 1675: 'Vain man is apt to think we were merely intended for the world's propagation, and to keep its human inhabitants sweet and clean, but, by their leaves, had we the same literature, he would find our brains as fruitful as our bodies ... Most in this depraved age think a woman learned enough if she can distinguish her husband's bed from another's.' In 1706 Mary Astell put forward the argument that men were destroying the possibility of marital companionship by depriving girls of a good education. 'How can a man respect his wife when he has a contemptible opinion of her and her sex ... so that folly and a woman are equivalent terms with him?' These women were no wild-eyed political or moral radicals, but devout Christians of impeccable virtue, and loyal subscribers to the standard doctrines about the naturally subordinate role of wives. All they wanted to see was their sex better prepared to be companions with their husbands.

One of the few late seventeenth-century male advocates of a more academic education for women was John Locke, who geared his plan not to companionate marriage but to improving the capacity of women to educate their children for the first eight or ten years. He therefore wanted them to be able to 'read English perfectly, to understand ordinary Latin and arithmetic, with some general knowledge of chronology and history'. But in upper-class households, the education was often left to governesses and tutors, and even Locke was forced to admit that there was 'an apprehension that should daughters be perceived to understand any learned language or be conversant in books, they might be in danger of not finding husbands, so few men, as do, relishing these accomplishments in a lady'.

Naturally enough, most men who publicly advocated a better education for women preferred Mrs Astell's argument that it would be to the benefit of husbands. 'I would have men take women for companions, and educate them to be fit for it,' said Defoe. He foresaw a millennium of domestic bliss that would result from improved female education. 'A woman well bred and taught, furnished with the additional accomplishments of knowledge and behaviour, is a creature without comparison ... She is all softness and sweetness, peace, love, wit and delight. She is in every way suitable to the sublimest wish, and the man that had such a one to his portion has nothing to do but to rejoice in her and be thankful.'

It is very doubtful whether this barrage of propaganda had much effect on improving female education before the middle of the eighteenth century, even though it was based on the self-interest of husbands. Male education had been shifting from the intensely scholarly classical education of the late sixteenth century to the shallower and more aesthetic training in the seventeenth century of the 'virtuoso', a dabbler in many arts and sciences. Similarly, the standard female education among the aristocratic elite had also become more purely ornamental. In the 1670s Anne Barrett-Lennard, who came from a very wealthy noble family, was regarded as very well bred. She had been taught singing by the famous Signor Morelli, and she could speak and read French and Italian. Her cousin Roger North considered her a highly educated woman, even though she apparently knew nothing of the classics, history, mathematics or the sciences. What he admired was her 'exceeding obliging temper' and 'a more than ordinary wit and fluency of discourse'.

Boarding-schools for girls had been fairly common in the seventeenth century, specializing in training in the social graces which it was thought would enable women both to attract husbands and to occupy their leisure hours once they were married. At a school run by a Mr Playford at Islington, 'the young gentlewomen may be instructed in all manner of curious work, as also reading, writing, music, dancing and the French language'. The 'curious work', which tended to bulk so large in the curriculum in the late seventeenth and early eighteenth centuries, consisted of embroidery and needlework, paper-cutting, wax-work, japanning, painting on glass, patchwork, shell-work, mosswork, feather-work, and similar time-consuming trivia, while the arts of housekeeping and polite conversation also figured prominently. It was a busy education, but not an intellectual one, being rather concerned with 'everything that was genteel and fashionable', and designed to provide time-consuming occupations for women of infinite leisure.

Like the private schools and academies for boys, which were growing rapidly in number throughout the eighteenth century, boarding-schools for girls also increased, so much so that it was alleged that in 1759 around London '2 or 3 houses might be seen in almost every village with the inscription "Young Ladies Boarded and Educated"' written in gold letters on a blue signboard. But the education these little schools provided in the early eighteenth century was no more intellectual than that of the seventeenth century. It was still primarily concerned with instruction in the social graces and such lady-like pastimes as embroidery and needlework.

Writing in the 1820s, Lady Louisa Stuart thought that in the first decades of the eighteenth century, 'the education of women had then reached its lowest ebb, and if not coquettes or gossips or diligent card-players, their best praise was to be diligent housewives'. The old school of seventeenth-century gentlewomen had been brought up to believe that they should occupy all their leisure time with needlework. The new generation of the early eighteenth century were still taught some of these skills, but tended to abandon them once they were out of school. They were as ignorant as their grandmothers, but now devoted themselves to parties, visits, cards, and the theatre – pursuits that characterized a far more leisure-oriented and pleasure-loving society. In 1714 an angry woman wrote bitterly about the life-style of her young nieces. 'Those hours which in this age are thrown away in dress, plays, visits and the like, were employed in my time in writing out recipes or working beds, chairs and hangings for the family. For my part I have plied my needle these fifty years, and by my good will would never have it out of my hand.

It grieves my heart to see a couple of proud idle flirts sipping their tea for a whole afternoon in a room hung around with the industry of their great-grandmother.' She was deploring the decline of the Puritan ethic of useful work among gentlewomen in the early eighteenth century, but had no vision of how their endless leisure hours could be put to more rewarding use.

One reason for the persistence of deportment in the boarding-school curriculum was that some of these establishments were now filling up with the daughters of the prosperous London bourgeoisie and professional men, and what these parents were seeking in return for their money was precisely training in the manners, graces and skills of a lady. By 1775 it was alleged that some of these schools now catered for the daughter of 'the blacksmith, the ale-house keeper, the shoemaker etc, who from the moment she enters these walls becomes a young lady'. Satires like D'Urfey's *Love for Money, or the Boarding School* of 1691 were quite incapable of stopping the trend, and indeed Defoe's plans in some ways tended in precisely this direction.

There is good reason to think that slowly over the eighteenth century their recommendations took effect, and the success of *The Tatler* and *The Spectator* in the first decade of the eighteenth century proves that there was a market, female as well as male, for semi-serious periodical literature on subjects of current interest. By 1770 the feminine reading market was now so large that there appeared the first successful women's periodical, *The Ladies' Magazine, or Entertaining Companion for the Fair Sex*, while the sales and circulation of novels, written mostly for and often by women, continued to soar. 'All our ladies read now, which is a great extension,' commented Dr Johnson in 1778. As a result, he believed that 'the ladies of the present age ... were more faithful to their husbands, and more virtuous in every respect than in former times, because their understandings were better cultivated'.

Contemporaries were well aware that things had improved. In 1753 Lady Mary Wortley Montagu contrasted favourably the current educational advantages of her grandchildren with those available in her own day. One of the best late eighteenth-century schools for girls was that run by the Misses Lee at Bath. Sarah Butt, the daughter of a wealthy naval doctor, was sent to the school in 1798 at the age of fifteen. It was a big school with fifty-two boarders and over twenty day-girls, a permanent staff of five and other specialist teachers. The curriculum covered the traditional areas of feminine deportment, namely music, dancing, drawing and needlework. But equal stress was laid on the more academic aspects of the curriculum, which included writing and grammar, arithmetic, geography and French. So seriously was French taken that it was the only language which was allowed to be spoken during working hours. This was because 'to speak French is necessary in order to appear genteel'.

By the end of the eighteenth century a consensus was emerging about the ideal education for women from the landed classes and from the higher ranks of the bourgeoisie. She was neither the frivolous, party-going, neglectful mother and possibly adulterous wife of the aristocracy, nor the middle-class intellectual blue-stocking who challenged and threatened men on their own ground of the classics. She was a well-informed and motivated woman with the educational training and the internalized desire to devote her life partly to pleasing her husband and providing him with friendship and intelligent companionship, partly to the efficient supervision of servants and domestic arrangements; and partly to educating her children in ways appropriate for their future. The girls stayed under her care for a prolonged period, so that she was well placed to mould them into her own useful but subordinate sex-role; the boys stayed until the age of seven, when they passed under masculine control of tutors and schoolmasters. The education of women now covered a broad sweep of subjects, including history, geography, literature and current affairs, and some women were now boasting, with reason, of the positive superiority of their education over the narrow classical linguistic training of their brothers. In 1790 *The Ladies Monthly Magazine* claimed that 'many women have received a much better education than Shakespeare enjoyed'. 'Boys at grammar school,' remarked Mrs Eliza Fox, 'are taught Latin and Greek, despise the simpler paths of learning, and are generally ignorant of really useful matters of fact, about which a girl is much better informed.' The change in women's consciousness from a humiliating sense of their educational inferiority in 1700 to a proud claim to educational superiority in 1810 is little short of revolutionary. Men also admitted the change, and in 1791 *The Gentleman's Magazine* could observe that 'at present . . . the fair sex has asserted its rank, and challenged that natural equality of intellect which nothing but the influence of human institutions could have concealed for a moment'. The standard male attitude towards women's intellectual capacities had also been significantly modified over the previous half century.

It seems likely that this broader education of women must have played its part in leading to demands for greater freedom of choice in mate-selection and a greater share in family decision-making. It certainly resulted in a greater capacity to participate in the life and problems of the husband, and it probably also resulted in a more relaxed attitude toward sexuality within marriage, and a greater desire to restrict births. On the other hand, it presupposed a growing number of women wholly withdrawn from productive work and with a great deal of enforced leisure on their hands. There is no doubt whatever that large numbers of bourgeois and even lower-middle-class wives were now being educated like their social superiors for a life of leisure, and were being withdrawn from useful economic employment in their husbands' businesses. As Dr Gregory explained in 1762, 'the intention of your being taught needlework, knitting and such like is not on account of the intrinsic value of all you can do with your hands, which is trifling, but to enable you ... to fill up, in a tolerably agreeable way, some of the many solitary hours you must necessarily pass at home'.

The improved education of upper- and middle-class women during the eighteenth century transformed English culture, stimulating not only the novel, but also the provincial theatre and the circulating library. It greatly increased the companionship element in marriage, now that wives were as well read as their husbands in all fields except the classics. But it carried a cost in increased female idleness and withdrawal from the world of work. This may not have mattered too much to happily married women, but to the growing number of life-long spinsters, it was a catastrophe.

4. CASE HISTORIES

The study of intimate domestic relations involves probing into an area of the human psyche where it is extremely difficult, and sometimes impossible, to distinguish reality from image, fact from fiction. This is particularly the case when, as is usual, there has survived only a one-sided record of the relationship, sometimes written down immediately in a diary or in letters, and sometimes reconstructed later in an autobiography. Even if the facts are accurately reported, human feelings are so changeable and evanescent that interpretation of them is a most hazardous exercise.

Take, for example, the bare facts – which are all we know – of the story of the two marriages of Captain Yeo in the mid-eighteenth century. Most of the period of his first marriage was spent at sea, where he reached the rank of captain in command of a ship. In the home, on the rare occasions he was there, he was 'a bashaw, whose single nod of disapprobation struck terror into the whole family'. And yet when he heard that his wife was dangerously ill at Plymouth, he steered his ship immediately for harbour, in defiance of Admiralty orders. He arrived at Plymouth just too late, for his wife was dead and her funeral had taken place a few hours earlier. He promptly indulged in the romantic gesture of having the coffin dug up again and opened so that he could take one last look at the face of his dead wife. For the serious breach of naval discipline by directing his ship to Plymouth without permission, Captain Yeo was punished by having to wait for nine years before again being given a command at sea.

So far, the story appears to be one of remarkable marital devotion, exercised at the cost of the ruin of a professional career. A mere nine weeks later, however, he married again, with 'a giggling girl of nineteen' who bore him five more children. It is an extraordinary story, and it is hard to know how to evaluate the motives of the captain and his true feelings for his first wife and the children he had by her. The difficulty is compounded by the fact that we only know the story as it is told by his daughter, who actively disliked her father.

There is good reason to suppose that Oliver Goldsmith's model of the ideal companionate marriage first developed as a norm among the more pious, often nonconformist, middle-class families of the late seventeenth century. The Presbyterian Richard Baxter and his wife married one another, not with a view to worldly advancement, but for their personal qualities. When his wife died in 1681, Baxter wrote her biography, in which he departed wholly from the traditional patriarchal attitude to women of early seventeenth-century society and of most of his contemporaries. He freely admitted that in practical matters, 'her apprehension ... was so much quicker and more discerning than mine ... I am not ashamed to have been much ruled by her prudent love in many things'. He even confessed that she told him – rightly – that he wrote too much, too superficially. He was also unusual in giving her free control of the disposal of her own fortune. When it was all over and she was dead, he wrote that 'these near nineteen years I know not that we ever had any breach in the point of love, or point of interest'. The Baxters clearly enjoyed a most intimate spiritual, intellectual and emotional relationship.

When the struggling Grub-street writer Richard Steele married in 1707, his affection for his new wife knew no bounds and broke through all the barriers of austere seventeenth-century convention. 'There are not words to express the tenderness I have for you,' he wrote in 1708. Two years later, 'I know no happiness in this life in any degree comparable to the pleasure I have in your person and society.' In 1716, nine years after marriage, he was still telling his wife 'I love you to distraction', including his four children in a paean of praise for the pleasures of domestic felicity. Unfortunately, however, these emotions were not fully shared by his wife, who soon became exasperated by Steele's financial irresponsibility, and the last years before her death in 1718 were full of tension caused by what Steele over-optimistically brushed aside as the 'little heats that have sometimes happened between us'. For all this, however, Steele's frank and open demonstrations and assertions of love over a long period of years are clearly not hypocritical and are in striking contrast to the formal relations that were so carefully maintained in the sixteenth and early seventeenth centuries. What makes them historically important is his influence in moulding eighteenth-century squirarchy attitudes to love and marriage through the pages of *The Tatler*.

An important distinction has to be made between the life-style and familial arrangements of smallholders, shopkeepers, artisans and the labour aristocracy on the one hand, and the masses of the propertyless labouring poor on the other. The former group, anxious to preserve its precarious economic foothold one rung above the poor, were probably more concerned with capital and property accumulation as a motive for marriage than any other group in society except the highest aristocracy. Prevailing affective relations between spouses were symbolized by the customary behaviour of the nineteenth-century French peasant, who gave 'his arm to his wife the day of their marriage for the first and last time'. The small shopkeepers, tradesmen and artisans in the towns were equally dependent on capital to get a start in life, and therefore equally influenced by material as much as affective considerations in marriage. Moreover, this was a social group much at the mercy of economic circumstances, which could very easily go wrong, and as a result plunge the whole family into embittered misery. Financial disaster was extremely common among them in the eighteenth century, the debtors' prison was an ever present threat, and the consequence of imprudent marriage could easily be

> a smoky house, a failing trade
> Six squalling brats and a scolding jade,

as the late eighteenth-century caricaturist James Gillray described *Les Plaisirs de Marriage*.

Some indication of the complexities of the situation is provided by the story of Thomas Wright. A poor Methodist, Thomas Wright's first attempt at courting was when he visited a young woman 'after the family were gone to bed', while his companion wooed the maidservant. It was not a pleasurable experience and years later Wright remembered that 'I was terribly embarrassed to keep up the conversation, she not being a very talkative girl.' She was probably disappointed at Wright's lack of sexual enterprise during the long night for she later became pregnant by another suitor, followed by a forced wedding, unhappy married life, and early death: 'Farewell poor Nancy Hopkinson.' Wright's next, more serious, attempt at courting turned out no better. The girl became pregnant by an apprentice, but her parents refused to let her marry him. The child was born but fortunately died. She later married and had six children, but cuckolded her husband, who therefore left her, went off to London and bigamously married another wife, which was easy enough to do in the eighteenth century. Despite overtures from two girls and one widow, Wright finally fell in love with an eleven-year-old, Miss Birkhead. He waited several years for her to grow up, although at some point he was also courting another girl. But in 1766, when she was still only nineteen, he proposed to Miss Birkhead and was accepted. Since her parents were opposed to the marriage because of Wright's lack of financial prospects, the pair ran away to Scotland and were married in an inn by a minister for a fee of two guineas.

The marriage turned out badly. His wife's parents never forgave him for the elopement, particularly since they found themselves obliged to lend him £100, interest free, to buy a lease of a small farm. But they succeeded, according to Wright, in alienating his wife's affection for him, while to add to his matrimonial troubles she took to drink, so much so that at one stage a gallon of rum a week was being consumed in the house. In 1777, eleven years after he married her, she died of galloping consumption, having given birth to seven children, three of whom died young.

After a lot of trouble with two thievish and drunken housekeepers who cost him some £50, Wright finally realized that he had no option but to remarry. The motives which guided his choice were illuminating:

Some people advised me to marry an old woman that would have no more children, and talked in such a manner as if they supposed that I might accommodate my fancy and affection to any old creature, with as much ease as I might choose a joint of meat to get my dinner upon. These people seemed to think, that if a person has been married once, and got some children, he must have lost all the finer feelings of the human heart; or, at least, that he could be justified by no other motives to a future marriage, than those mean and sordid ones, interest and convenience ... I therefore chose to take a young woman whom I could love, and with whom I could be happy, though attended with almost a certainty of being encumbered with more children, rather than take an old woman, to avoid that inconvenience, whom I could not love, and with whom I could not be happy.

So in 1781 after four years of widowhood and at the age of forty-five, he married the fifteen-and-a-half-year-old daughter of a neighbouring farmer, who 'had got a tolerable education, had very good hands, was very ingenious, solid and sensible'. The growing family, and the total hostility of the parents of his first wife, helped to drive him into deeper financial difficulties than ever, but he claimed that he judged them worth it. As Wright tells the story, the desire for love and affection were uppermost in his mind in both his marriages, even if the first disappointed his expectations, and the second added to his financial troubles.

The picture of married life among the lower-middle classes as presented in this randomly preserved record is a reasonably consistent one, in which economic calculation played an important part, but in which much weight was given to the often thwarted expectation of domestic felicity. This is a view supported by George Crabbe, the poet. He thought that although romantic love was almost unknown among the rural smallholder, companionship was common enough. He approvingly described a couple

> Blessed in each other, but to no excess,
> Health, quiet, comfort form'd their happiness.
> Love, all made up of torture and delight
> Was but mere madness in this couple's sight.

The same he thought was true of the more substantial tenant and freehold farmers.

> Our farmers too, what though they fail to prove
> In Hymen's bonds the tenderest slaves to love
> . . . .
> Yet, coarsely kind and comfortable gay,
> They heap the board and hail the happy day.

The urban tradesmen and artisans and the rural smallholders of the late eighteenth century were thus probably largely unaffected by the new demands of love, generated among their betters by the romantic movement of the age, although they had recognized the need for companionship as well as for economic partnership. As Crabbe pointed out, they therefore avoided some of the inevitable disappointments that accompanied the sharp rise among the upper-middle classes in expectations from the married state. In *Mansfield Park*, Jane Austen makes Mary Crawford, as the spokeswoman for worldly wisdom, declare that 'there is not one in a hundred of either sex who is not taken in when they marry. Look where I will, I see that it is so, and I feel that it *must* be so, when I consider that it is, of all transactions, the one in which people expect most from others and are least honest themselves.' There was undoubtedly a good deal of truth in her diagnosis of the practical results of romantic aspirations upon marriage arrangements. There was a very marked contrast between mid-seventeenth-century patriarchy and late eighteenth-century romanticism, and the result among the upper classes was confusion and a wide diversity of ideal models of behaviour. Lower down the social scale, the contrast and the confusion were far less severe.

It is not hard to find examples of affectionate couples among the upper squirarchy and nobility at any time in history; indeed, it would be surprising if this was not the case. But a purely subjective impression – and it can be no more – is that the proportion of such couples increased in the late seventeenth and eighteenth centuries, especially in the last half of the eighteenth century. But since we are dealing with real life, most cases are full of ambivalence. For example, Elizabeth and Richard Leigh of Lyme addressed each other in the fondest of terms in the 1660s – 'my dearest dear', 'my dear dear', etc., – but they had no compunction whatever twenty years later in putting very great pressure on their daughters to make loveless but financially and socially advantageous marriages.

Another case concerns the Duke of Newcastle and Henrietta Godolphin, whom he married in 1716. Despite the fact that this was a purely arranged marriage for money on the one side – the Duke had heavy debts to be liquidated – and for the social prestige of a dukedom on the other, the subsequent relations between the couple turned out exceptionally well, at any rate for Newcastle. The latter's political business kept him mostly in London and therefore often separated from his wife, but within two years he was writing the most affectionate letters to 'my dearest girl'. In 1759, after forty-four years of childless marriage, the now elderly pair had a serious quarrel, and the Duke wrote to 'Harriot' in near despair. 'Be the same to me as you ever was. For God's sake, my dear, consider the many happy years we have by the mercy of God had together, how much our mutual happiness depends on each other. You know, you must know, how much, how sincerely, I love and esteem you. You must know that if once your affection, your dear warm heart, is altered to me, I shall never have a happy moment afterwards. All other uneasiness and affliction I can get over; from that I never can, and that is *the most solemn truth*.' This was a marriage that began as a mere mercenary arrangement, but turned out to be truly companionate, except that the pair were separated for very long periods, she in the country occupied with music and card-playing, he in London absorbed in political patronage manipulation.

By the late eighteenth century, arranged marriages for money had fallen into disrepute. In 1776 Lady Sarah Lennox commented on an unhappy marriage that 'he had no more business to marry a girl he did not like than she had to accept of a man she was totally indifferent to'. This was a position to which she had arrived by bitter experience, having married at seventeen a man she could cheerfully accept and with whom she got on reasonably well. But there were no children, and her husband, though very fond of her, yet loved his racehorses more. She became dissatisfied and flirtatious, and, after six years of marriage, she eloped with a lover, only to leave him within a year to live in seclusion with her daughter by him.

A final example of the companionate marriage of the eighteenth century is that of Mary Hamilton, who was born in 1756. At the age of seventeen when she first came onto the marriage market, her guardian gave her some sound advice: not to accept the first suitor for fear of never having another and in hopes that 'love is to come afterwards', 'never to enter into engagements without the consent of her parents and friends', but also never to 'take the man her friends desire without consulting her own heart'. Hotly pursued by the Prince of Wales (later George IV), she rejected his amorous advances, but agreed to be his platonic friend and adviser. Finally, at the age of twenty-eight, she fell passionately in love with a suitably rich and virtuous young man, John Dickinson. She told him 'how much I love you', and a year later in 1785, soon after they married, she wrote, 'I love you as much as it is possible for one human creature to love another.' When a daughter was born a year later, she lavished similar affection and attention on 'our dear girl'. It was a most happy and enduring union, and after some fifteen years of married life, in about 1800, John Dickinson wrote to her that 'I have only time to say that I love you dearly – best of women, best of wives and best of friends.' Here was the epitome of the new companionate marriage among the upper classes of the late eighteenth century, exuding a warmth and an emotional commitment that is so very hard to find in the sixteenth and early seventeenth centuries, especially among men. There are fashions in love, as in everything else, and the Dickinsons were undoubtedly influenced in their use of language and in the sentiments they expressed by the rise of the romantic novel.

By way of contrast to these enduringly successful companionate marriages, it is fitting to conclude with one which began well, but eventually turned sour. It concerns Lord William Russell, younger son of the Duke of Bedford. In 1817 he made a socially suitable marriage with Miss Elizabeth Rawdon, with whom he was genuinely much in love. His father the Duke expressed his pleasure that 'you have every prospect of being happy with Miss Rawdon', and six years later, in 1823, Lord William told his wife, 'I love you more than anything in the world.' The evidence suggests that she was quite fond of him but had little respect for him, and there is little doubt that she invested all her emotional capital in her children. At the age of two in 1822, 'the child breakfasts, dines and lives with us as if he were 20 years old, to the horror and amazement of English mothers', and a year later was still sleeping in his parents' room, in his own bed, at any rate when they were travelling. As late as 1829, after twelve years of marriage, Lord William was still telling himself, perhaps to keep up his morale, that 'there is no happiness like that derived from wife and children, it makes one indifferent to all other pleasures'. It was not until 1830 that there was the first sign of marital tension, due to Elizabeth's imperious ways and her single-minded devotion to her children at the expense of her husband. It also seems that she was very anxious to limit the number of her children, and was very discontented in 1828 when she found herself pregnant with a third (surviving) child. Her husband's abject apology suggests that he may have forcibly raped her in his frustration, or failed to withdraw in time. 'I regret the affliction and mortification my fatal sin has brought upon you ... I think and hope I can never again be wicked.' They did indeed have no more children.

In 1835 Elizabeth became increasingly discontented with life in England, and to please her Lord William gave up his career in the army and parliament in order to go to live abroad with her. After all this, it is hardly surprising that soon afterwards, in 1835, he fell head over heels in love with a rich German Jewess, with whom he carried on a liaison without even pretence of concealment. Thereafter the pair in practice went their separate ways, with only fleeting visits home by the father to see his children. By 1846 Lord William was dead, as dead as his marriage had been for many years.

5. SINGLE PERSONS

This rise of the companionate domesticated marriage was accompanied by a rise in the proportion of unmarried in the society, caused partly by the postponement of marriage to a later and later age, and partly by an increase in the proportion who never married at all. The problem of adolescence, and the nuisance it causes to society, were familiar enough to Europeans since the fifteenth century, especially as the time-lag between sexual maturity and marriage got longer and longer. The shepherd in Shakespeare's *A Winter's Tale* must have struck a familiar chord when he remarked, 'I would there were no age between sixteen and twenty-three, or that youth would sleep out the rest; for there is nothing in the between but getting wenches with child, wronging the ancientry, stealing, fighting.' The idea that adolescence, as a distinctive age-group with its distinctive problems, was a development of the nineteenth century is entirely without historical foundation.

During the late seventeenth and eighteenth centuries, there was a very high proportion of lifelong bachelors among younger sons of the nobility and gentry. Unless they were lucky enough to catch an heiress, many could not afford to get married and still maintain themselves in the life-style to which they were accustomed. By this time, the property arrangements of the elite had hardened into custom: younger sons were now pushed out into the world with a small life annuity and some patronage leverage, rather than being given, usually for two lives but sometimes in perpetuity, one of the ancestral estates on which to live like country gentlemen. Failing this, many took to peripatetic professions such as the army, or remote and isolated ones such as service in the colonies where white women of the appropriate status were in very short supply. The result was that the proportion of sons (including some eldest sons, so that is a substantial underestimate for younger sons) who were still unmarried at fifty from the late seventeenth to the early nineteenth centuries was between one in four and one in six of the whole (Graph 2, p. 41). At the same time, the median age of marriage among children of the upper and professional classes was rising, reaching twenty-eight by 1800 (and thirty by 1870), so that even those who did eventually marry remained bachelors for some twelve or thirteen years after the time of sexual maturity (Graph 3, p. 43). In 1773 *The Lady's Magazine* complained that nowadays 'the men marry with reluctance, sometimes very late, and a great many are never married at all', the explanation offered being fear of the expense, now rendered insupportable by women's passion for caprice and extravagance. In 1799 it was alleged that 'Railing at matrimony is become so fashionable a topic that one can scarcely step into a coffee-house or a tavern but one hears declamations against being clogged with a wife and a family, and a fixed resolution of living a life of liberty, gallantry, and pleasure, as it is called.'

One possible consequence of a system of very late marriage and a large number of permanent bachelors is the development of a violence-prone society of bachelors who take out their sexual frustrations in military aggression. 'I am drunk with unsatisfied love. I must rush again to war ...', wrote William Blake, perceptively. Not only did these groups have a strong economic incentive to war and imperial conquest, but they also had a psychological incentive. Early nineteenth-century doctors were worried about the situation, and in the 1850s Dr William Acton wrote that 'I have daily cause to regret that in the present civilized age pecuniary considerations render the marriage tie so frequently beyond the reach of our patients.' All he could advise as a remedy for frustrated sexual desire was 'low diet, aperient medicine, gymnastic exercise and self-control'. It is no accident that the English Public School of Thomas Arnold tried all these expedients, for Arnold was advised by Dr Acton. The results were clear enough. Wayland Young has persuasively argued that

> If every value and every force surrounding an adolescent tells him that his bodily affections must at all cost be transformed and sublimated into physical effort, intellectual prowess, competitive zeal, and manly prowess, how can he not found empires? . . . The nineteenth-century British Empire was not acquired in a fit of absence of mind, it was acquired in a fit of absence of women.

As a result of the shortage of suitable males, owing to the low level of nuptiality among younger sons and to the rise in the cost of marriage portions, there developed in the eighteenth century a new and troublesome social phenomenon, the spinster lady who never married, whose numbers rose from under five per cent of all upper-class girls in the sixteenth century to twenty to twenty-five per cent in the eighteenth century (Graph 2, p. 41). As Moll Flanders complained, 'the market is against our sex just now'. This was especially true in the towns, and particularly London, where the sex ratio, due to the influx of young women from the countryside and perhaps the greater vulnerability of males to the plague, was thirteen women to ten men at the end of the seventeenth century. As a result, a London marriage broker of the period carried 'a catalogue of women wanting marriage, some young, some not, all tame as a city cuckold chid by his wife'. In economic theory, such an excess of supply over demand should have cheapened the price, but it did not work this way among the landed classes, where marriage portions continued to rise, causing many fathers to prefer to keep their daughters off the market altogether.

Another result of this situation was that in upper-class circles in the late eighteenth century, manoeuvres to marry off a daughter turned into a desperate man-hunt. A fictitious letter from a young girl to *The Lady's Monthly Museum* in 1798 gives some hint of the frantic quality of this traumatic experience:

My pappa and mamma have been trying for the last three years to match me, and have for that purpose carried me from our country seat to London, from London to Brighton, from Brighton to Bath, and from Bath to Cheltenham, where I now am, backwards and forwards, till the family carriage is almost worn out, and one of the horses is become blind, and another lame, without my having more than a nibble, for I have never yet been able to hook my fish. I begin to be afraid that there is something wrong in their manner of baiting for a husband or in mine of laying in the line to catch him.

It was not until the very end of the eighteenth century that another occupation opened up for well-educated spinsters from decent homes, when 'accomplished girls, portionless and homeless' could become governesses in wealthy households to young children under seven. But even this new opening offered no more than a frustrating and peripatetic career with few prospects or enduring satisfactions, since the emotional bonds with the children were constantly being broken as the latter were transferred to the care of a male tutor or went off to school. Moreover, governesses suffered from both economic hardship and social stigma. They were usually very badly paid, sometimes as little as £12 to £30 a year, although those who knew French and had the right graces and connections might earn up to £100 a year 'in a family of distinction'. The work was very hard, for they were on duty seven days a week from 7 a.m. to 7 p.m. 'more a prisoner than any servant in the house'. Worst of all was that their equivocal social status deprived them of any companionship or sense of belonging. 'A governess is almost shut out of society, not choosing to associate with servants, and not being treated as an equal by the heads of the house and their visitors.' Not a relation, not a guest, not a mistress, not a servant, the governess lived in a kind of status limbo. By reason of her position, she was also treated as almost sexless. Not a lower-class servant and so open to seduction, not a daughter of the house and so open to marriage offers, she was nothing. 'There are three classes of people in the world', remarked an anonymous writer in 1836, 'men, women, and governesses'.

One should be careful not to exaggerate the predicament of any social group on such fragmentary evidence as is at present available. But there can be no doubt that the spinster in the early eighteenth century, when the problem first became of serious proportions, enjoyed a reputation for malice and ill-temper. 'If an old maid should bite anybody, it would certainly be as mortal as the bite of a mad dog,' remarked Defoe in 1723, and from then onward the ill-natured old maid became a permanent feature of the English novel, and a subject of hostile comment by all writers of domestic handbooks. In 1774 Dr John Gregory warned his daughters about 'the forlorn and unprotected situation of an old maid, the chagrin and peevishness which are apt to infect their tempers'. Eleven years later William Hayley declared that the worst feature of the condition was 'that coarse and contemptuous raillery with which the ancient maiden is perpetually insulted'.

The three obstacles to any solution to the spinster problem were social snobbery, which made most business occupations beyond the pale for a girl of genteel upbringing; the non-vocational educational training of women; and the lack of openings in the professions, or even as clerks. In the early nineteenth century, John Stuart Mill saw the defects of female education as the root cause of the spinster problem. 'Women are so brought up, as not to be able to subsist in the mere physical sense, without a man to keep them ... They are so brought up as to have no vocation or useful office to fulfil in the world, remaining single ... A single woman, therefore, is felt both by herself and others to be a kind of excrescence on the surface of society, having no use or function or office there.'

6. CONCLUSION

The three most significant physical symbols of these profound shifts in psychological attitudes among the elite are the ha-ha, the corridor and the dumb waiter. The ha-ha, the substitution of an invisible sunken ditch for high brick walls, marked the triumph of romanticism, for it destroyed the seventeenth-century concept of the garden as an orderly symmetrical area of enclosed space, as man-made and artificial as the house itself. In the eighteenth century, the rooms became more secluded and more private, but the external view from the windows was now thrown open to carefully contrived parkland and grazing cattle and sheep. The corridor, which was a feature of all new houses in the eighteenth century and was progressively added to older buildings, made a major contribution to the rise of physical privacy by removing the ever-present and inhibiting threat of a stranger walking through one's bedroom to reach his own room. Four walls and a door are a better protection of privacy than the curtains of a four-poster. The dumb waiter, used in the small private dining-room, made possible the intimate family meal-time conversation, not only away from the crowd of servants in the great hall, but also free of the surveillance of waiters serving at table. The desire to give the false impression of nature in the raw lapping around the portico of the Palladian villa, the desire for privacy in the bedroom, and the desire to reinforce nuclear family bonding by excluding both servants and strangers at meal-times were the factors which stimulated the invention of these three convenient devices. All three, together with the abandonment of the suite of rooms and the removal of the bedrooms upstairs, the rise of maternal breast-feeding, the use by children into adolescence and adulthood of the words 'Mamma' and 'Papa', the use of first names between husband and wife, the opposition to flogging, and some limited but significant improvements in female education, were symptoms of a whole set of new attitudes towards nature, natural instincts, privacy, the affective character of the nuclear family and the education of children. Contemporaries were well aware of this major shift in human relations. 'The behaviour of ladies in the past age was very reserved and stately. It would now be reckoned ridiculously stiff and formal.' Even public figures like admirals now boasted on their tombstones of their domestic virtues, such as 'filial reverence, conjugal attachment and parental affection'.

Against these positive advances, there have to be set some serious negative features. In the first place, the series of developments from the sixteenth to the eighteenth centuries, including the rise of the state, the rise of Puritanism and then the rise of individualism, had the effect of stripping away from a marriage one by one many of those external economic, social and psychological supports which normally serve as powerful reinforcing agencies to hold together the nuclear family. Among the landed classes the assistance and/or interference of the kin were largely reduced, though not removed; the importance of property exchange, patrimony and dowry was undermined in all but the highest aristocracy by the quest for personal happiness. Among the middling and lower ranks, the social support of the neighbours was lessened as the intrusive and inquisitorial functions of village or parish community declined. All that was left of the old external props was the indissoluble nature of the marriage contract, and that could be evaded by concubinage by the rich or desertion and bigamy by the poor.

The nuclear family was thus left to stand far more than ever before on its own bottom, with little to hold it together but its own internal cohesion. There can be little doubt that in many cases this was not enough. Among the upper classes, the demand for romantic love and sexual fulfilment was stimulated – especially among women – by the reading of romances and love stories, which created exaggerated expectations of marital felicity which were very often frustrated. As early as 1712, long before the romantic movement got under way, *The Spectator* was complaining that the result of the 'half theatrical and half romantic' style of courting was to 'raise our imaginations to what is not to be expected in human life' (Plate 9). In the mid century Oliver Goldsmith was still more convinced of the damage caused by the exaggerated expectations raised by novels. 'How delusive, how destructive, are those pictures of consummate bliss. They teach the youthful mind to sigh after beauty and happiness which never existed, to despise that little good which fortune has mixed up in our cup, by expecting more than she ever gave.' To make matters worse, the readers of novels mostly came from the middle ranks, while the subjects were usually drawn from the squirarchy or nobility.

Wives of the middle and upper ranks of society increasingly became idle drones. They turned household management over to stewards, reduced their reproductive responsibilities by contraceptive measures, and passed their time in such occupations as novel-reading, theatre-going, card-playing and formal visits. This was because they had been taught to cultivate 'that refined softness and delicate sensibility which renders its possessor incapable of performing the active duties of humanity'. The result was that the custom of turning wives into ladies 'languishing in listlessness as ornamental status objects spread downward through the social scale. It was not long before more and more women found themselves utterly frustrated. In 1853 Marietta Grey complained in her diary that 'ladies, dismissed from the dairy, the confectionery, the store-room, the still-room, the poultry-yard, the kitchen garden and the orchard, have hardly yet found themselves a sphere equally useful and important in the pursuits of trade and art to which to apply their abundant leisure'.

This erosion of outside supports involved a reduction of sociability, of contacts and emotional ties with persons outside the nuclear group. Friends, neighbours and relatives all receded into the background as the conjugal family turned more in upon itself. Moreover, the decline of the kin involved a serious loss of identity with the lineage, with the concept of oneself as a link between past and future generations. Fewer and fewer knew who their great-grandfathers were, and fewer and fewer cared. There was a fragmentation of the familial aspect of the Great Chain of Being, leaving the individual as an atomized unit without a past. He was no longer linked to a piece of property or to tombstones in a graveyard, or to names in a family Bible, and it is not mere romanticism to argue that he lost his past in the process of achieving his autonomy and self-fulfilment in the present.

Moreover, a new tension now emerged to threaten the peace of domesticity. Many wives found themselves torn between the two sets of new affective responsibilities, towards their husbands and towards their children. This conflict appears again and again in the surviving records. Some wives were left behind by their husbands, who were pursuing their professional careers at sea or abroad, and solaced their loneliness by devoting themselves obsessively to their children. Others, faced with a choice of living with their husbands in London or with their children in the country, opted for the latter. Yet others never much cared for their husbands anyway, and lavished all their attention on their children, even to the point of hardly ever leaving them to go out to dinner or the theatre for years on end. But one way or another, this conflict between duty to a spouse and duty to children was a source of great domestic tension in the eighteenth century, and one which particularly affected wives.

A special manifestation of this tension must have been generated by the spread in upper- and middle-class circles of the practice of mothers breast-feeding their own children. This had always been recommended by doctors, who were equally insistent that resumption of sexual relations during lactation would spoil the milk and endanger the life of the child. Since sexual relations were an important component of the new companionate marriage, the dilemma of these unfortunate women torn between their husbands and their children must have been a cruel one. Nor was it one which could be resolved by contraception through *coitus interruptus*, since it was sexual excitement itself, not even leading to intercourse, which was thought to spoil the milk. Perhaps the growing doubts of doctors about the truth of this medical theory helped to solve this agonizing dilemma by undercutting its alleged scientific foundations.

Another reason for the frustration of many women was that this shift of motives for marriage from the concrete ones of power, status and money to the imponderable one of affection probably worked to the benefit more of men than of women. This was because social custom dictated that the initiative in the courtship process should be with the male and not the female. The former was, therefore, free to follow his personal inclinations wherever they might lead him, but the latter was, at any rate in theory, restricted in her choice to those who made advances to her. She had great latitude to encourage or rebuff, but she could not formally initiate a courtship. Dr John Gregory pointed out this problem to his daughter in a volume published posthumously in 1762. If a man 'should become extremely attached to her, it is still extremely improbable that he should be the man in the world her heart most approved of. As, therefore, Nature has not given you that unlimited range of choice that we enjoy, she has wisely and benevolently assigned to you a greater flexibility of taste on the subject,' by responding to any demonstration of interest by any man. 'If attachment was not excited in your sex in this manner, there is not one of a million of you that could ever marry with any degree of love.' Even under the new arrangements, successful marriage thus depended on the docility and adaptability of the woman, as it had always done in the past, which is one of the reasons that some women were so vociferous in their disappointment and frustration in the eighteenth century.

A further reason for the discontent of some wives in the eighteenth century was that the rise of the concept of the affective marriage, like that of the seventeenth-century 'holy matrimony', caught the more independent-minded women in something of a double bind. This dilemma was made crystal clear by Defoe's liberated heroine Roxana, when she discussed the proposals of her Dutch suitor. He argued that where there was mutual love there could be no bondage; that there was but one interest, one aim, one design, and all conspired to make both very happy. Roxana would have none of this. 'That is the thing I complain of,' she retorted, 'the pretence of affection takes from a woman everything that can be called herself: She is to have no interest, no aim, no view, but all is the interest, aim and view of the husband. She is to be the passive creature.' It was no good for the suitor to try to tell a woman like Roxana how lucky were the wives of rich men. 'The women had nothing to do but eat the fat and drink the sweet ... They had indeed much the easier part ... spending what their husbands get.' Roxana did not want to lead the life of an idle drone, and suspected that her husband's power of the purse would give him power over her will.

It was almost inevitable that the trend towards greater emotional and sexual freedom for elite women in the late seventeenth century should give rise for a while to a good deal of overt misogyny, as expressed in popular male fantasies. Thus one of the most successful plays of the period was Wycherley's *The Country Wife*, whose hero, or antihero, was that insatiable adulterer, Horner. But Horner was a prisoner of sex. He derived no sensual pleasure from his conquests, only sadistic satisfaction at the seduction and then betrayal of his victims: his gratification came from their private humiliation and public ruin. That for thirty years fashionable audiences should have found this sexual cruelty so attractive to see upon the stage indicates some of the tensions and anxieties aroused by the first tentative steps towards the greater liberation of women in the late seventeenth century.

Another problem that led to much marital unhappiness was caused by the education given to wealthy women. The girls were brought up permissively at home by nurses and governesses and not taught to curb their tempers or their tongues. In infancy and youth, boys were spoiled at home by doting mothers, sisters, nurses and governesses. They were then packed off to the rough-and-tumble male world of public school and college, and so deprived of experience of female company, apart from lower-class prostitutes and tavern girls. The anonymous female author of a marriage manual for the upper-middle-class young girl, published in 1846, warned her of the shock she would experience when 'her delicate and shrinking nature discovers the real and intense coarseness of the male character'. This was not a discreet allusion to the brutality of the male sexual drive, but rather to masculine selfishness, desire for autocratic domestic authority, and contempt for common little politenesses in the treatment of a wife: 'the courtesies of life soon – too soon – after marriage are changed into a careless and fluctuating attention'. A young married woman was advised to obey her husband, even if under protest, not to cry, to put on a cheerful expression and not to complain, *never* to refer to 'the rights of women', to curb her tongue and to try to avoid a quarrel, not to criticize her husband's friends or relatives, not to keep him waiting, and to be neat and elegant without being over-scrupulously fussy. It is the advice of someone with fairly low expectations of marital behaviour from a husband, and it describes a world far removed from the notions of married life supplied by the romantic novels of the time. The general conclusion is that wives make husbands unhappy through 'perverse tempers and cold hearts' and that husbands make wives unhappy through 'careless neglect', tyranny and adultery (Plate 10).

It is symptomatic of unresolved problems in the more companionate marriage that in the second half of the eighteenth century many of both sexes still felt more at ease in the company of their own sex, evidence of which is the persistence of the custom of the withdrawal of the women from the dining-room to the drawing-room after dinner (Plate 13). In the 1720s Swift remarked that 'it has sometimes moved me with pity to see the lady of the house forced to withdraw immediately after dinner ... as if it were an established maxim that women are incapable of all conversation'. He attributed this social custom to the inadequacies of female education, which left them uninterested in discussing anything but clothes. Even in the second half of the eighteenth century the custom persisted, despite the improvement in female education. One possible explanation is that it was customary in England for chamber-pots to be kept in the sideboards in the dining-room and for the men to relieve themselves openly while their companions went on drinking (Plate 12). Under such circumstances it was clearly desirable for the women to withdraw, to use close-stools or chamber-pots elsewhere in the house. Another possible explanation was the reluctance of well-bred women to listen to masculine postprandial bawdy conversation and to participate in their heavy drinking. Whatever the cause, the facts are clear. In 1762 it was reported that 'their drawing-rooms are deserted and after dinner and supper the gentlemen are impatient till they retire'. Another commentator remarked that 'the gloom that hangs over an English company while the ladies remain, and the reciprocal restraint that each sex seems to be upon the other, has been frequently a subject of ludicrous observation to foreigners'. In the 1770s Mrs John Parker saw relatively little of her husband while they were in London, although they were only recently married. She breakfasted upstairs in her room, he downstairs in the breakfast-room. And later, 'Mr Parker likes to play his game of whist at Boodles almost every evening, so that I have nothing else to do.' At the Duke of Bedford's seat at Woburn Abbey in 1820, a female member of the house-party reported that 'in the evening the men play at whist or billiards, and we sit in the saloon all very well together'.

A subject which still needs much further exploration is the way in which close female bonding persisted in the eighteenth century, parallel to the familiar bonding of the men. Males of the upper classes spent much of their waking hours at their work among men, and their leisure in all-male dining clubs and stag dinner parties. Their sanctums were the billiard-room, the smoking-room and the stables, and much of their time was spent with men, horses and dogs in the hunting-field. As we have seen, even the dining-room tended to become a male preserve, at any rate as soon as the main meal was finished. Female sanctums were the drawing-room and the boudoir, where they spent much of the day in feminine company, gossiping, doing needlework, playing cards, and exchanging endless visits. Many very close female friendships developed, closer in many cases than those with husbands. On the other hand, the ubiquitous and time-consuming habit of card-playing was a bisexual leisure activity, as was attendance at assembly-rooms, balls, masquerades, visits to the theatre and the performance of amateur theatricals at home. The development after about 1780 of the intellectual salons, hosted by a number of blue-stocking ladies and attended by the cultural elite of London, was a further step towards the social integration of the sexes at this somewhat exalted level. In 1765 Almack's Club was founded, which was open to members of high society of both sexes, the men elected by the women, and vice versa. This was apparently the first bisexual private club in London. More important were the assembly-rooms, which were springing up in the mid-century in so many provincial towns, and which provided a meeting place for both sexes which had not previously existed, thus facilitating the new mating arrangements based on prior knowledge and affection. In 1760 Lady Mary Wortley Montagu was satisfied that 'the frequency of assemblies has introduced a more enlarged way of thinking; it is a kind of public education, which I have always thought as necessary for girls as for boys'. There is therefore evidence that the sexes were mingling far more freely than before within the squirarchy, although the growth of exclusively male London clubs and the habit of ejecting the women from the dining-room after dinner remained as significant exceptions to this trend.

One clear victim of change was the aged. The decline in patriarchy involved not only a loss of authority by the old, but also a philosophical re-evaluation of the role and value of old people generally. The fate of King Lear at the hands of his daughters foreshadowed a century of change and uncertainty in family and societal attitudes towards old people. Finally, the growing independence of the nuclear group tended to destroy vertical family ties. In 1828 a foreign observer noted that 'grown-up children and parents soon became almost strangers, and what we call domestic life is therefore applicable only to husband, wife and little children living in immediate dependence on their father'.

There are thus many reasons to believe that the institution of marriage was undergoing very severe stresses – perhaps even a major crisis – as a result of the profound changes in domestic relationships which were taking place at this time. Affective individualism brought costs as well as benefits.

CHAPTER NINE

Parent–Child Relations

'The beast and bird their common charge attend
The mothers nurse it and the sires defend.
The young dismissed, to wander earth and air,
There stops the instinct and there ends the care.
A longer care man's helpless kind demands,
That longer care contracts more lasting bonds.'
(A. Pope, *An Essay on Man*, 1733, Epistle 3, lines 26–31.)

Slowly, at a pace which varied from class to class and from individual family to individual family within each class, there took place in England between about 1660 and 1800 a remarkable change in accepted child-rearing theory, in standard child-rearing practices, and in affective relations between parents and children. As early as 1697 a French visitor could detect that a change was taking place, and that English children were being treated in an extraordinarily affectionate manner. The new attitude was at first confined to the middle ranks in the society, neither so high as to be too preoccupied with pleasure or politics to bother with children, nor so low as to be too preoccupied with sheer survival to be able to afford the luxury of sentimental concern for them. As will be seen, by 1800 there were six distinct modes of child-rearing from which parents could choose. This chapter is devoted to the emergence of the only new one among the six, the maternal, child-oriented, affectionate and permissive mode that came to prevail among the upper ranks of the bourgeoisie and the squirarchy.

1. THE CHILD-ORIENTED, AFFECTIONATE AND PERMISSIVE MODE

i. *General Indicators of Change*

There are four possible views about the nature of the new-born child, the adoption of each of which profoundly affects the way he is treated. The first, and most common, was the traditional Christian view, strongly reinforced by Calvinist theology, that the child is born with Original Sin, and that the only hope of holding it in check is by the most ruthless repression of his will and his total subordination to his parents, schoolmasters and others in authority over him. This religious view merely reinforced the current secular position that it is the duty of inferiors, like children, to give full obedience to superiors, like parents, and that early socialization in the need for such obedience and deference is an essential preparation for life in a strictly hierarchical society.

The second view was the environmentalist one, that a child is born with a propensity towards neither good nor evil, but is a *tabula rasa*, malleable and open to being moulded by experience. As early as 1628 the Anglican John Earle observed that 'the child is ... the best copy of Adam before he tasted of Eve or the apple ... His soul is yet a white paper unscribbled with the observations of the world ... He knows no evil.'

The third view was biological, that the character and potentialities of the child are genetically determined at conception, that there is little that subsequent environmental influence and educational efforts can do except to reinforce good habits and restrain bad ones. This view was of course fundamental to astrological theory, according to which both character and fate are largely determined by the configuration of the planets at the moment of birth (or possibly conception). But in practice seventeenth-century parents do not seem to have acted on this assumption, despite their faith in astrology. They continued to break the will of children in the hope of remoulding character. It was a view which only began to affect child-rearing during the eighteenth century, and in 1744 Molly Lady Hervey wrote that children 'acquire arts but not qualities; the latter whether good or bad, grow like their features; time enlarges, but does not make them'. Education, she believed, is powerless to change nature, 'yet one may certainly help it'.

The fourth view was utopian, that the child is born good and is corrupted only by his experience in society. This was an idea which had been propounded by some Renaissance humanists, but it had disappeared under the onslaught of the Calvinist doctrine of Original Sin. Early evidence of its re-emergence in England appears in connection with the 'noble savage' in Mrs Aphra Behn's play *Oroonoko* in 1688: 'God makes all things good: man meddles with them and

255

they become evil.' The suggestion was ignored, until it was put forward with far greater publicity by Rousseau in the middle of the eighteenth century. Even then, however, it seems to have had little practical influence, although *Émile* was certainly widely read in England. In eighteenth-century England the environmental theory tended to supersede the Calvinist in middle- and upper-class circles, before it was overwhelmed again in the nineteenth century.

In 1693 John Locke gave wide currency to the second – 'piece of clean paper' – point of view in his extremely popular handbook on education. His book coincided with the overthrow of Divine Right monarchy, the rejection of the doctrine of Passive Obedience, the granting of limited religious toleration and the passage of the Bill of Rights. The general relaxation of deferential and hierarchical practices in society, as reflected in these political changes, combined with Locke's *Some Thoughts upon Education* to open the way for a new era in parent–child relations, and a much more relaxed and affectionate approach to the problems of child-rearing. The book was a success because the readership was already half prepared to accept its ideas. Its time had come.

Locke warned parents against excessive permissiveness, or 'fondness' as he called it, but he argued that education had to be a stage process adapted to the growing capacities and self-development of the child. At birth the infant is merely like an animal, without ideas or morals and ready to receive any imprint, but later, as he develops both a will and a conscience, the treatment of him has to change accordingly. 'Fear and awe ought to give you the first power over their minds, and love and friendship in riper years to hold it.' The result would be that 'you shall have him your obedient subject (as is fit) whilst he is a child, and your affectionate friend when he is a man'. Locke was clearly not an apostle of childish autonomy and parental permissiveness, but he differed widely from those theorists earlier in the century who advised constant distance and coldness, and the enforcement of deference and obedience by the use of force. After infancy, he advocated psychological manipulation rather than physical coercion. This is a change the significance of which should not be underestimated by those who have never been subjected to the latter, and who are obsessed with the fashionable mirage of complete childhood autonomy as an ideal goal. He also thought that parental authority ceased once the children reached the age of discretion. This cautious piece of advice, carefully balanced between the old repressive mode and the new more permissive one, heralded a series of changes in all aspects of child-rearing among the professional and upper classes in the late seventeenth and eighteenth centuries, beginning with the treatment of the child at birth and ending with the handling of his marriage.

The earliest evidence of greater attention being paid to infants and children was the tendency in England, beginning in the late sixteenth century, to record upon tombs erected decades later children who died in infancy — represented as tiny images wrapped up in swaddling clothes — or in youth — represented as children holding skulls. At Tettenhall in Staffordshire there is an Elizabethan tomb surrounded by images of no fewer than ten dead babies. At Fulham a dead wife is seated holding a dead baby, both having perished in childbirth (Plate 5). It is also very revealing that the omission from genealogies of very short-lived infants among children of the aristocracy is estimated to have fallen from fifteen per cent or more in the late sixteenth century to five per cent in the mid eighteenth century to under one per cent by the early nineteenth century. This cannot be entirely due to the improvement in record-keeping which is a feature of this period in all areas; it must also reflect a greater concern to register the existence on earth, however brief, of all infants born.

There is also evidence that, for the first time, parents were beginning to recognize that each child, even if it lived only for a few hours or days, had its own unique individuality. During the middle ages and the sixteenth century, it had been common practice to give a new-born child the same first name as an elder sibling, especially if it was the traditional name for the head of the family. The habit lingered on into the first half of the eighteenth century, and Edward Gibbon records that after his birth in 1737, 'so feeble was my constitution, so precarious my life, that in the baptism of my brothers, my father's prudence successively repeated my Christian name of Edward, that, in case of the departure of the eldest son, this patronymic appellation might still be perpetuated in the family'. More frequent in the seventeenth century was the practice of substitution, of giving a new-born son the same name as one who had recently died. When Sir Christopher Wandesford's eldest son Christopher died at the age of ten, the next child to be born a few months later was also named Christopher. Similarly when John Benjamin Wesley was born in 1703, both his names were those of elder brothers, who had died in 1699 and 1700. So far as I am aware, this practice died out by the late eighteenth century, indicating a recognition that names were highly personal and could not be readily transferred from child to child.

Indications of the trend towards a more child-oriented society can be found in many different areas. Special clothing, however, does not seem to have been one of them. Right through the seventeenth and eighteenth centuries middle- and upper-class boys passed through a critically important *rite de passage*, when they shifted out of the long frocks of their childhood into the breeches and sword-carrying of the adult world. Among the aristocracy in the seventeenth century this took place at about six or seven, the moment when they were transferred from the care of women to the care of men. It was a great moment for a child, 'to throw off the coats and write "man"'. What happened in the early eighteenth century was that the change of clothing took place at an earlier and earlier age. Boys were dressed like their fathers from the age of three or four, girls like their mothers from the age of two. Young Henry Thrale was put into breeches at two and a quarter in 1769 – an unusually early age. Conservatives complained that 'even misses at whose age their mother wore the backstring and the like, assume the dress of womanhood'. So far as girls are concerned, loose, informal clothing was developed for young children after 1760, to become the standard style of adult clothing forty years later. 'Skeleton suits' for boys also developed after 1780, and in 1782 a German noted that 'free and natural dress is worn until they are eighteen or twenty'.

There are, however, more revealing types of evidence than clothing to prove that the eighteenth century was a turning point in the recognition of childhood as a period with its own distinctive requirements. Between 1750 and 1814 some twenty professional writers of children's books produced some 2,400 different titles. Parents were now willing to spend money to buy children's books that were totally lacking in moral implications and were merely to amuse (Plate 15): a wholly new demand had given rise to a new industry to supply it. By 1800 there was a very large range of children's books, costing between a penny and sixpence, and therefore accessible to the humblest artisan who wished to indulge his children.

Educational games that combined instruction with fun were also introduced in the mid-eighteenth century, geographical jigsaws in

1762 and a geographical or travel game played with dice in 1759. This was the time when toy-shops were springing up in provincial towns, and were doing a brisk trade selling toys that were designed merely to give pleasure to the individual child, not to gratify its parents' desire for moral or educational improvement. It was now that dolls with changeable clothing and dolls' houses were first mass produced for a commercial market (Plate 10). The commercialization of the supply of goods specially designed for children was obviously only made possible by social and economic developments which created a large upper- and lower-middle-class market of parents with money to buy such relative luxuries in quantity for their children. As today, status competition undoubtedly also played its part in stimulating demand. But what is important is that large numbers of parents were now willing to pamper their children by buying them these frivolous toys and books. England was clearly moving towards a child-oriented family type.

By the middle of the eighteenth century, there is also visual artistic evidence of a growing solidarity between parent and children, as exemplified in the growing popularity of family portrait groups, no longer stiffly and formally posed, but with the children in postures and attitudes which indicate friendly and playful association with their parents. These pictures by Reynolds, Zoffany, J. S. Copley and others, are a genre especially popular in England in the late eighteenth century, although its origins lay in Dutch bourgeois art of the seventeenth century. This is how eighteenth-century noble-women, and even noblemen, wanted themselves to be remembered – as affectionate, even doting, mothers and fathers – and in many cases, as we shall see, the reality approximated to the ideal.

Other evidence of the change in attitude, this time as it affected both young and adolescent children, is provided by the fading away of those symbolic acts of deference, the kneeling, the standing, the doffing of the hat in the parents' presence, which were so noticeable in the sixteenth and early seventeenth centuries. The first categorical statement of the new parent—child relationship came from John Locke in the late seventeenth century when he wrote: 'he that would have his son have a respect for him and his orders, must himself have a great reverence for his son'. Locke was a bachelor and a philosopher, who did not have to put his ideas to the test of practice, but this is nonetheless a very remarkable observation. Admittedly he was only paraphrasing Juvenal, but no English author seems to have done so before. He was still very far in advance of his time. Conservatives naturally viewed such novelties with alarm, and in 1700 one complained that 'the expressions of outward honour from children to parents by the dissoluteness of the age are almost out of fashion, viz., to bow before them and desire their blessing or prayers'. A century later, in about 1800, Mrs Catherine Mary Howard explained the change as an inevitable concomitant of the greater familiarity of parents with their children. 'When children, like ours, live much with parents ... there is no longer that very great distance observed ... which engendered fear and was the bane of confidential intercourse.'

Modes of address from children to parents also support belief in a major change in personal relationships among the squirarchy and upper bourgeoisie. As we have seen, the early seventeenth-century convention was stiff, formal and deferential, parents being addressed as 'Sir' and 'Madam'. In the 1720s, however, the young John Verney, away at school for the first time, began his letters to his father 'Dear Pappy' or 'Dear Papa', and referred to his mother as 'dear Mamma'. Sir Richard Steele said of his five-year-old son, 'we are very intimate friends and playfellows', and told his daughters, 'my soul is wrapped up in your welfare'. By 1778, at the height of this trend to affectionate parent–child relations, the Countess of Bristol could talk ecstatically about her 'little fairies ... bleating ... that dear word "Mamma"'.

On the other hand, families varied very widely in the modes of address between children and parents, and generalizations from the particular are very dangerous in this regard. In 1737 Elizabeth Robinson at the age of eighteen still addressed her parents as 'Sir' and 'Madam', and in 1747 her brother Matthew, a Cambridge undergraduate, addressed his father as 'Honoured Sir'. In 1759 Dr Johnson addressed his dying mother, to whom he was greatly attached, as 'Honoured Madam', and 'Dear Honoured Mother'. But these seem to be exceptions to a more casually affectionate eighteenth-century norm. At the very end of the eighteenth century, however, the tide was slowly beginning to turn again, and in 1799 Richard Thackeray was addressing his parents as 'Pater' and 'Mater'. These new Latin words do not preclude affection, but they certainly suggest affectation, if not renewed formality, and their popularity was to grow enormously in the course of the nineteenth century.

Another piece of evidence of increased concern for the child as an individual is the beginning after about 1675 of contraceptive practices among the upper classes. In the sixteenth century, the upper classes had a higher rate of fertility than the lower. But between 1675 and 1775 there took place a striking decline in the fertility of the children of the nobility, just at the time when mortality was rising (Graphs 6 and 7, pp. 53 and 56). As a result, for a time they brought their effective generation replacement rate (the number of children reaching the age of fifteen relative to the number of adults) below the zero population growth level of 1·0. The rate fell from 1·6 in 1550–99 to 0·8 in 1700–25, rising again to 1·4 in the late eighteenth century. What induced late seventeenth-century and early eighteenth-century upper-class women and men to want to reduce the size of their families? There are four conditions to be fulfilled before contraception will be practised in a society. In the first place, it must be theologically and morally accepted both to make planned choices rather than to trust to the will of God, and to regard sexual pleasure within marriage as a legitimate aspiration without relation to the objective of reproduction. So long as the officially accepted view remained that of Tertullian that 'to prevent a child being born is to commit homicide in advance', and so long as the story of Onan in the Book of Genesis was used as evidence of God's vengeance on those who defied this rule, there could be no prospect of any change. In any case, sixteenth- and seventeenth-century Puritans (and Anglicans) had four distinct objections to marital birth control. First, it violated God's injunction to be fruitful and multiply; second, children were a blessing of God, and fecundity was God's will; third, it would, especially if practised by Puritans, reduce the number of the Elect in the next generation; and lastly, childbirth brought honour to women and aided them to achieve salvation.

The liberation of sexuality in the eighteenth century from the constraints of theology is evidence that the self and its satisfactions were now being regarded as of prime importance, even if the individual remained no more than a small cog in the huge biological machine of Nature. Few upper-class English families had reached this position before the late seventeenth century, and the attitude of helpless resignation of Mrs Alice Thornton in the 1660s was still the norm, even if her piety was of an extreme variety. After seven attempts, in 1662 she at last satisfied her husband by producing a healthy male heir, and would clearly have been more than content to have ceased childbearing then. But she endured two more painful and difficult – and futile – childbirths before her final liberation by the death of her husband. When she found she was pregnant for the ninth time at the age of forty-one in 1667, when she was in very poor health, she commented revealingly: 'if it had been good in the eyes of my God, I should much rather ... not have been in this condition. But it is not a Christian's part to choose anything of this nature, but what shall be the will of our heavenly Father, be it never so contrary to our own desires.' Until conscious family planning became theologically acceptable, no progress could be made in moving to a contraceptive society. It was not until the eighteenth century that the pleasure principle began to be clearly separated from the procreative function, both in theological tracts and in the minds of husbands and wives. Well into the seventeenth century, however, the idea that sexual intercourse within marriage was only legitimate if it led to conception, modified though it was by the concession that another end was mutual comfort, was so deeply embedded in the internalized value system of most women, especially pious women, that deliberate contraceptive practices were unacceptable to them. Up to a certain point, the higher the cultural level the greater the exposure to ideas of sexual resignation. As a result of the successful christianization of the household, the sixteenth and seventeenth centuries saw the development of a lay, private, internalized morality of sexual asceticism, which spread widely in the middle and upper classes. No change was possible until this morality began to break down. The 'mutual comfort' argument might possibly lead a pious Puritan couple to continue sexual activity during pregnancy in defiance of theological advice, but it would not permit deliberate contraceptive practices like oral or manual sex or *coitus interruptus*. But by separating pleasure from procreation, however tentatively and guardedly, Protestant theology opened the way for a new, more positive attitude towards contraception as its unintended legacy to the secularized world of the eighteenth century.

Moreover, husbands must begin to share in the anxieties and sufferings of their wives, subjected to the agonies and dangers of repeated pregnancies and painful childbirths, and to desire to help them. It was not enough for the wives themselves to begin to be willing to take positive steps to limit pregnancies, since what is assumed to have been the most widely practised method, *coitus interruptus*, depends on extraordinary measures of self-control on the part of the husband. By the middle of the century the ancient Biblical teaching about the sin of Onan and God's punishment of him had so far lost its strength that in Puritan Massachusetts in 1771 a young man accused in a paternity suit could openly claim in court (unsuccessfully) that he had practised *coitus interruptus*: 'I fucked her once, but I minded my pullbacks.' The companionate marriage thus helped to spread the desire for contraception from the wife to the husband.

Equally importantly, contraception will only develop where there is a clear economic incentive to reduce births, that is where the cost of bringing up and launching a child into the world exceeds the profit to be gained from his free labour in his youth, and from his support for his parents in their old age. It is significant that the first groups in Europe to practise contraception within marriage were the aristocracy and the urban elite, who did not depend on their children for labour in the fields or shop, or for support in their old age, and who were the first to experience the rising costs of education and marriage. They were, therefore, the class with the most to gain and the least to lose by restricting births. The decline of kin responsibility for welfare threw a greater burden for the economic upkeep of children upon the father, and therefore increased his incentive to restrict numbers.

The fourth factor necessary for the spread of contraception is, paradoxically enough, the development of a more child-oriented society. It is more likely to be practised if children are regarded as valuable individuals in their own right. So long as the futures of younger sons and of daughters are not a matter of primary concern to their parents, it does not matter too much how many there are. But once serious trouble has to be taken over their nurturance, maintenance, education, and launching into the world, they become competitors for a number of scarce resources, and any increase in numbers reduces the investment in quality per child. The decision to limit births is thus partly the result of a cost-benefit analysis, a trade-off between known parental resources and anticipated costs in both time spent by the mother in rearing and money spent by the father on education. It is also partly one of preference, the balance between the value placed on children as against other goods, especially that of the personal pleasures of the parents and of conspicuous consumption. Contraception is therefore only likely to happen in a child-oriented society in which bringing up the child and launching him into the world is becoming so burdensome in its demands for love, time, effort and money, that some reduction in numbers is highly desirable. The issue became a live one in the late seventeenth century as the cost of girls' marriage portions rose, and came out into the open in Sedley's play *Bellamira* in 1687. Merryman promised his future wife that: 'we will have two beds, for I will not come home drunk and get girls, without I know where to get portions for them. In this age they sour and grow stale upon their parents' hands.' A character in a play of 1705 by Richard Steele complained bitterly that 'the war has fetched down the price of women; the whole nation is overrun with petticoats. Our daughters lie upon our hands ... Girls are drugs, sir, mere drugs.'

The seriousness of this problem at this particular time can be demonstrated from an example. The Reverend Ralph Josselin was vicar of Earl's Colne, for some years served as schoolmaster at the local school, and was also the owner of a significant amount of farmland; all of which brought him the modest income of around £160 a year between 1641 and 1683. Of his total expenses over this forty-two-year period, including the purchase of land, no less than one third went on the rearing, education and marriage of his ten children, only five of whom lived to survive their parents. A third of this money was wasted, in the sense that it was spent on children who did not live to enjoy an adult life-span.

For a child-oriented society to develop, however, it is thus essential that children should be less liable to sudden and early death than they were in the early sixteenth or again in the seventeenth and early eighteenth centuries. To use the language of the economists, the value of children rises as their durability improves – although at the same time their maintenance cost also rises. There is reason to believe that the last two thirds of the sixteenth century was a period of relatively low infant and child mortality rates, although the rates rose again sharply in the seventeenth and early eighteenth centuries. One could hypothesize that the sixty years of low child mortality may have given an impetus to the growth of a new respect for and attention to, children, which could not be arrested by a fresh relapse into the old pattern of high mortality rates in the seventeenth century. The attitude survived into the new era of sustained decline in infant and child mortality, which seems to have begun in about 1750. It was perhaps this renewed fall which provided the final stimulus for the eventual development of the permanently child-oriented, and increasingly contraceptive, family type. Moral theology, economics, affect between spouses, and care for children were thus all involved in the growth of contraception among the elite.

For those lower down the social scale, the husbandmen, artisans, small tradesmen on the one hand, and the poor cottagers and common labourers on the other, the critical variable was probably not any change in attitude towards pleasure or consumption, but a balance between two purely economic considerations. On the one hand, everyone recognized that the time would come when, if they survived, they would be unable to work at the craft or in the field, and they and their wives would need to be provided with a pension if they were not to fall into complete destitution. Given the high mortality rates of the age, five or six children would be needed to guarantee that one breadwinner would survive to look after the parents in their old age. According to this hypothesis, the supply of a cheap labour force from the children when adolescents and the expectation that they would provide a pension for the parents in their old age were the prime reasons for multiple procreation. This second incentive only works for those with the foresight to look far ahead, with sufficient property, house-space and current income to be able to raise the children without economic hardship, and with the confidence of being able to place them in a situation where they will be able to afford a pension for their aged parents. In practice this means the husbandmen and small yeomen, and relatively prosperous artisans and small traders. For the propertyless, however, the cottagers and common labourers, the economic balance was different. In bad years, when the harvest failed and food prices were high, they could not afford to feed their children, while in their cramped two-room houses children were a nuisance and always underfoot. They did not cultivate land on a large enough scale to be able to put the children to useful employment, and the future job prospects were such that there was no reasonable expectation that the children would be in any position to look after their parents in their old age. Their houses would be too small to accommodate them, and their incomes too marginal and precarious to have any surplus with which to feed and clothe them. Except in clothing areas, where children from the age of four could earn their keep, the very poor had, therefore, no economic incentive to have many children.

Just how the reduction of births was achieved is not known for certain, but since sexual abstention is unlikely, except by the very poor suffering from malnutrition and physical exhaustion, it is presumed that the principal means was *coitus interruptus*, assisted no doubt by oral, manual and anal sex. One would have supposed that these are techniques which each generation can think up for itself, without any need for transmission of information. But in 1590 the Vicar of Weaverham in Cheshire was denounced as 'an instructor of young folks how to commit the sin of adultery or fornication and not beget or bring forth children'.

Condoms first appeared in the late seventeenth century, but did not become common until the early eighteenth. Even then they were hard to find outside London, and were apparently reserved largely – though probably not entirely – for extra-marital affairs as protection against venereal disease. In 1726 Lord Hervey sent his young bachelor friend, Henry Fox 'a dozen preservatives from claps and impediments to procreation'. A London advertiser of the sale of condoms in 1776 referred to them as 'implements of safety which secure the health of my customers', and another referred to the shop as the place where 'all gentlemen of intrigue may be supplied with those bladder policies or implements of safety, which infallibly secure the health of our customers'. It seems clear that in the eighteenth century the contraceptive function of the condom was at best secondary, and that its primary purpose was protection against venereal disease. James Boswell used them frequently, but only on one occasion for contraceptive purposes. When he was sleeping with a woman about whose health he felt reasonably secure, he preferred to promise to look after any possible child. Although Richard Carlile claimed in 1825 that the vaginal sponge and the sheath had been used by the English aristocracy to reduce their marital fertility for at least the previous century, there is no positive evidence that these methods were indeed in common use among upper-class married couples in the eighteenth century. Sponges were mentioned as being used by prostitutes as early as 1660, but only as prophylactics against venereal disease.

The only other methods of restricting births were medicines offered for sale in London in the eighteenth century both for contraceptive and for abortifacient purposes. One can safely discount the efficacy of recipes for the former purpose, as advertised by an early eighteenth-century London quack: 'If the party ... would not conceive, take one paper of powders in a glass of warm ale, every morning after the man has been with her, and she shall be out of danger.' It seems unlikely that either these desperate chemical remedies or surgical intervention were resorted to by more than a minority, although the traditional methods of inducing abortion by hot baths, heavy purges, jumping off tables and galloping on horseback were no doubt more frequently attempted, with varying results.

One early nineteenth-century attempt at abortion will serve to illustrate the point. Mary, wife of the second Lord Alderley, had a quiverful of children who were already a severe strain on her husband's resources, when in 1847 she found herself pregnant again. She hastened to inform her husband, who was appalled. 'This your last misfortune is indeed most grievous and puts all others in the shade. What can you have been doing to account for so juvenile a proceeding: it comes very opportunely to disturb all your family arrangements ... I only hope it is not the beginning of another flock, for what to do with them I am sure I know not. I am afraid, however, it is too late to mend, and you must make the best of it, tho' bad is best.' But he wholly underestimated his wife's resourcefulness, for she wrote to him triumphantly the same day: 'A hot bath, a tremendous walk, and a great dose have succeeded; but it is a warning.' The next day she added reassuringly that 'I was sure you would feel the same horror I did at an increase of family, but I am reassured for the future by the efficacy of the means.' This pious Victorian lady, who devoted twenty years of her life to her children, clearly saw nothing whatever wrong in inducing an abortion.

ii. *Changes in Child-rearing Practices*

Some time during the eighteenth century swaddling, like so many other traditional child-rearing practices, began to be abandoned in England. Swaddling goes back at least to Roman times, but in the late eighteenth century, both moral and medical advice in England and America was beginning to turn against it. At the end of the seventeenth century, Locke objected strongly to tight-laced stays, and had his doubts about swaddling. 'The child has hardly left the mother's womb, it has hardly begun to move and stretch its limbs when it is deprived of its freedom. It is wrapped in swaddling bands, laid down with its head fixed, its legs stretched out, and its arms by its sides, it is wound round and round with linen and bandages of all sorts, so that it cannot move.' In the 1740s Richardson's *Pamela* took Locke to be attacking swaddling directly, while strong criticisms were levelled in France by Rousseau in *Émile* and by Buffon in

his *Histoire Naturelle de l'Homme*, so that complaints by intellectuals and moralists are spread over almost a hundred years.

It is one thing for moralists, and even doctors, to preach, and
quite another for mothers to put their advice into practice. The speed
with which the new advice was followed in England is still not clear.
In 1707 Mme de Maintenon expressed her approval of the English
habit of removing the bands after three months, so that already England may have been in advance of the continent, at any rate in
reducing the duration of the swaddling. Moreover it seems to be
generally admitted that the practice was on its way out during the
third quarter of the century. In 1762 Rousseau stated that in England
it was already 'almost obsolete', and in 1785 *The Lady's Magazine*
thought that most of its readers would not even know how it was
done. The most influential books on the subject in England were two
enormously popular works on child care by Dr William Cadogan,
published in 1748 (ten editions in the next twenty-five years), and
Dr William Buchan, published in 1769 (twenty editions in the next
fifty years). Dr Cadogan presented to the fashionable mother a horrific picture of how her infant was being handled by the wet-nurse in
the village, while she enjoyed herself in town. 'At the least annoyance
which arises, he is hung from a nail like a bundle of old clothes and
while, without hurrying, the nurse attends to her business, the unfortunate one remains thus crucified. All who have been found in
this situation had a purple face, the violently compressed chest not
allowing the blood to circulate ... The patient was believed to be
tranquil because he did not have the strength to cry out.' Twenty
years later, Dr Buchan denounced in no uncertain terms the way
'the poor child, as soon as it came into the world, had as many
rollers and wrappers applied to its body as if every bone had been
fractured in the birth'. He admitted, however, that by now 'in
several parts of Britain the practice of rolling children with so many
bandages is now in some measure laid aside', an observation which
was also supported by Jonas Hanway in 1762. By the end of the
century the standard advice was to let infants exercise early and use
their legs.

In 1784 von Archenholz was surprised to find that in England 'the
children are not swaddled ... they are covered with light clothing,
which leaves all their movements free', and a year later an English
doctor agreed that 'the barbarous custom of swathing children like
living mummies is now almost universally laid aside'. England seems

to have been far in advance of the rest of Europe in abandoning a practice which had been standard throughout Europe for millennia and was to persist well into the nineteenth century through most of the rest of western Europe, and into the twentieth century in Russia.

Once again, one can only speculate about the true causes of this precocious change in eighteenth-century English child-rearing practices, but it falls into line with other similar changes at the time, all tending to the liberation of the infant and the child. These changes are symptoms of a profound shift of attitudes towards family life in general, and towards children in particular. One of the most significant results of swaddling is that it prevents the mother or wet-nurse from cuddling, hugging and caressing the child. It seems clear, therefore, that the change came about for ideological rather than scientific reasons, for the benefit of the parents rather than the infants. Recent research has shown that swaddled children are indeed more tranquil, sleeping a lot, crying little, and with reduced cardiac and respiratory rates, and that there is little evidence of later physical or mental retardation due to the lack of early stimuli. Swaddling was condemned in England since it was seen as an assault on human liberty, and its early disappearance there and in America, and its survival in Russia and elsewhere into the twentieth century, must be explained on grounds of different cultures and different political, social and psychological ideals. The arguments of Drs Cadogan and Buchan were not as scientifically proven as they pretended, nor those of Locke and Richardson as ethically incontrovertible as they believed.

In Early Modern Europe, breast-feeding seems usually to have lasted between one year and eighteen months, and it was therefore a severe burden on a mother. The time may have shortened later, for in the middle of the eighteenth century James Nelson alleged that 'the present fashion ... is to let children suck only three or four months', although he strongly advised six to twelve months, with nine as the ideal.

Although doctors had always advised against it, it had long been the custom of upper-class mothers to put children out to paid wet-nurses. There were many reasons for this practice. Many mothers were unable to produce an adequate milk supply, either because of exhaustion and sickness after childbirth or because of some congenital defect, or possibly because of psychological hostility towards the child. For others it was a painful process for the nipples, and in any case it was always a nuisance, interfering with sleep and the normal round of social engagements. Breast-feeding was a task entirely without social prestige, and many mothers were afraid that it would impair the shape of their 'pretty breasts, firm nipples, round and smooth', and, therefore, their sexual attractiveness. The compelling reason for this practice, however, lay elsewhere. In the early seventeenth century William Gouge, and in the middle of the eighteenth James Nelson, both thought that it was the insistence of the husbands rather than the desire of the wives which was the main reason for the employment of wet-nurses: 'Many a tender mother ... is prevented by the misplaced authority of a husband.' This was partly so that the child at the breast would not be a competitor for his wife's attention, but mainly so that he could continue to have access to her sexual services, since according to Galen, who was followed by sixteenth and seventeenth-century doctors, husbands ought not to sleep with nursing wives since 'carnal copulation ... troubleth the blood, and so in consequence the milk'. As late as 1792, when the practice was already dying out, Mary Wollstonecraft still thought that desire for sexual relations by the fathers was the main reason for the survival of wet-nursing: 'There are many husbands so devoid of sense and parental affection that, during the first effervescence of voluptuous fondness, they refuse to let their wives suckle their children.'

In the early seventeenth century the most popular and influential Puritan writers on household management, Perkins, Gouge, and Cleaver and Dod, strongly reinforced the traditional advice of the medical profession, and told mothers to feed their own children. They used the functional argument that nature had provided women with breasts to supply milk, not to serve as sexually exciting erogenous zones; they used the medical argument that mother's milk was best; and they used the ancient superstitious argument that by absorbing the wet-nurses' milk, babies would also pick up their lower-class, and probably evil, character traits, whereas the mother would pass on her own good traits. Even a few of the nobility began to accept these ideas in the early seventeenth century. In 1596 the ninth Earl of Northumberland declared that 'mother's teats are best answerable to the health of the child', and a generation later the Countess of Lincoln published a book which urged mothers to breast-feed their children themselves.

How far this growing propaganda took effect in the seventeenth century is not entirely clear, but it is significant that those mothers who fed their own children regarded it as something to boast about, as if it was an unusual occurrence. There is also some indication that it was the more puritanically inclined mothers who were the first from well-to-do families to try to nurse their own children. Benjamin Brand, who died in 1636, boasted on his tombstone that his wife bore him twelve children, 'all nursed with her unborrowed milk'. In 1658 the second wife of the second Earl of Manchester had recorded on her tombstone that, of her eight children, seven 'she nursed with her own breasts . . . Her children shall rise up and call her blessed.' In the middle of the seventeenth century, the pious, upper-gentry Mrs Alice Thornton repeatedly stressed her strong sense of obligation to try to nurse her own children, although she was often too ill after her confinements to be able to do so.

In the early eighteenth century, the propaganda in favour of mothers nursing their own children was powerfully reinforced by a fierce attack in *The Spectator* on so inhuman and physically dangerous a practice as handing children over to slovenly and dirty wet-nurses, even if they did only cost between three and six shillings a week. Addison, however, admitted that 'this cruelty is supported by fashion, and nature gives place to custom', and in 1756 James Nelson in his *Essay on the Government of Children* added his voice to the chorus, but also had to confess that 'I am not insensible how little probability there is that my advice herein will be followed by persons in high life.' It seems that Nelson was right. In 1716 even so independent a woman as Lady Mary Wortley Montagu was against maternal breast-feeding: 'I grant that Nature has furnished the mother with milk to nourish her child; but I maintain at the same time that if she can find better milk elsewhere, she ought to prefer it without hesitation.' Below this exalted level of the rich, however, it is probable that cost was a limiting factor, for according to Dr Cadogan a really good wet-nurse in 1748 cost £25 a year, which was a substantial sum, three times higher than Addison's estimate earlier in the century. In the 1740s Elizabeth Montagu was paying £50 a year for a very reliable wet-nurse. In 1813 in Ireland a wet-nurse for a countess cost £26 a year.

The conclusion seems to be, therefore, that the practice of using wet-nurses was largely confined to the wealthy classes. Although the proportion may have been declining, it seems that the majority of mothers in these classes, even devoted and child-oriented ones, were still not feeding their own children well into the middle of the eighteenth century. In 1748 Dr William Cadogan published his widely read *Essay upon Nursing and the Management of Children*. He argued that ninety per cent of children died who were reared on pap or fed by lazy wet-nurses with a poor or contaminated milk supply. He went so far as to claim that the children of the poor were healthier than those of the rich since they were breast-fed by their mothers and not kept shut up in stuffy rooms.

This weight of medical opinion was supported by the memoirs of several men, who blamed their adult ill-health on the negligence of their wet-nurses. Worst of all was the experience of J. G. Stedman, who was born abroad, the son of a military officer, in 1774:

Four different wet-nurses were alternately turn'd out of doors on my account, and to the care of whom I had been entrusted, my poor mother being in too weak a condition to suckle me herself. The first of these bitches was turn'd off for having nearly suffocated me in bed; she having slept upon me till I was smothered, and with skill and difficulty restored to life. The second had let me fall from her arms on the stones till my head was almost fractured, and I lay several hours in convulsions. The third carried me under a moulder'd old brick wall, which fell in a heap of rubbish just the moment we had passed by it, while the fourth proved to be a thief, and deprived me even of my very baby clothes. Thus was poor Johnny Stedman weaned some months before the usual time.

It was not until the second half of the eighteenth century that practice at last began to conform to propaganda, and wet-nursing quite rapidly went out of fashion. In the 1770s and 1780s one of the highest women in the country, the Duchess of Devonshire, breast-fed her eldest son for a period of nine months. In 1786 Countess Fitzwilliam was breast-feeding her infant son, and three years later the wife of Vice-Admiral F. W. Drake expressed her satisfaction that a friend was breast-feeding her child. That these mothers were now very numerous is confirmed by Lady Craven, who in 1789 reported that 'you will find in every station of life mothers of families who would shrink with horror at the thought of putting a child from them to nurse: a French custom with people of every degree'. 'Even women of quality nurse their children', von Archenholz remarked with surprise when he visited England in 1784, and in 1797 the popular handbook of Thomas Gisborne stated firmly that for a mother, 'the first of the parental duties .; . . is to be herself the nurse of her own offspring' (Plate 22).

There can be little doubt that the growth of maternal breast-feeding as an upper-class fashion saved many infants from death at the hands of negligent wet-nurses. The other consequence, the importance of which can hardly be exaggerated, was psychological. As Plutarch had pointed out in his *Moralia* centuries before, breast-feeding by the mother stimulates maternal affection. It also gives the child a greater sense of security and confidence about the world, and increases its attachment to its mother. This may well be a prime cause of that growth of affect in the eighteenth century which is central to the argument in this book.

There is reason to believe that in this shift to maternal breast-feeding, as in a number of other family matters, England was in the lead in Europe. The use of rural wet-nurses was more or less universal among all but the lowest classes in the towns and cities of eighteenth and early nineteenth-century France, causing a very high rate of infant mortality. The practice seems to have died out in France only in the late nineteenth century and in Germany only in the twentieth, to be replaced in many cases by bottle-feeding.

In noble families, there was a growing practice of educating the children at home, according to the advice of Locke, who recommended a private tutor in order to avoid the crude and vulgar rough and tumble and the strong temptations to vice of a public boarding-school. Home education also served to remove the noble child from social contamination by contact with those of lower social status than himself. Much more research is needed before a clear picture can be obtained of the development of this practice, but it was undoubtedly common throughout most of the eighteenth century, as the aristocracy withdrew their sons from the local grammar schools to educate them either by a private tutor in the home, or in private academies, or at one of the two most aristocratic public schools, Eton and Westminster. It was only at the very highest level of the court aristocracy that Locke's advice was ignored, and children were still largely neglected and sent early away from home. Many aristocratic children still went off to boarding-school as early as the age of seven, and did not return home again for decades, spending their holidays with close relatives, uncles or grown-up brothers or sisters.

The main cause for the withdrawal of the elite from the grammar school to the home was the same one as that which caused the withdrawal from the university, namely the fear of moral contamination from other boys, especially boys of lower social status. It was widely, and rightly, feared that the eighteenth-century school and college were training-grounds of vice, which tended in the minds of many parents to outweigh the benefits of political maturity by exposure to the rough and tumble of school life. This was why Squire Allworthy had Tom Jones and Master Blifil educated at home, 'where he thought their morals would escape all that danger of being corrupted to which they would be unavoidably exposed in any public school or university'. Defoe, who was bitterly hostile to home education by a tutor, thought that the reason was mainly one of social snobbery. ' "What," says the lady mother, "shall my son go to school? My son? no, indeed, he shan't go among the rabble of every tradesman's boys and be bred up among mechanics." ... And so the young gentleman has a tutor bestowed on him to teach him at home.'

This rise of education in the home meant that teaching methods became less brutal and authoritarian. As in many other areas of domestic relations, middle-class dissenters seem to have been in advance of the rest of the society. In the late seventeenth century the Quaker William Penn advised parents to 'love them with wisdom, correct them with affection, never strike in passion, and suit the correction to their ages as well as the fault'. If children were sinful or disobedient, 'show them the folly, shame and undutifulness of their faults rather with a grieved than an angry countenance'. In 1691 John Dunton, the Presbyterian-trained editor of the *Athenian Mercury*, was advising his bourgeois readers to educate their children at home. The mother, he argued, lacks 'that magisterial sourness which sticks so close to most pedagogues, and frightens more learning out of children than ever they can whip into them'. In the middle of the eighteenth century, James Nelson, in his popular handbook on the upbringing of children, advised strict moderation of chastisement in the home, although he was generally opposed to excessive permissiveness in child-rearing. His objections to brutality were both medical and social. 'Severe and frequent whipping is, I think, a very bad practice: it inflames the skin, it puts the blood in a ferment; and there is besides, meanness, a degree of ignominy attending it, which makes it very unbecoming.' Stress was laid now on the psychological carrot rather than on the physical stick. In 1798 mothers were told that 'the first object in the education of a child should be to acquire its affection, and the second to obtain its confidence ... The most likely thing to expand a youthful mind ... is praise.'

This advice was certainly followed in many upper-class households in the eighteenth century. The most explicit statement of the new attitude is contained in the instructions given by Philip Francis when in 1774 he entrusted his only son to a private tutor: 'since it is my purpose to make him a gentleman, which includes the idea of a liberal character and sentiment, I cannot think it consistent with that purpose to have him brought up under the servile discipline of the rod . . . I absolutely forbid the use of blows.' Henry Lord Holland gave similar instructions for the upbringing of his son Charles James Fox: 'Let nothing be done to break his spirit. The world will do that business fast enough.' This was not an unusual position to adopt by then. Arthur Young, born in 1741, was only once flogged by his naturally irascible father, a well-to-do and well-connected clergyman, and then only as punishment for an act of cruelty. Mrs Eliza Fox, born in 1793, the daughter of a local barrister, 'was seldom checked or chided at home', while Mrs Boscawen's son was only whipped once in the home, when he was still a child in long coats.

But there were clearly differences of opinion on this subject even among the most affectionate of parents (and indeed modern child psychologists are still far from united on the subject). The son of Robert Owen, the industrialist, who was born in 1800, recorded later that his mother, who was a Scotch Calvinist, and his father had different views on child-rearing. When as a baby he screamed for something, 'very gentle though she was, the doctrine of innate depravity, in which she had been bred, urged her to slap me into quiet'. But his father would not let her, preferring to allow the child to scream until he stopped. When he was older, his father said to him, 'I have never struck you. You must never strike anybody.' Mrs Howard of Corby Castle thought that 'the rod, if used with discretion, is of great use before they can perfectly discern right from wrong, and does much less harm to the child than a persevering cry'. The attitude to the beating of older children, however, was generally hostile. When in 1813 Ellen Weeton was employed as a governess in a wealthy industrialist's home, she struggled for some time to control 'the perverse and violent tempers of the children'. At last she 'resorted to the rod, notwithstanding it is so repugnant to the present mild system of education', and despite the 'sour looks and cool treatment' of both the parents. In those circles, at that time, flogging in the home was clearly frowned upon.

Some of the stories about parent—child relations in the late eighteenth century indicate a degree of indulgent permissiveness among parents and of spoilt arrogance among children which historically have no parallel except for conditions in the United States in the late twentieth century. When Mary Butt (later Mrs Sherwood) visited a doctor at Warwick in 1782, she found the son of the house lying on a carpet in front of the fire. When told by his mother to get up and greet the visitor, he replied, 'I won't', which was Mary's first introduction to this sort of licensed insubordination and bad manners. 'But I have lived to see this single specimen multiplied beyond calculation,' she added bitterly. Another woman recalled a disastrous dinner party at which 'the eldest boy was a perfect pest in the house, although only about five years old. A more uncomfortable dinner there could not be than the one we had that day, owing to the behaviour of that horrid child . . . he screaming every now and then and making such a noise. There was little conversation.' An equally disastrous dinner party was given in 1777 by Joshua Reynolds for David Garrick and Mrs Thrale. Unfortunately, Mary Countess of Rothes, who was also there with her second husband, Bennet Langton, spoilt the party for Boswell by bringing along her two babies: 'they played and prattled and suffered nobody to be heard but themselves . . . Langton and his wife with a triumphant insensibility kissed their children and listened to nothing with pleasure but what they said.' Boswell complained bitterly about the deplorable social consequences of this widespread practice.

This evidence of an injudicious fondness by parents for exhibiting children in company is supported by signs that parental authority had in some cases been virtually abdicated. It was in 1762 that Henry Lord Holland wrote a letter to his son at Eton which could hardly be matched in tone of deferential supplication from father to schoolboy son at any other period in history than the late 1960s. 'I much wanted to see your hair cut to a reasonable length and gentlemanlike shortness. You and some Eton boys wear it as no other people in the world do. It is effeminate; it is ugly; and it must be inconvenient. You gave me hopes that if I desired it, you would cut it. I will, dear Ste, be much obliged if you will.' Even by the standards of the day, Lord Holland was an exceptionally permissive parent, who brought up his precocious son Charles James Fox on 'a system of the most unlimited indulgence of every passion, whim or caprice'. A great dinner was given at Holland House to all the foreign ministers. The children came in at the dessert. Charles, then in petticoats, spying a large bowl of cream in the middle of the table, had a desire to get into it. Lord Holland insisted he should be gratified, and, in spite of Lady Holland's remonstrations, had it placed on the floor for the child to jump in and splash about at his pleasure. At the turn of the century, there were a few families, admittedly eccentrics, where permissiveness was carried to the ultimate extreme. In 1804 Admiral Graves and his wife at Exeter never had their children's hair cut. 'None of the children are allowed to be contradicted, and when 3 or 4 of them cry at once for the same thing and run tearing and screaming about the room together with their long tails, the effect on strangers is rather surprising.'

The conclusion one can draw from these diverse scraps of evidence is that in some high professional and landed circles in England by the late eighteenth century, there had developed an astonishingly permissive style of child-rearing. As a result, some parents were obliged humbly to cajole their adolescent children instead of ordering them about, and adult social occasions were often marred by those twin scourges of civilized conversation, the presence of undisciplined, noisy and talkative children demanding to be the centre of attention, and the habit of doting parents of 'repeating *bon mots* of babies among people of wit and understanding'.

The trend towards a more affectionate and permissive handling of children did not go unnoticed by contemporaries. Some welcomed the change, and in 1797 Thomas Gisborne pointed out that in the sixteenth and seventeenth centuries 'domestic manners were severe and formal. A haughty reserve was affected by the old, and an abject deference exacted from the young.' Even not so long ago, he observed, children were 'condemned to almost perpetual silence in the presence of their parents'. At the time he was writing, however, a quite different domestic atmosphere prevailed and a parent strove to 'preserve the confidence of a friend' of the children.

Many others, on the other hand, were increasingly worried that affection was leading to spoiling, and permissiveness turning into licence. By 1732 Richard Costeker was afraid that the sons of nobles were now 'degenerate into foppery and effeminacy ... Thousands are ruined by the very effect of maternal love.' Nowadays, he complained, a son was 'naturally under the conduct and tuition of his mama'. In the 1750s James Nelson, in his popular *Essay on the Government of Children*, was far more concerned about the dangers of excessive permissiveness, which he thought was current, than with the dangers of excessive strictness, which he regarded as now confined to a minority. He wasted little time in denouncing 'the cruelty of some parents who use everybody well but their own children', but devoted two hundred pages to damage done by excessive permissiveness. In the early years of the nineteenth century, even the caricaturists weighed in. One drawing entitled 'The Mother's Hope' shows a small boy screaming with rage before his complaisant and helpless mother, concluding his tirade with the statement: 'I will have my own way in everything' (Plate 18). Another shows two children torturing a cat and a dog, while their father remarks fondly, 'Dear little innocents, how prettily they amuse themselves.' There is an extraordinary contrast between these reiterated warnings in the eighteenth and early nineteenth centuries about excessive maternal influence and domestic affection, and the complaints in the late seventeenth century about excessive parental indifference and severity. It is a contrast that clearly had a firm basis in reality.

One of the most impressive pieces of evidence of a kindlier attitude towards children is the late seventeenth-century revulsion in many quarters against the brutal flogging that had been standard practice earlier, especially in the public grammar schools. In terms of pedagogy and psychology, there is an essential difference between constant flogging for academic lapses, such as stupidity, ignorance, inattention or idleness, and occasional flogging for serious moral faults, such as disobedience and lying. The prime objective of the reformers was the total elimination of the former practice, the secondary objective being to reduce the latter to the bare minimum necessary for social control and moral improvement.

The first onslaught on the extraordinary brutality of schoolmasters in the public grammar schools towards their pupils did not occur until soon after the middle of the seventeenth century. It was not only inspired by a spirit of compassion, but was also informed by a new understanding of the psychological motivation for the current practice of routinely and daily flogging boys severely for the most trivial lapses of memory or failure of understanding or performance in class. The Elizabethan poet Thomas Tusser had complained that his Eton master had once given him fifty-three stripes for 'fault but small or none at all' in learning his Latin. Critics noted that the frequency and severity of the punishment was vastly in excess of the cause, and that it took the form of beating boys with a birch on the naked buttocks while bent over and horsed on the back of another boy.

Samuel Butler in *Hudibras* hinted at the explanation of this ferocity but it was left to an anonymous author to spell it out. In a pamphlet of 1669 the boys are made to point out that 'our sufferings are of that nature as makes our schools to be not merely houses of correction, but of prostitution, in this vile way of castigation in use, wherein our secret parts ... must be the anvil exposed to the immodest and filthy blows of the smiter'. The author asked 'who can think that if the punishment were not suffered on those parts, that it were like to be so much?' Having demonstrated the homosexual sadistic motivation for the practice, he pointed out that it failed totally in its ostensible object of increasing the capacity to learn, while it was unworthy to treat a future gentleman in a manner fit only for a slave. Moreover, the terror induced could lead to stammering and other psychosomatic illnesses. He concluded, 'it is in truth a question rather worthy of the most mature deliberation whether children should ever be beaten at all about their books'. Flogging, that is, should be a rare punishment limited to moral crimes, not applied indiscriminately to minor intellectual deficiencies.

At just the same time that the sadistic motivation of flogging by schoolmasters was being analysed and exposed, the psychological opposite, the stimulus to masochism in some boys, was also first brought to public attention. In his play *The Virtuoso* of 1678, Thomas Shadwell portrayed an elderly man who in a moment of sexual excitement asks his mistress: 'Where are the instruments of our pleasure?' When she produces a couple of birch rods, he explains 'I was so used to it at Westminster School I could never leave it off since ... Do not spare thy pains: I love castigation mightily' (Plate 25). A contemporary poem alleged that Nell Gwyn specialized in flagellation, James Cleland included a mutual whipping episode in *Fanny Hill* in 1748, while Hogarth's print in 1732 of a whore's room in *A Harlot's Progress* showed a bundle of birch rods hanging on the wall over the bed. '*Le vice Anglais*' was well established by the eighteenth century, apparently among both sexes.

The late seventeenth-century view of the sexually and educationally harmful effects of flogging to enforce education gained enormous currency by being adopted by John Locke in his best-selling treatise on education of 1693, which had gone through twenty-five editions by 1800. He approved of physical punishment, in moderation, at an early age before a child had developed powers of reasoning. After that, however, he insisted on the almost exclusive use of the psychological stimulus of competition and emulation and the psychological punishment of shame at failure. He flatly declared that flogging was wholly ineffective as a means of moral or intellectual improvement. His arguments, which closely follow those of Plutarch in his *Moralia*, were twofold, practical and moral. The first was that it was counter-productive, because, 'this sort of correction naturally breeds an aversion to that which it is the tutors' business to create a liking to'. The second was that 'such a sort of slavish discipline makes a slavish temper', and is therefore unsuitable 'to be used in the education of those who would have wise, good and ingenuous men'.

Largely as a result of Locke's powerful advocacy, these ideas slowly became the conventional wisdom of the time. In 1711 the widely read and very influential *Spectator* contributed to the chorus. Swift alleged that it had now become a popular notion 'that whipping breaks the spirits of lads well-born'. Finally in 1769 Thomas Sheridan, senior, made a lively plea, based on the new spirit of the age, for the total abolition of corporal punishment in schools for the elite. 'Away with the rod ... Let pleasure be their guide to allure the ingenious youth through the labyrinths of science, not pain their driver to goad them on.'

These novel ideas naturally did not go without challenge from 'the party of the Thwackums'. Neither Dr Johnson nor Oliver Goldsmith was convinced by the new educational ideas, the latter concluding grimly: 'I do not object to alluring it [a child] to duty by reward, but we well know that the mind will be more strongly stimulated by pain.' On the other hand, in Smollett's *Roderick Random* of 1748, the hero led a rebellion of boys against a cruel master, on whom they turned the tables by tying him to a post and whipping him themselves – a fantasy of schoolboy revenge that must have appealed to many thousands of eighteenth-century readers.

The degree to which this new approach slowly affected practice in schools is not easy to determine with precision. Flogging at the university certainly died out altogether in the 1660s – the last known case at Cambridge was in 1667. It declined from a daily expectation in the classroom to a rare and solemn occasion in the fashionable public schools at some time between the post-Restoration Westminster School of Dr Busby – famous both for his pedagogic successes and for his enthusiasm for flogging – and the early nineteenth-century Rugby of *Tom Brown's Schooldays*. Neither *The Spectator* in 1711 nor Robert Campbell in 1747 thought that there had been much change, but there can be little doubt that flogging by masters was on the decline in the major elite public schools. The headmaster of St Paul's School between 1748 and 1769, George Thicknesse, was famous not only for his classical scholarship but also for his kindness to his pupils, many of whom became friends for life. He took the view that 'some boys had no talent for the acquisition of dead languages, and that a master must be content with their elementary instruction, as the birch and cane would not alter nature'. Things were also changing at the other, and more socially prestigious, London public school, Westminster, as well as at Harrow. As for Eton, the eighteenth-century headmaster Dr Barnard 'had a way of talking to boys who were taking their leave of him at once so tender and so full of admonition that many of them had been known to shed tears at parting'. As a result, in 1747 Thomas Gray looked back on his schooldays at Eton as the best years of his life, a concept unthinkable in the seventeenth century:

> Ah, happy hills, ah, pleasing shade,
> Ah fields beloved in vain
> Where once my careless childhood strayed,
> A stranger yet to pain.

Dr Johnson, who was on this issue extremely conservative, agreed that 'there is now less flogging in our great schools than formerly, but then less is learned there; so that what the boys get at one end they lose at the other'.

All that can be said about the lesser provincial grammar schools, which were increasingly abandoned by the squirarchy to the children of the middle and lower-middle classes, is that the concept of a grammar-school master as primarily a flagellant seems to have declined. The situation clearly varied greatly from school to school, depending on the temperament and character of the master. At Bury St Edmunds Grammar School in the 1730s and 1740s, an admittedly excellent master made full use of the rod and the ferule. In the 1750s in nearby Lavenham, Arthur Young received an inferior education, but was never beaten once. At Reading Grammar School in the late eighteenth century, George Hanger was brutally beaten for academic faults: the 'tyrant did but seldom use the rod; his favourite instrument was a long rattan cane, big enough to correct a culprit in Bridewell ... The shrieks of the boys who were writhing beneath his blows were music to his soul ... I declare to God I have seen wales on the sides, ribs and arms of boys of the bigness of my finger.'

There is some reason to suppose that brutality had always been less common in the many little private schools run by clergymen as a way of augmenting their income by taking in a few upper- or middle-class boarders and teaching them the classics, as well as in the larger and more professional academies, if only because their survival depended on their popularity with their middle-class clientele.. By the 1780s some private academies were boasting in their advertisements in the newspapers about their reliance on 'emulation excited by proper rewards at every reasonable opportunity', rather than 'corporal punishment'. As for girls' schools, physical punishment seems also to have died out by the end of the eighteenth century in the better-run establishments for the middle and upper classes. Mrs Boscawen, who was born in 1719, 'was never whipped at school', while at the Misses Lee's school at Bath in 1797, 'no one is ever allowed to be struck'.

John Locke seems to have been the first to protest vigorously against the encasing of young bodies in tight corsets reinforced with metal and whalebone. William Law, whose handbook on the upbringing of children ran to ten editions between 1729 and 1772, told the story of a mother whose daughters were laced as tightly as possible, stinted in their meals, and constantly given purges and enemas to maintain a fashionably pallid complexion. As a result not only were they all 'poor, pale, sickly, infirm creatures, vapoured through want of spirits', but the eldest daughter died at the age of twenty. At the autopsy it was found that 'her ribs had grown into her liver, and that her other entrails were much hurt by being crushed together with her stays, which her mother had ordered to be twitched so straight that it often brought tears into her eyes whilst the maid was dressing her'. Rousseau in *Émile* took a gloomy view of the biological and the aesthetic results: 'I cannot but think that this abuse, pushed in England to an inconceivable point, will cause in the end the degeneration of the race ... It is not agreeable to see a woman cut in two like a wasp.'

In practice, however, this was one area in which the combined criticism of philosophers and doctors had not the slightest effect. The reason that the most cruel physical restraints continued to be employed on girls, admittedly at school rather than in the home, throughout the more permissive and affectionate period of the eighteenth century, was that they were thought absolutely essential to create the physical attributes required to catch a husband. One victim of these contrivances was Mary Butt, the daughter of a parson, who grew very rapidly up to the age of thirteen, and had a tendency to stooping. 'It was the fashion then for children to wear iron collars round the neck, with a back-board strapped over the shoulders. To one of them I was subjected from my sixth to my thirteenth year. It was put on in the morning and seldom taken off till late in the evening, and I generally did my lessons standing in stocks with this stiff collar round my neck.' At about the same period Lucy Aikin underwent the same experience: 'There were backboards, iron collars, stocks for the feet, and a frightful kind of neckswing in which we were suspended every morning, whilst one of the teachers was lacing our stays, all which contrivances were intended and imagined to improve the figure and the air. Nothing was thought so awkward and vulgar as anything approaching to a stoop. "Hold up your head, Miss"', was the constant cry. I wonder any of us kept our health.'

Nor were stays and braces the only constraints imposed on fashionable girls. By the late eighteenth century, the ideal of feminine beauty and deportment was extreme slimness, a pale complexion and slow languid movements, all of which were deliberately inculcated in the most expensive boarding-schools. When Arthur Young's beloved daughter Bobbin caught tuberculosis in 1797, he blamed in part the school regime of inadequate food, no fresh air, and the forbidding of all running about or quick motions. By the late eighteenth century, the frail health induced by these constricted bodies and spare diets had become generally associated with the female sex. Women of 'the quality' were expected to be creatures whose 'whole frames [are] incessantly deranged by the most trivial shocks'. It was generally agreed that the ideal was a pale, languid and fainting belle, and that 'an air of robustness and strength is very prejudicial to beauty'. Dr Gregory advised that 'a wise woman enjoys her good health in grateful silence but never boasts of possessing it'.

By a strange twist of cultural fate, the sex which is the toughest and most resilient of the two became identified with both physical and psychological delicacy and debility — defects in fact artificially induced in the interests of conformity to the current ideal of beauty. The cultivation of feminine debility had the same symbolic significance as the crushing of the feet of upper-class Chinese women, and it survived the opposition of philosophers and doctors and was stimulated by the rise of a more child-centred society in the late eighteenth century. Loving parents now believed that their daughters' chances on the marriage market would be seriously impaired unless they had the correct, rigidly upright, posture, emaciated bodies, pallid complexion and languid airs, and were prepared to faint at the slightest provocation. The importance attached to these matters was a direct result of the decline of money and the rise of personal choice as the most important factor in the selection of a marriage partner. Girls were now competing with one another in an open market, for success in which physical and personal attributes had to a considerable degree taken over the role previously played by the size of the dowry. A straight back was now thought to be as important as a substantial cash portion in the struggle to catch the most eligible husband.

There can be no doubt that between 1660 and 1800 there took place major changes in child-rearing practice among the squirarchy and upper bourgeoisie. Swaddling gave way to loose clothing, mercenary wet-nursing to maternal breast-feeding, breaking the will by force to permissiveness, formal distance to empathy, as the mother became the dominant figure in the children's lives. These changes reflect a general easing of those tensions which justified the iron discipline of the post-Reformation century, and in their turn they helped to produce individuals less suspicious of the world at large, less prone to violence, and now capable of intense personal attachments to other individuals, in particular to their wives and children.

On the other hand there was a good deal of truth in the contemporary indictment of the permissive child-rearing patterns recently adopted by many middle- and upper-class parents. The critics argued that parents were failing in their prime responsibility to prepare their children to fit comfortably into the adult world that awaited them, and that the result was a generation of idle rakes, mannerless boors and social misfits. There was a partial breakdown of that essential process of the socialization of the child. Particular sufferers were those boys who were suddenly wrenched out of a home environment which was almost excessively affectionate and indulgent, and thrust into one of the great public boarding-schools, where the torture of younger boys by the older ones was common.

A further unfortunate consequence of the liberation of maternal love was that mothers found it almost impossible to let go of their children, especially their sons, when they reached adolescence. Childhood came to be regarded as the best years of one's life, instead of the grim purgatory it had been in the seventeenth century.

> Such, such were the joys
> When we all girls and boys
> In our youth were seen
> On the echoing green

wrote William Blake, whose attitude would have astonished John Aubrey and his contemporaries. But again and again it becomes apparent in the literature of the eighteenth century that this Golden Age of childhood under close maternal care had serious inhibiting consequences later on. As Professor Hagstrum has pointed out, 'the maternal orientation of romantic vision appears in the boyhood of the Man of Feeling', that archetypal hero of the late eighteenth century. Again and again the story is one of sexual love that goes unfulfilled, inhibited by an oedipal fixation on the mother.

2. CHILD-REARING MODES AND SOCIAL CATEGORIES

It cannot be emphasized too often that the changes in child-rearing which have been described were socially highly selective in their impact, affecting primarily the professional classes and the gentry, and later the nobility. The key to the story of the evolution of child-rearing is the principle of stratified diffusion, by which new attitudes first take hold among those classes which are most literate and most open to new ideas; and which are neither so very poor that economic circumstances often compel them to neglect, exploit or abandon their children; nor so very rich that their social and political life-style is too time-consuming to allow them to devote much time or trouble to child-rearing, and whose enormous economic assets encourage them to compel their children to marry persons selected for them on strictly economic or political grounds. The first to adopt the new attitudes towards children were professional people, wealthy merchants and the squirarchy, all of whom were economically entrepreneurial, often upwardly mobile, and united by a common literary culture. Parents from these classes did not personally attend to the day-to-day needs of their children, who were looked after by nurses, maids, governesses and tutors, but they did see them every day, and gave them their full attention during those periods. For many mothers, this took up a good deal of their time.

At the highest level of society, among the court aristocrats and among some of the wealthy squires, there were many families in the eighteenth century in which both husband and wife were too immersed in politics and the social whirl of London and the court to bother themselves with their children, who for the first six to eight years were left in the hands of wet-nurses, nurses, governesses and tutors. After that the boys were then sent off to school, the university and the Grand Tour. These were not harsh or cruel parents, merely indifferent ones who had little interest in their children and saw little of them. Between 1682 and 1698, from the age of six when he went away to school to the age of twenty-two when he was summoned back from Cambridge on the death of his elder brother, Robert Walpole had only spent a few weeks at a time, at rare intervals, at home with his parents. Similarly, when John, son of the first Earl of Bute, went off to school at Eton at the age of seven, he did not return home again until he was almost a man, for he spent his holidays with his uncles, who clearly acted as surrogate parents. Girls were kept at home, but were particularly undesirable, and expensive to get rid of in marriage. 'Lady Hervey is brought to bed of a nasty, shabby girl,' Lord Hervey told his intimate friend, Henry Fox, in 1734.

In the course of the eighteenth century many of the professional and landed classes of England seem to have evolved a very long way towards the child-oriented society as we know it today. As a professional man with little professional business to perform, James Boswell was in the exceptional position of having plenty of time at home to devote to his children. In his diary he was careful to record the lisping efforts of his young children as they learned to speak. 'Etti me see u pictur,' said his little daughter Veronica. When she rubbed Boswell's sprained ankle, 'with eager affection I cried "God Bless you my dearest little creature". She answered "od bless u, Papa".' The only fly in the ointment was that 'she loved her mother more than me'. He was delighted when, as he left home on a trip, the five-year-old Veronica 'cried very much and clasped her little arms around my neck, calling out "O Papa". Sandie cried too ...' He was equally pleased to find that on his return home 'the children were quite overjoyed to see me again. Effie and Sandie actually cried.

This was very fine.' His letters to his son Sandie are both affectionate and written as one equal to another. So far as the record goes, he only beat Sandie once in his life, and this was for telling a lie. As the children increased in number and grew up, Boswell took them on special outings for their pleasure, and every Sunday he listened to them reciting psalms and the Lord's Prayer. He found his younger son Jamie 'a delightful child', went out riding with his eldest son Sandie, and was very touched when in 1782, as he was leaving for a trip, the nine-year-old Veronica said 'Papa, write to me.' He and his wife made the Boswell home so much of a nest that the children found it difficult to leave. In 1783 the nine-year-old Phemie was sent to school in Edinburgh as a full boarder, while the ten-year-old Veronica for some reason attended only as a day boarder. But Phemie 'cried so much that after persisting for a week, we allowed her to come home every evening as well as her sister'. Three years later Boswell was busy helping Sandie with his Latin, and Veronica and Phemie with their French.

It should be emphasized that Boswell was by no means exceptional in his interest in his children, and some of the stories he tells about others clearly prove that affectionate child-centred family attitudes had spread in the late eighteenth century even to some fathers among the highest court aristocracy. When in 1778 Boswell visited the Earl of Pembroke in his London house, there was 'coffee and tea and little Lady Charlotte climbing on her father's knee ... I was delighted with the perfection of easy fashionable behaviour.' He was equally pleased to learn that the Duke of Gloucester 'put his little daughter to bed every night ... resembling myself and Veronica'. Another very affectionate and permissive father was Henry Fox, Lord Holland, who despite his heavy involvement in political affairs found time to write anxiously about the welfare of his children and spend some time with them. When his precocious son Charles was only three, his father was already fascinated by him. 'I dined at home today *tête-à-tête* with Charles, intending to do business; but he had found me pleasanter employment. I grow immoderately fond of him.' As a result, he spoilt the child, calmly ignored his temper tantrums, and refused to allow him to be disciplined. The boy grew into that charming, impetuous, wilful, brilliant, but erratic and dissipated statesman, Charles James Fox.

It is maternal rather than paternal affection which is most amply documented in the eighteenth century, and the intimate family groups of mothers and children depicted by Reynolds and Zoffany clearly had a firm basis in reality. Many wives and mothers, when faced with the choice of personally supervising their children, or leaving them to servants, nurses and governesses and accompanying their husbands on pleasure or business, unhesitatingly chose the former, despite the recognized probability that the decision would drive their husbands into the arms of a prostitute or mistress. Mrs Boswell was far from unique when in 1778 she was 'so anxious about her children that she thinks she should be unhappy if at a distance from them', and so let the highly unreliable Boswell go off to London by himself.

Nothing could be more unlike the harsh and remote seventeenth-century upper-class domestic relations or the cloyingly pious and morally oppressive Victorian ones than the warmth, affection and tact which enveloped the family life of Lady Sarah Lennox, wife of the Honourable George Napier, and their children. When in her old age in about 1820, one of her daughters-in-law questioned her about her relations with her children, her reply (as reported by her interrogator) was very revealing:

As they rose out of infancy, I left them to their father's management, and studied to become their friend, not the tutoress of my sons . . . In me they trusted to find sympathy, kindness, my opinion or advice if they sought it, knowing at the same time that it was unaccompanied by the necessity of adopting it . . . Then, left to decide for themselves, their actions (even if unknown to themselves) were somewhat of the hue of what they had just heard.

The reason for her influence, she thought, was that her children always recognized her as 'the object of their father's tender love and care, seeing me at the same time holding a high place in his estimation as his friend and companion'. The same warm relationships seem to have prevailed in the families of their children.

Some families within this same social class followed a different mode. A remarkably well-documented example of the caring but authoritarian parent of the eighteenth century who still resorted to physical force to break the will of her children is the case of Mrs Hester Lynch Thrale (Plate 16). Born in 1741 the daughter of an impoverished branch of the wealthy gentry family of the Salusburys, she was adopted by a rich, childless uncle and so became a desirable heiress. In 1763, at the age of twenty-two, the combined pressures of her mother and her uncle induced her to agree to marry a wealthy brewer, Henry Thrale, whose primary interest in her, it seems, was her £10,000 marriage portion from her uncle. In the next fourteen years, from 1764 to 1778, she had two miscarriages and produced twelve children. This was an exceptionally high fertility rate, no doubt helped by the use of wet-nurses to suckle the children, which exposed her very rapidly after birth to renewed sexual activity and liability to pregnancy. In 1779 she remarked 'five little girls and breeding again, and fool enough to be proud of it. Ah, idiot, what should I want more children for? God knows only to please my husband.'

A careful record Mrs Thrale kept from 1766 to 1778 allows a unique view of one mother's relations with her children. Mrs Thrale was far from being typical, but her story is firmly embedded in the culture of her time and her class. Old-fashioned views about total submission of the will by physical force – encouraged by Mrs Thrale's chief friend and advisor Dr Johnson, who spent much of his life living with the family – were coupled with a strong maternal ambition to produce a series of intellectual child prodigies. The tragedy was that her failure to breast-feed them, her harsh educational methods, and her selfish ambition to make her children exceptional in their learning and achievements alienated their affections, while her extraordinary fertility – one birth every fourteen months or so – produced a race of puny children who were constantly dying. For twelve years, however, all her energies were devoted to her children. She was lacking any emotional support from her husband, who followed his business, pursued his own gay social life and his extra-marital affairs, largely ignored his growing brood of children, and only paid sufficient attention to his wife in bed to keep her constantly pregnant in the hopes of getting a male heir to carry on his brewery. She was an energetic and dynamic woman, deprived of all emotional or functional outlets except her children, her mother, and her books. As she described it, 'We kept the finest table possible at Streatham Park, but [I] his wife was not to think of the kitchen. So I never knew what was for dinner till I saw it ... From a gay life my mother held me fast. Those pleasures Mr Thrale enjoyed alone ... Driven thus on literature as my sole resource, no wonder if I loved my books and my children.' She 'brought a baby once a year, lost some of them, and grew so anxious about the rest that I now fairly cared for nothing else but them and her' – her mother, whom she saw for several hours almost every day.

When her Children's Book opens in 1766, Mrs Thrale's eldest daughter Hester, or 'Queeney', was already a child wonder. The eighteenth century was an age which encouraged child prodigies, whose parents took pride in showing them off to visitors, and her mother treated her very much like a show animal. Queeney was indeed truly remarkable for her memory. At two and a half she could not read or write, but she already knew the compass, the solar system, the signs of the zodiac, the nations, seas and islands and European capital cities, the three Christian virtues, the first page of Lilly's *Grammar*, the names of colours, the days of the week and the months of the year, the two-times table, the Pater Noster, the Nicene Creed and the Decalogue, and could tell the stories of the Fall of Man, Perseus and Andromeda, and the Judgement of Paris. By the age of three, Queeney could repeat all the Responses, but still could not read, and was a poor speller. By four and a half she could read fairly well and knew her Latin grammar to the fifth declension.

Mrs Thrale's obsessive devotion to Queeney knew no bounds. In 1770, by which time Queeney was six, she recorded that she went to the theatre (taking Queeney with her) for the first time since the child was born. 'I have never dined out, nor ever paid a visit where I did not carry her, unless I left her in bed; for to the care of servants (except asleep) I have never yet left her an hour.' At the age of six and a quarter, in January 1771, her mother made her go through her paces before Mr Bright of Abingdon, who finally declared that if the examination had been in Latin, 'she would have qualified for a degree in the university of Oxford'. Queeney's emotional response to all this excessive maternal care and egotistical devotion – her mother was constantly showing off her child prodigy – was far from satisfactory. Her mother concluded that the girl was 'obstinate to that uncommon degree, that no punishment except severe smart can prevail upon her to beg pardon if she has offended'. 'A heart void of all affection for any person in the world, but aversion enough for many.' After ten years she noted that Queeney was 'sullen, malicious, perverse, desirous of tormenting *me*, even by hurting herself'.

Among all her many children, two were her particular favourites. Lucy was 'wonderfully amiable. I am accused of a partial fondness towards her, but she is so lively one cannot resist her coaxing.' Henry 'has charity, piety, benevolence . . . a desire for knowledge . . . He is so rational, so attentive, so good.' On the other hand, poor little

Susanna, the premature baby, was ugly, sickly, and whining. Her mother detested the child – 'her temper is so peevish and her person so displeasing that I do not love to converse with her' – and packed her off at the age of four to a private school in Kensington, where to her astonishment the girl immediately began to thrive. In 1775 Mrs Thrale decided to take the other girl, Sophy, back home since she was 'very amiable. I will keep her at home, Queeney and I can tutor her mighty well, and it will be an amusement.' This wholly self-centred attitude towards her children was coupled with the use of force to make herself obeyed. She beat her children with her 'Salusbury fist' to make them obey her orders at once and to learn their lessons. This aroused the disgust and hostility of their Italian teacher Baretti, who advocated an educational system based on permissiveness and love, and encouraged the children to oppose their mother. So there was constant friction in the home.

It was not until 1774, after eleven years of child-rearing, that Mrs Thrale first took an extended holiday away from them. Even then, she was a prey to anxiety and wept when no letters arrived from home to tell her how they were faring. What eventually soured her on her educational endeavours was partly the hostility towards her expressed especially by her prized pupil Queeney, and partly the constant attrition of the children by death. One child died within ten hours from respiratory trouble, one within two weeks of diarrhoea, one within six months of influenza; these deaths could be endured, but the beloved Lucy died at four of mastoiditis. One son, Ralph, was diagnosed as suffering from brain disease ('a thing to hide and be ashamed of whilst we live'), but fortunately died at under two; Henrietta died of measles at five; Susanna, as we have seen, was sickly and ugly, and was sent off to school at four. But their mother constantly worried about the health of the others, stayed up all night with them when they were sick, and doctored them herself to try to cure them. The greatest blow was the death in 1776, at the age of nine, of Henry, the talented, handsome and amiable only son and heir. He suddenly collapsed and died within hours of a ruptured appendix, leaving his mother 'childless with all her children – want an heir'. 'I was too proud of him,' she told herself, 'and provoked God's judgements by my folly. Let this sorrow expiate my offences, good Lord ... Suffer me no more to follow my offspring to the grave.' She, and even more her husband, desperately wanted a boy, if only for a simple economic reason. As her friend and advisor Dr Johnson put it, 'a son is almost necessary to the continuance of Thrale's fortune; for what can misses do with a brew-house? Lands are fitter for daughters than trades.' It was probably for this reason that she allowed herself to be constantly re-impregnated by her husband, although to no effect. 'Mrs Thrale is in hopes of a young brewer,' commented Dr Johnson when she once more became pregnant in 1777.

But the events of 1776 finally broke Mrs Thrale's determination to mould the lives of her children, and to turn them all into prodigies of learning who could be put on display. Within one year she had lost three of her six children, including the only boy, and became thoroughly disillusioned. 'I have really listened to babies learning till I am half stupefied – and all my pains have answered so poorly. I have no heart to battle with Sophy. She would probably learn very well, if I had the spirit of teaching I once had ... I will not make her life miserable, as I suppose it will be short ... At present I cannot begin battling with babies – I have already spent my whole youth at it, and lost my reward at last.' Of the three surviving daughters, two were sullen and hostile to their mother.

So at last, in 1776, she abandoned the struggle to subdue her children's wills and to cram book-learning down their throats, pushed the survivors off to school, and turned her energies to her literary pursuits, the cultivation of the blue-stocking coterie of London, and the creation of an intellectual salon of her own. Her children had defeated her either by dying or by ingratitude. In 1781 her husband died of apoplexy, leaving his widow with five surviving daughters (of whom one soon died). Mrs Thrale then at last faced the bitter truth: 'They are five lovely creatures to be sure, but they love me not. Is it my fault or theirs?' Two years later, she abandoned both her old friend Dr Johnson and her four surviving children for the sake of a passionate romance: she married their Italian music teacher Mr Piozzi and went off to Italy to taste, for the first time in her life, the pleasures of true married love.

What conclusions are we to draw from this story? It concerns a woman who directed all her driving ambition on to her children, for lack of any serious support from, or interest shown in her by, her husband. Dominant, authoritarian, demanding, possessive, and wholly selfish in her pursuit of ego-gratification through her children, as a mother Mrs Thrale/Piozzi was a total failure. She had not succeeded in turning any of her children into intellectual prodigies, and she had not attracted their affection. Lucy and Henry, the two to whom she had been most attached and who seemed both most closely to match her ambitions for them and to reciprocate her love, both died young, aged four and nine respectively. The two upon whom she had lavished most attention, the eldest Queeney and the youngest Cecilia, came to resent her most and even speculated that subconsciously she actually hated them because of her hostile feelings towards their father. The combination of the physically repressive parental mode of the seventeenth century with the child-oriented obsessions of the eighteenth, and the high intellectual ambitions of the contemporary female blue-stocking, together formed an altogether disastrous mix.

All the evidence hitherto put forward for an increasing concern for children is strictly confined to the upper landed and high professional or bourgeois classes, and there is no evidence that this attitude penetrated much lower down the social scale. One would suppose that stern Calvinistic ideas about upbringing persisted longest among the lower-middle class, but this is largely speculation.

It seems not unlikely that in many lower-middle-class homes, there was carried over from the seventeenth century the concept of the innate depravity of children and therefore the need and the incentive for an unremitting and stern effort to break the child's will and so repress his impulses to sin. There seems to have been an uninterrupted connection between the caring but authoritarian discipline of the Puritan bourgeois parent of the seventeenth century and the caring but authoritarian discipline of the Evangelical bourgeois parent of the late eighteenth and early nineteenth centuries.

The link between the two is provided by the methods of education of children adopted by John Wesley's mother Susanna at Epworth rectory in the early years of the eighteenth century and passed on by him to the Wesleyan movement. As she explained her policies in 1732, 'when turned a year old, and some before, they were taught to fear the rod and cry softly, by which means they escaped the abundance of correction they might otherwise have had, and that most odious noise of the crying of children was rarely heard in the house'. The children were drilled into strict obedience to parental instructions. 'In order to form the minds of the children, the first thing to be done is to conquer their will and bring them to an obedient temper.' 'Whenever a child is corrected, it must be conquered', for this provides 'the only strong and rational foundation of a religious education'. As a result, the children were made to eat everything that was put before them, even if it nauseated them, and were fully obedient to Susanna's wishes. She devoted her life to them, teaching them religion and the three Rs six hours a day. It was her policy to reward them for goodwill and effort, even if the results were unsuccessful, thus encouraging them to try their very best. It was a discipline not too far removed from that recommended by Locke. It was strict, intrusive, but supportive, rational and predictably consistent. Where it differed from that of Locke was that the object, so far as the parents were concerned, was to please God, and to bring up the next generation to internalize the same strong sense of piety and duty. The result of this upbringing was the adult John Wesley, a compulsive perfectionist, with a persistent desire to conform to authority, but with an overwhelming sense of his own role in history as one of the chosen of God. Half a century later, in 1783, Wesley was still preaching the same doctrines in his *Sermon on the Education of Children*. Although he admitted that in his degenerate age only one parent in a hundred had the resolution to go through with it, he insisted on the need to 'break the will of your child, to bring his will into subjection to yours, that it may be afterwards subject to the will of God'.

It is no surprise, therefore, to find a late eighteenth-century Evangelical like Hannah More, a middle-class educational reformer of the poor, echoing the ideas of Susanna Wesley, and writing in 1799 that it is a 'fundamental error to consider children as innocent beings, whose little weaknesses may perhaps want some correction, rather than as beings who bring into the world a corrupt nature and evil dispositions, which it should be the great end of education to rectify'. This could be interpreted to mean that Hannah More thought that the 'childish innocence' theory was very common among her audience, or that she was reinforcing and repeating accepted dogma. It seems at least likely that the lower-middle classes never accepted the Lockean view of the child as a *tabula rasa* upon which society could imprint its image, much less the Rousseauesque theory that he is born naturally good. They always knew about Original Sin and acted accordingly, using a combination of physical force and moral manipulation that varied from family to family.

Among the mass of the very poor, the available evidence suggests that the common behaviour of many parents towards their children was often unpredictable, and sometimes indifferent or cruel. It is not clear whether the reason was cultural, a result of deprivation of any property stake in society and displacement far from home and kin, or whether it was economic, in the sense that more humane feelings and a greater sense of sustained concern were luxuries which they could rarely afford. The culture of poverty did not encourage foresight or providence, since the lives of those on the economic margin of existence were too much at the mercy of sheer chance – a bad harvest, unemployment or sickness – to justify rational calculation for the future. They were in the habit of treating their children occasionally with rough, even extravagant affection in good times, and with casual indifference, and not infrequently with great brutality, when in drink or in bad times. If they were cruel to their children, it was because they needed to vent their frustrations on somebody, or because they failed to foresee the consequences of their actions, or because that was the way they themselves had been brought up, and they therefore regarded it as the normal and proper method of rearing children, or because they had no alternative due to economic circumstances. In a society which was generally horribly cruel to animals, children tended to be treated in a similar manner. As late as 1846, a sensible upper-class woman commented that 'anyone who has been accustomed to live in a country village must know that the children of the poor there are brought up with blows – with harsh words'. It was for this reason that she strongly advised against entrusting the power of punishment of upper-class children to a nurse or servant, since the latter would 'naturally carry the same system into execution'.

For those without property, security or prospects, children were sometimes an unmitigated nuisance. There was the cost of feeding and housing them and the opportunity cost in the removal of the wife for a time from productive labour in order to breast-feed and look after the children. Even if the child could be gainfully employed after the age of seven, which was possible in many rural areas for guarding animals, collecting firewood, frightening birds, etc., and became both more common and more profitable in the early stages of the industrial revolution, there were still seven years in which it would have to be fed. If the wife produced a child every two years, the family might therefore have to support three or four unproductive mouths, which was a burden that many simply could not afford. One is torn between pity and horror at the story of the poor man near Wakefield in 1674 who 'hanged his own child to death for taking a piece of bread to eat it; another child said, "father, you'll not hang me, I took no bread" '.

Neglect of children was particularly prevalent in areas where female employment was high and the demand for child labour was low. The mothers went out to work every day, leaving their children at home, exposed to malnutrition and maltreatment, and often dosed with opiates to keep them quiet. In these areas, child mortality was very much higher than in others where the women stayed at home, the cause being death by negligence. Where the women stayed at home and the children survived, hunger and deprivation was their lot, and William Huntingdon, a future Methodist preacher, had bitter memories of his childhood as the son of a day-labourer earning no more than 7s to 9s a week and with eleven children to support. 'Suffering with hunger, cold and almost nakedness so embittered my life in childhood that I often wished secretly that I had been a brute, for then I could have filled my belly in the fields.'

Even the industrious and sober labourer found himself in much the same plight as the feckless poor who drowned their despair in drink. Francis Place, who began his married life in the 1790s in London, living in one room in miserable poverty, repeatedly refers to the curse of many children. This was a situation which he apparently thought inevitable, for he seems to have had no knowledge whatever of contraception. He explains how desperate was the situation of the diligent labouring poor at that time, who could see no hope of improvement of their lot. 'How, as the number of their children increases, hope leaves them. How their hearts sink as toil becomes useless.' As for himself, 'I saw the certainty that I should have a large family, and that nothing but wretchedness awaited us', unless he could set himself up in business. His wife became pregnant at regular intervals, and looking after the first two children took her from productive labour as his helper. She, too, fell into despair as 'her fears of our ever doing well were increased by her again being pregnant'. Although she was up for the family dinner within three days of giving birth, the care of the children reduced her earning power, and the increase of mouths to feed dragged down the already marginal living standards of the family.

One consequence of the rise in the proportion of the propertyless in the society was a rise in the rates of illegitimate to legitimate births, for reasons which will be discussed later on. The rise in bastardy inevitably stimulated some deliberate infanticide and a great deal of abandonment, for the plight of an unmarried mother without means of support was bad enough to encourage a few desperate women to murder their newly born infants and many more to leave them in the streets either to die or to be looked after by a charitable passer-by, the parish workhouse, or a foundling hospital. There is a long history of fairly generalized infanticide in western Europe going back to antiquity, when it seems to have been extremely common. In the sixteenth and seventeenth centuries, as the Church strengthened its hold over the moral conduct of the population at large and enlisted the help of the state in law enforcement, infanticide became a much more serious offence. Since it deprived an infant of baptism, and so the opportunity for salvation, it now became a crime that carried with it the penalty of death. It therefore became a practice almost entirely confined to those most desperate of women, unmarried mothers. When the three witches in *Macbeth* were concocting their magic brews, among the many things they threw into their cauldron was a

> Finger of birth-strangled babe
> Ditch-delivered by a drab.

Finding this ingredient, which might be a little hard to come by in the twentieth century, should not have presented insuperable difficulties in Shakespearean England.

Deliberate infanticide – to become 'the butcher of her own bowels' – was a solution adopted by only the most desperate of pregnant mothers, and abandonment, both of illegitimate and of legitimate children, was infinitely more common. As Jonas Hanway observed in 1766, 'it is much less difficult to the human heart and the dictates of self-preservation to drop a child than to kill it'. During the eighteenth century rapidly increasing numbers of infants were simply abandoned in the streets, and left to become a charge on the parish. Most of them were sent off to the parish workhouses, which were built after 1722, and where the death rate was almost as high as if they had been left in the streets.

There is no wonder in this, when it is considered that these children were put into the hands of indigent, filthy and decrepit women, three or four to one woman, and sometimes sleeping with them. The allowance to these women being scanty, they are tempted to take the bread and milk intended for the poor infants. The child cries for food, and the nurse beats it because it cries. Thus with blows, starving and putrid air, with the addition of lice, itch, filthiness, he soon receives his quietus.

For the few who survived, the prospect was a grim one. The older females were frequently handed over to 'a master who is either vicious or cruel: in the one case they fall victim to his irregular passions (Plate 26); and in the other are subjected, with unreasonable severity, to tasks too hard to be performed'. These were the lucky ones, others being virtually enslaved by criminals and trained for a life of prostitution if female or of robbery and pick-pocketing if male. Some had their teeth torn out to serve as artificial teeth for the rich; others were deliberately maimed by beggars to arouse compassion and extract alms. Even this latter crime was one upon which the law looked with a remarkably tolerant eye. In 1761 a beggar woman, convicted of deliberately 'putting out the eyes of children with whom she went about the country' in order to attract pity and alms, was sentenced to no more than two years' imprisonment.

During the 1730s Captain Thomas Coram frequently walked from Rotherhithe through the East London slums to the City. These walks 'afforded him frequent occasions of seeing young children exposed, sometimes alive, sometimes dead, and sometimes dying, which affected him extremely'. As a result, he enlisted support from the wealthy, and in 1741 established the London Foundling Hospital, 'to prevent the frequent murders of poor miserable children at their birth, and so suppress the inhuman custom of exposing new-born infants to perils in the streets, and to take in children dropped in churchyards or in the streets, or left at night at the doors of church wardens or Overseers of the Poor'. The hospital was planned to accept a limited number of children each year, but in 1756 a well-meaning Parliament threw it open to the country as a whole. The results were catastrophic. Three or four thousand infants poured in every year, being collected in baskets from all over the country by itinerant baby transporters, who dumped the contents, dead, dying or half alive, on the doorsteps of the hospital. Travelling tinkers were paid a guinea to carry a child to the hospital, while another man took four infants from Yorkshire, two in each pannier, for eight guineas the trip. Of the 15,000 children dumped in the hospital in the first four years, some 10,000 died. It became 'a charnel house for the dead'.

Although many of this growing mass of abandoned children were illegitimate, a majority seem to have been legitimate children of couples who were financially unable to support them. Abandonment of infants was thus a product partly of rising rates of bastardy, but still more of a deepening economic crisis for the very poor. Partly also it was a population control device operating after birth for lack of the two alternatives – abortion of the foetus while in the womb or the prevention of conception. The paradox should also be noted that the practice of abandonment was partly stimulated by the setting up of charitable public institutions. It was easier for mothers to abandon their children if they knew that they would be picked up, even if the workhouses and foundling hospitals in which they were deposited in practice, and inevitably, became little more than licensed death camps.

By 1820 the situation, at any rate in London, was already greatly improved. Francis Place, who was a very well-informed observer of urban poverty in the metropolis, had no doubts about the changes which had occurred in the previous fifty years. Recalling conditions he knew in the 1770s, he denounced 'the ignorance, the immorality, the grossness, the obscenity, the drunkenness, the dirtiness, and the depravity of the middling and even a large portion of the better sort of tradesmen, the artisans, and the journeymen tradesmen of London in the days of my youth'. The causes of the change he attributed to the introduction of cotton underclothing which revolutionized the problem of personal cleanliness; a higher standard of living as the benefits of the industrial revolution seeped down to the poor; a greater sense of self-respect and equality as a result of the diffusion of the ideas of Tom Paine and the French Revolution; and the moral and literary education of children provided by the Sunday Schools. The result was a general elevation of 'the manners and morals of the whole community'. Bad as things were by the time Marx and Dickens were writing, they were very much better than they had been in the third quarter of the eighteenth century. In 1824 Francis Place had no doubt that in his lifetime, he had seen an 'increased knowledge of domestic concerns and the general maintenance of children'.

PART FIVE

Sex

'Knowledge gives like pleasure to the mind that Venus doth to the body.'

(Marginalia by King Charles I on a copy of F. Bacon, *Advancement of Learning*, in the British Museum. I owe this reference to Dr M. Smuts)

'I could be content that we might procreate like trees, without conjunction, or that there was any way to perpetuate the world without this trivial and vulgar way of coition; it is the foolishest act a wise man commits in all his life; nor is there anything that will more deject his cooled imagination, when he shall consider what an odd and unworthy piece of folly he has committed.'

(T. Browne, *Religio Medici*, 1642, Oxford, 1909, p. 163)

CHAPTER TEN

Upper-Class Attitudes and Behaviour

'The husband who, transported by immoderate love, has intercourse with his wife so *ardently* in order to satisfy his passion that, even had she not been his wife he would have wished to have commerce with her, is committing a sin.'

> (J. Benedicti, *Somme des Péchés*, 1584, quoted by J.-L. Flandrin, 'Contraception, Marriage and Sexual Relations in the Christian West' in *Biology of Man in History*, ed. R. Forster and O. Ranum, Baltimore, 1975, p. 35)

'Life can little else supply
But a few good fucks and then we die.'

> (J. Wilkes, *Essays on Woman*, 1763, ed. J. C. Hotten, London, 1871, p. 13)

1. INTRODUCTION: GENERAL CONSIDERATIONS

In terms of its sexual drive, the human species lies at the extreme end of the normal range of animal behaviour, in that the drive lasts all the year round, and even during periods when reproduction is impossible. This is caused by the biological fact that, at some very remote time in the past, the human female lost the oestrus, the brief but intense period of sexual receptivity. On the other hand, the abnormal size and development of man's cerebral cortex means that the sexual drive is stimulated or controlled by cultural norms and learned experience. Despite appearances, human sex takes place mostly in the head. The Freudian assumption that sex is an unchanging infrastructure, and that there has been no change in the strength of the libido over time, has therefore no basis in reality, so deeply is it overlaid by cultural norms.

It seems very likely that the levels of marital and extra-marital sexual activity revealed in late twentieth-century surveys are far higher than those normally achieved in the Early Modern period. In the first place, the general standard of personal hygiene, even among the elite, was very low. Samuel Pepys was a successful bureaucrat and a business associate of great nobles and courtiers in London of the 1660s. Yet he regarded it as a matter of course that he should have lice in his hair, for which his maid regularly combed him, and he only expressed surprise when one day his wife found no fewer than twenty of them. He hardly ever washed his body until February 1664 when his wife suddenly went to a bathhouse, temporarily discovered the pleasures of cleanliness and refused to allow him into her bed until he too had washed. After holding out for three days, he finally gave way to her whim and bathed in hot water. As for William Byrd, sixty years later in London, he washed his feet every few weeks, but bathed only when he took a woman to a bagnio for a night of sexual enjoyment – and then not every time. As late as the 1760s Topham Beauclerk, a man of charm and wit who moved in the highest aristocratic circles, was 'remarkably filthy in his person, which generated vermin'. Despite the fact that his wife, Lady Diana, slept in a separate bed and had her sheets changed daily, he was not in the least ashamed of his condition. When at a Christmas party at Blenheim, all the ladies complained to him that he was spreading lice in their hair, he retorted casually: 'Are they so nice as that comes to? Why, I have enough to stock a parish.' One or two private bathrooms existed at the end of the seventeenth century, but only in the most-up-to-date palaces of the enormously rich. For example, at Chatsworth in 1700 the Duke and Duchess of Devonshire had a sumptuous marble bathroom, with a marble bath large enough for two, fed by hot and cold water taps. The Duke and Duchess of Bedford had baths with running hot and cold water in their country seat at Woburn Abbey and their town house at Bedford House by about the middle of the century, and they installed a water-closet for themselves in 1771. But this was altogether exceptional, and most people, even in the highest social stratum, hardly ever washed anything, except their faces, necks, hands and feet. Lord Hervey seems to have been the earliest Englishman on record to have bathed daily, and this was in the early eighteenth century.

There is evidence to suggest that carelessness in personal hygiene was more common among upper-class women in England than abroad, and was something which greatly annoyed those men who took their sexual pleasures seriously. The first, and frankest, to complain was John Wilmot, Earl of Rochester, in the 1670s:

> Fair nasty nymph, be clean and kind
> And all my joys restore
> By using paper still behind
> The sponges for before.

In the early eighteenth century, Swift confirmed that English women neglected 'care in the cleanliness and sweetness of their persons', while in the middle of the century the rake John Wilkes echoed Rochester's complaint that 'the nobler parts are never in this island washed by the women; they are left to be lathered by the men'. In 1755 John Shebbeare also confirmed that among English women 'the parts concealed are more neglected than among the regions of Italy', and in 1792 Mary Wollstonecraft asserted that among English women 'that regard to cleanliness ... is violated in a beastly manner'. Half a century later in 1841, Dr William Acton was still complaining that in England women 'wash every other part of the body, but, unhappily for their own comfort as well as that of their husbands, they seem averse to let clean water reach the vagina'. To what extent this lack of personal cleanliness, particularly among women, acted as a disincentive to sexual play and intercourse is not an easy question to answer. It is certain that earlier societies were far less offended by smells than we are today. It is also a known fact that in the animal world female genital body odours – chemical substances called pheromones – play a critically important part in triggering male sexual responses, and that they also play some part, if only to a somewhat atrophied degree, in human sexuality. Body cleanliness is one thing, but use of the vaginal douche may well reduce rather than increase sexual desire in the male. On the other hand, contemporary complaints about the dirtiness of women, and the use of the bagnio as a place of sexual assignation, both suggest that men in the seventeenth and eighteenth centuries found cleanliness a positive asset to sexual activity. The bidet was introduced into upper-class French households in the early eighteenth century, but never spread to England. As early as 1752 it was known in England as a 'machine such as the French ladies use when they perform their ablutions'; but it was not adopted. English opposition to it, which was based apparently on moral rather than hygienic objections, supports the hypothesis of an association of cleanliness with foreplay and oral sex.

Another fact of Early Modern life which is easy to forget is that only a relatively small proportion of the adult population at any given time was both healthy and attractive, quite apart from the normal features of smell and dirt. Both sexes suffered long periods of crippling illness, which incapacitated them for months or years. Even when relatively well, they often suffered from disorders which made sex painful to them or unpleasant to their partners. Women suffered from a whole series of gynaecological disorders, particularly leuchorrhoea, but also vaginal ulcers, tumours, inflammations and haemorrhages which often made sexual intercourse disagreeable, painful or impossible. Both sexes must very often have had bad breath from the rotting teeth and constant stomach disorders which can be documented from many sources, while suppurating ulcers, eczema, scabs, running sores and other nauseating skin diseases were extremely common, and often lasted for years.

In addition, there was the ever-present risk of venereal disease, which seems to have been spreading steadily over the centuries. As we shall see, Boswell contracted gonorrhoea at least seventeen times during his life. In 1762–3 both Charles Churchill and his mistress had it, and the former was taking the dangerous remedy of mercury treatment to cure it. In 1787 Lord Herbert got it after serving as president at a military dinner. 'Curse great English dinners and military or civil clubs,' commented his father, 'all is drunkenness and pox afterwards with us.' As a result, Lord Herbert was ill for a considerable time with 'a wound in my groin which no one can persuade to heal', and which had to be cut by a surgeon five times. As we shall see, wives not infrequently found themselves sleeping with husbands suffering from venereal disease, as a result of which they developed the disease themselves. Not surprisingly, eighteenth-century newspapers were full of advertisements for such things as Dr Rock's 'Famous Anti-Venereal Grand Specific Pill'.

Among the poor, all the disincentives already listed were present to an exacerbated degree. Because of the cost of soap, the lack of facilities for washing, and from traditional habit, the poor were very much dirtier than the rich. Francis Place recalled that among the lower-middle and lower classes in the late eighteenth century, bed sheets were changed three times a year at most. Women wore stays made of bone or leather, which lasted for decades and were worn day in and day out without ever being washed. They also wore quilted petticoats which were also never washed and were worn until they disintegrated. As for children, 'when I was a boy . . . the children of tradesmen . . . all . . . had lice in their hair', which was combed once a week, while grown-ups, even in these more respectable circles, were not free from them. But in Place's opinion, the spread of cheap and easily washable cotton clothes in the early nineteenth century 'has done all but wonders in respect to the cleanliness and healthiness of women'.

Because of poor diet and lack of protection from the weather, it is probable that sickness was more common among the poor than among the rich. Many of the very poor also suffered from malnutrition, especially in years of harvest deficiency, and it is known that a severely reduced level of caloric intake will somewhat reduce the sexual instinct among males, and greatly reduce it among females. Even if adequately fed, sheer physical exhaustion from labour in the fields could reduce sexual desire.

At all social levels there were also psychological inhibitions as well as physical, quite apart from internalized restrictions imposed by moral theology. The poor seem in general to have been both more prudish and less imaginative about sex than the leisured classes. Reluctance to strip naked was especially prevalent among the poor. A French doctor confirmed that foreplay was largely unknown among the peasantry. As a result, lower- and lower-middle-class sexual activity in the Early Modern period has been described as 'man on top, woman on bottom, little foreplay, rapid ejaculation, masculine unconcern for feminine orgasm'. As such, it was a mirror of prevailing social relationships, where the patriarchal power of the husband for long remained in full force.

Among all classes, the fear of unwanted pregnancy must have been a very powerful deterrent to sexual pleasure, not only for wives who found themselves repeatedly giving birth painfully and dangerously, but also for husbands who had somehow to find the money for the upkeep of the growing brood of children. The best known method of contraception, the practice of *coitus interruptus*, or withdrawal by the male before ejaculation, requires great self-control and must therefore also act as a strong inhibiting factor to the male, while possibly affording little satisfaction to the female. The latter would often have had to choose between completing the sexual act and consequently running the risk of pregnancy, or withdrawal before she reached her climax, leaving her sexually aroused but frustrated. Nineteenth-century writers went to great lengths to stress the harmful effects of this practice on women, 'whose nervous system suffers from ungratified excitement', when 'the sensibilities of the womb and the entire reproductive system are teased to no purpose'. This merely added to normal female complaints about 'the hasty ejaculation of the husband'.

Furthermore it has been argued that the very late marriage pattern of north-west Europe, coupled with the low illegitimacy rate, meant that both parties at the time of marriage must have had some ten years' experience of masturbation, and that this habit was likely to inhibit satisfactory sexual relations in marriage. If to this is added the fact that, before the eighteenth century, most marriages among all levels of the propertied classes were loveless contracts of convenience either aranged by parents or chosen by the spouses on economic or other prudential grounds, the chances of mutually satisfactory sexual relations must have been reduced still further.

The obstacles against the mutual achievement of full sexual satisfaction by man and wife in the Early Modern period were thus both numerous and severe, and as a result both the quantity of sexual activity and its pleasurable quality were both probably significantly lower than they are today, even among the elite. On the other hand, there can be no doubt that the female orgasm was regarded as both medically desirable and morally legitimate. The idea that most women either were or were supposed to be frigid before the eighteenth century receives no support whatever from the evidence of medical literature, nor from current sayings and proverbs about the natural lustfulness of women.

There were certain features of sexual behaviour which were peculiar to Western man, at any rate in the seventeenth and eighteenth centuries, and distinguished him from members of other societies. The first, and hardest to explain, was the interval of ten years or more between the age of sexual maturity and the mean age of marriage, an interval which in most other societies is relatively short. The gap was most marked among the plebs, but it was also noticeable among the elite, and it was a gap which became wider and wider throughout the seventeenth and most of the eighteenth centuries. Moreover, there was a significant proportion – about ten per cent among the plebs and rising to twenty-five per cent among the elite in the eighteenth century – who never married at all, most of the females among the latter group probably remaining virgins all their lives.

The second characteristic has been the imposition on the sexual drive of an ideological gloss known as romantic love, which, thanks to nature imitating art, at times has taken on a life of its own. Beginning as a purely extra-marital emotion in troubadour literature of the twelfth century, it was transformed by the invention of the printing press and the spread of literacy in the sixteenth and seventeenth centuries. It was a theme which dominated the poetry, theatre and romances of the late sixteenth and seventeenth centuries and found its way into real life in the mid-eighteenth century.

The third, and in some ways the most salient, characteristic has been the predominance of a religion – Christianity – which has always been more or less hostile to sex as pleasure or play, and anxious to confine its legitimacy to the functional purpose of procreation. Though mitigated somewhat by the Protestant rejection of virginity as an ideal and the substitution of holy matrimony, this suspicion nonetheless persisted as a prominent feature of moral theology throughout the sixteenth and seventeenth centuries.

2. UPPER-CLASS CULTURE IN THE SIXTEENTH AND SEVENTEENTH CENTURIES

All known societies have incest taboos, and the only peculiarity about them in England was the restriction of their number at the Reformation to the Levitical degrees. On the other hand, the punishments meted out by Church courts in cases of incest in Elizabethan England were surprisingly lenient, and there is reason to think that sodomy and bestiality were more repugnant to popular standards of morality than breaking of the laws of incest, which must have been common in those overcrowded houses where the adolescent children were still at home. The sixteenth century inherited from the medieval church a strong hostility to homosexuality, which over time, particularly because of the affair of the Templars and the Albigensian crusade, had become closely associated in official thinking with religious heresy. In sixteenth-century continental Europe, waves of prosecutions of homosexuals seem to be closely correlated with waves of persecutions of witches, both being regarded as dangerous deviants whose existence threatened the well-being of society. For reasons which are still obscure, however, England escaped the worst excesses of these attacks on both sodomy and witchcraft, towards which a more pragmatic attitude seems normally to have prevailed.

Information about sexual conventions in Early Modern times, whether inside or outside the marriage bonds, is not easy to come by, since it was not a subject which contemporaries were in the habit of committing to paper. The evidence has, therefore, in the main to be derived from advice in medical treatises and didactic literature of moral theologians, or by inference from statistical data about observed behaviour. Both are risky procedures: the first since there is always a yawning gap between how people are supposed to behave and how they do in fact conduct themselves; and the second because it is highly speculative to infer motives and feelings from data about actions.

Sex manuals of the Early Modern period were few, mainly a compendium of received wisdom handed down from the classical authorities, and a mixture of physiological fact and fiction. Ovid's *Art of Love* is vague and imprecise for the ignorant seeker after truth. The most popular sex manual in the West in the Early Modern period, misleadingly called *Aristotle's Masterpiece or the Secrets of Generation*, ran to edition after edition in many languages over many centuries (there were eight registered editions in eighteenth-century England alone). Unlike the Chinese manuals, neither it nor its few rivals offered any advice whatever about methods and varieties of sexual foreplay, the wide options of positions for intercourse, or ways to prolong and maximize pleasure; these matters were left in decent obscurity. Those seeking purely technical information on such subjects would have been obliged to look for it elsewhere, namely in the French, and later the English, pornographic literature, which began in the sixteenth century with Aretino and Giulio Romano's famous *Postures* and grew from a trickle to a moderate stream in the eighteenth century. A pornographic pamphlet of 1660 reminded its readers that 'the several postures are necessary, because all do not affect one and the same riding', but avoided going into details. As a result, the average upper-class man, much less the average woman, would have had no easy access to precise information on sexual techniques before the mid-twentieth century.

On subjects other than techniques and positions of love-making, *Aristotle's Masterpiece* was full of facts and advice — some true, some false. For women, the menarche was placed at fourteen to fifteen and the menopause at forty-four. For men, sexual activity began at sixteen to seventeen, increased in 'force and heat' to between forty-five and fifty-five, and then died away. The sexual organs of the man were described, and the clitoris was clearly identified as the 'seat of venereal pleasure' in women, without which 'the fair sex neither desire nuptial embraces nor have pleasure in them nor conceive by them'. In 1724 De Mandeville noted that 'all our late discoveries in anatomy can find no other use for the clitoris but to whet the female desire by its frequent erections'. Vaginal, as distinct from clitoral, orgasm, however, was a discovery – or false hypothesis – which still lay in the future. Throughout the middle ages and the Early Modern period, woman had been regarded as the temptress, taking after her ancestress Eve, and, by her fickleness and liability to sexual arousal, as a constant threat to the monogamous nuclear family. When in 1621 Robert Burton asked 'of woman's unnatural, insatiable lust, what country, what village doth not complain?' he was doing no more than repeating the conventional wisdom of the age. Aphra Behn went so far in 1682 as to suggest that a young wife often sexually exhausted her husband, as evidenced by 'the paleness of his face, the lankness of his cheeks, the thinness of his calves'. The capacity of the female for multiple orgasms far exceeding the male ability to keep pace was a well-known fact, and provided the physiological basis for this popular belief. 'Though they be weaker vessels, yet they will overcome 2, 3 or 4 men in the satisfying of their carnal appetites,' observed the misogynist Elizabethan musician Thomas Wythorne, a proposition repeated a hundred and fifty years later by Dr Venette.

Advice about the ideal quantity of sexual activity was based on the Aristotelian principle of moderation in all things, and on theories about the nature of male semen, which was regarded as essential to good mental and physical health, and therefore to be expended only in moderation. Early marriage was therefore unwise since adolescent husbands might become 'so enfeebled and weakened that all their vital moisture was exhausted'. Even in adulthood, 'to eject immoderately weakens a man and wastes his spirit'. Dr Venette declared that sexual excess shortens life, and the great Swiss mid-eighteenth-century Dr Tissot, whose work was translated and reprinted for a century, was only repeating an old belief, but giving it a false statistical veneer, when he stated that the loss of one ounce of semen is the equivalent of the loss of forty ounces of blood – apparently a new version of Avicenna's medieval claim that one ejaculation is more debilitating than forty blood-lettings.

311

A second reason for moderation was the widespread and persistent medical theory that the constitutional characteristics of the child were determined by the physical condition of the parents at the moment of conception. It was believed that sexually exhausted fathers and/or sexually abused wives were likely to produce weakly children with low life expectations. The moment of copulation should occur, therefore, when both man and woman were in full sexual vigour, as well as being rested, sober, and free from mental worries. Early morning was therefore a propitious time.

As a result, from the fifteenth century to the nineteenth, lay commentators and the writers of marriage manuals unanimously recommended very restricted sexual activity in marriage. In addition to general advice about moderation, doctors advised total abstinence at the height of summer, since sex overheats the blood and 'infrigidates and dries up the body, consumes the spirits'; during menstruation, since procreation at this time was thought likely to produce diseased children (there was no knowledge of the female ovarian cycle and that conception was impossible); during the latter stages of pregnancy, since there was danger of crushing or aborting the foetus; and during the period of breast-feeding after birth, since sexual activity could spoil the mother's milk, and renewed pregnancy would cut off the milk supply altogether and so kill the infant child. We do not know how seriously any of these prohibitions were taken. The last was certainly believed in by the rich, which was one reason why upper- and middle-class husbands in the sixteenth and seventeenth centuries made their wives put their children out to a wet-nurse and why they tried to prevent the husband of the wet-nurse having sexual access to her. In view of the very long period of breast-feeding – usually twelve to eighteen months – it is certain that the poor, who for lack of money to hire a nurse had to breast-feed their own children, were unable to resist the importunities of their husbands for so long.

The standard medical view of sex in the Early Modern period was based on a plumber's view of the body, the maintenance of good health being determined by a nice balance between the production and discharge of fluids in the pipes so as to maintain an equilibrium. The medical profession also had some understanding of the twentieth-century boiler-maker's view of sex, as a release-valve for the letting off of psychological steam. This meant that before the nineteenth century, when medical opinion became more radically antisexual, doctors were as much concerned with the dangers of abstinence as with those of excess. Galen flatly stated that 'if this natural seed be over-long kept (in some parties) it turns to poison', and led to both physical disease and melancholia (although Robert Burton thought that melancholia was also 'exasperated by venery'). Most doctors recognized that sexual release had important psychological as well as physical benefits and regarded it as normally necessary for mental health. As Thomas Cogan put it in 1589, 'the commodities which come by moderate evacuation thereof [semen] are great. For it procureth appetite to meat and helpeth concoction; it maketh the body more light and nimble, it openeth the pores and conduits, and purgeth phlegm; it quickeneth the mind, stirreth up the wit, reneweth the senses, driveth away sadness, madness, anger, melancholy, fury.'

Just what the lay public made of all this advice from the medical profession is obscure. On the one hand, it was laity rather than doctors who took some of the most alarmist positions about the medical dangers of excess. One of the seventeenth-century lay commentators who indulged in hyperbole on medical grounds was John Evelyn, who thought that 'too much frequency of embraces dulls the sight, decays the memory, induces gout, palsies, enervates and renders effeminate the whole body, and shortens life'. This opinion was echoed in a pamphlet by Daniel Defoe, published in his crabbed old age in 1727, in which he too warned that sexual excess would lead to 'palsies and epilepsies, falling sickness, trembling of the joints, pale dejected aspects, leanness, and at least rottenness and other filthy and loathsome distempers', to say nothing of impotence in old age.

On the other hand, it is very doubtful how far married couples in the early eighteenth century actually practised the kind of restraint advised by *Aristotle's Masterpiece* and by Defoe. The two-thousand-year defiance by upper-class women of medical advice in favour of maternal breast-feeding suggests great caution in assuming that practice follows theory in such matters.

The attitude of sixteenth- and seventeenth-century theologians towards sexuality was one of suspicion and hostility, only very slowly and reluctantly tempered by the rejection of the ideal of virginity at the Reformation and the substitution of 'holy matrimony'. This attitude has a long history behind it, stretching back to the early Fathers of the Church, like St Jerome, to whom all sex was unclean. In England, the consensus of theological opinion stressed the prime importance of 'matrimonial chastity', as it was called, and identified breaches of it with breaches of the Seventh Commandment against adultery. This was not in conflict with the Protestant view of 'holy matrimony' as a source of mutual comfort as well as a means of satisfying lust and procreating legitimate children, although it was left to Milton to argue that 'copulation . . . is an effect of conjugal love', rather than the other way around.

By 'matrimonial chastity' was meant moderation of sexual passion, something which had been advocated not only by the Catholic Fathers but also by both Calvin and foreign humanists of the early sixteenth century, like Vives and Guazzo. The husband was expected to give his wife sufficient satisfaction to avoid her being obliged to seek consolation elsewhere, but not so much as to arouse her libido to the extent of encouraging her to seek extra-marital adventures. All passionate love-making was sinful, regardless of whether it took place inside or outside marriage. Sensuality itself, the lust of the flesh, was evil. The basic advice to a husband was that 'nothing is more impure than to love a wife like an adulterous woman'.

In the first place, intercourse was forbidden during periods when there could be no conception, which at that time were believed to be limited to the nine months of pregnancy. In addition, both the forty days of Lent and Sundays were regarded as periods of ritual sexual continence for married couples. In England in the late eighteenth century, the period on Sunday during which respectable couples were at their devotions in church was particularly sacrosanct. A popular obscene poem of the period, about a sexually over-demanding wife who reduced her husband to a pale emaciated skeleton, ended with the lines

> And for which I am sure she'll go to Hell,
> For she makes me fuck her in church time.

For Methodists, the whole day was taboo, and there is the (perhaps apocryphal) story of a Methodist in St Martin's Lane who on Saturday nights tied together the legs of his cocks so that they could not mount his hens on Sundays. The religious prohibition on sexual activity on Sunday was also a standard part of Victorian middle-class morality, at least up to 1870. On the other hand, by 1870 some medical advisors, such as A. K. Gardner, were recommending Sunday as the ideal day of procreation on the grounds that the sense of relaxation from the weekly round of work would produce healthier children. 'Never on Sunday' therefore has a long, complicated and still somewhat obscure history, involving conflicts between moral theology, medical theory, and social convenience.

Apart from restricting the times of intercourse, the theologians also interfered in the details of the sexual act. Variant sexual positions other than the standard 'missionary' position of the man on top and the woman supine underneath were rejected, since they were merely incitements to lust and designed for pleasure not procreation. Any approach from behind was condemned since it made man imitate the behaviour of animals; any position with the woman on top was condemned, partly since it inverted sex roles, making the female the dominant and active partner, and partly because it reduced the likelihood of conception, since the semen was running against gravity. For the same reasons there was total prohibition of the use of 'unnatural' orifices such as the mouth or the anus, and of contraceptive practices such as *coitus interruptus*.

Among the upper classes for most of the Early Modern period, the 'double standard' of sexual behaviour prevailed. According to this convention, the husband enjoyed full monopoly rights over the sexual services of his wife, who was expected to be a virgin on her wedding night. As Fielding's Mr Modern told his wife in 1732: 'Your person is mine: I bought it lawfully in the church.' Lord Sandwich's father put it, forcefully if crudely: 'He that doth get a wench with child and marries her afterward is as if a man should shit in his hat and then clap it on his head.'

On the other hand, the man was expected to have gained some sexual experience before marriage, and any infidelities after marriage were treated as venial sins which the sensible wife was advised to overlook. Thus, both fornication and adultery were exclusively male prerogatives at this social level, despite the fact that in current physiological theory and folk tradition women were regarded as more lustful in their appetites and more fickle in their attachments than men. 'All witchcraft comes from carnal lust, which in women is insatiable,' observed the authors of the *Malleus Maleficarum*, thus expressing no more than the conventional view. This dichotomy between women's physiological impulses and their social obligations to pre-marital chastity and post-marital monogamy was solved by the imposition on them of the strictest standards of sexual behaviour, enforced by all the legal, moral and religious pressures of which the society was capable. The explanation of this discrepancy lies firstly in the value attached to female chastity in the marriage market of a hierarchical and propertied society, and secondly in the necessity that there should be no legal doubts about the legitimacy of the heirs to property and title. As the Marquess of Halifax explained to his daughter in 1688: 'The root and excuse of this injustice is the preservation of families from any mixture which may bring a blemish to them; and whilst the point of honour continues to be so placed, it seems unavoidable to give your sex the greater share of the penalty.' If, on the other hand, the husband is unfaithful, 'do not seem to look or hear that way . . . such an indecent complaint makes a wife much more ridiculous than the injury that provoked her to it'. A century later, Dr Johnson was still saying the same thing, that upon female chastity 'all the property of the world depends' and that 'confusion of progeny constitutes the essence of the crime' of adultery. Consequently, 'wise married women don't trouble themselves about infidelity in their husbands', whereas wifely infidelity was unpardonable.

The third explanation of this durable phenomenon of the double standard is that women have for millennia been regarded as the sexual property of men and that the value of this property is diminished if it has been or is being used by anyone other than the legal owner. It was for these reasons that Mrs Manley's protests in the first decade of the eighteenth century that 'what is not a crime in men is scandalous and unpardonable in women' were entirely ignored. As late as 1825 Sir John Nicholls declared that 'forgiveness on the part of a wife is meritorious, while a similar forgiveness on the part of a husband would be degrading and dishonourable'.

Another explanation for the prevalence of the double standard lies in the stress in secular society on honour. In the sixteenth, seventeenth and eighteenth centuries, the concept of honour had a very clearly defined meaning, which was significantly different from that of today. The worst thing a man could say about another man was that he was a liar. 'Giving the lie' inevitably resulted in a challenge to a duel in genteel circles, and in a fight in peasant or artisan circles. The worst thing a woman could say about another woman was that she was unchaste, which might well result in a lawsuit for slander in an ecclesiastical court. Thus a man's honour depended on the reliability of his spoken word; a woman's honour on her reputation for chastity.

But the honour of a married man was also severely damaged if he got the reputation of being a cuckold, since this was a slur on both his virility and his capacity to rule his own household. He became the joke of the village, or at a higher level of his associates, and was defamed and thought unfit for public office. The Elizabethan Thomas Wythorne remarked bitterly on the injustice of a situation in which 'a man's honesty and credit doth depend and lie in his wife's tail'. In the village, the cuckolded husband and his delinquent wife were frequently victims of a 'skimmington', or public shame punishment.

The only period in which the double standard was seriously questioned was in the 1630s and 1640s. Courtiers like Sir Kenelm Digby, who led a chequered sex life, claimed that breach of chastity 'is no greater fault in them [women] than in men', while the Puritan John Milton adopted a similar position. But this was a temporary phenomenon, and did not survive the Restoration and the growing respect for property. Away from the hot-house atmosphere of the court, wives of the nobility and squirarchy of the sixteenth, seventeenth and eighteenth centuries usually felt themselves obliged to follow the rules of the double standard.

Even pious and chaste upper-class women in the late eighteenth century turned a blind eye to their husband's infidelities, so long as only sexual passion and not deep emotional attachment was involved. Mrs Thrale paid no attention to her husband's many liaisons with lower-class mistresses, though she was distressed when he fell in unconsummated love with one of her friends. Years later she protested vigorously to her daughter Cecilia when reports reached her that the latter's husband was sleeping with his wife's maid. But Cecilia brushed the matter aside as something of no consequence. ' "It is the way," she says, "and all who understand genteel life think lightly of such matters." '

Since few men of fashion were prepared to enter into a duel to avenge their wife's honour, the only serious danger to a wealthy gentleman from an adulterous relationship with a married woman of high status in the eighteenth century was that he might be sued for damages by the aggrieved husband on an action of 'crim. con.' (criminal connection). When in the late eighteenth century Colonel Sykes had heavy damages to the husband awarded against him for his adultery with a married woman, he subsequently always referred to his ex-mistress as '*dear* Mrs Parsloe, having a right, he said, to use the word after he had paid £10,000 for her'. The standard ethics of the late eighteenth-century elite indicated that a man should be discreet in his amours, so as not publicly to humiliate his wife. As the great courtesan Harriette Wilson put it: 'a man ought to be of royal blood before he commits adultery, except in private'. On the other hand, it was alleged at the time that some aged husbands married young wives with the deliberate purpose of making money by threats of legal proceedings against the latter's lovers: 'As most of us bargain to be husbands, so some of us bargain to be cuckolds.'

The prevailing attitude of women towards such matters in elite London circles in the late eighteenth century is perfectly summed up by an unknown lady who discussed the matter with Boswell one day in 1776. It shows how far the new contract theory of marriage had spread, and its consequences for the double standard. The lady

argued with me that marriage was certainly no more but a political institution, as we see it has subsisted in so many different forms in different parts of the world. 'Therefore,' said she, 'it is merely a mutual contract which if one party breaks, the other is free. Now', said she, 'my husband I know has been unfaithful to me a thousand times. I should therefore have no scruple of conscience, I do declare, to have an intrigue, and I am restrained only by my pride, because I would not do what is thought dishonourable in this century, and would not put myself in the power of a gallant.' I argued that the chastity of women was of much more consequence than that of men, as the property and rights of families depend upon it. 'Surely' said she, 'that is easily answered, for the objection is removed if a woman does not intrigue but when she is with child.' I really could not answer her. Yet she was wrong, and I was uneasy . . .

With marriage delayed for ten to twelve years after puberty, and with the practice of sending children out of the home at an early age to serve as apprentices or agricultural or domestic servants, living in other people's houses, it is hardly surprising that the problems of adolescence were a common preoccupation of the Early Modern period. The idea that adolescence only became a social problem in the nineteenth century is sheer historical fantasy, and there was constant anxiety about the danger to the social and moral order of the huge numbers of unmarried apprentices in London at this period. As Thomas Wythorne put it in the late sixteenth century, 'After the age of childhood [0–15], beginneth the age named adolescency which continueth until twenty and five . . . In this age Cupid and Venus were and would be very busy to trouble the quiet minds of young folk.'

Official attitudes towards masturbation provide perhaps the most illuminating insight into attitudes towards adolescent sexuality in general. Although the position of moral theologians in the middle ages was that both adult and child masturbation were mortal sins, eighteenth-century Catholic confession manuals treated the latter as no more than a venial sin. But the subject is not even mentioned in post-Reformation English child-rearing handbooks of the sixteenth and seventeenth centuries except in the most guarded terms. Current medical handbooks also largely ignored it, but medical theory pointed indirectly in its favour, if used in moderation. Based on the idea of balancing the humours, the standard doctrine was that for good health the human body needs occasional evacuation of superfluous fluids: blood by blood-letting; and semen by ejaculation. Both bachelors and widowers were, therefore, advised by doctors in the seventeenth century to follow a regime of moderate sexual activity. This being the case, the medical profession can hardly have disapproved of occasional pre-marital adolescent masturbation.

The only direct evidence on this subject comes from obscure hints about lustful thoughts and acts by seventeenth-century youths who later underwent a conversion experience. For example, George Trosse referred to his earlier practice of 'sin which too many young men are guilty of and look upon it as harmless, though God struck Onan dead in the place for it'. In general, however, post-conversion memoirs of the seventeenth century do not lay too much stress on adolescent masturbation, and Trosse's comment is revealing.

The most detailed account comes from a lapsed Calvinist of the mid-eighteenth century. James Boswell was brought up in Scotland by a fanatically Calvinist mother, and was in his youth a most pious child, oppressed with visions of hell-fire and eternal damnation. In an autobiographical fragment written years later to show to Rousseau, he explained that he was about thirteen in 1753 when he first learned from books and from a school friend about what he called, significantly, 'the fatal practice'. He had in fact already been masturbating without knowing it by climbing trees (which is apparently a rather common cause of spontaneous ejaculation among boys). His notes on the subject read: 'In climbing trees, pleasure. Returned often, climbed, felt, allowed myself to fall from high trees in ecstasy.' He asked the gardener about it, but got no enlightenment from him. At thirteen or fourteen, 'My youthful desires became strong. I was horrified because of the fear that I would sin and be damned.' At one moment he even considered self-castration as a solution, but promptly abandoned the idea. After all, 'I thought what I was doing was a venial sin, whereas fornication was horrible.'

From this very fragmentary evidence it would seem that in the seventeenth and early eighteenth centuries even the most Calvinistic of children, brought up in fear of hell-fire, nevertheless were not too deeply disturbed by the problem of handling their early impulses, no more so, at any rate, than children at any period in history; and that medical theory, parental pressure and moral lectures on the subject had not yet begun to approach the intensity of the nineteenth century. In this area of sexuality, at any rate, childhood and adolescence in the Early Modern period was a time of relaxation, compared with the intensification of repression in the late eighteenth, nineteenth, and early twentieth centuries.

As the interval between puberty and marriage became longer and longer, as the age of marriage was increasingly postponed in all classes of society, the problem of masturbation inevitably loomed larger and larger. It is characteristic of the prevailing silence on the subject, and the consequent uncertainty in the public mind, that in 1704 a gentleman wrote a letter to Defoe's *Review* asking whether or not 'self-pollution' was a mortal sin. Defoe replied in the affirmative, but added prudishly that the problem 'is not more fit to be shown in public any more than to be acted in private'.

The first popular pamphlet which spoke frankly about the terrible moral and physical dangers of masturbation was published in London in about 1710 by an anonymous clergyman. It was entitled *Onania or the heinous Sin of Self-pollution, and all its frightful Consequences in both Sexes considered.* Despite its vapid moralizing and implausible stories of resulting disease, the book was a great success. By 1760, thirty-eight thousand copies had been sold in nineteen English editions. It had also been translated into French and German, so that it clearly struck some hidden area of anxiety in early eighteenth-century Europe. Even Bernard de Mandeville accepted the theory and warned in 1724 that youthful masturbation, 'the first lewd trick that boys learn', could lead to impotence if practised in excess. In 1764 the internationally celebrated Swiss Dr Tissot weighed in with a learned medical treatise on the subject, which gave the problem the dignity of full authoritative medical recognition. His argument was ostensibly not moral but scientific, the old theory of the dangers from excessive loss of seminal fluid, on the subject of which he assembled an impressive list of authorities from Hippocrates to Galen to Boerhaave. He cited allegedly authentic cases of masturbating youths – and maidens – falling victims to lassitude, epilepsy, convulsions, boils, disorders of the digestive, respiratory or nervous systems, and even death. All he could suggest as remedies were low diet, short sleep, vigorous exercise, and regular bowel movements, but he seems in fact to have regarded the habit as more or less incurable.

This rise of anxiety about adolescent masturbation in the early and mid-eighteenth century is not easy to account for, since it coincides with the period of greater general adult sexual permissiveness. The late eighteenth- and early nineteenth-century epidemic of hysteria on the subject is more easily explained, since it coincided with the rise of Evangelical doctrine and the growing sense of horror and shame about sex that was current at that time.

Some have tried to argue that there is a close causal relationship between early industrial society with its need for saving for investment and the drive against masturbation – both demanded a reduction of 'spending'. Conversely, the argument runs that the consumer society of the twentieth century must inevitably also be a sexually active 'spending' society. This theory is attractive, but implausible. The drive against masturbation was led by clergymen and doctors, neither of whom can easily be identified with industrial society; the chronology is wrong since the first anti-masturbation publication was in 1710, half a century before industrialization made any impact on the scene; the propaganda was directed to the middle and upper classes, not the industrial classes; and it coincided with what was in all other respects a period of relaxation rather than a tightening of restrictions on sexual expression.

The most likely explanation of the rise of anxiety about masturbation in the early eighteenth century is that it was a by-product of the growing concern for the welfare of children and for their education to be socially and morally estimable persons. This would explain why the anxiety started first in England, which was in the vanguard in Europe in the development of the child-oriented family, and why it was repeated by Rousseau in his educational treatises. The anxiety may also have been encouraged by the rising median age of marriage, raising fears that masturbation was on the increase. More and more men were spending a longer and longer part of their sexual mature years with no other outlet for their libido but masturbation or prostitution. The rising age of marriage might help to explain the extraordinary success of Dr Tissot's learned and horrific treatise on the subject, since it was a problem of direct concern to more and more young men.

The second type of evidence about attitudes towards adolescent sexuality is provided by the degree of care taken to prevent homosexuality. In the sexually segregated academies and boarding-schools, which housed most upper- and middle-class children at that time, the children normally slept two in a bed, for reasons of economy, so that the first sexual experiments of most boys and girls may well have taken the form of mutual masturbation with a member of one's own sex, or some other form of overt homosexual activity. This is clearly what Mary Wollstonecraft was talking about when in 1792 she raised objections to sending children to boarding-schools: 'What nasty indecent tricks do they not also learn from each other, when a number of them pig together in the same bed-chamber, not to speak of the vices which render the body weak.'

It is astonishing to discover how apparently indifferent seventeenth- and early eighteenth-century parents were to what today would seem to be obvious temptations for the children that were better avoided. It was not until the 1770s that parents began to worry about the problem of adolescent homosexuality, and it was noted as a special feature of an extremely expensive private school, among whose pupils were two future dukes, that all the boys slept in separate beds. One school, which charged the substantial sum of forty guineas a year in fees, found it worthwhile to advertise in 1786 that the boys would share a room, but 'each will have a bed to himself'. In more normal schools, parents who wished their boys to sleep alone had to pay extra for the privilege. One such parent was Philip Francis; when in 1774 he prepared to send his son Philip to Harrow or some other boarding-school, he wrote: 'wherever he goes I insist upon his constantly sleeping *alone* ... for reasons that will increase with his years'.

Another piece of evidence of parental indifference to the dangers of adolescent homosexual contact is that in Oxford and Cambridge colleges in the sixteenth and seventeenth centuries it was normal practice for the tutor, who was usually a young bachelor in his middle twenties, to share his bedroom with several young students, aged perhaps fifteen to eighteen. One would have supposed that this was a situation which would have given great anxiety to parents, but in fact there is no evidence whatever that this is the case. In fact, parents were eager for their son to live with his tutor so that he could be more closely supervised. John Marston drew attention to the dangers, and he was ignored:

> Had I some snout-fair brats, they should endure
> The new found Castilian calenture
> Before some pedant tutor in his bed
> Should use my fry like Phrygian Ganymede.

The only evidence of homosexuality among the students comes from the confessional autobiography of David Baker, who alleged that it was common in Broadgate Hall in the 1590s, and generally in Oxford twenty years later.

It is not until after 1700, by which time the drastic fall in student numbers had put an end to the need for cohabitation of tutors and students, that there is evidence of parental anxiety on this score. As early as 1666 Anthony Wood alleged that the electors to a Fellowship at All Souls had chosen a handsome young man with a view to 'kissing and slobbering' him. In 1715 Dudley Ryder reported that 'among the chief men in some of the colleges, sodomy is very usual. It is dangerous sending a young man who is beautiful to Oxford.' And in 1739 there broke out a major scandal at Wadham College in which the Warden was accused, with a wealth of supporting evidence, of attempted forcible rape of a student, with less well-documented rumours of other homosexual activity between dons and students in the College. The Warden left the country hurriedly for France, and the episode was hushed up as rapidly as possible by heads of colleges. What this very fragmentary evidence suggests is that, whether or not the reality was changing, there was a growing concern among parents in the eighteenth century about the danger to their adolescent sons of homosexual advances from fellow-students or adults.

3. UPPER-CLASS BEHAVIOUR IN THE SIXTEENTH AND SEVENTEENTH CENTURIES

There is some evidence to suggest that throughout the Early Modern period, English attitudes to sensuality were more free than they were in most areas of Europe. One piece of evidence of actual behaviour is the staggering number of prosecutions in Church courts for sexual offences in the Elizabethan period. No doubt many of these accusations were the result of the malice and unfounded suspicions of neighbours, but a substantial proportion must have had some basis in fact. It has been estimated that in the one country of Essex, with a population of about 40,000 adults, some 15,000 persons were summoned to court for sex offences over the forty-five years between 1558 and 1603. This is an average of about 330 a year, or one per cent of the sexually mature population. In an adult life span of thirty years, an Elizabethan inhabitant of Essex, therefore, had more than a one-in-four chance of being accused of fornication, adultery, buggery, incest, bestiality, or bigamy. Even if only half the charges were well founded, it still suggests a society which was both sexually very lax and also highly inquisitorial, with a great readiness to denounce each other's transgressions. That malice and back-biting were prominent characteristics of village society has already been demonstrated, and this therefore comes as no surprise. The very high level of extra-marital sex, however, is more startling. Very many cases of fornication were between maidservants and either fellow-servants in the house or their masters. This temptation was greatly aggravated by the overcrowding in bedrooms, for the maid not infrequently slept in the same room as the master and mistress of the house. Some masters were frank about the services they expected, like the man who offered a girl '40s. to serve him by day and 40s. to lie with him on nights'.

If convicted, the Elizabethan penalties in Church courts for most sexual offences were not very severe. For fornication and adultery, they took the form of shame punishments of standing in a white sheet holding a white wand either in the town market place on market day, or in church before the full congregation. For pre-nuptial pregnancies, the penalty was open confession in church on a Sunday or at the time of marriage. As for bigamy, it was not even a civil offence at all before 1603, and many individuals ran away and married again without risk of being caught and often with a clear conscience. Thus in 1578 John Loggan formally put up the banns to marry Mary Hewitt, arguing that his first wife Jane was 'gone from him and married to another man now dwelling in Kent, wherefore he thinketh he might marry again'. The Church court naturally thought otherwise, but there is no reason to suppose that the delinquent first wife was tracked down. Apart from buggery and bestiality, which carried the death penalty, the one crime that was severely punished was not irregular sex itself, but its consequence. The production of a bastard child was likely to result in a drain on the financial resources of the parish and was, therefore, treated with exceptional severity. The father was served with a maintenance order – often very difficult to enforce – and up to about 1700 both mother and father were often stripped naked to the waist and whipped through the street at a cart's tail. It is hardly surprising that abortion potions made from the dried tops of the savin bush, or even more drastic remedies such as physical maltreatment of the womb, or postnatal infanticide and abandonment, were sometimes resorted to by desperate mothers.

Another indication of English attitudes is that foreign visitors from the late fifteenth to the late eighteenth centuries noted with astonishment and shock the freedom with which it was the custom in England for persons of different sexes to greet each other by a kiss upon the lips. Visiting England in 1499, Erasmus found it a most attractive custom: 'wherever you come, you are received with a kiss by all; when you take your leave, you are dismissed with kisses; you return, kisses are repeated. They come to visit you, kisses again; they leave you, you kiss them all round. Should they meet you anywhere, kisses in abundance; in fine, wherever you move, there is nothing but kisses.' In 1620 it was confirmed that 'for us to salute strangers with a kiss is counted but civility, but with foreign nations immodesty'. By the early eighteenth century, there were some doubts about the legitimacy of the practice, for in *The Spectator* a country gentleman, 'Rustic Sprightly', asked for 'your judgement, for or against kissing, by way of civility or salutation'. But the habit died hard and at the end of the eighteenth century, it was still 'the form of salutation peculiar to our nation'.

Finally there is the faint suggestion that in upper-class circles, at any rate in the late eighteenth century, the conversation was much more uninhibited than abroad. In 1784 La Rochefoucauld found after-dinner talk 'extremely free upon highly undecent subjects ... Very often I have heard things mentioned in good society which would be in the grossest taste in France.' He was probably referring to conversation after the ladies had left the room, a practice which did not occur in France.

Another piece of evidence about English attitudes towards sexuality, this time affecting all classes, is the retention in the official marriage service from the middle ages into the twentieth century of some very explicit wording which accompanies the ritual of the ring.

In this ceremony, the bride and groom exchange rings, accompanied by the following words: 'With this ring I thee wed, ... and with my body I thee worship ...' This was part of the marriage service in the middle ages, and was taken over by the Protestant Prayer Book in 1548. The Puritans objected to this wording in the *Admonition to Parliament* in 1572, on the not unreasonable grounds that they had not got rid of idolatry of images of the saints and the Virgin Mary in order to retain idolatry of a flesh and blood body. In the abortive Savoy Conference between Anglicans and Presbyterians in 1661, the latter asked that the ceremony be made optional, as a thing indifferent, and the Bishops conceded to alter the wording to 'with my body I thee honour'. But since the conference failed to reach agreement, the original wording was retained, and so has lasted until today.

Sexual modesty was a characteristic of the lower-middle class, but it is very doubtful whether it extended to their superiors. Richardson remarked that Pamela's bashfulness showed that she was 'not of the quality', while James Cleland's Fanny Hill, a respectable country girl, was genuinely shocked to discover that some men and women took all their clothes off in daylight to make love. When seeing it practised by a Genoese, she attributed it to 'a taste, I suppose, peculiar to the heat, or perhaps the caprices of their own country'. On the other hand, it is noticeable that in Thomas Rowlandson's pornographic caricatures of the late eighteenth century, which represent the upper and middle ranks disporting themselves, the women are all more or less stripped but the men are fully clothed, with only their breeches pulled down around their ankles to expose their genitals (Plate 26). In the divorce trial of Lord Grosvenor, it emerged that he would pay substantially more to a lower-class prostitute if she was willing to strip – which some were reluctant to do – than if she merely let him penetrate her. One who agreed to do so complained that his Lordship's breeches hurt her, which alone made him take off both them and his shoes.

4. THE BEHAVIOUR OF 'THE QUALITY' IN THE EIGHTEENTH CENTURY

In the sixteenth and early seventeenth centuries, there had been two parallel archetypes of sexual conduct in existence: one being conjugal, primarily for the procreation of a male heir; and the other being extra-marital, exclusively for love, companionship, and sexual pleasure. What happened in the eighteenth century was that the two archetypes became increasingly fused into one in certain key social strata, as religious opposition to the second declined or was increasingly ignored, and as companionate marriages of personal choice increased. But this fusion took a very long time to spread much beyond the middling ranks and the country gentry. The second development in the eighteenth century was one of the most conspicuous results of the collapse of moral Puritanism as a dominant influence in society after 1660 and of the general secularization of society. This was a release of the libido from the age-old restraints of Christianity, which had been particularly effective in the late sixteenth and early seventeenth centuries. By the mid eighteenth century there was emerging a new ideal, which now included sensual pleasure within its scope, if only as an unanticipated by-product of Lockean philosophy. In France some Jesuit theologians were also turning away from the doctrine of Original Sin, and urging the cultivation rather than the denial of human nature. Later some Enlightenment and post-Enlightenment thinkers, like Helvetius, Fourier and St Simon, were to make the same argument on a high philosophical plane, namely that pleasure and passion should be guides to conduct in life. It was John Wilkes, who admittedly was speaking only for a libertine minority, who put the new attitude in its grossest and crudest terms, and applied it to pure sensuality in his notorious *Essay on Woman* of 1763. Such frank and hedonistic eroticism was unthinkable in England before that period. Mrs Manley was only expressing current opinion when in the first decade of the eighteenth century she described sexual pleasure as 'those inestimable joys ... which ... are the greatest that human nature is capable of enjoying'. Her words were shocking to contemporaries merely because they came from the pen of a woman. The trend even affected that most prudish of classes, the *petite bourgeoisie*, and Richard Griffiths was a mid-eighteenth-century lower-middle-class husband trying to have the best of both worlds when he wrote his bride a hopeful epithalamium:

> Her air coquettish but her mind a prude,
> Her body wanton but her soul not lewd.

The late eighteenth-century upper classes were deeply affected by the trend to recognize the needs of the body and even Mrs Thrale in 1790 condemned the current practice of deferred marriages on these grounds. Early marriages, she argued, 'are the best (popularly speaking) for all ranks. Why should we straggle so very far, as 'tis now the fashion, away from the course of nature?' Earlier, the poet William Blake had wrestled with the same problem, accepting sexuality as an essential, if subordinate, element in civilization: 'Art and Science cannot exist, except by naked beauty displayed.' It was, he felt, better to burn sexually than to suffer 'in misery supreme' the torments of ungratified desire. His final advice was 'let men do their duty, and the women will be such wonders'. Freedom of sexual expression was one of the many by-products of the eighteenth-century pursuit of happiness.

It must be admitted, however, that there were some counter-currents at work in eighteenth-century culture. Daniel Defoe's *Conjugal Lewdness* of 1727 was, as has been seen, a very austere work which deliberately advised strict self-control over sensual pleasure. Wetenhall Wilkes, in *A Letter of Genteel and Moral Advice to a Young Lady*, which ran to eight editions between 1740 and 1766, told his audience that chastity – 'the great point of female honour' – includes 'a suppression of all irregular desires, voluntary pollutions, sinful concupiscence, and an immoderate use of all sensual or carnal pleasures'.

The first conspicuous results of the collapse of moral Puritanism after 1660 was not the fusion of marriage with sexual passion, but the release of the libido. A hundred years later, Sheridan commented on the extreme volatility of the English character as revealed in this sudden transformation. 'In Oliver Cromwell's time they were all precise canting creatures. And no sooner did Charles II come over than they turned gay rakes and libertines.' One manifestation of the change was the dramatic upsurge of extra-marital liaisons among members of both sexes of the court aristocracy, spreading slowly down into rural elite society. Mistresses and bastards once again became a matter of common gossip and accepted normal facts of social life in these circles. The memoirs of Count Grammont are eloquent testimony to the return to patterns of extra-marital sexual licence at the court of Charles II. It was not merely that the King himself kept mistresses and spawned bastards in ostentatious profusion, to the pious horror of middle-class bureaucrats like Pepys, but that the whole court was absorbed in an endless game of sexual musical chairs. 'Lady Middleton, Lady Denham, the Queen's and the Duchess' maids of honour, and a hundred others bestow their favours to the right and to the left, and not the least notice is taken of their conduct.' Sexual promiscuity became a hallmark of fashion at court and in high political circles. Lord Keeper North was urged to keep a mistress, since otherwise he would be 'ill looked upon for want of doing so' and 'lose all his interest at court'. In 1675 it was remarked that 'adultery is common and this age gives it the soft and gentle French names of gallantry and divertisement in apology for it'. It is indeed significant of the new attitude that the crude word 'adultery' was replaced by the rather attractive euphemism 'gallantry'. A century later, when efforts at the moral reform of the upper classes were again being made, Hannah More remarked that 'the substitution of the word *gallantry* for that crime which stabs domestic happiness and conjugal virtue is one of the most dangerous of all the modern abuses of the language'. At the same period, a whole new genre of adulterous court literature also sprang up, from the plays of Wycherley to the poems of Rochester.

Throughout the eighteenth century it remained quite common in upper-class circles for men of rank, position and quality to keep a mistress or series of mistresses. Wives at this social level seem to have been indifferent to the adulteries of their husband. When in 1735 King George II found himself a new mistress and told his wife all about it, her only comment was that 'she was sorry for the scandal it gave to others, but for herself she minded it no more than his going to the close stool'. The monthly periodical *Town and Country Magazine* entertained its readers in each issue with an illustrated account of the irregular sex life of some man of note. These stories add up to only twelve persons a year out of a potential population of many hundred and, therefore, cannot be taken as typical of upper-class life. But what is interesting about the accounts is the uniformity of the social pattern they reveal. The girls who, in return for a fixed allowance, became the mistresses of noblemen and wealthy gentlemen were nearly all women from a well-to-do professional or merchant background whose fathers had gone bankrupt, and who found this virtually the only way of maintaining the standard of living to which they were accustomed. Between 1781 and 1784 the mistress of the Earl of Surrey was the daughter of a bankrupt attorney; of Thomas Gage the daughter of a poor parson (who had begun her career as the mistress of a naval lieutenant); of the Earl of Aldeburgh the widow of a lieutenant killed in America; of Colonel Tarleton the daughter of a

THE FAMILY, SEX AND MARRIAGE

bankrupt solicitor; of Sir Hubert Pakington the daughter (already pregnant by the Duke of Dorset) of an eminent brewer; of the Lord Mayor of London the widow of a bankrupt merchant; of the fifth Duke of Bedford the daughter of a bankrupt physician; of Baron Sydney, later Duke of Queensbury, the daughter of a bankrupt apothecary; of W. W. Grenville the daughter of a bankrupt musician.

The economic uncertainties of professional and mercantile life, the improvement in the education of bourgeois daughters, and the lack of alternative career opportunities for girls suddenly reduced from genteel affluence to poverty meant that there was a reasonable supply of attractive and well-bred girls to form suitable companions and mistresses for men of means. It is also worth noting that it was in the late eighteenth century – in 1782 to be precise – that respectable London newspapers like *The Herald* were publishing advertisements by men openly 'soliciting female friendships', a phenomenon which has only reappeared in England and America in the last few years.

The case of Mrs Pendarves shows how in the eighteenth century even an upper-class girl, if married against her will to an obviously incompatible husband, was constantly subjected to invitations to adultery by married and unmarried men of her own social status. Moreover, bastards appeared once more in wills in the early eighteenth century and were tolerantly accepted into the household, at least by some wives. In his will drawn up in 1721, John, Duke of Buckingham, mentioned many bastards including a son by one mistress living abroad with a tutor in Utrecht, and two girls by another being brought up at home by his second wife with their legitimate children, and now away at boarding-school. These girls, 'to whom she has always been most generously indulgent', he left with full confidence to the care of his widow.

This easy-going attitude to sexual promiscuity among the higher aristocracy persisted, and may even have become more common, throughout the eighteenth century. An anonymous author claimed in 1739 that female adultery in high circles was now 'rather esteemed a fashionable vice than a crime'. The causes of this situation he attributed to the traditional free and easy ways of the English, corruption by foreign manners, the decay of religion, permissive education with too much stress on 'ornament of the body' for girls, marriages for money or sexual passion rather than settled affection, and the infidelity of husbands. It was a plausible list, and he was undoubtedly right when he observed that 'the middling people are certainly more happy in the married state than persons of a more elevated dignity'. Forty years later, nothing had changed. In 1780 the Earl of Pembroke commented that '*nos dames, douces commes des agneaux, se laissent monter par tout le monde*'. The children of the Countess of Oxford were known as 'the Harleian Miscellany', and in the 1790s there were brought up at Devonshire House and Chatsworth a whole collection of oddly assorted children: three were the children of the fifth Duke of Devonshire and his Duchess, Georgiana; and two were of the Duke and Lady Elizabeth Foster, the Duchess's most intimate friend and life-long companion; while one child of the Duke and Charlotte Spencer and one of the Duchess and Lord Grey were brought up elsewhere.

The tenth Earl of Pembroke had children by two mistresses, and his bastard son, who had a successful naval career, was on the best of terms with the legitimate son and heir, Lord Herbert, and also with the Countess. The latter's sole request, which was respected, was that the illegitimate children should not take the family name of Herbert. She also objected when her husband hung prints of his current mistress, the actress La Bacelli, in his bedroom in Wilton House, a protest the Earl rejected, declaring that it could not be taken as an open affront 'between two people who professedly never wish to cohabit together'. In these circles, illegitimate boys seem usually to have been well educated and to have suffered no social discrimination in terms of professional career or marriage. As Lord Mulgrave remarked in the House of Lords in 1800, 'bastardy is of little comparative consequence to the male children'. Illegitimate female children, however, 'have to struggle with every disadvantage from their rank in life', since the only career open to a woman of this class was marriage. Only a small minority were as successful as the illegitimate daughter of Sir Edward Walpole, who in 1759 married the second Lord Waldegrave, and on his death George III's brother, the Duke of Gloucester.

This casual acceptance of illegitimate children in the eighteenth century spread down quite far into the professional classes. In the 1770s Erasmus Darwin, a successful and respected Cambridge doctor, fathered two illegitimate children between the death of his first wife and the marriage with his second. He brought them up openly, giving them a good education, and they remained on intimate terms with his second wife and his children by her. A century later, his grandson commented with astonishment that this irregularity in no way damaged Erasmus Darwin's professional practice as a physician. This could not have happened in the late nineteenth century, or, for the matter of that, in the early seventeenth.

The memoirs of Casanova and other professional libertines support the suggestion that there was a very easy-going sexual morality prevalent in the growing bachelor element among the upper classes in the eighteenth century, after the impact of seventeenth-century Puritanism had died away. There was an ethical code which was supposed to govern such lives, one which was best stated by Richardson's rakish creation, Lovelace: 'to marry off a former mistress, if possible, before I took a new one; to maintain a lady handsomely in her lying in, to provide for the little one, if he lived, according to the degree of the mother, if she died.' This was an honour code of a kind, and the memoirs of William Hickey in the late eighteenth century show it in full operation among expatriate English officials in India with regard to their native mistresses. The code implied that women of lower social class, but not ladies of one's own rank, were fair game for sexual exploitation.

During the eighteenth century, the most striking manifestations of sexual libertinism, now heavily tinged with conscious anti-Christian ideology, occurred in France and were confined to the higher reaches of the aristocracy and some of the intellectuals. The erotic writings of Choderlos de Laclos and the Marquis de Sade are manifestations of this movement in France, while in England the Hell-Fire Club of Sir Francis Dashwood provides a notorious example of these ideas carried to extremes. Between 1779 and 1784, an ingenious quack entrepreneur, an Edinburgh medical student named James Graham, made a living from lecturing to fashionable London society on 'generation' – allegedly illustrated by a naked woman on the stage – and from renting out to the jaded rich at £50 a night his 'celestial bed'. This remarkable contrivance, first installed in a 'Temple of Health', later replaced by a 'Temple of Hymen', was marketed as a sovereign remedy for female sterility or male impotence. Harmonica, flute and organ music, 'stimulating vapours' and oriental perfumes were piped into the bedroom, where the couple was encouraged to warm up by elaborate washing, followed by singing, and drinking a patented aphrodisiac 'divine draught' costing a guinea a bottle. They were then to approach the 'electro-magnetic' bed – Graham had visited America and seen Benjamin Franklin's electrical experiments –

where they were expected to perform in the light of the moon, on a mattress impregnated with the essences of Arabia, while 'magnetic fluid' wrought up their nerves and 'celestial and electric fire' was pumped into the chamber from a pressure-cylinder next door. This prototype of Masters and Johnson in the art of sex therapy ran his business with enormous success for four years before closing down in 1784.

These sometimes bizarre upper-class manifestations were exaggerated reflections of more profound and widespread changes that were taking place in general attitudes and conduct. There are clear signs that during the middle years of the eighteenth century attitudes towards sex in England, especially in London, were unusually relaxed. It is an open question how far the attitude towards sexuality in a society can be judged from the amount of sexual provocation or sexual concealment in women's clothes. Assuming that there is some correlation, it is noticeable that in the mid-1780s the fashionable dress included grotesquely enlarged breasts and buttocks, the former created by wirework and the latter by cork attachments. Elegant women resembled the callipygous statues of prehistoric art. Within a decade this fashion was replaced by the flowing see-through style in which women floated about in diaphanous veils with bosoms exposed or lightly covered, and the contours of the body fully displayed (Plate 22). In their very different ways, both fashions reflected an identical desire to advertise sexual attractions, the one representing unrealistic male sexual fantasies, the other exhibiting the real thing.

While perhaps equally sexually provocative, when it came to courting or dalliance the latter fashion had one obvious advantage over the former. Colonel George Hanger commented in 1801:

I must confess, I am a great admirer of short waists and thin clothing; formerly, when the women wore strong stiff stays and cork rumps, you might as well sit with your arm round an oaken tree with the bark on, as around a lady's waist; but now, as you have seldom any more covering but your shift and gown of a cold day, your waist is extremely warm and comfortable to the feel.

The production of sexual hardware was partly the result of improved technology and greater specialization in manufacture. But their appearance is also evidence of a new demand, made possible by a new morality. It is thus no accident that it was in the 1660s that such sophisticated devices as dildoes (imported from Italy) first became available in London, along with the first condoms. The former were sold, according to Rochester, at the Sign of the Cross in St James's Street and were bought and used by aristocratic ladies of the court, although they were still unknown to the wives of the bourgeoisie further east in the city. A century later they were still being imported from abroad, much to the embarrassment of the customs officials, since neither were they listed as dutiable, nor were they prohibited goods. They nonetheless ordered a consignment to be burned.

As for condoms, London and Paris were said to have been the only capital cities in Europe in the second half of the eighteenth century where these devices, then used primarily for prophylactic rather than contraceptive purposes, were openly manufactured, advertised, sold and used. They were clumsy affairs made of sheep gut, and were secured to the wearer at the base with a red ribbon, which was tied around the scrotum. In the 1740s they were sold by a Mrs Lewis in a shop in St Martin's Lane. Later on in the century, the monopoly passed to a Mrs Phillips, selling them in a shop first at the Green Canister in Half Moon Street, and later at 5 Orange Court, Leicester Fields.

It is equally significant that it was only in the eighteenth century that there first developed the large-scale production of home-made English pornography, both in literature and in pictures. When in the 1660s Pepys wanted to read a pornographic book, he had to buy a French work called *L'École des Filles*, 'a lewd book, but what doth me no wrong to read for information's sake'. This was a somewhat lame excuse, for the reading gave Pepys an erection and led him to ejaculate once. He then burned the book, presumably to prevent his wife from finding it. France long continued to be a major source, and as late as 1753 there were complaints about 'that inundation of obscenity which is daily pouring in from France'.

Frankly erotic English poetry certainly occurred in the early seventeenth century, such as John Donne's lyrical exploration of a woman's body: *O America! O my new found land!* Poetry only began to be more physically explicit, and even pornographic, however, with the Cavalier poets like Lovelace, as in his poem *To Amarantha:*

Here we'll strip and cool our fire
In cream below, in milk-baths higher.

With Lovelace there surfaces a new sensibility, involving the open expression of the long-suppressed id, which paved the way for the eroticized court culture of the Restoration.

Native English pornography as a literary genre seems to have had its tentative beginnings in the scurrilous and mildly obscene poems about sexual life at the court in the 1620s, which circulated widely in manuscript. This unpublished material began again slowly after the Restoration, but became a torrent in the last years of Charles II, from 1679 to 1685. Although the authors included Lord Rochester and Sir George Etherege, the quality of the doggerel was if anything lower than before. The great difference from the output of the pre-war years, however, is in the tone, the moral sensibility displayed by the authors and the elite audience of both sexes, who avidly sought after, read and preserved this material. It was now frankly pornographic in content, both in the generalized use of four-letter words and in the explicit descriptions of different kinds of sexual activity attributed to the King and other members of the court.

These manuscript poems went hand in hand with more directly political satires, and in both types the chief villain was the King, who was depicted in the former as the leader of an endless debauch. The connection between political opposition and pornographic anti-court satire was seen at the time, and a poem of 1682 makes it very clear:

> The King, Duke and State
> Are so libelled of late
> That the authors for Whigs are suspected.
> For women in scandal
> By scribblers are damned all,
> To Court and to cunt disaffected.

The political significance of such material in destroying the charisma of kingship should not be underestimated. On all three occasions in Early Modern times when a king was deposed or executed – England in 1649 and 1688, France in 1793 – the event was preceded by decades of pamphlets and poems, depicting the court as a sink of financial corruption and sexual depravity, fit only to be destroyed by men of moral integrity.

But the key event in the development of native English pornography was the publication in 1748 of James Cleland's *Memoirs of a Woman of Pleasure*, a lively piece of cheerful and literate hardcore pornography which was the first of its kind to be written by an

Englishman, and one of the few which succeeded in being extremely graphic without the use of four-letter words. The author, printer and publisher were admittedly prosecuted, but it is noticeable that nothing serious in fact happened to them, and that the book was defended as not 'offensive to decency' by the *Monthly Review*. By 1750 the market had grown sufficiently large to justify the launching of a fortnightly pornographic magazine, but it did not last. In 1773, however, *The Covent Garden Magazine or Amorous Repository* began a more successful career. It contained sexually provocative stories, and advertisements for prostitutes and brothels, with the prices (five shillings 'for a temporary favour', and half a guinea 'for a night's lodging'). In 1795 there began publication of *The Ranger's Magazine, or the Man of Fashion's Companion*, which included, according to its own statement of contents, monthly lists of whores; annals of gallantry; the juicier parts of trials for adultery, 'crim. con.' and seduction; *doubles entendres*; animating histories of wanton frolics. Some years earlier, there had begun publication of *Harris' List of Covent Garden Ladies*, an annual directory of call-girls, with prices, specialities, and descriptions which combined lyrical enthusiasm with extreme anatomical precision. The issue of 1786, for example, listed 105 women, the attractions of one of whom were described by an obviously well-educated hack ad-writer. Despite seven years experience in the trade, 'the coral-tipped clitoris still forms the powerful erection . . . nor has the sphincter vaginae been robbed of any of its contractive powers; the propelling labia still make the close fissure'.

Another sign of the spread of the new erotic sensibility is the widespread production and distribution of pornographic prints in eighteenth-century England. An early but abortive attempt to supply the market was made by some young dons at All Souls College in 1675. They were caught in the act of using the Oxford University presses after closing hours to print off copies of Giulio Romano's engravings from Aretino's *Postures* – the most famous, indeed almost the only, illustrated how-to-do-it sex manual of the day. By the early eighteenth century pornographic prints were in wide circulation and even found their way into fashionable drawing-rooms by the 1740s. So popular was the demand that in the very late eighteenth and early nineteenth centuries – mostly in about 1812 – England's most famous caricaturist, Thomas Rowlandson, was turning out pornographic prints, some of them for special customers like the Prince Regent (Plate 26). Finally, we have some evidence of a phenomenon which may have been present from the days of Pompeii to the twentieth century, but which certainly varies in quantity over time and space, as travellers and elderly persons today can testify, namely the habit of scribbling obscenities in public places:

> In wicked sport they rudely scrawl
> Unseemly words on every wall,
> And underneath the well-spelt line
> The parts themselves at large design.

The authors were presumably drawn from all sectors of the literate classes including the elite.

By the eighteenth century homosexuality was apparently becoming more common, or at any rate more open, among the upper classes. It may perhaps be significant that the numbers of male heirs who inherited landed estates in three sample counties and who never married rose from about five per cent before 1650 to about fifteen per cent thereafter (Graph 1, p. 39). Since the incentive of a property owner to marry, if only to produce a male heir, was very great, this may possibly indicate a rise in the number of homosexuals in this class. By the early eighteenth century, homosexual clubs existed for the upper classes in London, and throughout the century there were well-known wealthy deviants, like William Beckford, who were never brought to book. In 1731 William Pulteney publicly accused Lord Hervey of being a homosexual, and the evidence indeed indicates that he was actively and physically bisexual. On the other hand the fact that there were so many trials indicates that the forces of order still tried to punish those accused of this offence, and as late as 1772 a Captain Robert James was executed for this crime. The normal punishment for attempted sodomy was the pillory, but in more than one case this was the equivalent of the death penalty. Such was the fury of the mob, apparently mostly women, that they would sometimes pelt, stone or whip the victim to death, shouting 'cut it off', 'shave him close', 'flog him', etc. It is very hard to draw any firm conclusions from the very fragmentary evidence. It certainly looks as if eighteenth-century upper-class society was becoming more tolerant of adult male homosexuality, although the violent prejudices of the poor did not alter. What is certain is that male homosexuality was practised and talked about more openly in the eighteenth century than at any previous time, except in the restricted court circles in the reign of James I.

The second feature of eighteenth-century sexual life, the fusion of the previously separate roles of wife and mistress – the one to run the house and provide a male heir, and the other for companionship and sexual pleasure – is more difficult to document. There is evidence of an urgent female desire in the late eighteenth century to obtain full scientific knowledge of the anatomy of female sexual organs of reproduction, and public waxwork exhibitions on this subject were thronged with respectable young women. They were representative of the modern girl,

> Who ere for wedlock ripe, is wild to see
> What must its joys, and what its pains must be;
> How in the womb the foetus is reclined,
> What passage thence by nature is designed.
> With every other circumstance beside
> That may inform her ere she be a bride.

She had, complained the conservatives,

> This bawdy itch of knowing secret things
> And tracing human nature to its springs.

Armed with this new knowledge, she was better equipped than any generation before her to handle the problems of marital sexuality. There is sufficient evidence from private correspondence to indicate that sexual passion was an essential ingredient of many marriages among the squirarchy and professional and bourgeois classes, and it was the frequent waning of this passion which led to the rise of extra-marital liaisons during this period. It is highly significant that in *The Lady's Magazine* in the 1770s, the constant advice is, firstly that sexual attraction is ephemeral and an inadequate basis for marriage by itself, but secondly that it is an essential ingredient of marriage and something that the wife should do her utmost to keep alive. Above all, she should not, after capturing her man, allow herself to become sluttish and neglect her appearance. A letter of advice by a brother to a sister on her marriage puts it in a nutshell: 'never lose the mistress in the wife – a text of bullion sense'; the word 'mistress' being clearly defined in the context as a sexual partner, not a household manager.

5. CONCLUSION

In the terms of the sexual attitudes of the upper classes, who more or less successfully imposed their values on their social inferiors, English society thus passed through several phases: a phase of moderate toleration lasting until towards the end of the sixteenth century; a phase of repression that ran from about 1570 to 1670; and a phase of permissiveness, even licence, that ran for over a century from 1670 to 1810. This was followed by a new wave of repression that began in 1770, was spreading fast by 1810, and reached its apogee in the mid-Victorian period. After about 1870 this wave in turn receded, to be followed by a new period of permissiveness that has perhaps reached its apogee in the 1970s. These long-term seesaw oscillations do not seem to be connected to economic or political factors, but rather to cultural – and particularly religious – changes. Both sexual repression and sexual permissiveness eventually generate extremist features, which in turn set in motion counterforces which by a process of 'social reversion' slowly turn the pendulum back in the other direction. The duration of each of these swings of religio-ethical attitudes towards sexuality seems to have been about a hundred years. There is no reason to believe that there is a cyclical law in operation, for the swings can be accounted for by specific changes in religious enthusiasm, and by the time it takes for excesses to generate their own opposites.

CHAPTER ELEVEN

Gentlemanly Sexual Behaviour: Pepys and Boswell

'My wife ... said it was leaving myself embowelled to posterity ... But I think it is rather leaving myself embalmed.'

'Is it preserving evidence against oneself? Is it filling a mine which may be sprung by accident or intention?'
(James Boswell about his diary in *Boswell: the Ominous Years, 1774–1776*, ed. C. Ryscamp and F. A. Pottle, New York, 1963, pp. 174–5, and *The Private Papers of James Boswell*, ed. G. Scott and F. A. Pottle, New York, 1932–4, 13, p. 275)

If the examination of sexual behaviour among the upper classes is to be studied in greater depth than in the previous chapter, it can only be done by taking well-documented case histories and examining them in detail. This is, admittedly, a dangerous procedure for a variety of reasons. In the first place, those who kept diaries which recorded their sexual experiences and fantasies were exclusively men, and secondly, the mere fact of keeping diaries of their sex lives marks them off from their fellows. Most men at most periods do not record their sexual experiences, and the few who do are likely to be exceptional in some way or another. The mere desire to record sexual experience is usually a sign of latent anxiety, not necessarily about the writer's sexuality, but about his moral and physical performance generally. Moreover the extreme egocentricity of all the diarists blocks the reader from a full understanding of the two-way physical and emotional relationships.

The number of examples from which to work for the Early Modern period is pitifully small. Only six major sexual records kept by Englishmen or Americans seem to have survived, all but one of them mostly confined to activity in London. These six are, in fact, among the very first in recorded history, so that there is nothing to compare them with for earlier periods. Since Dr Kinsey and others have amply demonstrated the enormous variety and range of human sexual behaviour, generalization from a handful of individuals is obviously very hazardous. On the other hand some of them, especially Boswell, record not only their own experiences, but also how their male and female friends and associates reacted to their comments and confessions about themselves. Their sense of guilt, which runs through several of the diaries, is also an illuminating indicator of current values. What interests the historian is not what are the normal sexual responses of men and women at all times, but what are peculiar to a given time, place and society. This chapter will therefore narrate the sexual experience of two of these six men, and will try to distil from them such generalizations as are specific to the culture.

1. SAMUEL PEPYS

Married in 1655 at the age of twenty-three to a fifteen-year-old girl, Elizabeth St Michel, Samuel Pepys's domestic life for the next fourteen years until her death was not an easy one. He was a rising young official in the Navy Office, rapidly gaining money, power and reputation for himself, after an initial push from his great patron the Earl of Sandwich. Elizabeth was childless and lonely, left at home in the constantly expanding house with more and more maids to do all the work. She was frivolous, extravagant and easily aroused to anger or the sulks. One problem for her was that she loved her husband and was very jealous of other possible women in his life, with far more reason than she ever suspected.

To make matters worse, she was sexually inadequate for long periods of time. Even in his early days, before he sought other diversions, Pepys's sexual relations with his wife do not seem to have been very frequent, his only complaint occurring when once he had not slept with her for ten days or two weeks. On another occasion he slept with her before she left him for an extended stay in the country, noting that 'we have [not] lain together because of the heat of the weather a good while'. The main use to which they seem to have put marital sex was to make peace after one of their not infrequent quarrels. One reason for Elizabeth's sexual inadequacy was that she

341

was often ill. Throughout the early 1660s she suffered badly from severe menstrual cramps, which put her into bed for several days at a time every month. In 1663 she developed an abscess in the vaginal area which at times made intercourse altogether impossible and at times very painful to her. Even when she was more or less cured, there were long periods when the Pepys's domestic sexual life seem to have ceased altogether while he pursued his amours elsewhere. On 12 August 1667, for example, he recorded that he had not slept with his wife for three months.

On the other hand, Elizabeth was a great beauty who was admired wherever she went and, as Pepys eventually discovered, was formally invited to a sexual liaison on at least two occasions, once by Pepys's great patron the Earl of Sandwich and once by his son Lord Hinchinbrook, both of which she virtuously refused. Pepys at times was extremely suspicious of her, especially when she was learning to dance with an attractive young dancing master. She was one of the few women of her age to wear drawers, and so jealous and irrational was her husband that he took to watching her closely as she undressed at night on days when she had been taking dancing lessons, to make sure that she was still wearing them. In fact his suspicions about her were as baseless as his wife's about him were well founded.

As for Pepys himself (Plate 19), his sexual activity went in bursts. He rarely seems to have had intercourse more than once at a time with either his wife or any of many women. Once in 1664 he took Mrs Betty Martin twice '*sous de la chaise*' (? in the sitting position), and two years later he had intercourse with her 'forwards and backwards, which is my great pleasure'. Nine days later, he did whatever he wanted – an obscure phrase he often uses – with Mrs Martin at Westminster, and then hurried down to Deptford to sleep with his other mistress Mrs Bagwell, who was waiting for him naked in bed. After one bout with her, however, his lust was satiated, and he was overcome with shame and disgust at his behaviour. He got up in the middle of the night and slunk off home.

Like most men, Pepys was an insatiable *voyeur* of pretty women. At the playhouse, he spent his time looking at the actresses and the court ladies and royal mistresses in their boxes. Indeed, he was so taken by Charles II's beautiful mistress Lady Castlemaine that he fell in love with her, although he never even managed to speak with her. He was fascinated when he saw her underclothes hanging out to dry in the Palace garden; whenever he got a chance, he 'glutted myself with looking on her', and he bought a print of her portrait and had it mounted in his house. On one occasion he dreamed that he had her 'in my arms and was admitted to use all the dalliance that I desired with her', an episode that led him to wish that one could perhaps dream in one's grave, 'then we should not need to be so fearful of death, as we are in this plague time' of 1665. Since he had earlier been told that she 'hath all the tricks . . . that are practised to give pleasure' to be found in Aretino's famous illustrated sex manual, it must have been an enjoyable dream. He knew himself well and was astonished at the 'strange slavery I stand in to beauty, that I value nothing near it'. Everywhere he went, every shop he visited, every party he attended, every street he walked down, he was forever on the look-out for a pretty face. Sometimes he would follow attractive women down the street and try to take them by the hand. He did his best to strike up a close acquaintance with the pretty wives of his vintner, his bookseller, and other tradesmen.

After an initial period of timidity, he grew bolder in his advances, and found to his surprise that most women were quite willing to be kissed and to allow their breasts to be seen and handled, an experience in which Pepys took enormous pleasure and over which, if he is to be believed, he could spend literally hours without proceeding to further intimacies. What he most enjoyed were prolonged tactile fondlings, leading sometimes to masturbation.

In his choice of the no fewer than fifty-odd women with whom he had some physical contact between 1660 and 1669, he was governed by four primary considerations, apart from their physical attractiveness. The first was a fear of venereal disease, which led him to avoid all relations with professional prostitutes, despite a week in which he was strongly tempted by one called Cocky of Fleet Alley. Fortunately, he had another amateur mistress available at that time.

The second consideration that guided his on the whole very prudent conduct was a fear of pregnancy. It is perfectly clear that neither he nor any of his women had any knowledge whatever of contraceptive devices, either as protection against venereal disease or as barriers to impregnation. It was for this reason that almost without exception he confined actual sexual intercourse to married women whose husbands were not too long absent, so that if pregnancy occurred he could not be held responsible. Thus he played to his heart's content on many occasions with his first mistress Betty Lane, the seamstress and haberdasher in a booth at Westminster Hall, but she dared not indulge in intercourse so long as she was unmarried, a resolution he praised her for. The nearest they allowed themselves to go was for Pepys to rub his penis on her breasts and belly. He therefore did his very best to get a subordinate in the Navy Office, one Mr Hawley, to marry her – 'God knows I had a roguish meaning in it' – but Hawley procrastinated, much to Pepys's irritation. The pair once succumbed to a moment of passion and had intercourse, but fortunately there was no pregnancy. It was only in 1664, after Betty had married a Mr Martin, that they were free to indulge in full sexual relations, a process that went on for years regardless of her pregnancies. On one occasion they slept together after her husband had been absent for a while, and for a week there was a panic when she thought she was pregnant and Pepys had to think wildly of some scheme to get her husband posted back home hastily from his ship, which was at sea off Scotland.

The third consideration which guided Pepys, in his prudent way, was not to get so absorbed in his pursuit of sexual pleasure that he neglected his business at the office. His career was based on making a name for himself as a most capable and devoted man of business, and again and again he forswore women, ale-houses and playhouses for a period in order to concentrate on his work. His sexual adventures were, therefore, a form of relaxation from a normal life of diligent drudgery in the Navy Office. A fourth consideration that governed him was his determination to conceal all traces of his adventures from his wife, of whose jealousy he was well aware. Although he moved in the vicinity of court circles where mistresses were openly flaunted and where wives accepted the situation and took lovers of their own, this was very far removed from the life-style of the bourgeois Pepys, and he was very anxious not to have a domestic row or a separation. After several narrow escapes from detection by his wife, it was almost inevitable that sooner or later he would be found out, especially since he could not keep his hands off the chambermaids in his own house. As we shall see, in the end this was his undoing. Finally, he was constantly torn between his nagging puritanical conscience and his irrepressible sensuality and love of pleasure. Forever making good resolutions, and forever breaking them, he lacked a strong moral centre to hold him together. Meticulous to a degree in his business affairs at the Navy Office, his private life was something of a mess, possibly because he pursued women as a form of relief from the tensions in the office.

One striking aspect of Pepys's adventures is the way he used his official position to extract sexual favours, while others used their sexual favours to extract official grants from him. It is never quite clear in these exchanges who was exploiting whom. As Clerk of the Acts and Commissioner of the Navy Board, he was able to exercise patronage over a vast range of jobs, both at sea and in the dockyards, and he did not hesitate to use it for his own ends. Indeed, all the women who actually went to bed with him were in some way or another dependent on him for the professional advancement of their husbands. His first and most durable mistress, Betty Lane, married Mr Martin, for whom Pepys got an appointment as a ship's purser, despite the low opinion he had of Martin's personal capacity. Mrs Martin continued to satisfy Pepys's sexual desires whenever he was in need, and her husband continued to rise in the world. Long after the diary ceases, Martin was made consul in Algiers, where he died in 1679, after which his widow, Pepys's old love, was given a handsome government pension of £100 a year. It is hard not to believe that it was the sexual availability and attraction of his wife which formed the basis of Mr Martin's successful career. Nor is there much doubt that Martin was well aware of his wife's relationship with Pepys, and used it for his own advantage. Thus on one occasion Pepys notes 'to Mrs Martin, and did what I would with her; her husband going for some wine for us. The poor man I think would take pains if I can get him a purser's place, which I will endeavour' – and he did.

The same story at a lower social level applies to William Bagwell and his pretty young wife. Pepys first met Mrs Bagwell in 1664 when she began lobbying him in his office to obtain promotion for her husband, who was then only an ordinary carpenter to a fifth-rate man of war, about the lowliest job a naval carpenter could have. She immediately discovered that Pepys liked kissing her, and she played her cards with calculated but measured encouragement and becoming modesty. She reproved him for his advances, but slowly gave way step by step, allowing Pepys to progress from kissing her mouth to fondling her breasts and then her vagina, at the same time continually reminding him about her husband's promotion. After some months of this sexual ballet, he got her to the stage of mutual masturbation, once in a tavern and once in her home while her husband discreetly took a walk. Finally, in February 1665, Pepys got her husband his promotion and came to the Bagwell house for his reward. There he finally got what he wanted, although Mrs Bagwell put up a token struggle in which Pepys strained his probing left fore-finger. After many years of this on-and-off procedure of Mrs Bagwell lobbying Pepys for her husband's promotion, rewarded always by semi-reluctant intercourse, Mr Bagwell ended his career as master carpenter of a first-rate man of war, with Pepys in 1689 still lobby-ing for him, now to be promoted to assistant shipwright. In this case, there can be no doubt that the Bagwell parents and Mr Bagwell him-self were aware of what was going on, and were perfectly content to let it happen. On 1 February 1667, for example, he visited the Bagwells' house by appointment, to find Mrs Bagwell expecting him. They went upstairs and she let Pepys do whatever he wanted with her. Only later did her husband discreetly come home, took no notice of his wife and Pepys being alone together in the house, and began to talk business. As for Mrs Bagwell, she mystified Pepys, who remarked: 'Strange it is to see how a woman, notwithstanding her great pretence of love to her husband and religion, may be con-quered.' It does not seem to have struck him that it is very uncertain who was using whom for his or her own purposes, the only certainty being that the coin in which the bribe was made was sex. It seems likely that both parties were well satisfied with their bargains.

One gets the impression that it became well known in naval circles that the best way to obtain a favour from Pepys as Commissioner of the Navy was to send a pretty wife or a daughter, who had to be prepared at the very least to be kissed and to have her breasts fondled. The young wife of the merchant Thomas Hill was kissed while lobbying for a naval cork contract for her husband. A Mrs Lowther, who was also after a favour, was similarly manhandled. Black Nan, the daughter of the paper-ruler in the office, allowed her-self to be kissed as often as she appeared with paper, which no doubt helped to keep her father employed. Old Delks the waterman artfully left his daughter in Pepys' office to be felt and kissed by him, in order to get his son released from impressment into the navy.

The women who fell most easy prey to his advances were tavern girls like Frances and Susan Udall of the Swan, whose mouth and breasts he would kiss until he climaxed, or Sarah and Frances Her-bert, who were equally willing. But there were also the wives or friends of the family or business acquaintances, like Mrs Pierce or Mrs Pennington, with whom he toyed for hours whenever he got the chance. Finally, there was the succession of maids in his own house, both chambermaids and the higher-class companions to his wife.

One of their duties was to comb his hair for lice and to help him dress; and on many occasions maid after maid had to put up with Pepys's hands exploring their breasts and thrusting up under their petticoats while they did their work.

Pepys's imagination was so vivid that he could ejaculate while merely engaged in sexual fantasies. Once he did it in church on Sunday while thinking of Betty Michell, a pretty young wife with whom he fell half in love, and pursued for years without succeeding in doing more than getting the use of her hand to rub his penis now and then when sitting close together in a coach or a boat. Once he even experienced orgasm while lying on his back in a boat, not using his hand but merely thinking about a woman. Much of his sexual activity was not directed to intercourse, but to dreaming about or handling women for masturbatory purposes.

He only fell even superficially in love twice, and on each occasion it was because his sexual desires were thwarted. In 1664 he fell in love with Jane Walsh, the maid of his barber, who double-crossed him and failed to turn up to every assignation he made. In 1668 he fell in love with his wife's young companion Deb Willett, his passion for whom at last led to the discovery by his wife of some of his doings. On 25 October, Elizabeth suddenly entered the dining-room to find Deb combing her husband's hair while one of his hands was well up under her petticoats, feeling her vagina. It was three weeks before his wife could bully Pepys into dismissing Deb from the house. The trouble was that, as he confessed to his diary, 'I love the girl'; or rather 'the truth is I have a great mind for to have the maidenhead of this girl', if only the opportunity to do so offered itself. Meanwhile, his wife Elizabeth alternately raged and stormed at him, her anger being temporarily appeased only by passionate sexual intercourse. Pepys was thoroughly bewildered by his wife's violent oscillations from fury to sexual frenzy, but noted in his usual objective manner that he had slept with her more frequently in those three weeks than in all the previous twelve months. Moreover, the quality had improved with the quantity, for his wife received this sexual activity 'with more pleasure to her than I think in all the time of our marriage before'. At last, after thirteen years of marriage, Elizabeth's discovery of just one of her husband's more minor peccadilloes had succeeded in arousing her libido.

Soon after this episode, the curtain falls on Pepys's sex life since failing eyesight forced him to discontinue his diary. Two years later, his wife died of typhus, still childless and at the early age of twenty-nine. Pepys never remarried, but formed a lifelong liaison with a cultivated woman, Mary Skinner, whom he kept as his mistress for the next thirty-three years. Towards the latter end, she was openly living in his house and being treated by his friends as the social equivalent of a wife. Since Mr Bagwell and Mr Martin continued to rise in their professions, one can assume that for some years at any rate, he also maintained, if only intermittently, his sexually satisfying connections with their wives. When he died in 1703, he left Mary Skinner a handsome life annuity of £200 a year.

Pepys's diary is a unique piece of historical evidence, which could only have been kept by a very unusual man. But his activities involved large numbers of other people, and to that extent his *Diary* provides reliable and illuminating evidence about current standards of behaviour in the circles within which he moved in post-Restoration London. The first conclusion is that few women put up much resistance to his sexual advances, most of which went no further than a fondling of their erogenous zones. At first Pepys's upbringing led him to be shocked when he saw or heard about Charles II fondling his mistresses in chapel or at the theatre. Later he successfully adopted the same tactics among his own circle of acquaintances. All the evidence suggests that such casual physical contacts, only rarely leading to actual intercourse, were acceptable to a wide variety of women in late seventeenth-century London, whether married or unmarried, and coming from a wide variety of social classes. Only once were his physical advances totally rebuffed, when a woman he was standing next to, listening to a sermon in St Dunstan's church, threatened to stick pins in him if he persisted in molesting her – and that may have been more a result of the unsuitability of the occasion and place than her general hostility to being touched.

Secondly, there is clear evidence that Pepys did not hesitate to use his power, both as master over his servants and as Commissioner of the Navy, to obtain consent from women for his sexual advances. He saw nothing wrong in this abuse of authority, nor did they. In any case, each was using the other for his or her own purposes. Nor was he surprised or shocked when he learned that his own patron, Lord Sandwich, had tried to seduce his wife. In a world of patronage, power and deference, a woman's body was within limits at the disposal of her or her husband's superior, a fact rammed home half a century later by Defoe in his stories of Moll Flanders and Roxana.

Pepys was a naturally prudent and cautious man, at the mercy of a growing sexual obsession, particularly with women's faces and breasts. It was not only his own personal charm, which was clearly considerable, but also the authority he wielded which enabled him to satisfy these longings with such a wide variety of women, from the middle, lower-middle and lower classes in post-Restoration London.

Pepys's story also points to the difficulties and inhibitions placed on extra-marital sexual life by the absence of contraceptives. The result was a great deal of very prolonged play, kissing and feeling, and in Pepys's case the careful selection of married women with whom to have full sexual intercourse. Pepys's love of sexual play, often prolonged for hours, makes the traditional courting practice of bundling more intelligible as a way of passing the time during the long hours of darkness, while his diary makes it clear that before the introduction of the brassière and underpants in the nineteenth century, women's erogenous zones were wide open to the roving hand of any man. Women before the nineteenth century must have been accustomed to being intimately fondled as they went about their business, and to being indecently exposed if they fell down.

Pepys tried his best to be very secretive, to achieve which a good deal of his sexual activity took place in coaches, which were very secure places once the blinds were drawn, or in private rooms in alehouses across the river in Lambeth or north of Tothill Fields where he was unlikely to meet an acquaintance.

Finally, the spread of the sexual habits of Charles II's court by rumour, observation and example downward through the social scale of London life is very clearly evidenced by Pepys's diary. He continued to express shock and disgust, but also prurient interest and envy, at the goings-on at court. And while carefully preserving his own wife from temptation from others and from knowledge of his own extra-marital activities, he slowly succumbed to the temptation to imitate – in a far more modest and guilt-ridden way – the sexual behaviour of his social superiors.

Pepys's sexual life seems not at all exceptional. He appears to have been the archetypal *homme moyen sensuel,* unusual only in the lack of satisfaction he derived from his wife and his consequent search for pleasure elsewhere. His sexual activities often went in bursts, with occasional days when he rushed frantically from one woman to another. It is not at all clear what triggered off these hectic bouts of activity, but some of them may have been caused by the build-up of tensions and conflicts at work in the Navy Office.

The diary records a ceaseless battle between the id and the super-ego, between Pepys's powerful appetites and his nagging, puritanical, bourgeois conscience. Unlike the court grandees with whom he associated professionally, he was unable to indulge in hedonistic adventures of sexual seduction without a twinge of guilt or remorse. He recorded what he regarded as his failings as an aid to his reformation, and at the New Year he would make futile good resolutions to be more chaste in the future. Pepys was a man at war with himself, and as such was an epitome of his time and his class. Unlike Boswell a century later, he told no one about his exploits, neither his wife nor his most intimate male friends. This difference between Pepys and Boswell is partly one of character and class, but still more it is one of time. In the 1760s both men and women talked far more freely about sex than they did in the 1660s outside a small circle around the court.

2. JAMES BOSWELL

The most revealing information of all about sexual mores in the eighteenth century comes from the diaries, notes, memoranda and letters of James Boswell, which cover all his adult thirty-seven years from 1758 to his death in 1795 (Plate 20). Boswell, who was born in 1740, was the son and heir of an ancient and status-conscious Scottish family, and his father, the laird of Auchinleck, was a Lord of Court of Sessions and a member of the High Court of Judiciary in Scotland, one of the most respected lawyers in Edinburgh. For him, as for many young men of his time from upper bourgeois or landed backgrounds, a key figure in his early life, who decisively moulded his later character, was his mother. 'My mother was extremely pious. She inspired me with devotion. But unfortunately she taught me Calvinism. My catechism contained the doctrines of that system. The eternity of punishment was the first great idea I ever formed. How it made me shudder!... I thought but rarely about the bliss of heaven, because I had no idea of it.' The experience left him with a lifelong sense of guilt about the sensual pleasures he sought so avidly.

But it was his own genetic make-up which was responsible for his most pronounced characteristic – his supreme egoism, his absorbing passion in all aspects of himself, which was the cause of his compilation of so staggering a quantity of notes, memoranda and journals of such a self-revelatory and intimate nature. 'I have a kind of strange feeling as if I wished nothing to be secret that concerns myself.' He was also a manic-depressive, forever oscillating between moods of exuberant zest for life and profound melancholy. This melancholia was an inherited family trait which virtually incapacitated both his brother and an uncle. Possessing so volatile a temperament, none of his declarations of mood are to be taken too seriously, since they rarely lasted very long. But as a reporter of facts and of immediate feelings, he is beyond compare.

From the age of sixteen in 1756 to the age of twenty-nine in 1769 when he finally got married, Boswell was in the throes of a complex identity crisis, of which there were three main components. The first was the problem of religion. Brought up as a strict Calvinist, he was under great pressure from his mother to have a conversion experience. But this he could not do. He studied logic and metaphysics at the University of Edinburgh, and was temporarily converted to Methodism. He then became for a time a Pythagorean vegetarian under the influence of an old man. A little later, at the age of eighteen, he fell in love with a Catholic woman, and in 1758 suddenly fled to London and was secretly admitted by a priest into the Roman Catholic Church. This lasted only a matter of weeks before he was converted to hedonistic Deism (and the pleasures of sex) by a young Scottish friend, Lord Eglinton. Finally, five years later, on Christmas Day 1764, he was admitted to communion in the Anglican Church, although since he had had his bastard son baptized in that faith in November 1762, he had presumably more or less settled his religious problems by then. The man he admired most in the world was that bigoted Anglican Dr Johnson, but he still delighted in talking with sceptics like John Wilkes and Voltaire, while maintaining fascination for an outright atheist like David Hume and a boundless admiration for a Deist like Rousseau. His religious anxieties seem to have been mainly generated by his fear of and preoccupation with death – he rarely missed a hanging in London – and his uncertainty about an after-life.

The second identity crisis concerned Boswell's career and his relations with his father. The latter was an aloof and frosty figure with whom he could never establish human contact, and who despised him for his indolence and instability of purpose. He wanted his son to stay in Edinburgh and follow the practice of Scottish law like himself, but Boswell had other plans. He loved the theatre and fine literature; he wanted to travel and to meet the intellectual world of Europe; and he wanted to become famous as a writer – just how, he did not then know. Above all, he did not want to be cooped up in the provincial town of Edinburgh under the stern and inquisitive supervision of his unsympathetic father. His first plan, therefore, was to try to get a commission in a Guards regiment, which would give him an adequate income with little to do, except an obligation to reside in London. 'I could in that way enjoy all the elegant pleasures of the gay world, and by living in the metropolis and having plenty of time, could pursue what studies and follow what whims I pleased, get a variety of acquaintances of all kinds, get a number of romantic adventures, and thus have my satisfaction of life.'

The third identity crisis concerned the problem of how to deal with his sexual impulses. It was the discovery of the pleasures of the flesh which, according to his own account to Rousseau, cured him of his religious crisis by diverting his mind into other channels. His father naturally wanted him to settle down and marry a suitably rich and well-connected Scottish heiress, but this was not at all to Boswell's taste. He found himself blessed or burdened with an overwhelmingly powerful sexual drive – crude, unrefined, and urgent – and a very large member. This was a combination which regularly overcame his fear of venereal disease, his contempt for the low women he resorted to, and his recurrent moral doubts. He told himself that 'I am of a warm constitution; a complexion, as the physicians say, exceedingly amorous.' Moreover, 'I am too changeable where women are concerned. I ought to be a Turk.' As a result, he was forever plotting new sexual adventures: in 1762, 'in the midst of divine service' – in fact listening to a sermon on the topic 'Wherewith shall a young man cleanse his way' – 'I was laying plans for having women, and yet I had the most sincere feelings of religion.' When he forced himself into Rousseau's presence in 1764, the main problem he wanted to discuss was his boundless sexual fantasies. He proposed to Rousseau: 'If I am rich, I can take a number of girls. I get them with child, propagation is thus increased. I give them dowries and marry them off to good peasants who are very happy to have them. Thus they become wives at the same age as would have been the case if they had remained virgins, and I, on my side, have had the benefit of enjoying a great variety of women ... I should like to follow the example of the old Patriarchs, worthy men whose memory I hold in respect.' Rousseau would have none of these ideas, telling Boswell that fleshly pleasures were ephemeral compared with spiritual ones and that virtue has its own reward, advice which the latter followed for about a month.

The trouble was that the sensual mysticism of Rousseau, the elevation of sexual passion to a kind of religious experience, was alien to Boswell's whole approach to the subject. He was driven by direct, uncomplicated physical needs, to him as simple and instinctive as urinating or excreting. He was therefore much more at home with the frank sensuality of John Wilkes, whom he met at Naples. Wilkes reassured him that sex and literary distinction went hand in hand, that dissipation and profligacy renew the mind, proof being that he had written his best pieces for *The North Briton* in bed with Betsy Green. Wilkes also told him to be grateful for his constitution. 'Thank heaven for having given me the love of women. To many she gives not the noble passion of lust.' This was the sort of thing in which Boswell fundamentally believed, although, unlike Wilkes, his Calvinist upbringing continued to worry him about the propriety and the morality of his behaviour. Once in 1764 he referred to Cupid as Satan and later told himself to 'think if God really forbids girls'. In Berlin he even tried to frighten himself by writing a discourse against fornication along the hellfire and brimstone lines of his early education by his mother. But none of these doubts, and constant spasms of guilt and remorse, had more than temporary effects on his actual behaviour.

To sum up in purely quantitative terms Boswell's sex life from the ages of twenty to twenty-nine, he laid unsuccessful siege to more than a dozen ladies of quality – Scottish, English, Dutch, German and Italian; he made three married women of quality his mistresses; he had liaisons of varying length with four actresses, and a brief but passionate affair with the lifelong mistress, friend and attendant of Rousseau; he kept at least three lower-class women as mistresses, and he produced two illegitimate children, one in 1762 and one in 1767; he made a brief but successful assault early one morning on the pregnant wife of one of the King of Prussia's guards at Potsdam; and last but by no means least, he had sexual relations with well over sixty different prostitutes in Edinburgh, London, Berlin, Dresden, Geneva, Turin, Naples, Rome, Florence, Venice, Marseilles, Paris, and

Dublin. As a result, he suffered from at least ten outbreaks of gonor-rhoea before his marriage, and seven after, although it is certainly possible that some of them may have been recrudescences of latent old disease rather than altogether new infections.

The chronology of Boswell's sexual experiences was as follows. He lost his virginity during his first runaway visit to London to join the Roman Catholic Church at the age of twenty in March 1760. This took place in a room in the Blue Periwig in Southampton Street with a woman called Sally Forrester. This introduction into 'the melting and transporting rites of love' was an experience to which Boswell always looked back fondly, and he immediately embarked, under the tutelage of his older mentors Lord Eglinton and the Duke of York, on a series of debauches which ended in his first attack of gonor-rhoea, the cure for which lasted ten weeks. On his forced return to Edinburgh, he missed both the intellectual and the sensual pleasures of London. In May 1761 he consoled himself with a visit to a brothel in Edinburgh, where he promptly caught an even worse infection of gonorrhoea, which put him out of action for four months. On his recovery, he flung himself into a variety of intrigues, carrying on no fewer than four active liaisons at the same time. The first was with Mrs Jean Heron, the seventeen-year-old wife of a close friend and the daughter of one of his father's friends and his own patron, Lord Kames. She flung herself at him within a month of her marriage, and his notes contain unambiguous memoranda such as 'Tea, angel, two.' He naturally was consumed with guilt at his treachery, but Jean made a clear distinction between marriage and sexual passion, and was totally indifferent to such scruples. At the same time, he carried on active liaisons with two middle-aged actresses – one of them the wife of his second best friend – and picked up a lower-class girl as a steady mistress: one Peggy Doig, a 'curious young little pretty'. By November 1762, when he at last persuaded his father to let him go to London again to seek a commission in the Guards, Peggy was preg-nant. Before he left, he made proper gentlemanly arrangements for her lying-in, the baptism of the child, and its care by a foster-mother.

Boswell thus arrived in London in November 1762, at the age of twenty-two, with a wide variety of sexual experience already be-hind him. He had experimented with prostitutes in two cities; he had visited a brothel; he had had two intrigues with 'that delicious sub-ject of gallantry, an actress'; he had conquered the heart and used the body of a young married woman of his own social class; he had

kept a lower-class mistress and got her with child; and he had contracted venereal disease twice. The next seven years were to be no
more than variations on these established themes.

He began his visit to London full of wise resolutions: 'I determined to have nothing to do with whores, as my health was of
great consequence to me.' In London he could take his pick of hired
women, 'from a splendid Madam at fifty guineas a night down to the
civil nymph ... who tramps along the Strand and will resign her
engaging person to your honour for a pint of wine and a shilling'.
But he could not afford the one and planned to keep away from the
other for fear of 'the loathsome distemper'. What he wanted was a
renewal of what he had enjoyed in Edinburgh, 'the most delicious intrigues with women of beauty, sentiment and spirit, perfectly suited
to my romantic genius'. He therefore fastened his attention upon a
pretty twenty-four-year-old actress at Covent Garden Theatre,
'Louisa', or Mrs Lewis, who came from respectable parents and was
separated from her husband. On 17 December, he thought that he
'felt the fine delirium of love', and every day he pressed his suit more
closely. Three days later she borrowed two guineas from him, and he
offered up to ten, consoling himself with the reflection that although
not cheap, 'it cost me as much to be cured of what I contracted from
a whore, and that ten guineas was but a moderate expense for women
during the winter'. At the end of the month, mutual attraction was
clear. Mrs Lewis asked him what would happen if she became pregnant, and he promised that he would behave like a gentleman and
see the child taken care of. On Sunday, 2 January 1763, while the
landlady was out, she offered herself to him, but he felt impotent for
a while. At last his energies revived, and he hurried her into the bedroom and 'was just making a triumphal entry when he heard her
landlady coming up'. Thwarted on this occasion, Louisa promised
to spend the night with him at an inn on a Saturday, since she did
not have to act in the theatre on Sundays. The meeting took place
on 12 January, when Boswell excelled himself. 'Five times was I fairly
lost in supreme rapture', for him an unsurpassed feat of which he
was extremely proud. Six days later, however, Boswell felt 'a little
heat in the members of my body sacred to Cupid', and by the next
day it 'too, too plain was Signor Gonorrhoea' again. When taxed
with this unpleasant fact, Louisa confessed that she had been very
bad three years ago, but had felt no symptoms for eighteen months,
and had slept with no one but Boswell for six. It seems more than

likely that she was telling the truth and was an unsuspecting carrier, but Boswell was naturally furious and broke off all relations. 'Thus ended my intrigue with the fair Louisa ... from which I expected at least a winter's safe copulation.'

This mishap forced Boswell to retire to his room to live on bread and water and broth and to take physic for five weeks. He was visited by friends, but none of them took his predicament very seriously. The Judge Advocate of Scotland even made a pun about it, asking 'Who in the performance of a manly part would not wish to get claps?' But it spelt the end of Boswell's hopes of liaison with an amiable and reasonably cultivated woman with whom he could both talk and make love. In March, therefore, as soon as he was cured, he visited Mrs Phillips's shop at the Green Canister in Half Moon Street and bought himself some condoms as a protection against the prostitutes he would henceforth be obliged to resort to – his 'armour', as he called them. On 25 March he went into St James's Park, picked up a whore, and 'for the first time I did engage in armour, which I found but a dull satisfaction'. Every four or five days thereafter the physical urge became irresistible again and out he would go in search of a whore and 'copulated ... free from danger, being safely sheathed'. From time to time he made good resolutions 'against low street de-bauchery', but he could never put them into practice for long. Once he picked up 'a fresh agreeable young girl' and took her down a lane to 'a snug place'. 'I took out my armour, but she begged that I might not put it on, as the sport was much pleasanter without it.' Boswell was foolish enough to agree, a decision he much regretted the next day, but which fortunately brought no serious consequences. Once he found some willing amateurs, when he ran into two pretty girls 'who asked me to take them with me'. He offered them no more than his company and a glass of wine, which they accepted. He escorted them to a room in an Inn, fondled them, sang some songs, and then took them 'one after the other, according to their seniority'.

Encounters of this type – one of which took place on Westminster Bridge – went on all throughout the spring and summer of 1763, despite the reproaches of his friend Temple and his own self-disgust, not at the immorality of his behaviour, but its brutishness. What he really longed for was 'a genteel girl' as a mistress, but he could not find one. It was in June that he first met and became friendly with Dr Johnson, whom he enormously admired and to whom he confided his sexual problems. Dr Johnson gave him stern moral advice, and

Boswell resolutely concluded that 'Since my being honoured with the friendship of Dr Johnson ... I have considered that promiscuous concubinage is certainly wrong.' Even this did not stop him from a few further adventures, but his moral fibre was certainly being stiffened.

In August he left London on the Grand Tour of Europe, starting with Holland for the rest of 1763 and proceeding on through Germany and Switzerland in 1764 and Italy, Corsica and France in 1765–6. The moral lessons of Dr Johnson and the reproaches of his friend Temple had made a profound impression on Boswell. In Holland he was plunged into depression until on 15 October 1763 at Utrecht he drew up an 'Inviolable Plan' of moral reform and regeneration. 'For some years past, you have been idle, dissipated, absurd and unhappy,' he told himself. Henceforward, he would be industrious, purposeful, dignified, and chaste. The plan was hardly inviolable, but he certainly worked at the law at Utrecht and turned away from dabbling with whores and scheming for liaisons with ladies to a more serious study of a possible matrimonial prospect. The result was that on 23 July 1764, almost a year after leaving London, he could boast to Temple that 'since I left England, I have been as chaste as an anchorite'.

By September his matrimonial schemes had collapsed and he was in Berlin, where temptations were more plentiful. But he successfully resisted them until early one morning when a woman came to his room to sell chocolate. 'I toyed with her and found she was with child. Oho, a safe piece. Into my closet. *"Habst du ein Manne?"* *"Ja, in der Guards bei Potsdam."* To bed directly. In a minute – over ... Bless me, I have now committed adultery? ... Let it go. I'll think no more of it. Divine Being, pardon the errors of a weak mortal.'

As he proceeded onward on his journey, he was torn between lust and fear of disease. 'Chase libertine fancies,' he told himself; 'Swear solemn with drawn sword not to be with women *sine* condom *nisi* Swiss lass.' In Dresden he tried to buy condoms but failed, and was, therefore, obliged to content himself with picking up girls and ejaculating between their thighs without penetration for fear of infection. His visit to Rousseau, whom he then admired as much as he did Dr Johnson, did much to fortify him with renewed good resolutions to remain chaste in his forthcoming visit to Italy and France. But, as usual, it did not last, and in December, while at Geneva preparing to cross the Alps, his concern was not with chastity but with health. He was repelled by the masturbation he had again resorted to in desperation: 'Swear with drawn sword never pleasure but with woman's aid. In Turin and Italy you will find enough. But venture not but with perfect sure people.'

In Turin he attempted to gain access to two noble ladies, but he bungled both affairs and was rejected with humiliation. His approach to the Contessa di San Gillio was nothing if not direct. 'I am young, strong and vigorous. I offer my services as a duty and I think that the Comtesse de St Gilles will do very well to accept them.' She told him brutally, 'You should not attempt the profession of gallantry ... for you don't know the world.' Thus rebuffed, he consoled himself with whores, to his anxiety and disgust. From Turin he proceeded to Rome, where all scruples disappeared. 'Be Spaniard: girl every day,' he told himself – and he did. At Naples he slept with an opera singer, and others. As he confessed to Rousseau, 'I ran after girls without restraint. My blood was inflamed by the burning climate, and my passions were violent. I indulged them; my mind had almost nothing to do with it. I found some very pretty girls. I escaped all danger.'

Back in Rome in time for Easter week in 1765, he was not so lucky. After a series of orgies with whores, he had to confess on 29 April, 'Alas, real disease.' The infection was mild but persistent, the beginning of a urethric condition that lasted, on and off, for the rest of his life, despite the advice of many doctors and surgeons. Undeterred by this warning symptom, he continued throughout May to make an intensive study of classical art and architecture all day and to chase girls in the evening. At Rome he became acquainted with Lord Mountstuart, the eldest son of Lord Bute, the English Prime Minister, who invited him to join his party (consisting of himself, an ex-colonel as a governor, and a crotchety Swiss historian as a tutor) on a trip to Venice. At Venice Boswell's imprudence led to serious consequences. He allowed Lord Mountstuart to accompany him 'to take a look at the girls', as the result of which 'a pretty dancer was our common flame, and my Lord catched a tartar as well as I. A fine piece of witless behaviour.'

Lord Mountstuart was soon afterwards summoned home by his father, but Boswell, defying the instructions and expectations of his father, proceeded on to Florence and then Siena in a last attempt to bag an Italian countess. He first tried Porzia Sansedoni, the wife of the Chamberlain of the Grand Duke of Tuscany, who had earlier been the mistress of his friend Mountstuart. Once again his approach was a direct one: 'I should like to be with you, late at night, and in a modest darkness, to receive a tender pledge of your favour for an eternal friend' – i.e. Mountstuart. Rebuffed in this quarter, he turned to Girolama Piccolomini, the wife of the Mayor of Siena, who promptly fell in love with him. The first encounter was not a success, according to Boswell's notes: 'Girolama. Quite agitated. Put on condom; entered. Heart beat; fell. Quite sorry, but said "A true sign of passion." ' Later he recovered his virility, and there followed eighteen days of passionate love-making. But, as usual, Boswell soon tired of this new love, and resolutely left Siena never to return. For Girolama, however, this was the great emotional experience of her life, and she continued to write to her unfaithful lover for at least another four years.

There followed a visit to Corsica and the rebel General Paoli, his account of which was later to make Boswell famous at last. Paoli, whom he admired as much as he did Rousseau and Dr Johnson, was consulted by Boswell in his usual frank way about his sexual problems, and advised chastity and an early marriage. En route back home, Boswell stopped in December at Marseilles, where he had an introduction from a friend to a girl who had been his friend's mistress for about a year. He looked her up and, on the basis of his friendship with her ex-lover, persuaded her to spend the night with him. This episode sapped his Corsican resolve, and on his arrival in Paris he made straight for the best brothels in town, where he seems to have spent most of his time. While in Paris he met Rousseau's mistress and companion of twenty years, Thérèse Le Vasseur, who was on her way to join the philosopher in his English exile. She and Boswell therefore joined forces for the trip. Just what happened during the first eleven days of February between Paris and Dover is not known for certain since these pages of the journal have been destroyed. All that is left is Boswell's entry for 12 February, the day after their arrival at Dover: 'Yesterday morning had gone to bed very early and had done it once. Thirteen in all. Was very affectionate to her.' There seems to be no doubt that when he left Paris Boswell had no intention of seducing the lifelong companion of his hero Rousseau, but there can equally be no doubt that this is what happened. One scholar, who claimed to have read the missing pages before they were destroyed, said that the liaison began when they were forced to share a bed at an inn. After the usual period of impotence, Boswell finally succeeded. But when he boasted to her of his prowess, she told him bluntly that 'you are a hardy and vigorous lover, but you have no art' and proceeded to give him a series of lessons in the techniques of foreplay and the variations of posture. Once she rode him 'agitated, like a bad rider galloping downhill', while Boswell was vainly trying to pump her about details of her life with Rousseau.

Back in London and then in Edinburgh, Boswell continued to frequent whores, all his good resolutions having disappeared. In 1766, however, he formed a serious liaison with a pretty young woman of his own class, a Mrs Dodds, whose husband had left her. This was just what Boswell wanted: 'In this manner I am safe and happy, and in no danger either of the perils of Venus or of desperate matrimony.' Moreover, 'she has the finest black hair, she is paradisial in bed'. She was his mistress for about a year, and in April 1767 she became pregnant with Boswell's second illegitimate child. Meanwhile, he was extremely busy both cultivating his legal practice at the Scottish Bar and at last looking for a wife in real earnest. Despite this pressure of business and despite Mrs Dodds's willingness to give him every sexual satisfaction he asked for – on one occasion dressing in black and leaving the candles lit – Boswell nevertheless from time to time indulged in the grossest and stupidest behaviour, now largely due to a new vice, a propensity to get drunk.

On 8 March 1767, Boswell gave a bachelor party to pay a debt of honour to his friends with whom he had, before he left Scotland in 1762, made a bet of 'a guinea that I should not catch the venereal disorder for three years'. He got so drunk that he staggered off to a whore and spent the night with her, with the inevitable result (despite some half-hearted precautions) of a recrudescence of his gonorrhoea. Since the reaction was so fast, it seems possible that he was by now suffering from chronic gonorrhoeal infection of the prostate, which was reactivated by venereal or alcoholic excess. He still did not learn his lesson, and in June the same thing happened again. He spent the evening with his friends drinking the health of Miss Blair, his prime matrimonial choice at the time, and again got drunk and spent the night with a whore. This time the disease was really serious, and he passed it on to the now pregnant Mrs Dodds. Fortunately she recovered quickly, but it took Boswell all the summer in retreat and under a strict regime of diet and physic to clear up the infection.

In December he again slept with an Edinburgh whore, with the same result, and in January, while still infected, he was sleeping again both with whores and with Mrs Dodds. One of the whores was an illegitimate daughter of Lord Kinnaird, which gives some insight into the wide social spectrum from which the profession of prostitution was then drawn. He was no longer in love with Mrs Dodds, who in December had given birth to his daughter Sally, and was simply using her as a sexual convenience, usually after a heavy drinking party when he was inflamed with wine. On 7 February 1768 he arrived drunk at Mrs Dodds's house at 2 a.m., slept with her, and then went off to make a proposal of marriage to Miss Blair, who had the good sense to refuse him. Soon afterwards Mrs Dodds drops out of the picture, to be replaced by 'a pretty lively little girl', but one in whose constancy Boswell had no confidence. He gave her some money before he left for London, but asked two of his friends to test her by trying to seduce her, which they found only too easy. In March he was in London again, where in a manic mood he promptly 'sallied forth like a roaring lion after girls'. At first he was careful to use his 'armour', but General Clark told him that oil was a good protection, and he tried it out with a girl he had known before. He performed twice, paid her only four shillings and noted that 'I never saw a girl more expert at it', so it was a successful experiment. He had now acquired a taste for two girls at a time, and – no doubt because of his use of oil instead of condoms – he found himself re-infected for the ninth time. This time he was only cured by a retreat which lasted six weeks, and the experience inspired a vow of chastity for six months, taken in St Paul's Cathedral just before leaving for Edinburgh.

By the spring of 1769 his matrimonial choice, which was still focused on an heiress with at least £10,000, had narrowed down to two; and in June he visited Dublin in pursuit of one, during which he once more had the folly to visit a brothel, with the usual result of a new gonorrhoeal infection. So severe was it this time that he had to go to London for the cure, which consisted of a camphor liniment and mercury plaster on the affected parts, a daily draught of a pint of 'Kennedy's Lisbon Diet Drink' – at half a guinea a pint – and finally some minor surgery. In October the doctors reassured him that he would recover: 'By sleeping with the same woman all would come right.' A month later, on 25 November 1769, he married his final choice, his old friend and cousin Margaret Montgomerie, to whom he had become engaged before leaving for London for medical treatment. She was an intelligent and sensible woman, two or three years older than Boswell, without fortune, but whose physical proportions well suited the latter's gross appetites: she was 'a heathen goddess painted al fresco on the ceiling of a palace at Rome'. She was also deeply devoted to him, despite his manifold defects of character which she knew only too well (Plate 21).

It was a marriage which permanently alienated his father, who had set his heart on some well-connected heiress who would substantially increase the family fortunes. As a cousin with a portion of a mere £1,000, Margaret brought neither wealth nor additional political connections. Boswell had married in defiance of his father's wishes, and for long-standing settled affection, not family interest. It was thus on both counts a classic example of the new marriage in the eighteenth century. If the filial challenge was common, the paternal response was unusual in its brutal psychological impact. A sixty-two-year-old widower, his father suddenly announced his intention of remarrying. Not only did he not attend Boswell's wedding, but he arranged for his own to take place on the same day. A more obvious attempt at the sexual castration of his son could hardly be imagined.

But it was not only his father who disapproved of his marriage. Even his two bachelor friends were none too enthusiastic about it at first. Temple warned him that 'you are born to a fortune not inconsiderable, of a family of some note in your country. These are circumstances you must consider . . . If by marriage you do not both add considerably to your fortune and increase your influence by your wife's connections, the world will deem your generosity weakness and imprudence.' Dempster was just against marriage on principle: 'I think marriage is setting up a child-manufactory, at which one must drudge like a horse. Children are a commodity which requires great pains in the raising, and then you are miserable until you get them disposed of.'

In retrospect it is clear that Boswell's marriage to Margaret Montgomerie was the most – perhaps the only – sensible thing he ever did, and for some years thereafter his life was a model of domestic virtue and happiness, monogamy, sobriety and professional diligence. She loved him deeply, understood him, and was patient with all his weaknesses and follies. In his own odd way he loved her in return, and paid her the compliment of always being frank and honest with her, confessing all – or nearly all – of his constant infidelities. He kept a notebook entitled 'Uxoriana or my Wife's excellent Sayings', and after her death he carefully preserved her purse, a lock of her hair, her wedding-ring, and 'two stalks of lily of the valley which my dear wife had in her hand the day before she died'.

She had known him and been his confidante for years, and the ties of cousinhood no doubt reinforced Boswell's narcissism. He was almost marrying himself. This is not to say that he and his wife were temperamentally identical, for they were not. She had less of a sexual drive than her husband, and lacked both his ebullience and his melancholy. She was a plain, solemn, sensible woman. Once in 1775 she complained to him that he never talked seriously to her 'but merely childish nonsense'. Boswell admitted the truth of the charge. 'The reason of it may be partly indolence, to avoid thought; partly because my wife, though she has excellent sense and a cheerful temper, has not sentiments congenial with mine. She has no superstition, no enthusiasm, no vanity; so that to be free of a disagreeable contrariety, I may be glad to keep good humour in my mind by foolish sport.'

Mrs Boswell worked hard to satisfy her husband and to produce the son and heir he so badly wanted. A son was born in August 1770, but only lived two hours; a daughter Veronica arrived in March 1773; another daughter in May 1774; and at last a son Alexander in October 1775. In the next five years there followed two more sons (one of whom died almost immediately), one miscarriage and one daughter.

So happy was Boswell after his marriage that he abandoned his diary for almost three years, only taking it up again in the spring of 1772, when he left home for an extended trip to London in order to renew his association with old friends, and especially with Dr Johnson. He was reluctant 'to part with a valuable friend and constant companion', and his wife was equally sorry to see him go. Hardly had he reached London when the old temptations presented themselves. Boswell walked up and down the Strand, looking at the whores and 'indulging speculations about ... the harmlessness of temporary likings, unconnected with mental attachment'. But he controlled himself and 'resolved never again to come to London without bringing my wife along with me' – a resolve he never kept. He was also tempted by the pretty maid at his lodging, who as she bade him goodnight would ask him, 'Do you want anything more tonight, sir?' but he kept his desires to himself. During the two months he was in London, he wrote thirty-five letters to his wife, and he only faltered once in April when for two nights he 'went with bad women a little'.

On the other hand, he had a disturbing conversation with an old and intimate friend of his wife, the Honourable Mrs Stuart, wife of James Archibald Stuart, younger brother of Boswell's old travelling companion Lord Mountstuart. Somehow or other the breakfast talk got around to the subject of marital infidelity. Mrs Stuart

candidly declared that from what she had seen of life in this great town she would not be uneasy at an occasional infidelity in her husband, as she did not think it at all connected with affection. That if he kept a particular woman, it would be a sure sign that he had no affection for his wife; or if his infidelities were very frequent, it would also be a sign. But that a transient fancy for a girl, or being led by one's companions after drinking to an improper place, was not to be considered as inconsistent with true affection. I wish this doctrine may not have been only consolatory and adapted to facts. I told her I was very happy; that I had never known I was married, having taken for my wife my cousin and intimate friend and companion; so that I had nothing at all like restraint.

Despite this reassurance, Boswell was clearly thrown into some confusion by these remarks by a woman in whose judgement he had some confidence.

It was not until he was back in Edinburgh in the autumn of 1772 that he committed adultery for the first time after his marriage. On this occasion, it was caused by the vice of very heavy drinking, which was growing steadily on him during these years. More and more frequently he would go off on all-night drinking bouts which would deprive him of all self-control. Because of illness after a miscarriage the previous winter, Mrs Boswell was unable to satisfy her husband's sexual needs, and in late October after a drunken evening he visited an Edinburgh prostitute. He promptly confessed his folly to his wife, who made him send for a doctor at once. 'She is my best friend and the most generous heart,' he noted, justly. In January 1773, by which time Mrs Boswell was far gone with child, he lapsed again, contracted gonorrhoea once more and had to place himself in the surgeon's hands.

The birth of Veronica in March 1773 and the shame and pain of the disease seem to have made him get a grip on himself for over a year, but in the summer of 1774 alarming symptoms of loss of self-control reappeared. Six times in six weeks he went on all-night drinking orgies, returning home dead drunk to his waiting wife in the early hours of the morning. It seems likely that these drinking bouts were a substitute for sexual frustration, for he did not resume relations with his wife after the birth of the second child in May until 19 August. Boswell's sexual drive far exceeded that of his wife and she did not let him sleep with her again for another five weeks. A week before he had got dead drunk again, returned home, cursed his wife, and threw a candlestick at her with a lighted candle – an episode which filled him with contrition the next morning.

She probably realized the pressures that were tormenting her husband, and in late September 1774 he persuaded her to leave the two children at home and go off with him on a brief holiday. The first night he took her three times, and once on each of the three succeeding nights. He tried, but failed through excess of alcohol, a week later, but this was the last period for a long while during which he could obtain full sexual satisfaction from his wife. If his record is complete, they slept together only four times between 23 October 1774 and 22 January 1775, although by January she was again with child. On 8 March 1775, they finally had a frank discussion about their sexual problems, the result of which was to throw poor Boswell into a flurry of indecision, with temptation battling against moral qualms, and with a host of religious and literary witness on both sides.

I was quite in love with her tonight. She was sensible, amiable, and all that I could wish, except being averse to hymeneal rites. I told her I must have a concubine. She said I might go to whom I pleased. She has often said so. I have not insisted on my conjugal privilege since this month began, and were I sure that she was in earnest to allow me to go to other women without risk either of hurting my health or diminishing my affection for her, I would go. Thus I thought; but I was not clear, for though our Saviour did not prohibit concubinage, yet the strain of the New Testament seems to be against it, and the Church has understood it so. My passion, or appetite rather, was so strong that I was inclined to a laxity of interpretation, and as the Christian religion was not express upon the subject, thought that I might be like a patriarch; or rather, I thought that I might enjoy some of my former female acquaintances in London. I was not satisfied while in this loose state of speculation. I thought this was not like Isaak Walton or Dr Donne. But then the patriarchs, and even the Old Testament men who went to *harlots*, were devout. I considered indulgence with women to be like any other indulgence of nature. I was unsettled.

Ten days later, on his way to London for another extended visit, Boswell was still worrying over the morality of concubinage. He explained in a letter to his friend Temple, 'that no man was ever more attached to his wife than I was, but that I had an exuberance of amorous faculties, quite corporeal and unconnected with affection and regard, and that my wife was moderate and averse to too much dalliance. Why might I not then be patriarchal . . .?' As soon as he got to London, he put the problem to his friend the Honourable Mrs Stuart, who seemed to agree with him: 'the difference between men and women was that men could have connections with women without having their hearts engaged. Women could not with men.' This psychological explanation of the double standard Boswell found comforting, but not conclusive. He was as usual tempted by whores, but kept away from them. But by April his good resolutions had failed again.

By May Boswell was back in Edinburgh, and in October his son Alexander was born, for whom a wet-nurse was promptly introduced into the house. In November and December he visited a woman, apparently in her room in his house, who was probably Mrs Ross, the wet-nurse to his infant son. At the same time the tensions were rising again, and he was indulging in wilder drinking bouts, after one of which he came home and smashed all the dining-room chairs, throwing them at his poor wife. Moreover a new vice of all-night gambling at cards was growing steadily upon him.

Back in London on his usual spring jaunt in March 1776, he renewed relations with an old lover, probably the actress Mrs Love who had been his mistress back in 1761–2, a proceeding which he justified to himself on the grounds that 'these are Asiatic satisfactions, quite consistent with devotion and with a fervent attachment to my valuable spouse'. Not content with Mrs Love, he relapsed into casual promiscuity made easier by alcohol, picking up cheap whores in the street. The main thing he was afraid of was catching venereal disease, 'which there could be no doubt was an injury to her'. On 1 April he had another encounter with a whore and indulged in a new perversion – 'a kind of licence I never had'. By early April he had inevitably contracted gonorrhoea again and was in the hands of doctors and surgeons, who promised to cure him quickly with a new injection.

Back in Edinburgh again, Boswell was acutely depressed, and plunged into an endless round of alcoholic excess, all-night card playing, and promiscuous whoring. In the eight months from August 1776 to March 1777, he was hopelessly – sometimes helplessly – drunk twenty-six times, usually followed by terrible hangovers which made him quite incapable of business. His legal career in Edinburgh was getting nowhere, and he was profoundly bored by the vulgar provinciality of his job and his existence. His wife was not well. She gave birth to a son in November 1776, who soon died; had a miscarriage the following July; and gave birth to their second son James in September 1778. In 1777 she began to spit blood, first evidence of the tuberculosis which was to kill her twelve years later. Boswell's relations with his father remained strained, and until the old man died and he came into the estate, he was condemned to drudgery at the Edinburgh Bar, a situation which merely exacerbated his inherited tendency to bouts of profound melancholia. One cause for depression was a visit he paid to the dying David Hume on 21 August 1776. He hoped to find Hume reconciled to the Christian religion, only to discover that he was stoically resigned to the prospect of everlasting annihilation. This deeply upset Boswell, who had an intense fear of death and whose hold on religion was none too secure; after the visit he 'ranged awhile in the Old Town after strumpets, but luckily met with none that took my fancy'. At other times, alcohol clouded his discrimination, and anything female would serve the purpose: on 28 August he drunkenly ranged the streets, met with 'a comely fresh-looking girl, madly ventured to lie with her on the north brae of Castle Hill. I told my dear wife immediately.' A week later he discovered that the fresh-looking girl was a common whore, which made him afraid of gonorrhoea and obliged him to stop all sexual relations with his wife for fear of passing the infection on to her in her seventh month of pregnancy. Fortunately, this was a false alarm, but meanwhile he was falling in love with the children's nurse living in the house, his wife's penniless orphan niece Annie Cunningham. In November his child was born, but he continued to slake his appetite with casual encounters after heavy drinking bouts. Once he took 'a plump hussy who called herself Peggy Grant' in a field behind the Register Office on 'one of the coldest nights I ever remember', and on another occasion in a mason's shed in St Andrew's Square.

Always confessing to his long-suffering wife, always repenting, always relapsing, Boswell dragged through a wretched year. On 8 December even his wife had had enough. She insisted on reading his journal and found not only these brutish couplings with whores, which she could forgive if not understand, but evidence of love for her niece Annie Cunningham, which she could not. She 'told me she had come to a resolution never again to consider herself my *wife*, though for the sake of her children and mine, as a *friend* she would preserve appearances'. But a week later, as usual, she relented and forgave him. On 7 April 1777, his last day in Edinburgh before a trip to see his father, he was drunk again and met an old 'dallying companion', now pregnant, who encouraged him to penetrate her. But he contented himself with 'a lesser lascivious sport', came home to bed, stripped, 'enjoyed my dear wife excellently', and at dawn set out on his journey.

In September he set out on a trip to Ashbourne in Derbyshire to meet Dr Johnson, but on the way he lost no opportunity to feel the maids in every inn. At Liverpool he toyed with the chambermaid in the evening, and the next morning while she was taking his sheets off the bed he took further liberties, but was denied full penetration. At Leek he felt both the chambermaid and the maid who brought him tea, meanwhile reflecting: 'How inconsistent ... is it for me to be making a pilgrimage to meet Dr Johnson, and licentiously loving wenches by the way.' Once in the presence of the doctor, however, the latter's intellectual conversation effectively replaced 'the pleasure of enjoying women'. On 2 October, he was back home and lay with his wife, but she was 'justly displeased' on reading his journal to find out about his manhandling of the maids at the inns. That winter his wife was ill again and spitting blood, but she gave him satisfaction whenever she could, on 5, 6 and 17 December. She did it again on 5 January, but this brought on an alarming fit of spitting of blood in the middle of the night. Boswell, therefore, found solace with 'a fine wench' in a room in Blackfriars Wynd, and by February 1778 he had contracted gonorrhoea again. This was the twelfth time in his life, the second since his marriage in 1769 and the first in five years. As he left for London on 12 March, he noted that when they parted 'my wife having had reason to be offended with me, we were at present in a state of coolness'.

In London he renewed his acquaintance with the actress Mrs Love, his old mistress of sixteen years before, and now in her late fifties. As soon as the doctors declared him fit again, he pressed her to sleep with him, and she reluctantly agreed, saying it was only to oblige me or be agreeable to me or some such phrase'. As they climbed into bed, Boswell asked, 'What harm in your situation?' to which she replied, 'To be sure. Or in yours, provided it does not weaken affection at home.' Although she was clearly a very sensible and decent woman,

Boswell commented unkindly to his journal, 'What a slut, to be thus merely corporeal.' But two days running Mrs Love satisfied his physical needs, and sent him on his way with the much appreciated compliment that 'I was better than formerly'. When Boswell consulted his venereal doctor Sir John Pringle before he left London, the latter got him to admit his adventure with Mrs Love. Sir John advised him to 'add one more sin and deny it to Mrs Boswell. I insisted on preserving my truth.' Boswell might have been incapable of being a faithful husband, but he still prided himself on being an honest one.

Back in Edinburgh in May 1778, all was once more forgiven, as usual, and for a while Boswell lived a chaste and sober life. On 15 September, his son James was born, but only after great difficulty. Mrs Boswell had suffered so severely that she expressed a wish that 'she might have no more. I was satisfied to think that she should not.' Despite this agreement, and despite Margaret's obviously failing health, there are no signs that Boswell took any contraceptive precautions, either by using the condoms with which he had been so familiar before his marriage or by the practice of withdrawal. Before Margaret was fit for sex again, Boswell was already sneaking off to a house in the suburb of Portsburgh, where he had found a complaisant and, he hoped, disease-free widow woman. On 11, 19, and 21 October he resumed relations with his wife. But the occasions were rare, occurring not at all in November and only twice in December and three times in January. Boswell, therefore, filled in the gaps by visits to Portsburgh, although on one occasion he had an unwelcome surprise. He had slept with his wife on 25 January 1779 and had visited Portsburgh on the 29th. But his appetite was so whetted that he was back on the doorstep at Portsburgh early the next morning between 7 and 8 a.m. Boswell's staccato notes tell the story: 'Tedious waiting for the door to open. Found man in closet. Wonderful presence of mind. Bade him to be at it. The man went off. I was going, but was allured back, and twice.'

Boswell's record of the annual jaunt to London in the spring is very incomplete, but he must have been fairly chaste, for he slept with his wife the first and second day after his return home in late May. On 7 July, however, he visited a brothel called 'The Pleasance', and on the 8th came home dead drunk and was put to bed by the patient Margaret. On the 9th he was relieved to find he had not contracted disease from his visit to the brothel, but his subsequent forced abstinence from relations with his wife made her guess what had happened, and she forced him to confess. 'I was sorry for it. She was very good,' and they made it up in bed, although Margaret was angry a few days later when she found that Boswell had been cold sober when he made his unfortunate visit. He also confessed to his visits to the obliging widow at Portsburgh, but Margaret again forgave him, a forgiveness once more sealed in bed. On 15 July Boswell noted: 'I vowed fidelity ... It is amazing how callous one may grow as to what is wrong by the practice of it.'

The autumn and winter of 1779–80 was a happy time for the Boswells. Boswell was in good health and spirits, reasonably sober, busy at his legal work, and entirely faithful, except 'only once with a coarse Dulcinea, who was perfectly safe'. By early December Margaret was pregnant again, and they slept together twenty-one times in the three months from 13 December to 14 March, despite Margaret's increasing coughing and spitting of blood. Possibly their common anxiety about the prospect of her early death may have drawn them closer; possibly the progress of the disease may have stimulated Margaret's libido; possibly the fact that she was already pregnant made her more willing to satisfy her husband's desires. In April, however, Boswell lapsed again into heavy drinking, and on the 10th he staggered through the streets of Edinburgh and 'dallied with 10 strumpets ... I told my valuable spouse when I came home. She was good humoured and gave me excellent beef-soup which lubricated me and made me feel well.' The child Elizabeth was born on 13 June 1780, and the last time Boswell slept with Margaret before the birth was 21 May. Thereafter he was on his own, and an assignation with a black prostitute a week after the birth was followed by another slight attack of venereal disease. The rest of the year was a gloomy period of melancholia, drunkenness, and whoring, which apparently ended with yet another mild dose of gonorrhoea. However on 28 December 'at night when in bed with my dear wife, I was wonderfully free from gloom, and trusting to Mr Wood's opinion that I had no infection, I prevailed upon her to allow me to enjoy her'. He then rounded out the old year triumphantly by sleeping with her on the three following nights.

The spring of 1781 found Boswell back in London to renew the acquaintance of Dr Johnson, Sir Joshua Reynolds, Edmund Burke and his other literary and artistic friends. But their conversation was not enough to keep him happy, and he could not resist pursuing a variety of street girls, until once again he caught gonorrhoea. With his passion for confession, he confided his troubles to his old friend the Honourable Mrs Stuart 'and was calmly consoled'. Returned to Edinburgh, and presumably cured, he must have resumed relations with his wife, for she miscarried again in October, and was for a long time very ill as the tubercular symptoms got steadily worse. His misery, fear and sexual frustration drove Boswell back into the streets and backyards of Edinburgh, despite his own clear-headed self-appraisal: 'I am quite sensual, and that too, not exquisitely, but rather swinishly.' On 18 February 1782 he sank to a new low of alcoholic and sexual debauchery, and he confessed on 26 February that 'I am really in a state of constant, or at least daily, excess just now. I must pull the reins. But I feel my dull insignificance in this provincial situation.' The next day his wife read the (now missing) account of the debauch on 18 February and for the second time in her life told her husband that 'all connection between her and me was now at an end, but that she would contrive to live with me only for decency's sake and for the sake of her children'. Less than a fortnight later, however, all was forgiven, and they made it up in bed. So they drifted through the next six months, Margaret now rallying and eagerly renewing sexual relations, and now sinking, Boswell faithful and sober for a while, and then setting out on one of his drunken sprees in pursuit of Edinburgh whores.

His father's death on 30 August 1782 transformed Boswell's life, since he at last came into his substantial inheritance, and was also freed from the psychological burden of this stern, forbidding father, who regarded him as a good-for-nothing fool and wastrel. Two days later Boswell tried to sleep with Margaret, but was checked by the thought, 'What! When he who gave you being is lying a corpse?' Once the old man's body was safely underground, however, Boswell's spirits rose, and despite Margaret's constant coughing and spitting blood, he slept with her eight times between 9 September and 4 October. In February 1783, he could tell himself that he had been sober for over seven months – in fact, ever since his father died. If only temporarily, a great psychological weight had been lifted off him by his father's death.

After 1783 the story now goes blank for two years until 1785, when Boswell was on another of his spring visits to London. There he struck up with a 'pleasing and honest' girl, Betsy Smith, of whom he became very fond. On one occasion they visited a friend of hers and made it a threesome: 'I insisted she should repeat the Lord's

Prayer. Strange mixture. Wondrous fondness.' Two days later, 'Something not right appeared', and once again poor Boswell was in the hands of doctors, swallowing sulphurated pills and mercury pills and confined to his rooms. So concerned was he about Betsy that he paid 10s 6d to get her admitted to St Thomas's Hospital, but the girl was unhappy there, and soon went home to resume her normal career as a prostitute. 'I told her I was ashamed, but I loved her.'

In the autumn and early winter of 1785, Boswell was again in London and, despite Sir Joshua Reynolds's warning, in November he became the lover of a notorious but fashionable woman, Mrs Rudd. He returned to Edinburgh on 28 December, and in the first eight days of January he slept with his wife six times. But in February he was back in London for a long stay and was a regular visitor to Mrs Rudd. During this year in London, Boswell at last tried – and failed – to establish himself at the English Bar. By July it was clear even to him that his career as a lawyer in London had no future. No one would give him a brief, and anyway he was totally ignorant of English law and made no serious effort to learn it. The next three years were ones of great misery, as Boswell busied himself mostly in London collecting materials for his *Life of Johnson,* while harassed by poverty, deeply distressed at the relentless progress of his wife's tuberculosis which was finally reaching the terminal stage, and drinking heavily. On 17 March 1788, Margaret said to him on one of his now rare visits north, 'O Mr Boswell, I fear I'm dying.' Ten months later in January 1789, she finally died alone, while Boswell was away in London in a typically foolish and hopeless effort to carve out a political career for himself by attaching himself to the entourage of the cruel and tyrannical Lord Lonsdale. Before her death he had explained his behaviour to himself: 'I sometimes upbraid myself for leaving her, but tenderness should yield to the active engagements of ambitious enterprise.'

His wife's death, his failure to make a career either as a lawyer in London or as a politician, and the death of Dr Johnson all deeply depressed Boswell, and the years after 1789 are ones of increasing misery and degradation. In London in 1789, he entered into a liaison with 'C', a beautiful woman of fashion. But, as usual, when he was dealing with women of his own class, he sometimes suffered from impotence. The first encounter was a 'delicious night'. Two days later he returned home dead drunk and staggered out again into the night in pursuit of 'C', only to be fetched back home again by his young son James. The next night went badly, 'with love and wine oppressed'. He was 'weakly deficient; only one; ineffectual wishes'. Although one day later the familiar indications of infection reappeared (probably the disease was now chronic, so that 'C' may not have been responsible), the liaison lasted through December. But on 21 December, Boswell dreamed of his late wife and awoke in tears: 'It seemed to me impossible that I could ever again love a woman except merely as gratifying my senses.' And yet he thought that there remained the faint chance that he might yet discover 'a sensible, good-tempered woman of fortune' to make a second wife. He consulted his old friend Temple, who in view of 'my warm propensities', thought that 'a contract with any decent woman' was 'an insurance against some very imprudent connection'.

But no such paragon appeared, and Boswell became a habitual drunken lecher, a familiar figure staggering through the less reputable streets of London. Despite increasing urethric trouble, once causing total stricture necessitating surgical intervention, his sexual virility remained unimpaired – in June he visited a new girl three times in the course of a single day – but he became more and more reckless, and the attacks of gonorrhoea more frequent. To whet his now jaded palate, he once 'tried an experiment on three', although he is careful not to explain what the experiment was. Three years later, in September 1793, his friend Temple again advised him to marry, as the only way to sober him up. But he warned Boswell that any wife 'would be very unhappy with a man of such a disposition and such a life as I was'. So Boswell continued his dissolute ways, although now at rarer intervals, until the end came in May 1795, when he fell ill and died of a tumour in the bladder, probably the result of the spread of urinary tract infection. One can reasonably speculate whether the repeated ingestion of mercury pills to cure his bouts of gonorrhoea may not have contributed to his mental deterioration, while his early death was almost certainly caused ultimately by the disease.

A man plagued by inherited manic depression, an evident failure as a husband, a father and a lawyer, driven by a lust for female flesh that he was unable to control, constantly more inebriated than was seemly, Boswell nevertheless had two extraordinary gifts. The first was for making friends. In 1781 Dr Johnson said, 'Mr Boswell was never in anybody's company who did not wish to see him again', and when he died the Shakespearean editor Malone remarked, 'I . . . now miss and regret his noise and his hilarity and his perpetual good humour.' The second was his passionate introspective honesty, which makes his notes and diary perhaps a more revealing record of a man's life than any other of any time or any age. We now know Boswell, with all his faults, better than we know any man who has ever lived. Sometimes narcissistic, sometimes moralistic and guilt-ridden, sometimes a device to drive away his ever-threatening melancholia, the record served a variety of purposes. But above all, it carries the ring of truth, even though the final version is a polished literary product, often written up after the event from rough jottings taken down at the time. It was Boswell's greatest (and only) legacy to posterity, and he knew it. From it he quarried his published works, his account of General Paoli of Corsica, the journal of his tour of the Scottish Highlands with Dr Johnson, and his great biography of the latter. The recent discovery and publication of these records has at last brought him the fame that largely eluded him in life.

There can be little doubt that the liberation of Boswell's libido was caused by his rejection of the strict Calvinist upbringing of his youth and his rapid passage through Methodism and Catholicism into scepticism and then to a somewhat lukewarm Anglican Episcopalianism. He continued to feel guilt, embedded in him from his Calvinist past, particularly noticeable in his rejection of masturbation, which was the deepest area of conflict between Calvinism and his sexual urges during his adolescence. The result was that his attitude to his sexual behaviour oscillated wildly between lacerating self-reproach and swaggering machismo.

His main problem, with which he wrestled all his life, was his failure to link *Eros* and *Agape*: lust and love. It was a problem that did not bother him very much so long as he was a bachelor, but after his marriage in 1769 it became acute. He was deeply attached to his wife, and as late as 1776 could tell himself, 'I could not have been so happy in marriage with any other woman as with my dear wife.' She in her turn loved him, and suffered with extraordinary patience and good humour his habitual sexual infidelity, his growing alcoholism, and his growing passion for all-night gambling. On the other hand, as she frankly explained to him on 8 March 1775, she could not fully satisfy his sexual appetites, which may well have been partly a cause not only of his whoring, but also of his drowning his frustrations in alcohol and gambling. But other, perhaps more important, causes were his congenital manic-depressive melancholia, which was exacerbated by the open contempt of his father, his sense of failure as a professional man and as an author, his hatred of his job as a lawyer at the Scottish Bar and his disgust at the vulgar provincialism of Edinburgh society in comparison with the glittering intellectual circles in which he moved in London. Dr Johnson probably had Boswell in mind when he generalized that 'Melancholy and otherwise insane people are always sensual; the misery of their minds naturally enough forces them to recur for comfort to their bodies.' Boswell certainly pursued whores most avidly in his depressive troughs, and when his sense of guilt was anaesthetized by alcohol. By pursuing only the cheapest whores, with the consequent near certainty of disease, it almost looks as if he were deliberately seeking to punish himself for his sensuality.

It seems likely that what with her prolonged illness, her pregnancies, her miscarriages and her generally low libido, Margaret was for considerable periods something of a sexual disappointment to Boswell. He may have been thinking of her when he remarked in 1777, 'I have my own private notions as to modesty, of which I would only value the appearance: for unless a woman has amorous heat, she is a dull companion, and to have amorous heat in elegant perfection, the *fancy* should be warmed with lively ideas.' The only solution, and one which came easily to him, was to dissociate sexual desire and affection altogether, as two totally different human passions. He had always treated women as purely sexual objects, so this presented no problem to him. An even more extreme position on the issue was advanced on high theoretical grounds by his friend Lord Monboddo, who 'would not allow a philosopher to indulge in women as a pleasure, but only as an evacuation; for he said that a man who used their embraces as a pleasure would soon have that enjoyment as a business, than which nothing could make one more despicable'. Boswell had an uneasy feeling that he might fall into that category.

What bothered Boswell most was guilt about his own infidelity to his wife, and he sought advice on the subject wherever he could find it, from his friend Temple, from the Honourable Mrs Stuart, who agreed with him, and from Dr Johnson, who took a stern moral line against adultery in any form. He tried to think through the problem rationally, but never succeeded. Once he mused: 'I thought of my valuable wife with the highest regard and warmest affection, but had a confused notion that my corporeal connection with whores did not interfere with my love for her. Yet I considered that I might injure my health, which there could be no doubt was an injury to her.' This question of whether his infidelity to his wife was morally acceptable was one which always worried Boswell, and he never did resolve it to his satisfaction. On the other hand, unlike many other eighteenth-century husbands, he was scrupulous in keeping away from her when there was any fear that he might have contracted venereal disease.

The other two areas of guilt concerned the seduction of young virgins and married women. Despite his fantasy proposal to Rousseau for the use of a series of young girls of low birth, later to be married off to peasants, he was in fact unusual for his class and his time for never, so far as one can tell, attempting to seduce a virgin. In 1766 he boasted, justifiably, about 'my principle of never debauching an innocent girl'.

He was always very uneasy about sexual relations with married women. Mrs Jean Heron threw herself at him, but he felt very guilty about his conduct, and followed Dr Johnson's advice to keep away from her in future. His liaison with Mrs Dodds he did not regard as adultery, since her husband had left her and was living with another woman. His sudden assault on the pregnant wife of the Potsdam guardsman seriously upset him for a while. His liaison with Girolama Piccolomini he excused on the grounds that all Italian upper-class women were married off against their will by their parents, and it was the custom of the country for them to take lovers.

The final area in which Boswell's sexual life was governed by a clear set of principles was concerned with the treatment of any possible illegitimate offspring. Mrs Heron assured him that she was sterile, which relieved part of his anxieties; when Peggy Doig produced a child of his, he made arrangements for the lying-in and for its maintenance with a foster-mother. When Mrs Lewis discussed the possibility with him, he reassured her that he would meet his obligations; and when Mrs Dodds gave birth to Sally, we have no reason to suppose that he did not also take responsibility for her upkeep, although she probably did not live long. With Signora Piccolomini, he was careful to use a condom. In this respect he was like most of the great aristocrats of his period, who normally took care of their illegitimate children, although there were exceptions, such as Lord Kinnaird, whose bastard daughter Boswell met in Edinburgh plying her trade as a prostitute.

On the other hand, he was very strict in refusing to treat them as social equals to legitimate children, the way his friend the tenth Lord Pembroke treated his. When Lord Chancellor Thurlow invited

Boswell and his daughter to a musical soirée with his lordship's illegitimate daughter Kitty, Boswell was careful to decline to go since 'I have always disapproved of putting them on a level with those lawfully born.'

There is a good deal of evidence from Boswell's diary that most women of the period accepted the double standard with resignation. Even in eighteenth-century pseudo-Calvinist Scotland these principles were more or less accepted. Boswell mused that 'an abandoned profligate may have a notion that it is not wrong to debauch my wife, but ... if I catch him making an attempt ... I will kick him downstairs or break his bones'. But he regarded his own case as somehow different. Mrs Boswell knew about Boswell's affairs before she married him; she several times advised him to satisfy his sexual appetites with a concubine, and although she was often disturbed when she found out about his amours, she always forgave him. On his side, although he was constantly sexually unfaithful, he never lied to her, never infected her, and was usually prompt to tell her about his innumerable lapses. Given his nature, it was the only fidelity he could offer her, and he was remarkably scrupulous in using her as his confessor. As a result, she realized that at bottom he loved her as he loved no other woman, and she was prepared to tolerate his almost insatiable promiscuity on condition that it never spilled over into any hint of love for another woman. Right up to the end, as she was slowly being consumed by tuberculosis, she continued to provide him with what sexual pleasure she could, which sometimes fully satisfied his needs. Boswell's diary is the work of a man obsessed with himself and his feelings, who is consequently not much interested in how others felt. But despite the agonizing pregnancies, the frequent miscarriages, the slow wasting of her lungs, and the often intoxicated condition of her husband, there are indications in her husband's notes that Mrs Boswell occasionally enjoyed, as well as loyally fulfilled, her wifely duties.

What other general conclusions can be drawn from Boswell's extraordinary story? It is obvious that he was in very many ways, not least in his egotistical absorption in his own affairs, a most unusual man. But he moved not unsuccessfully through the noble, intellectual and professional society of western Europe, and his adventures shed a dazzling searchlight upon sexual attitudes and practices among these classes. Boswell's sexual drive was clearly very different from that of Pepys, who was content to kiss and fondle women's lips and breasts for hours on end without orgasm. Boswell's appetite was stronger and grosser. His main need was frequent and violent intercourse without preliminary foreplay or even conversation. He was consquently especially attracted to the cheapest of whores, and he was liable to find himself impotent at the first sexual encounter on the rare occasions when he had to deal with women of his own social class.

Boswell was not a reticent man, and he poured out the details of his sexual life not only in his notes and journals but also in correspondence and conversation with his close friends like Temple and with the three men he most admired: Dr Johnson, Rousseau, and General Paoli. No one seems to have been particularly shocked by his indiscretions and infidelities, or by the grossness of his appetite. Dr Johnson advised chastity; General Paoli and Temple marriage, and Rousseau a mystical view of sexual passion which would exclude his brutish couplings. Because of his moral doubts he tended to be very solemn on the subject, and Wilkes told him that 'you like the thing almost as well as I do, but you dislike to talk and laugh about it.'

Although Boswell found it difficult to discover a regular genteel mistress in London, the level of marital infidelity among the upper classes of Europe seems to have been fairly high, as many other reminiscences confirm. Those married women who refused him were not shocked by his advances, but merely put off by his lack of tact, and a few, like Mrs Heron, Signora Piccolomini and Mrs Dodds, simply threw themselves into his arms. Some lower-class women were equally receptive, like the wife of the Potsdam guard and a woman at a Swiss inn who offered to accompany Boswell to Scotland. But pregnancy was an ever-present risk, which is why married women, and especially pregnant ones, were so much sought after, by both Pepys in the seventeenth century and Boswell in the eighteenth, although the latter always felt guilty.

The greatest risk from promiscuous sexual activity in the eighteenth century was clearly gonorrhoea, which Boswell contracted at least seventeen times, possibly more. Boswell's friends found these repeated attacks no more than a joke, although they certainly warned him to take more care. When his father complained of his son's recurrent infections to a Scottish lady, Mrs Montgomerie-Cunningham, she reassured him, 'telling him that what occasioned it was now become quite common'. Not even women took venereal disease very seriously any more, despite the fact that the medical results were quite serious. The treatment was almost as dangerous as the disease, since the most reliable cure was the ingestion of mercury, itself a dangerous poison, the other remedy being strict diet and sweating in a sweating-tub (Plate 23). On the other hand, syphilis does not seem to have been a serious threat. The ubiquity of gonorrhoea and the rarity of syphilis seems to have been an established feature of England at least by the late sixteenth century.

3. CONCLUSIONS

Various general conclusions about upper-class sexual behaviour and attitudes in eighteenth-century England may be drawn from these two case histories. In the first place, tolerant although at this time society was towards venereal disease, there were limits to what some wives would put up with. Mrs Boswell was far more long-suffering than other wives of their husbands' venereal infections. In 1776 Mr Thrale showed his wife a greatly enlarged testicle, a condition he tried to explain away as the result of bruising when he jumped out of a carriage some months before. Mrs Thrale refused to believe this improbable story, and she immediately recalled her father's remarks when she first got engaged to Mr Thrale thirteen years back. 'If you marry that scoundrel he will catch the pox, and for his amusement set you to make his poultices,' he warned her. She told herself that 'this is now literally made out, and I am preparing poultices like he said and fomenting this elegant ailment every night and morning for an hour together on my knees'. Similarly, the famous actress Mrs Siddons took it very badly in 1792 when her husband gave her the pox. After her recovery, 'an indignant melancholy sits on her fine face . . . ; she is all resentment'.

In view of the prevalence of the disease, and the pain and mental anguish that it caused, it is hardly surprising to find that the three most common subjects in the advertisment columns of eighteenth-century periodicals were cures for venereal disease, cosmetics and books – in that order. Take, for example, two fashionable London newspapers for 1785, *The Morning Chronicle* and *The Whitehall Evening Post*. They advertised aphrodisiacs for the jaded, like 'Hunter's Restorative Balsamic Pills', described as 'the first medicine in the world of restoring and invigorating the constitutions of persons weakened by a course of dissipated pleasures, or indeed by any other causes'; or 'The Bath Restorative', for 'those who have been almost worn out by women or wine', those who 'are not early happy in their conjugal embraces . . . and those who have impaired their constitution by the act of self-pollution'. They also advertised the addresses of obstetricians who would take care of 'ladies whose situation requires a temporary retirement'. But mostly they advertised nostrums for venereal disease, such as 'Leake's Genuine Pills', 'The Specific', 'Lisbon Diet Drink', 'Dr Solander's Vegetable Juice' and 'Dr Keyser's Pills'.

It is surprising to discover how difficult it was in the late eighteenth century, a hundred years after their introduction, to buy condoms as a prophylactic against venereal disease. Mrs Phillips's shop in London seems to have been the only place where Boswell could buy them without difficulty. He also sometimes expected his London whores to carry them, but they rarely, if ever, did. In all the other capitals of Europe, he drew a blank, which was why he so constantly caught venereal disease. He did have one on him in Siena, however, which he used, interestingly enough, for contraceptive rather than prophylactic purposes during his liaison with Signora Piccolomini. By the 1760s Boswell knew all about condoms and their uses, unlike Pepys in the 1660s who was wholly ignorant of their very existence. On the other hand, there is no sign that Boswell used them for contraceptive purposes in relations with his own wife, despite her weakening physical condition and unwillingness to bear any more children after the first three.

Finally, the journal of James Boswell throws a flood of light on the sexual underworld of eighteenth-century London. Beginning at the top, there was always a chance of finding a respectable married woman with whom to strike up an affair, although they seem to have been in short supply. Failing that, there was the *demi-monde* of the theatre, whose actresses, then as today, seem to have led more sexually permissive lives than the rest of the population. Then there were the milliners and shirt and ruffle makers, some of whom seem to have been willing to provide occasional sexual services as well as shirts and ruffles in return for their monthly retainer. Below them there were high-class houses of assignation, like that of Mrs Smith in Queen Street, where expensive call-girls could be had. There were also both general and specialized brothels, like the all-black one Lord Pembroke told Boswell about in 1775 (although by then it also had some white girls) (Plate 27). At the bottom of the ladder of the professionals there were the common street whores, clustering along the Strand or in St James's Park, who could be picked up and taken into a coach or down a dark alley for a few minutes, or to a bagnio for a bath, dinner, and a night of pleasure. And finally, there were the poor amateurs, the ubiquitous maids, waiting on masters and guests in lodgings, in the home, in inns; young girls whose virtue was always uncertain and was constantly under attack (Plate 26). These last were the most exploited, and most defenceless, of the various kinds of women whose sexual services might be obtained by a man of quality in eighteenth-century England. There were also the long-term mistresses taken on to satisfy the needs of men before marriage, like Boswell before 1769; or widowers, like Pepys after 1671. Some of them were educated and respectable women, like Pepys's Mary Skinner; others were lower-class girls who had been seduced and abandoned, and were therefore more or less unmarriageable; others were mere sluts, like some with whom Boswell lived before his marriage. Increasingly, however, it was possible for rich men to discover for themselves well-educated and attractive women of the middling ranks, whose fathers had gone bankrupt.

Almost all aspects of the late eighteenth-century upper-class sexual scene are displayed in a caricature by Rowlandson of 1786 (Plate 24). A shipload of pretty, well-dressed but impecunious girls anxious to find a rich husband or lover has just arrived on the dockside, presumably in Calcutta or Bombay, and is being inspected for purchase by wealthy nabobs and by an agent for the Governor. In the foreground are goods unloaded from the ship: one box of surgeon's instruments and seven casks of 'Leake's Pills', the best-known cure for gonorrhoea; a case of books labelled 'For the Amusement of Military Gentlemen', and containing such titles as *Fanny Hill* and *Female Flagellants*; a large bale of condoms labelled 'Mrs Phillips (the original inventor), Leicester Fields, London. For the Use of the Supreme Council'; and finally a case marked with crossed birch-rod bundles and labelled 'British Manufacture'. In the 'Warehouse for Unsaleable Goods' lie damaged barrels with broken bottles of 'Hunter's Restorative', the well-known stimulant for jaded sexual appetites. Here in one picture are young girls for sale, medicine against venereal disease, condoms, pornographic literature, aphrodisiacs, and instruments to satisfy the peculiarly English taste for sado-masochism.

CHAPTER TWELVE

Plebeian Sexual Behaviour

1. THE FACTS OF CHANGE

When dealing with the sexual behaviour of the lower orders, the historian is forced to abandon any attempt to probe attitudes and feelings, since direct evidence does not exist. He is obliged to deduce such things from legal records, the comments of literate contemporaries, and the stark demographic facts which can be laboriously extracted from parish registers of marriages and baptisms. Since in this area practice only faintly corresponded to the ideal norms of the society, almost the only indicator available to the historian is the type and amount of extra-marital sexual activity, either before marriage or outside it altogether. Among the plebs, sex within marriage – which is where most sex inevitably took place – is a world closed to the historian. This is the reason why a chapter on plebeian sexual behaviour is almost exclusively devoted to areas which by the norms of the day were generally regarded as sinful. If it can be demonstrated that there were significant changes in the type and amount of such theoretically deviant behaviour, then it may perhaps be possible to make some deductions about changes in attitudes towards sexuality among the lower orders of society. Thus evidence can be found for a possible decline in pre-marital and extra-marital sexual activity from the sixteenth to the early seventeenth century and for a certain and very striking increase in the late seventeenth and eighteenth centuries. Since there is no correlation with the rise and fall in the age of marriage, which one might suppose would have affected the amount of pre-marital sexual activity, the explanation of the growth first of tighter and then of very much laxer sexual behaviour must lie in changing attitudes.

As has been seen, in the middle ages the institution of marriage was very imperfectly controlled by the Church, which meant that the lower classes were allowed a wide degree of freedom in their sexual arrangements. In the fourteenth century, betrothal followed by intercourse was recognized by the Church as a binding marriage contract; children born after betrothal but before marriage were usually recognized as legitimate; bigamy was common and almost impossible to detect, given the absence of formal marriage registers, and clandestine marriages were equally common.

In the most remote areas of the highland north extremely ancient customs may have lasted well into the sixteenth century. In the middle of the fifteenth century an Italian cleric and diplomat (later Pope Pius II), travelling from Scotland to England through Northumberland, spent the night in a village just across the Border. After dinner all the men and the children withdrew to a fortified tower, leaving the Italian and all the women to take their chance with Scottish bandits. They justified the exclusion of the women from the safety of the tower on the grounds that the worst that could happen to them was rape, which they did not count as a wrong. When the Italian retired to sleep, he was accompanied to his room (which was bare except for straw on the floor) by two young women, who proposed to sleep with him if he wished, which he found to be a customary gesture of hospitality to an honoured guest. The Italian refused the offer, for fear of having his throat cut in the night while still in a condition of mortal sin. If this account is to be believed, in Northumberland in the mid-fifteenth century men did not prize the chastity of their women, and women offered their favours freely to strangers, both attitudes which have been observed in several very primitive societies in other parts of the world.

The failure of the medieval church to impose either its traditional hostility to sex except for the purpose of procreation, or its own religious ceremony as the one binding ritual to legitimate a sexual union, combined with the habitually casual ways of the population to make the medieval approach to marriage and sex very different from that of seventeenth-century England. The introduction of registers of births, marriages and deaths in 1538 was evidence of a tightening of both lay and clerical controls over the private lives of the population. The missionary activity of the Protestant Church over the following century did more than bring the institution of marriage under effective regulation by the public authorities, apparently for the first time; it also brought Puritan attitudes to sexuality to the attention of the public, and enforced them with the full sanctions of Church and state.

A final general observation that needs to be made is that for the poor, sexual privacy was a luxury which they neither possessed nor could have desired. Living conditions were such that among the bulk of the population before the second half of the nineteenth century, whole families lived, worked, ate and slept in one or two rooms. Under such conditions sexual privacy for parents, or for married children living at home was impossible, and children from an early age must have been familiar with the sight and sounds of the physical act of love. Only in summer – and then only on a dry day – was sexual privacy obtainable out of doors in the fields and woods.

Courting customs are obviously closely related to the amount of pre-marital sex. In many parts of north-west Europe in the seventeenth and the eighteenth centuries, there was a general practice among the labouring classes of the type of intimate courting known as 'bundling'. Bundling meant paying court to a girl, in bed, in the dark, half naked. In Wales in the eighteenth century, the man retained 'an essential part of his dress', and the women had 'her underpetticoat fastened at the bottom by a sliding knot'. In America, as an extra precaution, a wooden board was often placed in the bed to divide the pair. This practice was apparently almost universal amongst the poor on the north-western fringes of Europe, in Wales, Scotland, Holland and Scandinavia in the eighteenth and even early nineteenth centuries, as well as in Germany, Switzerland and certain limited areas of France. In 1761 John Adams was prepared to state publicly that 'I cannot wholly disapprove of bundling', and it was certainly common all over New England in the eighteenth century, and still practised in New Jersey in 1816 and on Cape Cod in 1827.

The conclusion seems inescapable that 'this pleasing but dangerous habit was probably imported from abroad'. The wide prevalence of this custom in eighteenth-century New England makes it hard to believe that it was not also fairly common in England itself, although the evidence on this point is scanty. The practice of lying clothed on a bed, talking and petting, which is what bundling in its simplest form amounts to, was certainly practised in seventeenth and eighteenth-century England. It is noticeable that when Thomas Turner was courting his second wife in 1765 – a very respectable girl – he twice spent all night with her, although he was shocked at a case of pre-nuptial conception in the village. On an early visit, he sat up with her until five in the morning, and on a second visit he stayed with her again till dawn – whether seated or lying down is not stated. Turner's courting methods strongly suggest that bundling –

meaning at least all-night conversations – was then a current custom in Sussex. On finding the custom in Wales in 1804, William Bingley remarked that 'within the last few years [it] was scarcely even heard of in England', which suggests that it had existed in the eighteenth century. As in many primitive societies, it was a custom which in the seventeenth century did not lead to much pregnancy. In Wales, 'the lower order of people do actually carry on their love affairs in bed, and ... they are carried on honourably'. In short, in the seventeenth century it was 'a practice ancient, general and carried on without difficulty'. It also made a good deal of sense. An all-night conversation allowed both parties to explore each other's minds and temperaments in some depth, while the physical propinquity provided a socially approved means of obtaining sexual satisfaction in the decade between maturity and marriage, and of experimenting in sexual compatibility with a series of potential spouses without running the risk of pregnancy and without commitment to marriage.

The most reliable indicator of the level of pre-marital chastity in a society without contraceptives is the proportion of first children who are born less than eight and a half months after marriage. The index of pre-marital conceptions is as good a guide to the realities of pre-marital sexual behaviour as the historian is likely to find, particularly if the trends are sufficiently clear. But before examining the facts, it is first necessary to establish exactly what the phenomenon means. If it is to leave evidence in the historical record of parish registers, pre-marital pregnancy must involve four distinct acts. There must be conception before the wedding, and since the chances of conception from a single random act of intercourse of a healthy young couple are only between two and four per cent, this must therefore probably be the result of several weeks, and perhaps months, of unprotected intercourse. Secondly, it involves a marriage ceremony in a church after conception, normally, but not necessarily always, with the father of the unborn child. Thirdly, the pregnancy must run its course and produce a live infant; and fourthly, that infant must be baptized, and so be recorded. It is obvious that any one of these last three steps could fail to take place. If this definition is accepted, it is evident that bastardy is merely a sub-branch of pre-nuptial conception in which intercourse before marriage took place, the child was carried to term (and was baptized), but there was no marriage.

It is possible to construct a typology of pre-nuptial pregnancies, based on the motives which might lead a couple to follow all four stages. The first type is when there was a formal betrothal in front of witnesses, followed by regular cohabitation before the church ceremony, carried on with the full knowledge and consent of parents and the community. There can be no doubt that this was a normal custom among the poor in some parts of England at this period, and probably also in New England. It probably accounts for a considerable number of those pregnancies which occurred within four months of marriage. It should be remembered that many brides who were only one or two months pregnant may well have been unaware of their condition. In any case, these are pre-nuptial conceptions which carried with them no stigma or guilt. A variant on this type could occur when the parents were obstructing the marriage. The pair could then betroth themselves in secret, begin to sleep together, and then confront their parents with the necessity for consent, since the girl was pregnant.

The second main type was the seduction of the girl by the man, with or without a secret or even public promise of marriage. The man then tried to repudiate his promise but was forced to the altar by the pressure of parents, neighbours, clergy, magistrate and the threat of legal action. This type probably includes many of the marriages of girls who were seven to nine months pregnant, and was mostly a rural phenomenon, since in the cities these pressures were more easily evaded. Another variant of this type was the result of a plot by the girl to force the man to marry her by deliberately letting herself become pregnant, relying on these community pressures to force the man into marriage later on. The third main type was when a lower-class girl, often a servant, allowed herself to become the mistress of a rich man. When she got pregnant, her master would arrange to have her married off to a poor man, perhaps his own manservant, who would be paid handsomely to take her on and to accept the child as his own. Another variant of this type, reportedly quite common in a seventeenth-century French village, was when a peasant married a girl already pregnant by another man, merely in order to lay hands on her dowry of money and sheep.

It has now been established that the level of recorded pre-nuptial pregnancies in England was low in the late sixteenth century and declined lower still in the seventeenth century, certainly well below twenty per cent, while scattered evidence suggests that it was even lower, below ten per cent, in New England (Graph 10). During

GRAPH 10: Prenuptial Conception Ratio

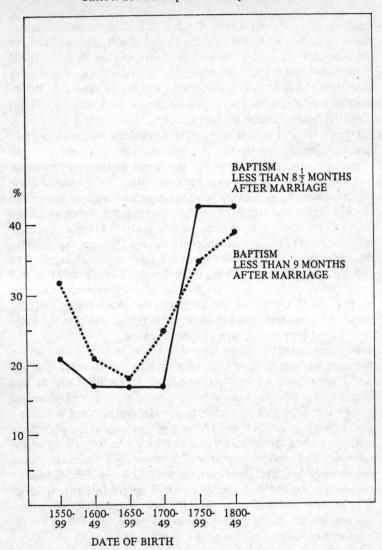

BAPTISM
LESS THAN $8\frac{1}{2}$ MONTHS
AFTER MARRIAGE

BAPTISM
LESS THAN 9 MONTHS
AFTER MARRIAGE

%

40

30

20

10

1550-   1600-   1650-   1700-   1750-   1800-
99   49   99   49   99   49

DATE OF BIRTH

the first half of the eighteenth century, however, a startling change took place. The rate of recorded pre-nuptial pregnancies shot up, reaching over forty per cent in the last half of the century in many places on both sides of the Atlantic. From these figures one can only conclude that among the English and American plebs in the last half of the eighteenth century, almost all brides below the social elite had experienced sexual intercourse with their future husbands before marriage. By then pregnancy was preceding – if not actually causing – marriage, not marriage pregnancy.

Francis Place remarked that 'want of chastity in girls was common' in late eighteenth-century London right up to the class of respectable small property owners, tradesmen and master craftsmen, and was not then regarded as a bar to marriage. By the time he was writing, however, in the 1820s, these practices were now confined to the daughters of wage-earners, journeymen and labourers, at the very bottom of the economic and social scale. If Place is right, the continued rise of pre-nuptial conceptions (and illegitimacy) well into the early nineteenth century conceals a significant shrinkage of the social classes which were responsible for these statistics. More and more the respectable lower-middle class were rejecting the permissive sexual morals of the propertyless wage-earners, but the graph of pre-nuptial conceptions went on rising, owing to the great increase in the numerical size of the latter group.

The bare statistics can be fleshed out a little by the diary of the Reverend William Cole of Bletchley, Buckinghamshire. In the one year 1766 he baptized the son of the local blacksmith, whom he had married to his bride six months before; he married the pregnant maid of a local gentleman to a soldier in the Life Guards; and in a single day he married a pair, baptized their newborn baby and churched the mother, the last two rituals being carried out in the privacy of his parlour, despite the incongruity of performing a 'churching' in a private room. It is clear from these stories that a considerable number of these pre-nuptial pregnancies occurred long before the wedding, and therefore had nothing to do with any change of custom to cohabitation after the betrothal, but rather were caused by a breakdown of community controls on pre-marital sex.

The evidence for illegitimacy is far less secure than that for pre-nuptial pregnancy since it may be affected by changes in the habits of unmarried women in practising primitive birth control, in procuring abortions, in encouraging infanticide, and in baptizing their bastards, as well as by changes in the habits of clergy both in agreeing to baptize children born out of wedlock and in recording them as illegitimate. The figures also, of course, fail to record as such the illegitimate offspring of married women. It is certain, therefore, that all the recorded levels of illegitimacy are underestimates of the reality, in some periods perhaps seriously so.

Bastardy, which is a sub-branch of pre-nuptial conceptions, also can be given a typology according to the circumstances of the conception. The first type was the result of the seduction of a girl by a fellow-servant or worker or neighbour, probably after a vague promise of marriage. When pregnancy occurred, the man repudiated the promise, if he had made one, and ran away. The second was the seduction of a girl, often a living-in maidservant, by someone of higher social status and in a position of authority over her, usually the master of the house, or one of his sons or friends. This could take place with or without a promise of marriage, the girl giving her consent for fear of losing her job. In this case, social custom made it impossible for any such promise to be honoured. If the girl became pregnant, she was either discharged or married off to another poor man who would accept her and her prospective child. The third, and rarest, type was the notoriously promiscuous girl who sooner or later became pregnant. She was liable to be repudiated and scorned by the community, and would be hard put to it to identify the father with any certainty.

In the Elizabethan period the rural illegitimacy ratio had been running at the modest level of under four per cent. Between 1590 and 1660, however, the recorded ratio fell steadily to the astonishingly low point of one half per cent at the height of the period of Puritan control, in the 1650s. It picked up a bit thereafter, but was still under two and a half per cent in the 1720s. It then took off, rising to four and a half per cent in the 1760s and over six per cent after 1780 (Graph 11). Since for the majority of the population the average age of marriage was twenty-six to twenty-eight and rising, this evidence suggests that during the sixteenth, and especially the seventeenth centuries, most men must have exercised extraordinary sexual self-control during the first twelve to fourteen years of optimum male potency.

Despite the rise of bundling, pre-nuptial pregnancy, and bastardy, the late and rising age of marriage meant that at all periods from the sixteenth to the eighteenth century most men of the lower classes

389

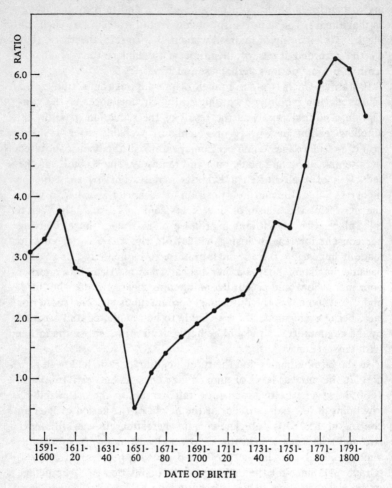

GRAPH 11: Illegitimacy Ratio

DATE OF BIRTH

passed twelve years or more of their most sexually virile period unmarried, and therefore in a condition of considerable sexual frustration. During the late sixteenth and early seventeenth century, internalized repression was undoubtedly aided by the moral pressures of Puritanism. Simon Forman, the late sixteenth-century astrologer, records that he did not sleep with a woman before the age of thirty, and his case may not have been as exceptional as one might suppose.

Repression was not the only solution, however, and it would be unreasonable to conclude that a low level of pre-marital conceptions necessarily meant an equally low level of all kinds of sexual activity. The 'double standard', with its toleration of male sexual experimentation and its insistence on female virginity before marriage for respectable girls, when coupled with the growth of lifelong bachelordom for younger sons of the upper classes and the general delay in marriage for young men to the age of twenty-six or more, created an acute socio-sexual problem which was partially relieved by a substantial increase of the ancient profession of prostitution.

Most of these women were concentrated in the bigger towns, which for country boys might involve a long journey and a not insignificant expense. In 1681 it was reported that Norwich swarmed with ale-houses, 'and every one of them, they tell, is also a bawdy-house'. On the other hand, Elizabethan legal records show that there was also a certain amount of casual, semi-amateur prostitution in the villages. Some poor families let out a room in their house to a whore, and the occasional married woman indulged in casual fornication in the fields for 4d a time, partly to earn money, and partly, it would seem, for mere pleasure. Sex was, therefore, rather more readily available to rural bachelor youths than one would have suspected without this evidence. Prostitutes congregated in London in profusion, partly to supply the needs of the twenty to thirty thousand bachelor apprentices in the city (Plate 28). The apprentices both used and abused these women, and in the seventeenth century were accustomed to work off their frustrations on Shrove Tuesday by rioting and pulling down bawdy-houses, ostensibly to remove temptation during Lent. In 1668 a panicky government reacted strongly to the rioting, which of course worsened the situation and caused two nights of serious disturbances. Charles II, himself the most practical of men, could not understand the ambivalence that underlay the apprentices' behaviour. 'Why? Why do they go to them then?' he asked, not unreasonably.

The increase in the supply of prostitutes to meet the demand was generated by 'Place's Law' that 'chastity and poverty are incompatible'. The ranks of the prostitutes were fed not only by poverty, but by the growing culture of sexual promiscuity in the large submerged class of the very poor. For some girls, selling their bodies was a preferable way of earning a living to working fourteen to sixteen hours a day as a seamstress or mantua-maker. Very many recruits to the profession presumably began as unwed mothers, and the rise of illegitimacy must, therefore, have increased the supply of prostitutes. Other recruits were said to be the cast-off mistresses of men of fashion, their seducers dumping them in brothels when they were tired of them. Many more, according to Defoe in 1725, were members of the huge class of young maidservants in London, who found themselves temporarily out of a job and were forced to 'prostitute their bodies or starve'. 'This is the reason why our streets are swarming with strumpets. Thus many of them rove from place to place, from bawdy-house to service, and from service to bawdy-house again ... nothing being more common than to find these creatures one week in a good family and the next in a brothel.' Defoe disapproved of this amateurish way of life, claiming that the girls 'make neither good whores nor good servants'. But the harsh fact about eighteenth-century employment opportunities was that apart from slaving as a seamstress, those were the only two major occupations open to an uneducated girl from a poor family. Because of the irregularity of employment, the two often tended to get mixed up.

In 1724 Bernard de Mandeville launched a vigorous protest against the Society for the Suppression of Vice, which was then very busy trying to close down brothels and to drive prostitutes off the streets. His solution was the establishment of publicly licensed and medically supervised brothels under state control, with different classes of girls and houses catering for different social groups, the cost varying from two shillings and sixpence to one guinea. Needless to say, his plea fell on deaf ears, and all the evils to which he drew attention became more and more common and serious as the eighteenth century progressed.

There were clear gradations in the profession, which it is important to recognize, and which come out very clearly in the sexual diaries of men like Boswell. The main distinctions are between the common street prostitute; the selective call-girl with her own rooms visited by gentlemanly clients; and the kept mistress set up in her own apartment, who might also make a little extra money on the side. In the 1780s Francis Place was apprenticed to a London leather-breeches-maker named Mr France, who had had three daughters by a first wife. 'His eldest daughter was and had been for several years a common prostitute. His youngest daughter, who was about seventeen years of age, had genteel lodgings where she was visited by gentlemen; and the second daughter . . . was kept by a captain of an East India ship, in whose absence she used to amuse herself as such women generally do.' Mr France's three daughters thus represented all three levels of the profession.

The only thing known about marital sexual activity among the poor is that it varied from month to month. An annual 'conception cycle', with quite strong fluctuations over the year, has been discovered in France and New England during the Early Modern period, although it has yet to be proved conclusively for England. In a society that does not use contraceptives, this cycle must reflect significant changes in the level of sexual activity among married couples. There was a fairly general trough in conceptions during March and another during August and September. The periods of peak conceptions, and therefore of peak sexual activity, were the spring and early summer, from April to July, and especially June. Only the March low can be explained by a taboo, being almost certainly the result of abstention from sexual intercourse during Lent, and to a very minor extent the absence of marriages during that period. Indications that this trough was weaker in England than in France and New England suggests that the power of the English clergy to regulate the sexual habits of their flock was weaker – which seems very plausible. The late spring and early summer peak may have been caused by the greater privacy afforded by warmer weather, but this is pure hypothesis. The low in the harvest months of the mid-summer is very puzzling: possible explanations are physical exhaustion due to very heavy labour in the fields, the separation of families for migrant labour, and malnutrition since food prices were always high before the new harvest came in. On the other hand food prices peaked as conception peaked in May and June, while the cycle applies to townspeople as well as to agricultural workers. Doctors were advising sexual abstention during the heat of summer, but it seems unlikely that this would have influenced any but the wealthy elite, who read or listened to them. Since the cycle slowly disappears with urbanization and modernization, there is no reason to suppose that the evidence supports any theory of a natural human female fertility cycle. The fact is that we do not know the explanation for this curious phenomenon.

Between the late seventeenth century and the very beginning of the nineteenth, exceptional freedom was provided for the popular expression of sexuality. Compared with the Puritan period that preceded it, or the Evangelical period that followed, it was a time when the authorities made very little effort to curb displays and products that reflected the pagan admiration for virility common to all folk culture. In the late seventeenth century, the nonconformist minister Oliver Heywood was a horrified observer of what he regarded as a moral collapse in rural Yorkshire. In 1673 he noticed a large, highly obscene sign-board, erected during a 'Priapic feast' and set on posts straddling the main road from Halifax to Bradford; it depicted, it seems, a naked man and woman in, or just before, the act of copulation, and all travellers on the road were obliged to pass beneath it.

In London this taste was catered for by the growth of a flourishing industry in popular pornography. In 1773 the energetic London magistrate Sir John Fielding protested to a grand jury about 'the exposing to sale and selling of such indecent and obscene prints and books as are sufficient to put impudence itself to the blush'. Francis Place confirms this from the point of view of the consumer. In his youth in the 1780s, respectable stationery shops sold pornography. At the one he frequented, the owner, Mrs Roach, 'used to open a portfolio to any boy or to any maidservant; ... the portfolio contained a multitude of obscene prints; ... she encouraged them to look at them ... This was common to other shops' (Plates 25, 26). Pornography, like the standard sex manual *Aristotle's Masterpiece*, was 'at that time sold openly on every stall'. Very obscene songs were commonly sung at mixed parties given by respectable tradesmen, and the streets of London apparently swarmed with singers – many of them women – of 'infamous and obscene songs and ballads'. The two romantic heroes of the poor were the highwayman, who preyed exclusively on the rich and inevitably ended his days in the awesome ritual of the gallows; and the sexual athlete; while the greatest hero of all was the man who was both. These were antique types of hero, going back to Robin Hood and beyond, and both of them violated the moral norms of the bourgeoisie, who believed in the sanctity of property and in chastity. According to Place, these ballads were the only ones to be heard on the London streets before the moral reformers, aided by fear of the spread of French revolutionary ideas, led police and magistrates to suppress them at the end of the century. In any case by 1800 public toleration for such things was declining, as middle-class morality spread down to the respectable poor through the Sunday Schools.

2. THE CAUSES OF CHANGE

It is clear that what needs explaining is a three-stage shift in the sexual behaviour of the English poor in the seventeenth and eighteenth centuries; first to an increase of pre-marital chastity in the early seventeenth century; then in the eighteenth century to greater visual and verbal permissiveness, far more pre-nuptial intercourse (usually followed by marriage), and a more or less simultaneous increase in the proportion of couples who failed to marry after pregnancy had occurred. Later still, in the very late eighteenth and the nineteenth centuries, a new wave of sexual prudery spread downwards from the lower-middle classes to the respectable poor, leaving unaffected only the very lowest elements of the society, the *lumpenproletariat*.

The shifting attitude towards sexuality in western Europe in Early Modern times can be studied at three levels, that of the official moral theologians, that of the religious radicals, and that of an increasingly secular society. It seems likely, however, that the first was of critical importance only during the early seventeenth-century Puritan drive and that thereafter it was modified to conform to attitudes among the laity, and is thus a secondary variable from 1660 until the renewed Evangelical drive after 1770. As for the second, it had little or no temporary or permanent influence whatsoever in its own time or afterwards.

There is every reason to believe that the chief cause of the unusually high and rising standard of sexual morality in early seventeenth-century England was the external pressure of Puritan organization and Puritan preaching, which slowly affected the attitudes of nearly all the propertied classes, whether Puritan, Anglican or Arminian. It became part of the generally accepted pattern of internalized and enforced social discipline, and thus seeped downwards through the social hierarchy to the plebs. To give but one example from a not especially devout Elizabethan, the gentleman musician Thomas Wythorne, he resisted the idea that he should attempt to seduce before marriage the young widow he was wooing, on the grounds that 'we should have provoked God's heavy displeasure and wrath, to have lighted upon us for our wickedness'. This phrase conveys something of the sense of God's looming presence, which was so powerful a force for sexual restraint in the late sixteenth and early seventeenth centuries. These internalized values, and the powerful system of punishments for transgression to which they gave rise, must have been the principal causes of the low level of pre-nuptial pregnancy and of illegitimacy in early seventeenth-century England.

In the late seventeenth century, however, there was both an evident decline in the enthusiasm of the upper classes to repress the sexual exuberance of the poor and a shift in attitudes of the poor themselves. One possible explanation of this relaxation of attitudes towards sexuality is a change in moral theology, obviously mainly affecting the middle- and upper-class reading public, but also presumably penetrating down to the poor through sermons.

Protestant theologians of all persuasions had long since identified mutual comfort and endearment as two of the purposes of the sexual act within marriage. By the mid-seventeenth century, this was a common assumption of everyone from Jeremy Taylor to John Milton. The explicit recognition of the legitimacy of these two objectives opened up a new stage in the evolution of official Christian attitudes to sexuality within marriage, and by extension – although not by intent – was bound eventually to have its effect on pre-marital sexuality as well. By legitimizing the sexual act within marriage for the purpose of mutual comfort and endearment, Protestant theology began the slow separation of sexual pleasure from procreation that ended in the late seventeenth-century spread of both contraception and libertinism. This was the last thing that the theologians had in mind, but it was in fact one of the legacies of the concept of holy matrimony to a more secularized world.

Far more important in loosening popular conventions about sexual behaviour in England was the reaction after 1660 to the Draconian imposition by military rule in the 1650s of the more austere anti-pleasure principles of the Puritans. Stage plays, horse-racing, cock-fighting, maypoles and brothels had all been suppressed; alehouses had been severely limited in numbers, and adultery made punishable by death. The result was exactly the opposite of what the Puritan leaders had expected. Instead of producing a regenerate nation of the godly, they created a society bitterly resentful of public interference with their normal recreations, one which regarded all enthusiasm with distaste, and which eventually came to reject the Puritan vision of man's relation to nature and God, and to deny the sinfulness of pleasure.

There are three different ways in which this cultural change may have affected the pre-marital and extra-marital sexual behaviour of the poor in the late seventeenth and eighteenth centuries. The first is merely the result of the relaxation in the external controls on sexual behaviour imposed by Church and state; the second is a decline in respect by children for established moral standards of sexual behaviour expected by their parents; and the third is a change in those internalized standards themselves. According to the first, the strict code of honour which had hitherto governed the common practice of intimate courting now broke down due to a relaxation of religious and secular penalties. According to the second, there developed a severe inter-generational conflict in which children were rejecting the moral code of their parents. According to the third, there was a spread – or more likely a revival – of the recognized medieval custom by which sexual intercourse was permitted to take place immediately after the formal betrothal, but before the wedding.

It does appear that the custom of marriage in church partly broke down after the Restoration, and when it was again universally reinforced after about 1720, and especially after the Marriage Act of 1753, it was probably no longer regarded as the decisive event in forming a union. There is one piece of evidence to suggest that clandestine marriages, contracted outside the Church altogether, were very common indeed between 1680 and 1720: in the small market town of Tetbury in Gloucestershire in the 1690s, they amounted to at least twenty per cent of the total, and possibly a good deal more.

The key to the change, therefore, is a change in recognized standards of honour. The gigantic rise of pre-nuptial conceptions in the late eighteenth century was not caused by a massive violation of accepted standards of sexual behaviour, but rather by a change in those standards. Only the minor phenomenon of the rise of bastardy involved a violation of social norms. In the eighteenth century it looks as if the spousals again became the generally accepted moment at which sexual relations could begin, the marriage ceremony occurring later, often when the bride was quite far advanced in pregnancy. The man's honour was not damaged in the public consciousness, provided that he lived up to his promise to marry despite any possible second thoughts he might subsequently have had; and the woman's honour was not damaged in the public consciousness merely for having commenced sexual relations after the spousals but before the marriage.

If, on the other hand, the man repudiated his promise or ran away, one may legitimately assume that the honour of both was ruined in the eyes of the community: the man was then a liar, and the woman unchaste. If the woman allowed herself to be seduced without any promise, her reputation was ruined, but the man's was not. Community interest was limited to ensuring that it was the father who paid for the support of the bastard child, rather than the parish poor rate, and that the child was taught a trade by which to earn its living. The rise of pre-nuptial conceptions therefore represents primarily a shift in community standards of honour; the rise of bastardy represents social disintegration and a collapse of all standards of honour, primarily among social groups too poor to afford or comprehend such things.

Within the rural community, where traditional ideas about honour and morality persisted, there was an economic incentive for the prospective father to marry the pregnant girl since, as a commentator on Wales in 1804 remarked, 'both parties are so poor that they are necessarily constrained to render their issue legitimate, in order to secure their reputation and with it a mode of obtaining a livelihood'. This economic incentive was powerfully reinforced by legislation passed in 1733. Designed to relieve the poor rate of the responsibility for maintaining bastards, it added legal to community pressures for marriage by making any man identified by the mother as the father of an illegitimate child liable to arrest to enforce payment for its upkeep. This meant that the prospective father – or alleged father – was forced to choose between marriage, imprisonment, and the payment of an allowance, which varied from one to seven shillings a week for seven years. It also meant that if he was without means, his marriage would make him eligible for a child's allowance from the poor rate in his own parish. But if it strengthened the man's incentive to marriage, the Act may also have weakened the woman's motives for premarital chastity. A girl now had less reason to refuse a man's sexual advances, since if she became pregnant she retained this powerful weapon to enforce marriage. As the poet Crabbe put it in 1807,

next at our altar stood a luckless pair
Brought by strong passions and a warrant there [Plate 29].

The most obvious sign of this major shift of values after 1660 was a progressive separation of sin from law, which resulted in a marked decline in attempts to enforce the laws concerning sexual behaviour. In the half-century before the civil war, the Church courts had been more and more actively engaged in the struggle to control sexual behaviour. Cases of sexual immorality more than doubled between 1595 and 1635, and comprised anything up to half of all the business with which the courts dealt. The commonest form of penalty for fornication imposed by these courts, whether or not it led to bastardy, was shame punishment, which took the form of being forced to stand publicly, dressed in a white sheet, before the congregation on Sunday or in the market-place of the local town on market-day. On the other hand, the powers of enforcement of these courts were limited. About half of all the accused preferred to live in excommunication than to obey the summons of the court, and only a small proportion of those accused of sexual deviation ever did public penance. In the face of an obstinately recalcitrant poor laity, the Church courts before the civil war were therefore of only limited effectiveness in curbing sexual immorality.

In the late seventeenth century there took place a slow shift in attitudes, which eventually distinguished private sin from public law. This shift took place despite the continuity of values stressed by moral theologians running from Richard Baxter's *Christian Directory* of 1673 through William Law's *Serious Call to a Devout and Holy Life* of 1728 to Henry Venn's *Complete Duty of Man* of 1763. Anxious critics saw the moral dangers of an erosion of legal authority to repress sin and warned that 'if there be no power in the church sufficient to enforce a regularity of life, and the civil magistrate be remiss and negligent, great confusions and disorder will ensue in that state'. But popular though these writings were, all of them running into many editions, their readers seem to have been more the pious bourgeoisie than the landed elite who ruled the country. In the eighteenth century, the cases brought before the Church courts concerning sexual morality declined drastically as the power of the courts declined in a secularized society. In 1743 in one Yorkshire village, both parson and churchwardens were afraid to report sexual delinquents to the Archdeacon for fear of reprisals from the parishioners. Not only did the number of immorality cases drop markedly after 1660, but by 1740 shame punishments for fornication or pre-nuptial conceptions had virtually disappeared altogether. Although a thin trickle of public penances for fornication show up after 1770, pre-nuptial conception was abolished as an offence by statute in 1787.

In England in the late sixteenth and early seventeenth centuries, the deficiencies of the Church courts were made up by the zeal of the Justices of the Peace. The problem of preventing bastardy had long attracted the attention of Parliament, where the members, most of whom were also JPs, passed Act after Act to try to deal with what they believed to be both a moral scourge and a financial burden on the community. In the late sixteenth and early seventeenth centuries, the justices did not hesitate to use their authority to punish mere fornication as well as bastardy. Particularly in the north of England, the woman convicted of fornication was often whipped in the nearest market town 'as a deterrent to others', while at the second offence she was often committed to the House of Correction for hard labour under the lash. Bastardy cases tended to be treated severely, although sentences varied from place to place and justice to justice. In 1601 the Lancashire Quarter Sessions condemned the father and mother of an illegitimate child to be publicly whipped and then sat in the stocks, still naked from the waist upwards, with a placard on their heads, reading 'These persons are punished for fornication.' This kind of shame punishment by public exposure in the stocks was normal practice in the north, although it was already dying out near London.

After the Restoration in 1660, however, the gentry, in their dual capacities as JPs and MPs, were neither eager to police sexual behaviour themselves, nor willing to allow the clergy to police it for them. They became exclusively preoccupied with the economic problem of transferring the maintenance costs of a bastard child from the poor rate of the parish to the father, or failing that to some other body. Shame punishments were no longer imposed; all prosecution stopped at once if the child died, and further Acts of 1662 and 1733 were exclusively concerned with the economics of child maintenance and no longer with the morality of fornication *per se*. This did not mean, however, that the situation of the unmarried mother improved. Indeed, it may have worsened, as the parish authorities tried desperately to ensure that the baby was not born within their boundaries, and thus did not become a burden on the local rates. There were frequent cases, like that recorded by Oliver Heywood in 1662, in which a pregnant mother about to deliver was hastily bundled out of town. In this case, the woman 'was delivered in the town field, in cold frost and snow; the child died, the woman is distracted'. Failing physical deportation, the parish authorities put tremendous pressure on the mother to reveal the identity of the father, who could then be required to pay for the child's maintenance. A common practice was for the midwife and some local women to cross-question the mother during labour, refusing to come to her help in her agony until she revealed the name of the father. Indeed the midwives' oath of 1726 imposed this duty upon them. The only satisfactory solution for a pregnant mother was falsely to assert that the father was some rich man, who would then be forced by the Justices to pay a generous maintenance for the upkeep of the child (Plate 30).

The penalties of pregnancy without marriage in the eighteenth century were thus very heavy for both mother and child. The former was likely to lose her job, might be sent to the House of Correction, and eventually be driven into prostitution. Because of the tremendous incentive to the mother to conceal the birth, the child was likely to be murdered in the first few hours, or abandoned in the street, either to die there or to be dumped in a workhouse, where the prospects of survival were not much better.

The second plausible explanation for the rise in the eighteenth century of pre-nuptial conceptions and illegitimate births is not cultural but economic. Anthropologists tell us that the value attached to chastity is directly related to the degree of social hierarchy and the degree of property ownership. Pre-marital chastity is a bargaining chip in the marriage game, to be set off against male property and status rights. Pre-marital female sexual repression is thus built into the social system, since male and female are bargaining on the marriage market with different goods, the one social and economic, the other sexual. The withholding of sexual favours is a woman's only source of power over men, as Aristophanes pointed out in *Lysistrata*. The system serves the interests of both parties, since the male is guaranteed that he is purchasing new and not second-hand goods, while the female has a powerful lever to obtain marriage. Both the principle of pre-marital female chastity and the double standard after marriage are, therefore, functional to a society of property owners, especially small property owners. It follows that the most sexually inhibited class in the population is likely to be the lower-middle class of small property owners, among whom rigid ideas of patriarchy, extreme loyalty to the authoritarian state, and extreme sexual inhibitions tend to be the norm, among both husbands and wives. The poor were under no such constraints, and the rise of a class of landless rural labourers and urban workers without property or status meant the rise of a class to whom virginity was not important, and foresight, prudence and planning were irrelevant to their dismal economic future. The developments of the eighteenth century, with the progress of enclosures, the amalgamation of farms, the development of cottage industries and the growth of towns, were causing a considerable increase in the size of such a class.

The second economic explanation for the dizzy rise in pre-nuptial conceptions lies in the spread of cottage industry, and later of factories, which enabled a young couple to earn enough to live on at an early age. They were therefore for the first time in a position to defy both their parents and community norms, and to indulge in full premarital sex, secure in the knowledge that if pregnancy occurred there would be no economic obstacle to an early marriage. 'The decay of agriculture has been followed by that of morals,' lamented a Swiss observer in 1801. The rise of illegitimacy was caused by fathers defying custom and evading their responsibility to marry the pregnant girls. This may be attributed in large part to the growth in number of rural landless males who were obliged by poverty to postpone marriage and so to repudiate any marriage promises they may have made. Many of this class were forced by demographic pressures to leave the village and seek casual labour in the town, while more and more young women were also forced to move further away from home to go into urban domestic service or the dressmaking trade.

There is also evidence to suggest that there was a small segment of the population, at the lowest social level, which failed to conform to the prevalent norms from generation to generation: a bastardy-prone minority group. Many were drawn from the most wretched dregs of the population, those drifting homeless vagrants whose growing number had increasingly preoccupied the authorities in the late sixteenth and seventeenth centuries. Large numbers of these girls ended up on the streets of London, and the confession of one such woman, arrested and whipped for vagrancy and bastardy in Southwark in 1603, can stand for them all.

Frances Palmer, a vagrant . . ., having two children begotten and born in whoredom, says that one Thomas Wood, servant with Sir Edward Wotton, is the father of them; and the place where she was delivered was openly in the street, two or three doors off the Cross Keys; and they died and were buried in Allhallows parish in Gracechurch Street.

This was the group for whom the policy of open admission to foundling hospitals in the mid- and late eighteenth century proved a godsend. If as a result of their promiscuity they became pregnant and gave birth to a child, it was morally much easier to abandon it, now that it could be disposed of (in fact mostly killed by neglect) by a charitable institution, out of sight and out of hearing. Those who argued that the system of open admissions to foundling hospitals encouraged promiscuity and illegitimacy probably had a point. Thomas Bernard commented in about 1818 that it had 'a direct and uncontrollable tendency to encourage vice and increase the mortality of our species'.

One may conclude, therefore, that the principal cause of the rise of illegitimacy in England in the late eighteenth century, as in the rest of Europe, was not any change in the nature of the work young girls performed, for only a tiny minority went to work in factories, but rather to a collapse of resistance by more young women to full pre-marital intercourse due to a rise of the proportion of the property-less with no economic stake in the value of their virginity, and a rise in the proportion of men removed from the pressures of family, community and priest which previously would have contrived to force them into marriage. There was thus a change of attitudes towards pre-marital sex on the part of some working-class women; a change of economic circumstances which left them more exposed to entice-ment and coercion to seduction; a change in social circumstances which deprived them of the moral stiffening provided by older relatives; and a change of economic and social circumstances which left the male seducers more free to refuse their traditional obligation to marry the girls whom they had impregnated.

The story of the love life of the radical Samuel Bamford lends some support to this theory. He first fell in love with a girl called Catherine, but her mother said that 'no one should marry her daughter who could not fetch her away on his own horse', a piece of property Bamford did not possess. He then got a Yorkshire girl pregnant. It is significant of changing attitudes that the girl did not insist on marriage, and was quite content with a financial settlement for the maintenance of the child in the parish workhouse. Finally, he married another girl, but only some months after she had produced her first child by him. This was probably a not untypical story of life among the propertyless young in the late eighteenth century, involving both bastardy and pre-nuptial conception and birth.

An important and tragic result of this decline of family and community protection of single girls, especially in domestic service or a small workshop, was that they were increasingly exposed to sexual exploitation. Without protection from parents, kin, neighbours, ministers or local opinion, these girls were easy victims of seduction by their masters, who then dismissed them when they became pregnant. As William Acton remarked in 1865, 'there are few women more exposed to temptation to immorality than domestic servants, especially those serving in houses where menservants are also kept ... A woman found pregnant is usually dismissed from her employment without a reference.' 'Men who themselves employ female labour, or direct it for others, have always ample opportunity of choice, compulsion, secrecy and subsequent intimidation should exposure be probable and disagreeable ... They can at any moment discharge her.' The rising tide of pregnant and abandoned young women, many of whom drifted into the disease-ridden and futureless profession of prostitution, were tragic victims of sexual exploitation, particularly since there is evidence of an association of pre-nuptial pregnancy not only with economic dependence and low social status but also with illiteracy.

PART SIX

Conclusion

CHAPTER THIRTEEN

Facts, Interpretations, and Post-1800 Developments

> 'What is good for the individual can be destructive to the family; what preserves the family can be harsh on both the individual and the tribe to which the family belongs; what promotes the tribe can weaken the family and destroy the individual; and so on upward through the permutations of levels of organization.'
>
> (E. O. Wilson, *Sociobiology: the New Synthesis*, Cambridge, Mass., 1975, p. 4)

1. THE FACTS OF CHANGE, 1500–1800

The family as it evolved in England during the Early Modern period was always limited in its options by certain unyielding demographic facts. The first was the very high level of mortality, particularly an infant and child mortality rate of between thirty and fifty per cent, which affected all classes of society, although the poor suffered more than the rich. Until this mortality rate began to fall in the late eighteenth century, family limitation was a gamble with death, since at any moment all the children might be wiped out by an epidemic disease, leaving none to inherit the property and family name. Continued high mortality among young adults also meant that few marriages outlasted the child-bearing period. On the average, they endured for only about twenty years at most, because of the early death of husband or wife. This meant that grandparents were relatively few in number, either as a support to help in child care or as a burden in their old age. The omnipresence of death coloured affective relations at all levels of society, by reducing the amount of emotional capital available for prudent investment in any single individual, especially in such ephemeral creatures as infants. One result was the neglect of infants by their parents, which in turn reduced the former's

407

prospects of survival. This was a situation which encouraged the concept of the family as a group of replaceable surrogates, both spouses and more particularly children.

Secondly, this was a society with relatively low nuptiality, in which a significant and rising proportion of population, especially from the upper classes, never married at all, being forced out of the marriage market by the iron law of primogeniture and by the need to earn an arduous living in a profession if status was to be maintained. Even among the poor, some ten per cent never married, and remained bachelors or spinsters all their lives.

Thirdly, western Europe and America were unique among all known societies in the extraordinary delay in the age of marriage some ten or more years after the age of puberty, a feature of family life common to all classes, except the male heirs and the daughters of the landed nobility and gentry. Dictated by the need, itself caused by the custom of separate residence for the newly married, to inherit or accumulate some capital and furniture before marriage, this delay involved severe sexual abstinence at the period of maximum sexual drive. The sublimation of sex among male adults may well account for the extraordinary military aggressiveness, the thrift, the passion for hard work, and the entrepreneurial and intellectual enterprise of modern Western man. The withdrawal of women from the reproductive cycle for ten of their twenty-five fertile years was a critical factor in slowing down population growth. Delayed marriage also meant that household formation from generation to generation tended to be consecutive rather than concurrent. This facilitated social and intellectual change, since the parents of those who married were often already dead, and thus no longer in a position to impose their will and their values on the new household.

Changes in the family from 1500 to 1800 were limited primarily to two important status groups, the upper bourgeoisie of the towns and the squirarchy of the country. These two lead sectors in society provided a pattern which was followed, at varying intervals of time, by the propertied lower-middle class and by the highest levels of the court aristocracy.

The late medieval and sixteenth-century family welcomed both aid and direction from the kin and the community. There was no sense of domestic privacy, and inter-personal relations within the conjugal unit, both between husbands and wives and between parents and children, were necessarily fairly remote, partly because of the ever-present probability of imminent death, partly because of cultural patterns which dictated the arranged marriage, the subordination of women, the neglect and early fostering out of children and the custom of harsh parental discipline. Child-rearing practices, especially swaddling, the lack of a single mothering figure, and the crushing of the supposedly sinful will by brute force at an early age, tended to create special psychological characteristics in adults: suspicion towards others, proneness to violence, and an incapacity to develop strong emotional ties to any one individual. The result was a family type whose characteristics of psychological distance, deference and publicity were congruent with the basic values and organization of the hierarchical, authoritarian and inquisitorially collectivist society of Early Modern England.

In the late sixteenth and early seventeenth centuries, this family type was modified by the loss of a sense of trusteeship to the lineage, by the decline of kinship and clientage, and by the concurrent rise of the power of the state and the spread of Protestantism. The most important consequence was the substitution of loyalty to state or sect for loyalty to lineage or patron. This weakened the diffuse affective network of kin and neighbours which had surrounded and sustained the loosely bound family structure, and tended to isolate the nuclear core. This process exposed that core to stresses it was often not yet strong enough to sustain, despite the fact that its internal psychological cohesion was steadily improving. This cohesion was stimulated by a flood of propaganda from the pulpit and printing press, making the household responsible for, and the symbol of, the whole social system, which was thought to be based on the God-given principles of hierarchy, deference and obedience. This almost hysterical demand for order at all costs was caused by a collapse of most of the props of the medieval world picture. The unified dogma and organization of the Catholic Church found itself challenged by a number of rival creeds and institutional structures, the role of the priests as the only authorized intercessors between God and man was undermined, and the reliance upon the intellectual authority of the Ancients was threatened by the new scientific discoveries. Moreover, in England there occurred a phase of unprecedented social and geographical mobility which at the higher levels transformed the composition and size of the gentry and professional classes, and at the lower levels tore hundreds of thousands of individuals loose from their traditional kinship and neighbourhood backgrounds. Protestant preaching in the late sixteenth century caused large numbers of the English to be effectively christianized for the first time, but the concurrent high geographical mobility also left them a prey to acute insecurity and anxiety. The material world was more threatening and unpredictable than it had ever been, and the Devil and his agents were everywhere, but the ancient remedies for human ills in magic and 'wise women' were now denounced as mere satanic witchcraft.

In an atmosphere of heightened religious enthusiasm, the only hope of salvation was thought to lie in the ruthless persecution of dissidents. Traitors were hanged, drawn and quartered; religious radicals and gypsies were exterminated like vermin; witches were denounced, tortured and burned; children were beaten; wives were subjugated. Passive Obedience and the Divine Right of Kings seemed to many to be the only theories that promised hope of avoidance of political chaos. For the state, Passive Obedience to the husband and father in the home was the model for and guarantee of Passive Obedience to the king in the nation. In Protestant England there took place a partial transfer of the functions of the Church to the family, of the priest to the head of the household. The spiritual sanctity of the family was particularly stressed by the Puritans, and the gathered Churches of the sectaries finally substituted a free association of godly families for the traditional religious organization of the parish which included both saints and sinners.

Paradoxically, although the institution of marriage was becoming more sanctified in the late sixteenth century and although there was a growing stress by the moral theologians on the importance of marital and parental love, at the same time power relations within the family were being theoretically urged to become more authoritarian and patriarchal under the strong encouragement of both Church and state. The propaganda for – and the reality of – this internal authoritarianism within the family, which was so marked among the propertied classes, applied to pre-marital relations between young people, which were strictly limited and controlled by their parents, to husband–wife relations, where the principle of wifely obedience was constantly stressed, and to parent–child relations, where the breaking of the child's will was thought to be the paramount purpose of infant and child training.

In the lower–middle and the labouring classes, economic cooperation in the running of the family business dictated a certain measure of sharing of responsibility, if only for the sake of joint survival. But leisure activities were mostly conducted in sexually segregated groups and very clear status lines continued to be drawn on the basis of sex. Working wives were subjected to a crushing burden of toil, both outside the home and in the household management, while still kept in a thoroughly subservient position. Engels's theory that work brought equality between the sexes, and that the subordination of wives was a product of their transformation into a kept leisured class in the home, is not supported by the historical evidence. On the other hand, children in the propertyless class had greater freedom of choice in marriage. Adolescents had mostly long since left home to work as servants or apprentices in other people's homes and were, therefore, physically free to make their own mate selection, and even to indulge in some sexual experimentation during the courting process. Nor were they tied down by the burdens of property exchange and so dependent on parental consent for marriage, since neither partner had much to give.

On the other hand, since the children were also part of the family economic unit, they were probably subjected to physical and moral coercion from an early age in order to maximize their productivity before they left home. Secondly, the need to accumulate household goods and working capital to set up an independent household forced the children of the poor to postpone marriage until later and later, to some ten to sixteen years after sexual maturity. Their freedom of choice in timing and person in marriage was thus severely limited by economic considerations.

The third stage in the evolution of the nuclear family in the middle and upper classes began in the late seventeenth century. It was characterized by a continuation of the emphasis on the boundary surrounding the nuclear unit, and a progressive decline in the influence on that unit of both the neighbourhood and the kin. This of necessity led to greater stress on internal bonding within the family both as emotional ties to outsiders diminished, and as pressures from external organized groups relaxed. On the other hand, there was a marked reversal of the previous trend towards domestic patriarchy. Neither the absolute monarch nor the patriarchal father was any longer necessary for the maintenance of the social order, as Locke deliberately pointed out in his assault on Robert Filmer's last-ditch stand in his *Patriarcha*.

By 1700 there was clearly emerging among the bourgeois and landed gentry a new family type inspired by the principle of Affective

Individualism, whose particular manifestations were as follows. The strength of the kin ties had declined and those that survived were increasingly limited to close relatives. Mate selection was determined more by free choice than by parental decision and was based as much on expectations of lasting mutual affection as on calculations of an increase in money, status or power. Except in the highest aristocratic circles, the financial considerations of the dowry and the jointure became less decisive elements in marriage negotiations than the prospect of future personal happiness based on settled and well-founded affection; as a result there were fewer marriages to heiresses, fewer marriages within the ramifications of the kin, and fewer marriages of young men to significantly older women. The authority of husbands over wives and of parents over children declined as greater autonomy was granted to, or assumed by, all members of the family unit. There were the beginnings of a trend towards greater legal and educational equality between the sexes, and the claims of each child to some part of the inheritance were carefully protected, although there was no decline in the emphasis on primogeniture. Professional, upper-bourgeois and gentry families became much more child-oriented, and some adopted remarkably permissive attitudes to child-rearing. Among the upper tradesmen and shopkeepers, yeomen and tenant farmers, more and more wives were being educated in the social graces of their betters, and were withdrawing from active participation in family economic production. Instead, they were occupying themselves with the supervision of the servants, child care and a round of status-enhancing leisure activities, whether time-consuming pursuits like tea parties and card playing, or good works, or visits to the local theatre and the circulating library. Although the economic dependence of these women on their husbands increased, they were granted greater status and decision-making power within the family, and they became increasingly preoccupied with the nurturing and raising of their children.

The higher social groups whose life-style these women were aping were now clearly distinguished by an elaborate set of culturally induced manners that marked them off as 'the quality'. The key was conformity to elaborate rituals of behaviour involving an increasing privatization of one's body, its fluids and its odours. The substitution of forks for fingers in eating, the supply by the host of separate plates and utensils for each course, the substitution of handkerchiefs for fingers or clothes for nose-blowing, the control of spitting, the wearing of nightclothes, the introduction of washbasins, portable bath-tubs and soap, the substitution of wigs for lice-ridden natural hair, are all symptoms of the same evolution. Knowledge of the classics for men, and music, dancing and needlework for women, were additional glosses on this deeper evolution of elite manners based on the refinement and elegance of body and mind. There was now a civilization of Western manners for the elite, defined by a set of internationally recognized patterns of behaviour.

In some quarters there was a glorification of the sexual aspects of love in art, literature and life, now channelled as much inside marriage as outside it: the role-models of wife and mistress were united, and the libido was released from its long period of religious containment. Among the higher aristocracy, adultery by both sexes again became extremely common, while men of all classes made much use of the growing army of prostitutes in the cities. Among the propertyless poor, and to a lesser extent the smallholders, artisans and small tradesmen, sexual relations before marriage became normal, pre-nuptial conceptions rose as high as forty per cent and the illegitimacy ratio greatly increased from a previously very low level. The first two are evidence of a weakening of parental, clerical and community controls over old customs of pre-marital petting, and of a willingness by young girls far from home to attempt to entice men into a stable relationship by taking a promise of marriage rather than the wedding as the moment to allow full sexual relations to begin. The third is evidence that a growing minority of men were exploiting their power as masters of servants or their position as drifting and lonely fellow workers, in order to take their sexual pleasure and evade the consequences.

Among the upper bourgeoisie and squirarchy the eighteenth century thus saw the emergence of a new family type playing a new role and experiencing new internal relationships: a family serving rather fewer practical functions, but carrying a much greater load of emotional and sexual commitment. It was a family type which was more conjugal and less kin and community oriented; more bound by ties of affection or habit, and less by ties of economic or political partnership; more morally and religiously sanctified and less utilitarian; more internally liberal, and less patriarchal and authoritarian; less responsible for the helpless who were now looked after by public authorities, but more concerned for their well-being; more sexually liberated, preferably within marriage, and less sexually repressed;

more concerned with children and their needs and less adult-oriented; more private and less public; and finally, more desirous and capable of controlling procreation, and less willing to leave such matters to the will of God.

These are, of course, trends and not absolutes, and older customs and values survived for a very long time. The degree to which, if at all, this new family type was adopted varied enormously from one class and one family to another. Most features took root first among the urban bourgeoisie, and spread a little later to the landed classes. Many never penetrated the poor at all until the nineteenth or even the early twentieth centuries. The outcome was not so much the replacement of one family type by another as the widening of the varieties. There was a growing diversity of family types, a widening pool of cultural alternatives.

Particular aspects of the new family type struck deeper and more immediate roots in some classes than in others. Thus the higher aristocracy clung longest to the arranged marriage with an eye to property, but were the first to welcome the new attitude towards sex as one of the supreme pleasures of life; the professional and bourgeois classes were probably the first to adopt the ideal of married love, but the last to build frank sexual passion into the marital relationship. The upper gentry seem to have been the pioneers in the creation of the permissive child-oriented family, and yet they continued to tolerate the brutal barbarities of English public-school life. The labouring classes had long been accustomed to a family with shared economic responsibilities, but were the last to develop strong internal emotional bonds, to admit a greater sense of equality of status between husband and wife, and to invest love or money in their children.

2. INTERPRETATIONS OF THE CHANGE 1640–1800

What needs explaining is not a change of structure, or of economics, or of social organization, but of sentiment. People within the nuclear family in certain circles treated one another quite differently in 1780 from the way their great-grandparents had done in 1600, and their attitude towards outsiders, whether kin or neighbours, was also substantially different. There was a shift in a whole cultural system, defined as the growth of affective individualism, the symptoms and causes of which have been spelt out at length in Chapter 6.

If the facts are correct, if the change to the new family type began as early as the mid-seventeenth century, and if the lead was taken by the mercantile and professional upper bourgeoisie and by the squirarchy, then certain common explanations for the evolution of the modern family cannot be true.

For one thing, the early and erratic chronology and social specificity of these developments make it impossible to accept any general sociological theory of modernization as applied to the family. There are numerous definitions of modernization theory, but one of the best and most relevant, a synoptic view of a century and a half of sociological work, has been made by R. Nisbet. He has argued that there has taken place a progressive erosion of five traditional values. The first of these values is the sense of community, which decays as the village neighbourhood gives way to the floating urban migrant mass. The immigrants are said to be detached physically from the ties of kin and friends and to be thus freed to evolve new values and ideologies of their own about virginity, pre-marital sex, marriage for love, individual autonomy, and so on. There seems to be a good deal of truth in this. The second value is the all-pervasive sense of authority and deference which enveloped late medieval man. This was ritualized by the repeated gesture of doffing the hat on all occasions to all superiors, and was internalized by constant indoctrination at every turn. The Great Chain of Being, the hierarchical ordering of the universe, made it natural to look on the monarch as a super-patriarch, and the father as a mini-sovereign. These values, too, were allegedly destroyed by the social, economic and political changes of the sixteenth century onwards. In fact, however, they were positively reinforced for over a century, from 1530 to 1660, as a buttress against anarchy, and they only finally gave way when the rate of change slowed down and they became superfluous to the maintenance of political stability.

Of the other traditional values, that of social stability was allegedly undermined by increased geographical, social and occupational mobility. But this is called into question when it is found that mobility among the propertied classes may have been on the decline after 1660. Increasing, not decreasing, proportions of apprentices in English towns in the late seventeenth and eighteenth centuries were admitted by virtue of their fathers' freedom of the city and membership of the guild. Urban immigration was increasingly short-range, from neighbouring areas. On the other hand more and more of the population were becoming propertyless, and as the demographic expansion of the eighteenth century picked up momentum, more and more flocked into the towns. Among these classes social disintegration certainly occurred, and to this extent the sociologists are right.

The fourth traditional value, the concept of the sacred, was certainly undermined by the secularization of society. But this is a change to be handled with extreme attention to chronology, in view of the rise of Protestant (and Catholic) religious enthusiasm between 1550 and 1650, and its revival again after 1780: secularization was squeezed in between two phases of religious zeal among all sections of the propertied classes. England in 1650 was probably less secular than it ever had been, and in 1780 it was probably more secular than it was ostensibly to be again for over a century.

The final alleged loss of traditional values, the cutting of modern man from his psychological roots, his purchase of autonomy and independence at the price of alienation and anomie, is also open to question because of faulty chronology and failure to specify the class under discussion. Familial change towards greater autonomy and equality took place among the squirarchy and upper bourgeoisie in the eighteenth century, whereas it was part of the labouring classes who were drawn into the dark satanic mills which by Marxist theory created the condition known as 'alienation'.

In view of these chronological and class discrepancies, the logic of a sociological theory based on an overarching concept of modernization marching relentlessly through the centuries appears less than convincing. It is merely one more example of the many pitfalls of any unilinear theory of history, which ignores the ups and downs of social and intellectual change, the lack of uniformity of the direction of the trends, and the failures of the various trends to synchronize in the way they ought if the paradigm is to fit. Above all, by sweeping broadly across the vast spectrum of highly distinctive national cultures, status groups and classes, these theories reduce the enormous diversity of social experience to a uniformity which has never existed in real life.

Yet another explanation of the evolution of the new family type is that it was a product of industrial capitalism. Capitalist society, it is said, stresses achievement, uniformity, functional specificity and geographical mobility, whereas the traditional family stressed ascription, particularism, diffuseness, and geographical stability. The latter, therefore, had to be modified to fit the former. It was Engels who argued that the free-contract system of labour relations, on which industrial society in the West was based, presupposed a free-contract system of marital relations. He recognized the prior importance of Protestantism in fostering possessive individualism and personalized morality, but stressed that it was industrialization which brought the love marriage to the working classes. Under this theory he was obliged to assert that the new family type was confined to the lower classes, and, unlike all other civil rights in the society, excluded the property classes.

There are many factual historical errors in this hypothesis, which has recently become the accepted dogma of Parsonian functionalist sociology. The main objection is that the class analysis is wrong. It was among the landed, professional and upper-bourgeois classes, not among the propertyless industrial poor, that an individualistic ideology first changed the character of internal and external family relationships. The second objection is that the chronology is wrong, since the new family type developed in New England and in England well before industrialization even began. Since both the social class distribution and the chronology fail to fit the model, it seems evident that there can have been no direct connection between the two developments. A third objection is that there is mounting evidence that the factory did not break up the family as an economic unit. Engels thought that 'the modern industrial family is founded on the open or concealed domestic slavery of the wife' and that the early factory caused the destruction of family life, since it drove work out of the home and separated husband, wife and children in different occupations in different locations. But it now looks as if the first phase of industrialization in the eighteenth century had little effect on the employment of married women in cottage industries in the home, and that the later stages of factory industrialization in the nineteenth century actually drove them back into the home.

What is certain is that the traditional female occupations of domestic service, textile manufacture and garment-making remained the three largest until the early twentieth century, while the family continued to act as a unit of production far into the nineteenth century in major areas of the economy, in domestic industry, agriculture and even in early industrial workshops. Thirdly, it is very

417

doubtful whether the factory did much to increase the employment of married women outside the home. There are good reasons to think that in the seventeenth and early eighteenth centuries a very high proportion of married women took part in productive labour, especially in labour-intensive drudgery in agriculture, petty trading, spinning, lace-making and other cottage industries. The demand for this labour was seasonal and erratic, and the women were paid only one half to one third the wages of men. But the work existed, and it served to ease some of the stresses of abject family poverty. In 1690 William Petty remarked that 'all women over 7 are to labour, except among the upper tenth'. It was only in 1820, when industrialization had been under way for over forty years, that employment opportunities for women in factories increased, and then only in the cotton trade. Even so, most of these women were unmarried girls, who mostly left the factory as soon as they set up a family; only seventeen per cent were married women in 1883. The only employment for women that continued to increase through the nineteenth century was as domestic servants to the increasing number of affluent middle class, but this again was a form of employment largely confined to unmarried girls. The evidence that industrialization in the eighteenth and nineteenth centuries substantially and progressively increased the job opportunities for married women outside the home is thus on balance very dubious indeed. If this is so, the link between the new family type and industrialized society becomes extremely tenuous.

It cannot be denied that for those married women who worked in factories, industrialization was highly destructive of family life. A report of 1833 noted that these girls had had little or no opportunity to learn domestic duties, and that they were forced to abandon the home for very long hours. 'Here is the young mother absent from her child about twelve hours daily. And who has the charge of the infant in her absence? Usually some little girl or aged woman, who is hired for a trifle, and whose services are equivalent to the reward.' But these were a tiny minority of all married women, and a small minority even of the women who worked in factories. Although the effect of the industrial revolution on the employment opportunities of married women was not very marked, except possibly in the limited area of the cotton towns, both cottage industry and factory industry everywhere increased the earning potential of children, in the period before the introduction of child-labour laws. If children could be put to regular productive work from the age of six or seven, and if the bulk of their wages could be appropriated by their parents until their early twenties, they could be transformed from an economic burden to a major economic asset to the family: three or four children out at work could double the family income. There can be little doubt about the effects of this on raising fertility rates, increasing nutrition in the home, and generally in improving the living standards of the poor. But the improvement must have been limited to that period in the family life cycle when the children were mostly over six and under twenty-six, and to the period in time before the new laws came into force.

There is no evidence as yet about the way in which this use of child-labour changed either power or affective relationship within the nuclear family or among the kindred. It should be pointed out that parental love, which was one of the central features of the new family type as it developed in the middle classes, was hardly conducive to early industrial work practices. As Marx and Engels were at pains to document, young children were exploited unmercifully in factories and mines in the early phases of industrialization. But it was their parents who consented and indeed actively encouraged this exploitation in order to obtain an early economic profit from these otherwise useless mouths that had to be fed. This is certainly true, although it is not established that the juvenile wage slaves of the factory were in fact worse off than the children employed in small family crafts carried on in the home.

The final blow to the theory that industrialization created the new family type is the recent empirical evidence which strongly indicates that the fit between the two is far less perfect than was previously supposed. Admittedly, the custom of independent residence for the nuclear family facilitates geographical mobility into new work areas and the breaking of ties with the kin. Partible inheritance facilitates the mobility of capital (although primogeniture drives younger sons out of the countryside into the city in search of work). Greater internal freedom within the nuclear family increases psychological adaptability to new situations and new work routines. But recent studies of family life among the poor during industrialization in the nineteenth century, or in the post-industrial urban world of the twentieth century, show conclusively that a variety of family types are compatible with industrialization and that kin relationships still remain very close in industrial urban societies, and indeed are positively reinforced as life-savers in times of high geographical mobility or economic hardship. A detailed case study of the relations between the family and employment in the largest textile factory in the world in Manchester, New Hampshire, in the late nineteenth and early twentieth centuries shows a very close interrelationship between the traditional family structure and modern factory needs. What emerges is the paradoxical discovery that it was the very old-fashioned family of the French Canadians, patriarchally controlled, enlarged and extended, with close kin ties and high fertility rates, which was best adapted to recruit, house and discipline a reliable labour force for this great modern industrial plant. Dependent on the changing conditions of supply and demand for labour, the modern factory managers and the traditional family patriarchs manoeuvred and bargained to control employment and recruitment to suit their own internal needs. Under these hard facts, the causal model that makes industrialization the independent variable in creating the modern nuclear family collapses completely.

It does appear, however, that the new family type is first associated with the upper levels of the urban bourgeoisie and professional classes. To this extent there is certainly a connection with the spirit of capitalism, though not with industrialization. It was early commercial capitalism as it affected the wealthy patriciate, the entrepreneurs and merchants, first in Florence in the fifteenth century, then probably in Amsterdam in the early seventeenth century, then in London in the late seventeenth century, which was a necessary, although not a sufficient, cause of the emergence of the new family type.

What seems to have happened in the late eighteenth and early nineteenth centuries is that the new family already adopted by the upper-middle and landed classes now spread downwards into the labouring classes. It was the Sunday Schools and other agencies which created a diligent, thrifty and sober labour force, mobile in relation to parents but centred around the family home, which was the ideal of every industrial entrepreneur. This new family type was in theory perfectly adapted to the economic changes of the period.

It is not being claimed that industrialization had no effect whatever upon family structure. As Marx demonstrated in the first volume of *Capital*, early factory industrialization was certainly destructive of cohesive family life as it then existed. Thus the modern family fitted the modern factory far better than the modern factory fitted the modern family. What is here being argued is that the relationship is not a simple one, that most of the features of the modern family appeared before industrialization and among social groups unaffected by it, and that even those exposed to it responded in different ways. Moreover meritocratic rather than patrimonial and kin-oriented systems of recruitment and promotion are not essential to the efficient working of a modern factory, as the Japanese example indicates. It is only when meritocratic values become paramount in hiring and promotion decisions that a very important aspect of traditional and early modern family structure disappears. But recent studies suggest that even in societies with rigorously impartial systems, there persists a strong built-in hereditary bias, which tends to preserve elite positions for children of elite families, while lower down in the class structure certain trades and occupations tend to be handed down from father to son, with the active help of modern trade unions.

Another explanation of the trend towards a new family type was formulated a century and a half ago by Alexis de Tocqueville, when in 1835 he surveyed the pre-industrial American scene. To him, the key to the change was what he called 'the democratic spirit', and is here called the spirit of individualism. Writing just before the Victorian revival of patriarchy, he remarked that it was now a commonplace that 'in our time the members of a family stand upon an entirely different footing towards each other: that the distance which separated a father from his sons had been lessened, and that paternal authority, if not destroyed, is at least impaired'. Here he is speaking in the same terms as Dr Johnson used about England sixty years before. He also noted the striking change in the affective character of private correspondence between family members, the change in legal obligations, and the early emancipation of young people from parental control. Tocqueville found the change particularly noticeable in the two Anglo-Saxon societies of America and England for exactly the reasons which have here been put forward. He believed that the spirit of independence was the result of a major cultural shift, fostered by Protestantism and reinforced by the rights of self-government. 'Freedom is then infused into the domestic circle by political habits and by religious opinions.' What he omitted to mention was first the enormous influence of the growth of a large, independent and self-confident middle class, equipped with a genteel education and enjoying sufficient affluence to support a life-style based on privacy and leisure; and second the cultural homogeneity of this class and the landed squirarchy since many of the former were younger sons of the latter. Both are essential to explain why the lead in these vast changes in *mentalité* occurred first in England and New England.

3. POST-1800 FAMILY TYPES

Historical change is not a one-way street, and even in the West over the last five hundred years, continuous linear development has only occurred in the one field of technology. The trend towards the isolated nuclear family, greater personal autonomy, and emphasis on affective ties has not run a steady course from the sixteenth century to the twentieth. In terms of both sexual attitudes and power relationships, one can dimly begin to discern huge, mysterious, secular swings from repression to permissiveness and back again. In England an era of reinforced patriarchy and discipline lasted from about 1530 to about 1670, with the high point in the 1650s. This in turn gave way to an era of growing individualism and permissiveness which was dominant in the upper-middle and upper classes from about 1670 to about 1790. The next stage in the evolution of the family was marked by a strong revival of moral reform, paternal authority and sexual repression, which was gathering strength among the middle-classes from about 1770, and continued for over a century.

The causes of this second tidal wave of moral regeneration and repression seem to be very similar to those that caused the first. There was a sense of social and political crisis, a fear that the whole structure of social hierarchy and political order were in danger. In the first period the fear had been of religious wars and peasant revolts. Now the fear was that under the inspiration of 1789 the impoverished and alienated masses in the industrial cities would rise up in bloody revolution. Secondly, two rival factions, one established and one nonconformist, were in competition for the allegiance of the population. In the sixteenth century, it had been the Anglicans and the Puritans, now it was the Evangelicals and the Methodists. In each case, both sides stressed the enforcement of patriarchy and obedience, and the crushing of the libido.

There were, however, some features which were peculiar to the middle-lower-class Victorian family. For one thing, it was the first family type in history which was both long-lasting and intimate. Child mortality had dropped markedly, and so had the mortality of young adults, so that children now survived more often, and fewer marriages were terminated prematurely by death. Moreover the practice of fostering out was now less common than it had been, except in those growing numbers who sent off their sons to public boarding-schools. Within this more durable unit, there developed a combination of repression of wives and children and an intense emotional and religious concern for their moral welfare. The subordination of women and the crushing of the sexual and autonomous drives of the children took place in a situation where the total emotional life of all members was almost entirely focused within the boundaries of the nuclear family. The psychodynamics of this family type have been well described as 'explosive intimacy'.

After this second phase of repression, which was at its peak from about 1800 into the 1860s or later, the tide slowly turned again. Since then there has developed a second and far more intense phase of permissiveness, beginning slowly among the middle classes in the 1870s, and spreading to the social elite in the 1890s; then, in the 1920s and more dramatically in the 1960s and 1970s, spreading for the first time to all sectors of the population. The influence of the family on job placement has declined as meritocracy has increased. The influence of the parents in the determination of the marriage choices of their children has all but disappeared. Patriarchal power, of husband over wife and father over children, has been severely eroded. Love has now become the only respectable and generally admitted motive for mate selection, whatever the secret reality may be. Aspirations for sexual and emotional fulfilment through marriage have mushroomed; pre-marital sexual experimentation has become increasingly respectable, thanks partly to a dramatic improvement in contraceptive technology which has at last more or less successfully isolated sexual pleasure from procreation, and partly to a shift of attitude to one favourable first to contraception and now also to abortion. The period has been characterized by rising divorce rates, moving in waves followed by periods of stability, by increasing numbers of consensual unions, by open demands for free sexual expression and unrestrained sexual fulfilment by both men and women, by growing permissiveness in child-rearing, and now by rising demands for female equality with men in all spheres of life. During this last stage the astonishing success of modern medicine in all but eliminating death among children and young adults has transformed the whole character of family life. Children no longer die, and it is worth while to lavish profound affection upon them and to invest heavily in their education, while their numbers have necessarily to be restricted by contraception. Young adults now rarely die naturally, and in consequence affection is a necessary bond for persons likely to be together for a period of over fifty years, while divorce is equally necessary as a safety valve when the bond fails. Marriage is now a high-risk enterprise.

4. GENERAL CONCLUSIONS:
FAMILY CHANGE AND HISTORICAL DEVELOPMENT

The key to family change in middle- and upper-class circles is the ebb and flow of battle between competing interests and values represented by various levels of social organization, from the individual up to the nation state. The evolution of the family, from the early sixteenth and the late eighteenth century, has faithfully reflected the changing positions in the tug-of-war between these various interests and the values attached to them. At first it was recognized that the kin took priority over the state, the nuclear family and the individual: the interests of 'the house' were regarded as paramount. In the sixteenth and early seventeenth centuries, the nation state and the national Church began to assert their own claims, to undermine the authority of the kin, and to reinforce patriarchy in an increasingly nuclear family. The individual continued to be expected to subordinate his own will to the interests and desires of others, although certain ideas were already germinating in Puritan moral theology and in politico-psychological theory which were eventually to help to bring about a fairly rapid recognition of his aspirations to autonomy. At the same time, the school was taking over much of the socialization function hitherto performed by family and kin, the result being to isolate childhood and youth as a special, and increasingly prolonged, period of social moratorium, of subordination and lack of adult responsibilities. By the late eighteenth century, the happiness of the individual, his untrammelled pursuit of ego gratification, was being equated with the public good, with the good of all those older rivals for priority, the nuclear family, the patriarch, the kin, the Church and the state. This was a wholly unrealistic assumption, and in the nineteenth century the interests of the family, the patriarch, the school, the religion and the state all reasserted themselves for a while, before the final thrust of affective individualism in the twentieth century.

Because family change has depended on this eternal conflict of interests and values, with victory swaying back and forth between the various contestants for priority, it is wholly false to assume that there can have been any such thing as straightforward linear development. There is no reason to assume that the end-product of affective individualism, namely the intensely self-centred, inwardly turned, emotionally bonded, sexually liberated, child-oriented family type of the third quarter of the twentieth century is any more permanent an institution than were the many family types which preceded it. This is strongly suggested by the fact that the cause of change lies in an unending dialectic of competing interests and ideas; by the historical record showing the highly erratic course of this evolution; by its very variable impact on different classes; by the strains to which it is currently being subjected; and by its very restricted geographical spread around the world. The only steady linear change over the last four hundred years seems to have been a growing concern for children, although their actual treatment has oscillated cyclically between the permissive and the repressive.

Nor is there any reason to assume that the family which has emerged in the late twentieth century must necessarily, in all respects, be more conducive to either personal happiness or the public good than the family types which preceded it. Affective individualism is a theory which lacks any firm foundation in biological, anthropological or sociological data. As Philip Slater has pointed out, 'the notion that people begin as separate individuals, who then march out and connect themselves with others, is one of the most dazzling bits of self-mystification in the history of the species'. As an ideal it has produced several unfortunate results, as well as many good ones. How else can one explain the peculiar fact that the two trends to a more individualistic family type among the middle and upper classes in the eighteenth and twentieth centuries were both preceded and separated by two other centuries of patriarchy during the Puritan and the Victorian periods? Why is it that at least twice the lead sectors of Western society have found this family type unsuitable for their needs and incompatible with their values?

There can be no doubt that the changes themselves had serious negative as well as positive features. For one thing, power is a zero-sum game, so that increased autonomy of wives and children meant a decrease in the respect and authority previously accorded to elderly males, whose status and prospects necessarily diminished. Further, the decline of ties with the kin deprived the wife of much external help which had previously been available to her in the difficult tasks of adjusting to life under a husband, and of child-rearing and child-care. She now lacked support in case of marital conflict, and advice in case of serious incompatibility; her life became more isolated and more tedious while the children were young for lack of relatives to share the burden of baby-sitting and education; and her existence was more empty and lacking in social or economic function when the children had left home. Moreover, the decline in respect for lineage and ancestry, in the concept of oneself as a trustee for the handing on of blood, property and tradition, resulted in some loss of identity, while the progressive postponement of the entry of children into the adult life of work, from seven when they started chores around the home, to fourteen when they became servants or apprentices in other households, to twenty-one when they finished their education, transformed the nature of childhood and created the problem of how to deal with large numbers of adolescent children with the drives and capacities of adults, but denied their responsibilities. Finally, the highly permissive child-rearing practised in many middle- and upper-class households in the late eighteenth century and again in the late twentieth century bred a large number of ill-disciplined and poorly socialized children who grew up to be adults with demands for instant gratification which could not be satisfied. Some wasted their lives in life-long dissipation, while others eventually found a solution in the conversion experience of Evangelical religion.

The distribution of affective ties, like that of power, is also something of a zero-sum game, although affect, unlike power, changes in quantity over time. The highly personalized, inward-looking family was achieved in part at the cost of, and perhaps in part because of, a withdrawal from the rich and integrated community life of the past, with its common rituals, festivals, fairs, feast days and traditions of charity and mutual aid. 'Privacy and community are antithetical needs and cannot simultaneously be maximized.' Thus the middle and upper classes, where the affect-bonded family developed most strongly, reduced their voluntary contributions to village charity and increased their physical, social and cultural isolation from the poor. They withdrew to their own world behind their park walls or inside the grounds of their Palladian villas. Any solution to the problem of boundary awareness has its benefits and its drawbacks. Optimum adaptation to the outer world of kin or community is achieved only by some limitation on internal affective bonding within the nuclear family. Conversely, optimum internal integration is achieved only at the cost of some mal-integration into wider social networks.

Despite its many virtues, the rise in the West of the individualistic, nuclear, child-oriented family which is the sole outlet of both sexual and affective bonding is thus by no means always an unmixed blessing. This intense affective and erotic bonding is no more permanent a phenomenon than were the economic ties of property and interest that united families in the past, even if this is the rough general direction in which Western society has been moving over the last three hundred years. Today parents can expect to live twenty or thirty years beyond the departure of the children from the home, the number of children is declining fast, and the number of mothers with small children who go out to work is rapidly growing. The separate economic preoccupations of each parent are beginning to detach them both from the home and from their dependence on each other. Already, moreover, the peer-group is almost as important as the family in the social life of children. It therefore seems possible that a new, more loosely structured, less emotionally and sexually cohesive, and far more temporary family type is already being added to the number of options available. The frustrated and lonely housewife, the over-possessive mother and the oedipal relationship of the son with the father may all be transient phenomena of a particular time, place and social class – to be replaced, no doubt, by a different set of pathological types. Furthermore, the historical record suggests that the likelihood of this period of extreme sexual permissiveness continuing for very long without generating a strong back-lash is not very great.

It is an ironic thought that just at the moment when some thinkers are heralding the advent of the perfect marriage based on full satisfaction of the sexual, emotional and creative needs of both husband and wife, the proportion of marital breakdowns, as measured by the divorce rate, is rising rapidly. Just at the moment when some thinkers are heralding the advent of the perfect parent–child relationship, based on the permissive theories of A. S. Neill, many American and

English young are losing interest in children and are choosing not to have any at all. When they do have them, they are also, it seems, either turning away from treating them permissively in the home, or else dumping them in day-care centres at the earliest opportunity. The cycle of history is revolving once more.

One hundred and fifty years ago, before the transformation of the family had run the full cycle that we have now witnessed, Tocqueville was cautiously but moderately optimistic in assessing the gains and losses to mankind: 'I do not know, on the whole, whether society loses by the change, but I am inclined to believe that man individually is a gainer by it. I think that in proportion as manners and laws become more democratic, the relation of father and son becomes more intimate and more affectionate . . . It would seem that the natural bond is drawn closer in proportion as the social bond is loosened.' Such a cautiously favourable final judgement about the results of the rise of affective individualism seems best to fit the confused and conflicting evidence about the evolution of the family. However one assesses it in moral terms, for better or for worse, it is certainly one of the most significant transformations that has ever taken place, not only in the most intimate aspects of human life, but also in the nature of social organization. It is geographically, chronologically and socially a most restricted and unusual phenomenon, and there is as little reason to have any more confidence in its survival and spread in the future as there is in that of democracy itself.

Index

Abergavenny, Lady, 122
abortifacients, 266–7
abortions, 52, 59, 266–7, 325, 388, 423
academics, 282, 322
Acton, Dr William, 243, 305, 404
Adams, John, 384
Addison, Joseph, 175, 184, 185, 271
Admonition to Parliament, 1572, 326
adolescents, homosexuality, 322–3;
    sexuality, 318–23, 411; *see also*
    apprentices; children
adultery, 391; aristocracy, 328–31,
    413; and double standard of sexual
    behaviour, 315–18; as grounds for
    divorce, 34; institutionalization of,
    33; as male prerogative, 315–16;
    prohibited by Church, 30;
    punishments for, 324, 400; Puritan
    attitude towards, 396
aged, 48, 50, 252–3
Aikin, Lucy, 283
Albigensian crusade, 309
Aldeburgh, Edward Augustus, Earl of,
    329
Alderley, Henrietta Maria (Mary),
    Lady, 267
Alderley, Edward John, Lord, 267
All Souls College, Oxford, 323, 336
Almack's Club, 252
almshouses, 107
America, age at first marriage, 44,
    408; birth rate, 52; bundling, 384;
    changes in family type, 417;
    'conception cycle', 393; duration of
    marriage, 46; individualism, 421–2;
    pre-nuptial pregnancies, 386, 388;
    pursuit of happiness, 161; rejects
    swaddling of children, 267, 269; size
    of families, 52
American Revolution, 227

Anabaptists, 157
anal sex, 266, 309, 315, 324, 337
Anglican Church, control of marriage
    laws, 30–32; objections to birth
    control, 261; and remarriage, 33,
    34; treatment of children, 125–6;
    view of marriage, 101–2; *see also*
    Church
Anglo-Saxons, 158
aphrodisiacs, 379–80
Aplin, Mr, 193
apoplexy, 65
apprentices, and age at first marriage,
    44; occupational mobility, 415–16;
    as part of household, 28, 84, 170;
    and prostitutes, 391; social control
    of, 120, 318
archdeacons' courts, *see* ecclesiastical
    courts
Aretino, *Postures*, 310, 336, 343
aristocracy, adultery, 328–31, 413;
    arranged marriages, 186–7, 414;
    child-rearing, 286, 287–8; choice of
    marriage partner, 50–51, 131–2;
    companionate marriage, 238–9;
    contraception, 263; and divorce,
    34–5; and double standard of sexual
    behaviour, 317; generation
    replacement rate, 261;
    homosexuality, 337–8; honeymoons,
    224; kinship and clientage, 94–5,
    99; life expectancy, 57, 58; lineage
    loyalty, 29, 69–70; and 1753
    Marriage Act, 32–3; marriage
    arrangements, 199–200, 202–3, 212,
    214, 216; orphans, 48; permissive
    treatment of children, 276–7;
    relations between spouses, 81
Aristophanes, *Lysistrata*, 401
Aristotle, 143